READINGS
IN
CLASSICAL
CHINESE
PHILOSOPHY

READINGS IN CLASSICAL CHINESE PHILOSOPHY

edited by

Philip J. Ivanhoe
University of Michigan

and

Bryan W. Van Norden
Vassar College

SEVEN BRIDGES PRESS
NEW YORK • LONDON

Seven Bridges Press
135 Fifth Avenue
New York, NY 10010-7101

Publisher: Ted Bolen
Managing Editor: Katharine Miller
Composition: Rachel Hegarty
Cover design: Stefan Killen Design
Printing and Binding: Victor Graphics, Inc.

LIBRARY OF CONGRESS CATALOGING-IN-PUBLICATION DATA

Readings in classical Chinese philosophy / edited by Philip J. Ivanhoe,
    Bryan W. Van Norden.
    p.   cm.
    ISBN 1-889119-09-1
    1. Philosophy, Chinese--To 221 B.C.   I. Ivanhoe, P. J.   II. Van
Norden, Bryan W. (Bryan William)
    B126 .R43 2000
    181'.11--dc21   00-010826

Manufactured in the United States of America
10   9   8   7   6   5   4   3   2   1

▪ CONTENTS ▪

▪ PREFACE ▪

Readings in Classical Chinese Philosophy introduces the seven most widely read and important thinkers of the "classical period" (roughly the sixth to the end of the third century B.C.E.) of Chinese philosophy. Each chapter begins with a very brief introduction to the text and the thinker it concerns and concludes with a short and lightly annotated, selective bibliography. The volume is intended to serve as an introduction to and source book for these texts and not as a philosophical primer for the thought of these authors. Introductory and interpretive material is kept to a minimum, but the volume includes four indices—*Important Figures, Important Periods, Important Texts* and *Important Terms*—that describe mythical and historical figures, periods of time, classical texts and specialized terms that regularly appear in the texts translated here. There is also a map of China during the *Spring and Autumn Period* that shows the approximate locations of the major states and rivers. Readers are encouraged to turn to these reference materials whenever they encounter terms or names in the text that are not explained in footnotes. Explanatory notes are provided at the bottom of each page in cases of a single occurrence of an obscure term or name or when more explanation appeared to be warranted. Those who wish to pursue additional secondary literature in English concerning the texts and thinkers included in this reader are encouraged to consult the web page that is maintained in support of this volume at our publisher's web site, www.sevenbridgespress.com.

A knowledge of the Chinese language is not in any way required for making full and thorough use of this volume. However, Chinese characters are provided for important references and terms of philosophical art in order to help the beginning student of Chinese and for the common edification of all. We do not provide characters for textual emendations or other textual notes as these issues require advanced facility in the classical Chinese language and other basic research languages of sinology. Readers interested in pursuing textual issues are encouraged to consult the appropriate sections of the web page mentioned above.

We have used the *Pinyin* romanization system throughout this volume, although we have chosen to romanize the common formal names of Chinese thinkers—their surnames and the honorific title *zi* 子 (literally "Master")—as one word rather than two. So, for example, *Zhuang Zi* (literally "Master Zhuang") is written as *Zhuangzi* and *Han Fei Zi* ("Master Han Fei") appears as *Han Feizi*. All romanizations in the bibliographies and notes remain in their original form in order to facilitate locating these sources. We have provided a complete table comparing the Pinyin and older Wade-Giles systems of romanization following this Preface.

We, the editors, have tried to balance a desire for consistency in the use of specialized terms with the variety of senses many of these terms have within the range of texts presented here, as well as with the different sensibilities and styles of the individual translators. In cases when a certain important term of art is rendered in different ways, we have provided notes alerting readers and directing their attention to the other occurences and translations.

We would like to thank the contributors to this volume for their work and their patience with us throughout the editorial process. Edward G. "Ted" Slingerland, a member of the Department of Religious Studies and the Department of East Asian Languages and Cultures at the University of Southern California, translated *The Analects* of Kongzi ("Confucius"); Paul Kjellberg, Chair of the Philosophy Department at Whittier College, contributed selections from the *Zhuangzi*; Eric L. Hutton, from the Philosophy Department of Stanford University, translated parts of the *Xunzi*; and Joel Sahleen, from the Department of Asian Languages at Stanford University, contributed selections from the *Han Feizi*. We, the editors, contributed the remaining translations of the *Mozi*, *Mengzi* (Mencius) and *Laozi* (The "*Daodejing*").

We would also like to thank Robert B. Rama and Jeremy R. Robinson for their help in preparing the manuscript for this volume. De-nin Lee provided invaluable assistance in locating and helping to reproduce the illustrations of individual philosophers that appear at the beginning of each chapter. T. C. "Jack" Kline III and Mark Csikszentmihalyi offered very helpful corrections and comments on various parts of earlier drafts of the manuscript. We would also like to thank the Center for Chinese Studies at the University of Michigan for a grant to help in the preparation of this volume, and Ted Bolen of Seven Bridges Press for the vision and perseverance he has shown from the inception to the completion of this project.

▪ COMPARATIVE ▪ ROMANIZATION TABLE

The following conversion table is provided in order to allow the reader to keep track of and convert between the Pinyin and Wade-Giles system of romanization.

Pinyin	Wade-Giles
b	p
c	ts'/tz'
ch	ch'
d	t
g	k
ian	ien
j	ch
k	k'
ong	ung
p	p'
q	ch'
r	j
si	ssu/szu
t	t'
x	hs
you	yu
yu	yü
z	ts/tz
zh	ch
zhi	chih
zi	tzu

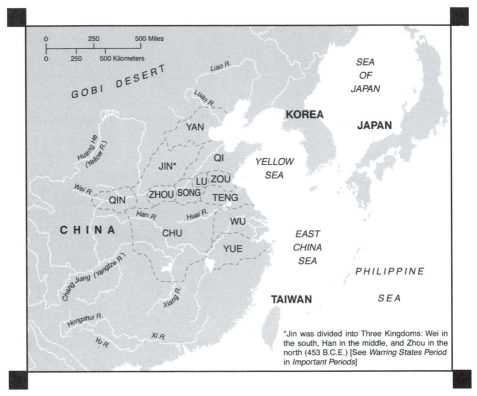

*Jin was divided into Three Kingdoms: Wei in the south, Han in the middle, and Zhou in the north (453 B.C.E.) [See *Warring States Period* in *Important Periods*]

▪ INTRODUCTION ▪

Chinese history and thought extends much farther back in time than the period covered in this volume, though it is fair to say that philosophy—in the sense of self-conscious reflection upon, modification, and defense of one's views—begins with the debate between Kongzi and Mozi. But at least a general sense of the trajectory of Chinese thought prior to this period and some understanding of the shape of the intellectual landscape on the eve of the age represented here will help the reader to appreciate more deeply the views of the thinkers presented.

The earliest substantial written documents we have from China are carved onto bone and shell or etched onto ritual vessels of bronze. These incised inscriptions, together with other modern archeological discoveries, have allowed scholars to reconstruct speculative yet intriguing pictures of very early Chinese society and culture.[1] Most of the so-called oracle bone inscriptions date from around the twelfth to mid-eleventh century B.C.E., the closing years of the Shang dynasty.[2] They record the queries of royal diviners—often the king himself—who sought the advice and assistance of various ancestral and Nature spirits. Ritual vessel inscriptions, which date from the Shang and continue, in their high form, through the eighth century B.C.E., in the period known as the Western Zhou dynasty, also provide a wealth of information concerning very early Chinese elite culture, particularly many of their religious views.[3]

---

[1]The best introductions to this period of Chinese civilization are: Kwang-chih Chang, *Shang Civilization* (New Haven, CT: Yale University Press, 1980) and David N. Keightley, ed., *The Origins of Chinese Civilization* (Berkeley, CA: University of California Press, 1983).

[2]For a remarkably edifying introduction to Shang oracular inscriptions, see David N. Keightley, *Sources of Shang History : The Oracle-bone Inscriptions of Bronze Age China* (Berkeley, CA: University of California Press, 1978).

[3]The most illuminating and thorough introduction to early bronze inscriptions is Edward L. Shaughnessy, *Sources of Western Zhou History: Inscribed Bronze Vessels* (Berkeley, CA: University of California Press, 1991).

These sources describe a precarious world, saturated with unruly and unpredictable spiritual powers. Above there was *Shang Di* 上帝, "The Lord on High," a powerful and only vaguely understood spirit who controlled the forces of nature and determined the fate of human beings. Unlike ancestral spirits and even the spirits of Nature, *Shang Di* was so remote from human concerns and so far from human understanding that he could not be approached directly. However, other spirits and particularly ancestral spirits could appeal to *Shang Di* on behalf of their living descendants and solicit his support for their all-too-human endeavors.

The majority of oracular and bronze vessel inscriptions record attempts by the ruling members of Shang and Zhou society to influence the spirits through ritual supplication and sacrifice. Those appeals that are directed specifically at ancestral spirits are among the clearest early expressions of "ancestor worship" and, given our concern with the development of philosophy, it is interesting that even at this early stage we find an explicit concern with the inner life of the worshipper. For they make clear that sacrifice was not simply an external behavior; in order for one's sacrifice to be accepted by the appropriate spirit, one had to offer it with the proper inner attitudes and feelings of respect and reverence. Moreover, it was thought that with enough effort of the right sorts, one could cultivate the appropriate attitudes and feelings.

In early Chinese religious thought, ancestral spirits bridge what in other traditions often looms as an abyss between the spiritual and human worlds. There is no fundamental metaphysical rupture in the cosmos; at the very least, living human beings have concerned representatives in the spiritual world who can temper and appeal to more remote and recalcitrant forces. This gives early and even later Chinese religious thought a distinctively "this-worldly" orientation, and it had a profound influence on the shape and style of later philosophical reflection.

Another fascinating and productive aspect of this complex of beliefs, attitudes, and practices is the attention early diviners paid to keeping track of their past interactions with the spiritual world. Shang diviners kept extensive records of their oracular activities, and these often included notes concerning the results they obtained by following the advice derived through divination. K. C. Chang argues[4] that they did so in the belief that, by studying these past records, thoughtful individuals could discern the most reliable patterns of productive human-spirit interaction. He further sug-

---

[4]See Chang, *Shang Civilization*, p. 90.

gests that such practices deeply influenced later Chinese conceptions of and attitudes toward history and in particular the value and role of historical precedent.

Together, these beliefs about the role of ancestral spirits and the wisdom of historical precedent laid the foundation for beliefs and attitudes that shaped and endured throughout the Chinese tradition, particularly in the tradition of the Erudites or "Confucians." They in particular preserved and elaborated on the idea that by keeping the lessons of the past in one's mind and the ancestors in one's heart, one could find a way through a dangerous and unpredictable world. These ideas find various expressions in the later philosophical literature. Different thinkers defend tradition on a variety of grounds, extending from a fundamental faith in a past golden age preserved in traditional cultural forms to a more subtle defense of the accumulated authoritative force of efficacious precedents. As Benjamin Schwartz has pointed out,[5] the unique part the ancestors played as mediators between the human and spiritual world lends itself to a form of life in which finding and fulfilling one's designated familial and social roles—whatever these might be in a particular case—allows one to take one's proper place in a harmonious universal scheme that worked for the benefit of all. The fact that such family-based roles also appear to be "natural" further reinforces this general conceptual scheme and opens up a way—that was taken by some of the thinkers we present here—to provide a more naturalized account of this early conception of the good human life.

When the Shang were overthrown and their conquerors founded the Zhou dynasty[6] we find the beginning of a tendency to "naturalize" and in a certain sense domesticate aspects of earlier Shang belief. By "naturalize" we mean a preference for accounts of actions and events in terms of systematic, natural phenomena rather than spiritual power. For example, while the early Zhou rulers appear to have promoted the idea that their supreme deity *Tian* 天 (literally, "Heaven" or "sky") was identical to the earlier *Shang Di*, with the passage of time, *Tian* came to be thought of as the structure or disposition of the universe itself, as opposed to an entity or being with consciousness and intention. This transition is clear in texts such as the *Analects*, where one finds both conceptions of Heaven as an ac-

---

[5]See Schwartz (1985), p. 23.

[6]Most contemporary scholars recognize that the traditional date of the Zhou conquest (1122 B.C.E.) is too early by about one hundred years, though there is still no clear consensus on exactly when it occured.

tive agent and conceptions of Heaven as the natural order of things. Another idea that manifests what we are calling the trend toward naturalized accounts is the notion of *Tianming* 天命, "Heaven's Mandate," which the Zhou invoked to justify their conquest of the Shang. The idea was that Heaven confers its "mandate" to rule on those who best represent its interests and concerns for humankind. The last Shang kings were depicted by the Zhou as drunken, self-serving despots who had forsaken their role-specific obligations and indulged their passions, thus bringing chaos to the world. As a consequence of this ethically reprehensible behavior, they were stripped of the mandate to rule.[7] This "naturalizes" the earlier scheme in the sense that now an individual's intentional actions and chosen way of life directly defines their relationship with the spirit world and determines who secures and maintains Heaven's favor. The shift to a new conception of Heaven and the appeal to Heaven's Mandate also domesticate earlier Shang beliefs in the sense that they open up the workings of the world to broader human understanding and control. In Shang times, the spirit world was largely beyond direct human understanding; oracular inquiries were like scouting parties, sent out into potentially hostile territory in search of strategically useful information. And even such indirect knowledge and limited control of the spiritual world was limited to royal diviners. In the emerging Zhou world view, anyone was potentially capable of understanding and harnessing the ethical power of Heaven.[8]

Later thinkers offer very different and at times conflicting accounts of the Western Zhou and its exemplary individuals but there is broad agreement that this period was one of remarkable internal stability, peace, and prosperity. And there is as yet no evidence available that would cause one to doubt such a claim. But given the newly developed views discussed above—which claim that an ethically superior ruler is necessary for sustained and successful government—such an age was destined to come to an end, for there is always the threat of moral rot. According to traditional accounts, the fall of the Western Zhou was the result of its last king's lack of virtue. It seems that King

---

[7]This idea remains sedimented in the modern Chinese word for "revolution," which is *geming* 革命, "stripping the mandate."

[8]Early Chinese society restricted women to primarily domestic vocations. However, there were exceptions to this general rule and there was a developed literature on woman's virtue quite early in Chinese history. See Lisa Raphals, *Sharing the Light: Women and Virtue in Early China* (Albany, NY: SUNY Press, 1999). Moreover, one does not find explicit arguments about purported reasons that prevented women from developing complete forms of the full range of virtues, as one finds, for example, in the writings of Aristotle.

You was deeply enamored of his concubine Bao Si and indulged himself by amusing her. Bao Si in turn was terribly fond of having the king light the series of beacon fires that were supposed to be used to summon his vassals from surrounding territories in times of attack. And so, even though there was no danger of attack, he would have the fires lit for her amusement. His vassals would gather their forces and rush to the capital, only to find that it was a false alarm. After a number of such false alarms, they stopped coming and hence were not there when the real attack came that toppled his regime and forced the remnants of the Zhou court to flee and found a new capital far to the east.[9] From this we are to see how self-indulgence weakens the power of a ruler, and that eventually such conduct will result in the loss of Heaven's Mandate to rule. Political failure follows close upon the heals of moral decay, and both are regarded as being largely within an individual's control.[10] These distinctive characteristics of Zhou religious, ethical, and political thought became central features of much of later Chinese philosophy.

From the perspective of the present work, the Eastern Zhou marks the dawn of the "classical period" of Chinese philosophy. It begins with Kongzi ("Confucius"), in a period when China consisted of a number of increasingly independent states, and culminates with Han Feizi, with the unification of central China under a new dynasty known as the Qin.[11] Of the seven thinkers covered, three—Kongzi, Mengzi, and Xunzi—are from what came to be called the *Ru* ("Erudite" or "Confucian") tradition, and two—Laozi and Zhuangzi—are from the more loosely affiliated group of thinkers later called the *Daojia* ("Daoist School").[12] In addition, there are selections from Mozi, founder and leader of the fascinating, powerful, and highly organized movement known as the *Mojia* ("Mohist School") and from Han Feizi, an incisive, eloquent, and influential representative of the *Fajia* ("Legalist School").

As will be clear from the notes and appendices included in this volume, this selection of writings by no means exhausts or even fully represents the

---

[9]For a discussion of the figure Bao Si, see Raphals, pp. 64–66.

[10]Uncontrollable and inexplicable factors could still affect one's overall destiny but as these were beyond one's choice and conscious control they received very little attention in the developing literature.

[11]It is from "Qin" that China gets its English name.

[12]For brief descriptions of these "schools" of thought, see *Important Terms*.

range of thinkers who lived, thought, argued, and wrote during this period.[13] There was a remarkably wide variety of thinkers active during this time in early China, a fact reflected in an another name for this age: the *baijia* 百家, "hundred schools," period. Even among the thinkers we present here, one finds a broad range of philosophical views. There are reflective defenders of tradition, ethical sensibility theorists, nature mystics, consequentialists, as well as those who present a purely political theory of state organization and control. One finds a variety of visions of the good life, ranging from those who insist that only the right kind of society presents human beings with a way to live complete and satisfying lives, to those who argue that *any* attempt to produce a good life will inevitably be contaminated and undermined by the hypocrisy of self-conscious effort. For proponents of this latter view, the only solution is to *stop* trying to find a solution and allow ourselves to fall back into the preexisting harmony of Nature. Many of these different views rest on explicit or implied views about the character of human nature and here again we see remarkable variety. This is true even in the case of the founder and first two most eminent defenders of Confucianism—Kongzi, Mengzi, and Xunzi—who shared a significant number of commitments and looked to a common historical and textual heritage.

The thinkers of the hundred schools period not only disagreed in theory, they disagreed with each other. That is to say, their views were not only in conflict but they themselves often argued with one another. Such exchanges led to greater philosophical sophistication, with thinkers responding to and often adapting each other's views in order to enhance their own positions. The careful reader will be able to see numerous examples of such disagreement and mutual borrowing in the selections presented here, and understanding this aspect of philosophical life during this period is important for a full appreciation of the lively and creative spirit of the time.

The intellectual variety seen among the early philosophers represented here did not stop with this first "classical period." Throughout subsequent history, Chinese thinkers continued to produce philosophical views of stunning originality and power. While certain early schools of thought died out, their influence remained, and is clearly reflected in the thought of their more long-lived competitors.[14] And over time other, non-Chinese tradi-

---

[13]This is true even if one counts only the thinkers for whom we have at least some samples of their work. Extant bibliographies and references in texts that we do have point to an immensely rich and extensive literature that is either lost or has not yet come to light.

[14]For example, the Mohist school died out around the time of the Qin conquest but it left a deep and indelible influence on both Daoist and Confucian thought.

tions of thought came and often profoundly influenced indigenous traditions. For example, Buddhism, which arrived in China some time around the first century C.E., generated a fundamental and enduring transformation of every active philosophical school.

The most important lesson to take away from this rich and complex history is that "Chinese philosophy" is not a single theory, thinker, or tradition but rather a diverse and lively conversation that has been going on for more than 2,500 years and that is still active and evolving in our time. And so our *Readings in Classical Chinese Philosophy* might more accurately be entitled, *Readings in Classical Chinese Philosophies*. In any event, it is the hope of the editors and other contributors to this volume that this work serves to facilitate an engagement with and appreciation of the wealth of philosophical ideas found in early China.

Philip J. Ivanhoe
Ann Arbor, Michigan

Bryan W. Van Norden
Poughkeepsie, New York

SELECTIVE BIBLIOGRAPHY

1. Chan, Wing-tsit. tr.

  1963   *A Source Book in Chinese Philosophy*. Princeton, NJ: Princeton University Press.

2. Fung, Yu-lan.

  1983   *A History of Chinese Philosophy*. 2 vols. Derk Bodde, tr., reprint. Princeton, NJ: Princeton University Press.

3. Graham, A. C.

  1989   *Disputers of the Tao*. La Salle, IL: Open Court Press.

4. Ivanhoe, Philip J.

  2000   *Confucian Moral Self Cultivation*. Indianapolis, IN: Hackett Publishing Company.

5. Munro, Donald J.

  1969   *The Concept of Man in Early China*. Stanford, CA: Stanford University Press.

6. Nivison, David S.

  1996   *The Ways of Confucianism*. Chicago, IL: Open Court Press.

7. Schwartz, Benjamin I.

  1985   *The World of Thought in Ancient China*. Cambridge, MA: The Belknap Press.

READINGS
IN
CLASSICAL
CHINESE
PHILOSOPHY

▪ CHAPTER ONE ▪

KONGZI (CONFUCIUS)

"The Analects"

Introduction

The *Analects* (*Lunyu* 論語—literally, the "Classified Teachings") purports to be a record of the teachings of Kongzi 孔子 or "Confucius" (551–479 B.C.E.) and his disciples.[1] Kongzi believed that the Golden Age of humankind had been realized during the height of Zhou dynasty, from c. 1045–771 B.C.E. (the so-called Western Zhou period). Personified by the cultural heroes King Wen (d.c. 1050 B.C.E.), his son King Wu (r. 1045–1043) and the virtuous regent, the Duke of Zhou (r. c. 1043–1036 B.C.E.), the early Zhou rulers established and maintained a special relationship with *tian* 天, "Heaven," by properly and sincerely observing a set of sacred practices collectively referred to as the *li* 禮, "rites" or "rituals." The scope of the rites was quite vast, including everything from grand state ceremonies to the proper way to sit or fasten one's lapel—details that we might think of as issues of etiquette. In return for such formal obedience to Heaven in all matters great and small, the Zhou royal line was rewarded with a *ming* 命,

---

[1]Some scholars have questioned the traditional view of the text as a unified work, arguing that it represents many different chronological strata and even incompatible viewpoints. The Chinese have nevertheless read it as a coherent whole for thousands of years, and this is the perspective on the text that we adopt here. This said, the reader will note that our selection gives greater weight to those portions of the text generally agreed to be earlier and most authoritative, Books 1–9.

"Mandate,"[2] to rule China, manifested in the form of a charismatic *de* 德, "Virtue," or power.

By Kongzi's age, the Zhou kings had been reduced to mere figureheads, and real political power was in the hands of various local rulers. In Kongzi's eyes, the "scholars" of his day—those who should properly be motivated by a love for learning and a devotion to the culture of the Zhou—were interested only in self-aggrandizement and sensuous pleasures, and the people, thereby bereft of moral leadership and grown unruly, could only be controlled through strict laws and harsh punishments. Despite the bleakness of this world, Kongzi believed that there was still hope for humanity, because the traditional Zhou ritual forms and written classics—which had been carefully preserved by a small group of cultural specialists, the *ru* 儒, "Erudites,"[3]—could serve as a sort of blueprint for rebuilding the lost Golden Age. Kongzi thus dedicated his life to both transmitting these cultural forms to his contemporaries and striving to embody them in his own person, hoping in this way to lead his fallen world back to the *dao* 道, "Way," of Heaven.

Involving lifelong and sincere devotion to traditional cultural forms, Kongzi's Way is to culminate eventually in a kind of intuitive mastery of those forms, and one who has attained this state of consummate mastery—the *junzi* 君子, "gentleman"—is said to possess the supreme virtue of *ren* 仁, "true humaneness" or "humanity." Originally referring to the strong and handsome appearance of a noble warrior, *ren* designates for Kongzi the quality of the perfectly realized person—one who has so completely mastered the Way that it has become a sort of second nature. Such a state of spiritual perfection is referred to as *wuwei* 無為, "effortless action" or "nonaction": a state of spontaneous harmony between individual inclinations and the sacred Way of Heaven. Through the power of Virtue accruing to one so perfectly in harmony with Heaven, this state of individual perfection is to lead to the spontaneous and effortless ordering of the entire world. There will be no need for raising armies, instituting laws, or issuing governmental decrees, for the entire world will be as inexorably drawn to a ruler with true Virtue as the heavenly bodies are bound to their proper circuits in the sky.

---

[2]By the time of the *Analects*, the term *ming* had taken on the additional meaning of "fate" or "destiny," but was thought to be similarly decreed by Heaven. For a discussion of this term, see Edward (Ted) Slingerland, "The Conception of *Ming* in Early Chinese Thought," *Philosophy East & West* 46.4 (1996), pp. 567–81.

[3]See *Important Terms* and *Analects* 6.13 for Kongzi's criticism of the "petty *ru*."

Book One

1.1 The Master said, "To study, and then in a timely fashion to practice what you have learned—is this not satisfying? To have companions arrive from afar—is this not a joy? To remain unrecognized by others and yet remain free of resentment—is this not the mark of the gentleman?"

1.2 Youzi[4] said, "It is unlikely that one who has grown up as a filial son and respectful younger brother will then be inclined to defy his superiors, and there has never been a case of one who is disinclined to defy his superiors stirring up a rebellion.

"The gentleman applies himself to the roots. Once the roots are firmly planted, the Way will grow therefrom. Might we thus say that filiality and brotherly respect represent the root of *ren*?"

1.3 The Master said, "A glib tongue and an ingratiating manner are rarely signs of *ren*."[5]

1.6 The Master said, "A student should be filial toward his parents when at home and respectful toward his elders when abroad. Careful in action and truthful in speech, he should display an expansive care for the multitude and seek to draw near to those who are *ren*. If in the course of his duties he finds himself with energy to spare, he should devote it to study of the *wen* 文, 'cultural arts.'"

1.9 Zengzi[6] said, "Be meticulous in observing the passing of those close to you and do not fail to continue the sacrifices to your distant ancestors. This will be enough to cause the Virtue of the people to return to fullness."

1.10 Ziqin said to Zigong,[7] "When our Master arrives in a state, he invariably finds out about its government. Does he actively seek out this information? Surely it is not simply offered to him!"

---

[4] A disciple of Kongzi.

[5] A suspicion of those who are overly glib or outwardly pleasing is a common theme in the *Analects*. In *Analects* 15.11, the danger presented by *ningren* 佞人, "glib people," is compared to the derangement of morals brought about by the decadent music of the state of Zheng.

[6] A disciple of Kongzi.

[7] Both disciples of Kongzi.

Zigong answered, "Our Master acquires it through being cordial, good, respectful, frugal, and deferential. The Master's way of seeking it is rather different from other people's way of seeking it, is it not?"[8]

1.12 Youzi said, "In the application of ritual, it is harmonious ease[9] that is to be valued. It is precisely such harmony that makes the Way of the Former Kings so beautiful. If you merely stick rigidly to ritual in all matters, great and small, there will remain that which you cannot accomplish. Yet if you know enough to value harmonious ease but try to attain it without being regulated by the rites, this will not work either."

1.15 Zigong said, "Poor and yet not obsequious, rich and yet not arrogant—what would you say about someone like that?"

The Master answered, "That is acceptable, but it is not as good as being poor and yet full of joy, rich and yet fond of ritual."

Zigong said, "In the *Odes* we read,

As if cut, as if polished;
As if carved, as if ground.[10]

Is this not what you have in mind?"[11]

The Master said, "Zigong, you are precisely the kind of person with whom one can begin to discuss the *Odes*. Informed as to what has gone before, you know what is to come."

Book Two

2.1 The Master said, "One who rules through the power of Virtue might be compared to the Pole Star, which simply remains in its place while receiving the homage of the myriad lesser stars."

---

[8]That is, Kongzi does not actively pry or seek out information, but rather is so perfected in Virtue that what he seeks comes to him unbidden, in a *wuwei* fashion.

[9]That is, a state of *he* 和, "harmony," between inner emotions and outward form.

[10]*Mao* # 55.

[11]That is, a person whose character has been arduously shaped and perfectly transformed in such a manner.

2.2 The Master said, "The three hundred poems in the *Odes* can be judged with a single phrase: 'Oh, they will not lead you astray.'"[12]

2.3 The Master said, "If you try to lead the common people with governmental regulations and keep them in line with punishments, the laws will simply be evaded and the people will have no sense of shame. If, however, you guide them with Virtue, and keep them in line by means of ritual, the people will have a sense of shame and will moreover reform themselves."

2.4 The Master said, "At age fifteen I set my heart upon learning; at thirty I took my stand;[13] at forty I became free of doubts;[14] at fifty I understood the Heavenly Mandate;[15] at sixty my ear was attuned;[16] and at seventy I could follow my heart's desire without overstepping the bounds of propriety."

Confucius' spiritual biography; A lifetime of submission to rigid, external forms (of ritual & study) to achieve autonomy in the end.

2.7 Ziyou[17] asked about filial piety. The Master said, "Nowadays, 'filial' is used to refer to anyone who is merely able to provide their parents with nourishment. But even dogs and horses are provided with nourishment. If you do not treat your parents with reverence, wherein lies the difference?"

2.9 The Master said, "I can talk all day long with Yan Hui[18] without him once disagreeing with me or asking questions. In this way, he seems a bit dim-witted. And yet when he retires from my presence and I observe his behavior in private, I see that it is in fact worthy to serve as an illustration of what I have taught. Hui is not so stupid after all."

---

[12]*Mao* # 297. The original reference is to powerful war horses bred to pull chariots, who are trained not to swerve from the desired path. The metaphorical meaning is that one committed through study to the *Odes*—"yoked" to them, as it were—will not be led astray.

[13]That is, through mastery of the rites; cf. *Analects* 8.8, 16.13, and 20.3.

[14]Cf. *Analects* 9.29.

[15]Cf. *Analects* 16.8, 20.3.

[16]Some interpretations take this to mean that Kongzi at this point immediately apprehends the teachings he hears, others that there is no conflict between his inner dispositions and the teachings of the sages. The latter seems more plausible, as it more clearly links this stage with the stage that follows.

[17]A disciple of Kongzi.

[18]Kongzi's favorite disciple, who tragically died at an early age (see *Analects* 5.9, 6.3, 6.7, 6.11, and 11.9).

2.10 The Master said, "Pay attention to the means a man employs, observe the path he follows, and discover where it is he feels at home.[19] How can his character remain hidden? How can his character remain hidden?"

2.11 The Master said, "A true teacher is one who, keeping the past alive, is also able to understand the present."

2.12 The Master said, "The gentleman does not serve as a vessel."[20]

2.15 The Master said, "To learn without *si* 思, 'thinking,' will lead to confusion. To think without learning, however, will lead to fruitless exhaustion."[21]

2.21 Someone asked Kongzi, "Why is it that you are not participating in government?"[22]

> The Master answered, "We read in the *History*:
> Filial, oh so filial as a son, a friend to one's brothers,
> both younger and elder; [in this way] exerting an
> influence upon the government.[23]

Thus, in being a filial son and good brother one is already taking part in government.[24] What need is there, then, to speak of 'participating in government'?"[25]

---

[19]Cf. *Analects* 4.2.

[20]*Qi* 器, literally a ritual vessel or implement designed to serve a particular function, is also used by extension to refer to officials who are specialized in one particular task. The gentleman is not a narrow specialist (cf. *Analects* 5.4, 6.13, 9.2, 9.6, 13.4 and 19.7).

[21]Cf. *Analects* 15.31.

[22]*Wei zheng* 為政 (literally, "doing government"). The reference is to Kongzi's lack of an official position.

[23]Cf. James Legge, trans., *The Chinese Classics, Volume III, The Shoo King*, reprint (Hong Kong: Hong Kong University Press, 1970), p. 535.

[24]Cf. *Analects* 1.2.

[25]The point is that one should be "doing government" through *wuwei* 無為, "not doing,": that is, by perfecting oneself—as Youzi puts it in *Analects* 1.2, establishing the "root" of virtue—and letting the rest follow naturally.

Book Three

3.1 Kongzi said of the head of the Ji clan, "He uses eight rows of dancers in his courtyard.[26] If this man can be tolerated, who cannot be tolerated?"

3.3 The Master said, "A man who is not *ren*—what has he to do with ritual? A man who is not *ren*—what has he to do with music?"[27]

3.4 Lin Fang[28] asked about the roots of ritual practice.

The Master exclaimed, "Noble indeed are you to ask such a question! When it comes to ritual, it is better to be frugal than extravagant. When it comes to mourning, it is better to be overwhelmed with grief than overly composed."

3.8 Zixia[29] asked, "[The *Odes* say,]

> Her artful smile, with its alluring dimples,
> Her beautiful eyes, so clear,
> The unadorned upon which to paint.[30]

What does this mean?"

The Master said, "The task of applying colors comes only after a suitable unadorned background is present."

Zixia said, "So it is the rites that come after?"[31]

The Master said, "Zixia, you are truly one who can anticipate my thoughts! It is only with someone like you that I can begin to discuss the *Odes*."

---

[26]Later ritual texts describe this as a ritual prerogative of the emperor; presumably in Kongzi's time it was viewed as a prerogative of the Zhou kings.

[27]This comment is probably also directed at the head of the Ji clan criticized in *Analects* 3.1. Cf. *Analects* 3.12 and 17.11.

[28]Lin Fang is usually identified as a man of Lu, and presumably shares Kongzi's concern that his fellow citizens were neglecting the "roots" and attending to the superficial "branches" of ritual practice.

[29]A disciple of Kongzi.

[30]The first two lines appear in the present version of *Odes* (*Mao # 57*), while the third does not.

[31]That is, the adornment provided by the rites is meant to build upon appropriate native emotions or tendencies. Just as all of the cosmetics in the world are of no avail if the basic lines of the face are not pleasing, so is the refinement provided by ritual practice of no help to one lacking in *zhi* 質 "native substance." Cf. *Analects* 3.4, 5.10 and 6.18.

3.11 Someone asked for an explanation of the *di* 禘 sacrifice.[32] The Master said, "I do not fully comprehend it. One who truly understood it could handle the world as if he had it right here," and he pointed to the palm of his hand.

3.12 "Sacrifice as if [they were] present" means that, when sacrificing to the spirits, you should comport yourself as if the spirits were present.[33]

The Master said, "If I am not fully present at the sacrifice,[34] it is as if I did not sacrifice at all."

3.14 The Master said, "From the vantage point of the Zhou, one's gaze can encompass the two dynasties that preceded it.[35] How brilliant in culture it was! I follow the Zhou."

3.17 Zigong wanted to do away with the practice of sacrificing a lamb to announce the new moon.[36]

The Master said, "Zigong! You regret the loss of the lamb, whereas I regret the loss of the rite."[37]

3.18 The Master said, "If in serving your ruler you are careful to observe every detail of ritual propriety, others will [wrongly] think you obsequious."[38]

---

[32]An important sacrifice to the earliest known ancestor of the reigning dynasty, the performance of which was the prerogative of the presiding ruler. By Kongzi's time, the performance of this ceremony had degenerated to a point that he could no longer bear to look upon it.

[33]That is, with an attitude of reverence and awe. There is no attribution for this line, and its form (cryptic text followed by an expanded, explanatory version) suggests that it might be a fragment from a lost ritual text interpolated by a later editor. Whether the Master's words or not, it nonetheless clearly harmonizes with the comment from Kongzi that follows.

[34]Although some commentators take "not being present" in the literal sense (i.e., not being physically present at the sacrifice, and sending a proxy in one's stead), the preceding comment would suggest that what is at issue is psychological or spiritual presence.

[35]That is, the Xia and Shang dynasties.

[36]Apparently this sacrifice had originally been part of a larger ritual to welcome the new moon. By Kongzi's time the ritual itself had fallen into disuse in Lu, whereas the sacrifice—being the responsibility of a particular government office—had survived. Zigong does not see the point of continuing this vestigial, materially wasteful practice in the absence of its original ritual context.

[37]Continuing this vestigial practice is Kongzi's way of mourning the loss of the original rite and keeping its memory alive, which in his view is worth the cost of an occasional lamb.

[38]Ritual practice had so degenerated by Kongzi's age that a proper ritual practitioner was viewed with suspicion or disdain.

3.20 The Master said, "The 'Cry of the Osprey'[39] expresses joy without becoming licentious, and expresses sorrow without falling into excessive pathos."

3.23 The Master was discussing music with the Grand Music Master of Lu. He said, "What can be known about music is this: when it first begins, it resounds with a confusing variety of notes, but as it unfolds, these notes are reconciled by means of harmony, brought into tension by means of counterpoint, and finally woven together into a seamless whole. It is in this way that music reaches its perfection."[40]

3.24 A border official of Yi requested an audience with the Master, saying, "I have never neglected to obtain an audience with the gentlemen who have passed this way." Kongzi's followers thus presented him.

After emerging from the audience, the border official remarked to the gathered disciples, "You disciples, why should you be concerned about your Master's loss of office?[41] It has been too long that the world has been without the Way, and Heaven intends to use your Master like the wooden clapper in a bell."[42]

Book Four

4.1 The Master said, "With regard to neighborhoods, it is the presence of those who are *ren* that makes them desirable. Given a choice, then, how could someone who does not choose to dwell in *ren* be considered wise?"

4.2 The Master said, "Those who are not *ren* cannot remain constant in adversity and cannot enjoy enduring happiness. Those who are *ren* find their

---

[39]The first of the *Odes*, and sometimes used to refer to the *Odes* as a whole.

[40]Music thus serves as a model or metaphor for the process of self-cultivation: starting in confusion, passing through many phases and culminating in a state of *wuwei* perfection.

[41]This loss of office is presumably the reason that Kongzi and his disciples are leaving the state.

[42]That is, to wake up the fallen world. Some commentators believe that the bell referred to is the kind used by itinerant collectors and transmitters of folk songs, and that the border official's point is thus that Heaven has deliberately caused Kongzi to lose his official position so that he might wander throughout the realm, spreading the teachings of the Way.

repose in *ren*; those who are wise follow *ren* because they know that they will *li* 利, 'profit,' from it."

4.4 The Master said, "Having merely set your heart sincerely upon *ren*, you can be sure of remaining free of odium."

4.5 The Master said, "Wealth and honor are things that all people desire, and yet unless they are acquired in the proper way I will not abide them. Poverty and disgrace are things that all people hate, and yet unless they are avoided in the proper way I will not despise them.

"If the gentleman abandons *ren*, how can he be worthy of that name? The gentleman does not violate *ren* even for the amount of time required to eat a meal. Even in times of urgency or distress, he does not depart from it."

4.6 The Master said, "I have yet to meet a person who truly loved *ren* or hated a lack of *ren*. One who loved *ren* could not be surpassed, while one who hated a lack of *ren* would at least be able to act in a *ren* fashion, insofar as he would not tolerate that which is not *ren* being associated with his person.

"Is there a person who can, for the space of a single day, simply devote his efforts to *ren*? I have never seen one whose strength is insufficient for this task. Perhaps such a person exists, but I have yet to meet him."[43]

4.7 The Master said, "People are true to type with regard to that which they overlook. Observe closely what a person overlooks—then you will know whether or not he is *ren*."[44]

4.8 The Master said, "Having in the morning learned the Way, one could die that evening without regret."

4.9 The Master said, "A true *shi* 士, 'scholar,' is one who has set his heart upon the Way. A fellow who is ashamed merely of shabby clothing or meager rations is not even worth conversing with."

4.10 The Master said, "Acting in the world, the gentleman has no predispositions for or against anything. He merely seeks to be on the side of what is *yi* 義, 'right.'"

---

[43]Cf. *Analects* 7.30.

[44]That is, it is often in unpremeditated, unconscious actions that one's true character is revealed.

4.12 The Master said, "If your conduct is determined solely by considerations of profit you will arouse great resentment."

4.13 The Master said, "If a person is able to govern the state by means of ritual propriety and deference, what difficulties will he encounter? If, on the other hand, a person is not able to govern the state through ritual propriety and deference, of what use are the rites to him?"[45]

4.14 The Master said, "Do not be concerned that you lack an official position, but rather concern yourself with the means by which you might take your stand. Do not be concerned that no one has heard of you, but rather strive to become a person worthy of being known."

4.15 The Master said, "Zengzi! All that I teach[46] is unified by one guiding principle."

Zengzi answered, "Yes."

After the Master left, the other disciples asked, "What did he mean by that?"

Zengzi said, "All of what the Master teaches amounts to nothing more than *zhong* 忠, 'loyalty,' tempered by *shu* 恕, 'sympathetic understanding.'"[47]

4.16 The Master said, "The gentleman understands what is right, whereas the petty man understands profit."

4.17 The Master said, "When you see someone who is *xian* 賢, 'worthy,' concentrate upon becoming their equal; when you see someone who is unworthy, use this as an opportunity to look within yourself."

---

[45]Cf. *Analects* 13.5.

[46]The word rendered here as "teach" (*dao* 道) also means "the Way," and a *double entendre* is almost certainly intended: "all that I teach" is also "my Way."

[47]To be *zhong* "loyal" or "dutiful" involves fulfilling the duties and obligations proper to one's ritually defined role (see *Analects* 5.19 below for a description of someone deemed *zhong* by Kongzi). This virtue is to be tempered by the virtue of *shu* "sympathetic understanding": the ability, by means of imaginatively putting oneself in the place of another, to know when it is appropriate or *yi*, "right," to bend or suspend the dictates of role-specific duty. Cf. *Analects* 5.12, 6.30, 12.2 and 15.24.

4.18 The Master said, "In serving your parents you may gently remonstrate with them. However, once it becomes apparent that they have not taken your criticism to heart you should be respectful and not oppose them, and follow their lead diligently without resentment."

4.19 The Master said, "When your parents are alive, you should not travel far, and when you do travel you must keep to a fixed itinerary."[48]

4.20 The Master said, "One who makes no changes to the ways of his father for three years[49] after his father has passed away may be called a filial son."

4.21 The Master said, "You must always be aware of your parents' age. On the one hand, it is a cause for rejoicing, on the other, a source of anxiety."[50]

4.22 The Master said, "People in ancient times did not speak lightly, and were ashamed lest their actions not measure up to their words."[51]

4.23 The Master said, "Very few go astray who comport themselves with restraint."

4.24 The Master said, "The gentleman wishes to be slow of speech and cautious with regard to his actions."

4.25 The Master said, "Virtue is never alone; it always has neighbors."[52]

Book Five

5.1 The Master said of Gong Yechang, "He is marriageable. Although he was once imprisoned and branded as a criminal, he was in fact innocent of any crime." The Master gave him his daughter in marriage.[53]

---

[48]So as not to give your parents undue cause for worry.

[49]The length of the mourning period for parents, equivalent to 25 months by Western reckoning. Cf. *Analects* 17.21 and the note to that passage.

[50]The age of one's parents is a cause for rejoicing in that they have lived so long, while also a source of anxiety because of their advancing years.

[51]Cf. *Analects* 14.27.

[52]The reference is to the attractive power of Virtue.

[53]The social stigma attached to former criminals in early China was enormous and inescapable, since criminals were prominently branded or tattooed. In giving his daughter in

5.4 Zigong asked, "How would you characterize me?"

The Master answered, "You are a *qi* 器, 'vessel.'"

"What sort of vessel?"

"A precious ritual vessel."[54]

5.8 Meng Wubo[55] asked, "Is Zilu *ren*?"

The Master said, "I do not know."

The question was repeated.

The Master said, "In a state that can field one thousand chariots, Zilu could be employed to organize the collection of military taxes, but I do not know whether or not he is *ren*."

"What about Ranyou?"

"In a town of one thousand households, or an aristocratic family that can field one hundred chariots, Ranyou could be employed as a steward, but I do not know whether or not he is *ren*."

"What about Zihua?"

"With his sash tied, standing in his proper place at court, Zihua could be employed to converse with guests and visitors, but I do not know whether or not he is *ren*."

5.9 The Master said to Zigong, "How would you compare yourself with Yan Hui?"

Zigong answered, "How dare I even think of comparing myself with Hui? When Hui learns one thing, it allows him to immediately grasp ten. When I learn one thing, I am able to grasp two."

The Master said, "No, you are not the equal of Hui. You or I—neither of us is the equal of Hui."

---

marriage to a former criminal, Kongzi is flouting conventional mores and making a powerful statement concerning the independence of true morality from conventional social judgements.

[54]Cf. *Analects* 2.12 and see the note to that passage.

[55]The son of a minister of Lu, who also appears in *Analects* 2.6 (not included in this volume). The three figures he asks about—Zilu, Ranyou, and Zihua—are all disciples of Kongzi.

5.10 Zaiyu[56] was in the habit of sleeping during the daytime. The Master said, "Rotten wood cannot be carved, and a wall of dung cannot be beautified. As for Zaiyu, what would be the use of reprimanding him?"[57]

The Master added, "At first, when evaluating people, I would listen to their words and then simply trust that the corresponding conduct would follow. Now when I evaluate people I listen to their words but then closely observe their conduct. It is my experience with Zaiyu that has motivated this change."

5.12 Zigong said, "What I do not wish others to do unto me, I also wish not to do unto others."

The Master said, "Ah, Zigong! That is something quite beyond you."[58]

5.13 Zigong said, "The Master's cultural brilliance is something that is readily heard about, whereas one does not get to hear the Master expounding upon the subjects of *xing* 性 'human nature' or *tiandao* 天道, 'the Way of Heaven.'"[59]

5.19 Zizhang[60] said, "Prime Minister Ziwen[61] was rewarded three times with the post of prime minister, and yet he never showed a sign of pleasure; he was removed from this office three times, and yet never showed a

---

[56]A disciple of Kongzi.

[57]That is, Zaiyu obviously lacks the *zhi* 質, "native substance" (see *Analects* 6.18), that serves as the background upon which the "color" of Confucian self-cultivation is to be applied (see *Analects* 3.8).

[58]Zigong's aspiration—what has been referred to as the "negative Golden Rule"—is a formulation of the virtue of *shu*, "sympathetic understanding": the ability to temper the strict dictates of loyalty to one's *zhong*, "duty" by imaginatively placing oneself in another's place. See *Analects* 4.15. Zigong's aspiration to the virtue of *shu* is particularly amusing to Kongzi because Zigong is the most unimaginative and rigid of all the disciples. In *Analects* 5.4, for instance, his fastidious adherence to the rites leads Confucius to dub him a "ritual vessel" of limited capacity, and in *Analects* 14.29 he is criticized by Confucius for being too strict and judgmental with others (i.e., for not moderating his duty-defined demands upon others with understanding). Zigong thus functions in the *Analects* as an excellent example of how the virtue of loyalty goes awry when not tempered with sympathetic understanding, and this is perhaps why Kongzi singles out Zigong in *Analects* 15.24 for his message that "sympathetic understanding" is the one teaching that can serve as a life-long guide.

[59]That is, in his teachings Kongzi did not concern himself much with such theoretical, esoteric subjects as human nature or the Way of Heaven, but rather tried to focus his disciples' attention upon the task at hand, acquiring the cultural refinement necessary to become gentlemen.

[60]A disciple of Kongzi.

[61]A prime minister of the state of Chu who was reknowned for his integrity and devotion to the state.

sign of resentment. When the new prime minister took over, he invariably provided him with a complete account of his previous policies. What do you make of Prime Minister Ziwen?"

The Master said, "He certainly was *zhong*, 'loyal.'"

"Could he not also be said to have been *ren*?"

"I do not know about that—what makes you think he deserves to be called *ren*?"

"When Cuizi assassinated the Lord of Qi, Chen Wenzi—whose estate could field ten chariots—abandoned all that he possessed and left the state.[62] Upon reaching another state, he said, 'The officials here are as bad as our Great Officer Cuizi,' and thereupon left that state. Again, after going to another state, he said, 'The officials here are as bad as our Great Officer Cuizi,' and thereupon left that state as well. What do you make of Chen Wenzi?"

The Master said, "He certainly was pure."

"Could he not also be said to have been *ren*?"

"I do not know about that—what makes you think he deserves to be called *ren*?"

5.22 When the Master was in the state of Chen, he sighed, "Oh, let us go home! Let us go home! Our young followers back in Lu are wild and ambitious—they put on a great show of brilliant culture, but they lack the means to prune and shape it."[63]

5.26 Yan Hui and Zilu were in attendance. The Master said to them, "Why don't each of you speak to me of your aspirations?"

Zilu said, "I would like to be able to share my carts and horses, clothing and fur with my friends, and not become resentful if they are returned damaged."

Yan Hui said, "I would like to avoid being boastful about my own abilities or exaggerating my accomplishments."

Zilu said, "I would like to hear of the Master's aspirations."

The Master said, "To bring contentment to the aged, to have trust in my friends, and to cherish the young."[64]

---

[62]Cuizi and Chen Wenzi were both officials in the state of Qi. The former is said to have assassinated Lord Zhuang of Qi in 548 B.C.E.

[63]Cf. *Mengzi* 7B37.

[64]Cf. the more elaborate version of a similar conversation in *Analects* 11.26.

5.27 The Master said, "I should just give up! I have yet to meet the man who is able to perceive his own faults and then take himself to task inwardly."

5.28 The Master said, "In any town of ten households you will be certain to find someone who is as *zhong* 忠, 'loyal,' or *xin* 信, 'trustworthy,' as I am, but you will not find anyone who matches my love for learning."

Book Six

6.3 Duke Ai[65] asked, "Who among your disciples might be said to love learning?"

Kongzi answered, "There was one named Yan Hui who loved learning. He never misdirected his anger, and never repeated a mistake twice. Unfortunately he was fated to live a short life, and has since passed away."

6.5 Yuan Si was appointed as steward. He was allocated a salary of nine hundred bushels of grain, which he declined. The Master said, "Do not decline it! [If you do not need it yourself], could you not use it to aid the households in your neighborhood?"[66]

6.7 The Master said, "Ah, Yan Hui! For three months at a time his heart did not stray from *ren*. The rest of them could only achieve such a state by fits and starts."

6.10 Bo-niu[67] fell ill, and the Master went to ask after his health. Grasping his hand through the window, the Master sighed, "That we are going to lose him must be due to *ming*, 'fate!' How else could such a man be afflicted with such an illness? How else could such a man be afflicted with such an illness?"

---

[65]Duke Ai (r. 494–468 B.C.E.) was the nominal ruler of Lu, which was in fact controlled by the Ji family.

[66]In light of the many injunctions against seeking office for the sake of material benefit found in Kongzi's teachings, the disciple Yuan Si no doubt expected to be praised by the Master for declining to be paid a salary. Kongzi's response reflects the fact that the proper course of action cannot be determined by a simple formula, but should rather be the result of careful reflection and consideration of the needs of others. The Master may also have detected a note of spiritual pride in Yuan Si's grandiose gesture and seen the need to deflate his feeling of self-importance.

[67]A disciple of Kongzi.

6.11 The Master said, "What a worthy man was Yan Hui! Living in a narrow alley, subsisting upon meager bits of rice and water—other people could not have borne such hardship, and yet it never spoiled Hui's joy. What a worthy man was Hui!"

6.12 Ranyou said, "It is not that I do not delight in the Master's Way, it is simply that my strength is insufficient."

The Master said, "Those for whom it is genuinely a problem of insufficient strength end up collapsing somewhere along the Way. As for you, you deliberately draw the line."[68]

6.13 The Master said to Zixia, "You must become a gentlemanly *ru*, not a petty *ru*."[69]

6.17 The Master said, "Who is able to leave a room without going out through the door? How is it, then, that none of you follow this Way?"

6.18 The Master said, "When *zhi* 質, 'native substance,' overwhelms *wen* 文, 'cultural refinement,' the result is a crude rustic. When cultural refinement overwhelms native substance, the result is a foppish pedant. Only when culture and native substance are perfectly mixed and balanced do you have a gentleman."

6.20 The Master said, "One who knows it[70] is not the equal of one who loves it, and one who loves it is not the equal of one who takes joy in it."

6.22 Fan Chi[71] asked about wisdom.

The Master said, "Devoting yourself to transforming the values of the common people, to serving the ghosts and spirits with reverence and yet keeping them at a distance—this might be called wisdom."

---

[68]That is, Ranyou has already decided he cannot do it, and so does not even really try. For a discussion of this passage and its relationship to the problem of "weakness of will," refer to Nivison (1998), pp. 80–82.

[69]The term "petty *ru*" refers to someone content to serve as a narrow technician or "vessel" (*Analects* 2.12) or to a moral hypocrite such as the "village worthy" (*Analects* 17.13). See also *ru* under *Important Terms*.

[70]That is, the Way.

[71]One of Kongzi's younger disciples.

He then asked about *ren*.

The Master said, "One who is *ren* sees as his first priority the hardship of self-cultivation, and does not think about attaining any results or rewards. Yes, this is what we might call *ren*."

6.23 The Master said, "One who is wise takes joy in the rivers, while one who is *ren* takes joy in the mountains. The wise are active, while the *ren* are still. The wise are joyful, while the *ren* are long-lived."[72]

6.25 The Master said, "A *gu* 觚 that is not a *gu*—is it really a *gu*? Is it really a *gu*?"[73]

6.27 The Master said, "A gentleman who is broadly learned with regard to culture and whose comportment has been disciplined by the rites can, I think, rely upon this training and so avoid straying from the Way."

6.28 The Master had an audience with Nanzi, and Zilu was not pleased.[74] The Master swore an oath in Zilu's presence, saying, "If I have done anything contrary to the Way, may Heaven reject me! May Heaven reject me!"

---

[72]This is a famously cryptic passage. Perhaps the most plausible interpretation is provided by the Han dynasty commentator Bao Xian 包咸: "The wise take joy in actively exercising their talent and wisdom in governing the world, just as water flows on and on and knows no cease. The *ren* take joy in the sort of peace and stability displayed by mountains, which are naturally nonactive and yet give birth to all of the myriad things."

[73]A *gu* was a ritual drinking vessel, and commentators generally agree that Kongzi's sigh of displeasure was provoked by the fact that the sort of *gu* being used by his contemporaries was not a proper *gu* (i.e., not in accordance with Zhou dynasty standards), although there is disagreement over the question of what precisely was wrong—some claiming that the offending *gu* was not of the proper shape, others that it was not of the proper size. In any case, this passage serves to illustrate Kongzi's strict adherence to ancient practices, his dissatisfaction with the practices of his contemporaries, and his concern for the proper use of names (cf. *Analects* 13.3). For an image of a *gu*, see the web page for this volume.

[74]Nanzi was the wife of Lord Ling of Wei, and a woman of bad repute. Zilu is not pleased that Kongzi would seek an audience with such a person. As many commentators point out, however, it is likely that ritual dictated that when arriving in a state one request an audience with certain minor local officials. In having an audience with Nanzi upon arriving in Wei, Kongzi was therefore merely observing the dictates of ritual propriety, which is more important than avoiding unsavory company. Zilu might thus—like Chen Wenzi in *Analects* 5.19 above—be characterized as "pure," but such rigid fastidiousness falls rather short of *ren*.

6.29 The Master said, "Acquiring virtue through use of *zhong* 中, 'the mean'—is this not best? And yet for some time now such virtue has been quite hard to find among the people."

6.30 Zigong said, "If there were one able to universally extend his benevolence to the people and bring succor to the multitudes, what would you make of him? Could such a person be called *ren*?"

The Master said, "Why stop at *ren*? Such a person should surely be called a sage! Even someone like Yao or Shun would find such a task daunting.

"Desiring to take his stand, one who is *ren* helps others to take their stand; wanting to realize himself, he helps others to realize themselves. Being able to take what is near at hand as an example[75] could perhaps be called the method of *ren*."

Book Seven

7.1 The Master said, "I transmit rather than innovate. I trust in and have a love for antiquity. I might thus humbly compare myself to Old Peng."[76]

7.2 The Master said, "Remaining silent and yet comprehending, constantly learning and yet never becoming tired, encouraging others and never growing weary—these are tasks that present me with no difficulty."

7.3 The Master said, "That I fail to cultivate my Virtue, that I fail to delve more deeply into that which I have learned, that upon hearing what is right I remain unable to move in that direction, and that I prove unable to reform my faults—such [potential] failings are a source of constant concern to me."

7.4 In his leisure moments, the Master was proper and serious and yet fully at ease.

---

[75]This sounds like a formulation of the virtue of *shu*, "sympathetic understanding." See *Analects* 4.15.

[76]There is a great deal of commentarial controversy concerning the meaning of this reference but the most plausible explanation is that of Bao Xian, who takes the reference to be to one person: "Old Peng was a great worthy of the Yin dynasty who was fond of transmitting ancient tales. In comparing himself to Old Peng, Kongzi indicates his reverence for those who merely transmit [and do not innovate]."

7.5 The Master said, "How seriously I have declined! It has been so long since I have dreamed of the Duke of Zhou."[77]

7.6 The Master said, "Set your heart upon the Way, rely upon Virtue, lean upon *ren*, and explore widely in your cultivation of the arts."

7.7 The Master said, "I have never denied instruction to anyone who, relying upon their own means, was able to offer as little as a bundle of silk or a box of cured meat."[78]

7.8 The Master said, "I will not enlighten a heart that is not already struggling to understand, nor will I provide the proper words to a tongue that is not already struggling to speak. If I hold up one corner of a problem and the student cannot come back to me with the other three, I will not attempt to instruct him again."[79]

7.9 When the Master dined in the company of one who was in mourning, he never ate his fill.

7.12 The Master said, "If wealth could be pursued in a proper manner, I would pursue it, even if that meant serving as an officer holding a whip at the entrance to the marketplace. If there is no proper manner in which to pursue it, however, then I would prefer to follow that which I love."

7.14 When the Master was in the state of Qi he heard the Shao music,[80] and for three months after did not even notice the taste of meat. He said, "I never imagined that music could be so sublime."

---

[77]Ideally, one's immersion in the culture of the Zhou is to be so complete that it penetrates even one's dream-life.

[78]There is some debate over the exact meaning of this passage, with some (such as the Han commentator Zheng Xuan 鄭玄) claiming that it refers to the fact that Kongzi would not deny instruction to anyone over fifteen years of age, and others arguing that the term *shuxiu* 束脩 (usually taken to mean "bundle of silk and cured meat" or "bundle of cured meat") actually refers to the *bearing* of the person seeking instruction—that is, an attitude of respect and self-discipline.

[79]Cf. *Analects* 15.16.

[80]The court music of the sage king Shun.

7.16 The Master said, "Eating plain rice and drinking water, having only your bent arm as a pillow—there is certainly joy to be found in this! Wealth and fame attained improperly concern me no more than the floating clouds."[81]

7.17 The Master said, "If I were given a few more years, so that by the age of fifty I could complete my studies of the *Changes*, this might enable me to be free of major faults."[82]

7.18 The Master used the classical pronunciation when reading from the *Odes*, the *History*, and when conducting ritual. In all of these cases, he used the classical pronunciation.

7.19 Lord She[83] asked Zigong about Kongzi. Zigong had no reply.

[Upon Zigong's return], the Master said, "Why did you not just say something like this: 'He is the type of person who becomes so absorbed in his studies that he forgets to eat, whose joy renders him free of worries, and who grows old without noticing the passage of the years.'"

7.20 The Master said, "I am not the kind of person who is born with knowledge. Rather, I am the kind of person who loves antiquity, and who diligently looks there for knowledge."[84]

7.22 The Master said, "When walking with two other people, I will always find a teacher among them. Those who are good I seek to emulate, and those who are bad provide me with reminders of what needs to be changed in myself."

---

[81]Cf. *Analects* 7.12.

[82]There is a great deal of commentarial controversy over how to understand this passage, and many textual emendations have been suggested. The most plausible interpretation—requiring no emendation—is that these words were spoken by Kongzi in his mid-forties, before he had reached the stage of "understanding the Heavenly Mandate" (*Analects* 2.4). Some scholars, doubting that Kongzi studied or even was aware of the *Changes*, prefer to follow an alternate version of this passage and read *yi* 易, "*Changes*" as *yi* 亦, "an intensifying particle": "Given fifty years of study, this might indeed enable me to be free of major faults."

[83]An official in the state of Chu.

[84]Cf. *Analects* 7.1 and 16.9.

7.23 The Master said, "It is Heaven itself that has endowed me with Virtue. What have I to fear from the likes of Huan Tui?"[85]

7.30 The Master said, "Is *ren* really so far away? If I merely desire *ren*, I will find that *ren* is already here."

7.32 Whenever the Master was singing in a group and heard a beautiful voice, he inevitably asked that person to sing again, and would then harmonize with him.[86]

7.33 The Master said, "There is no one who is my equal when it comes to *wen* 'cultural refinement,' but as for actually becoming a gentleman in practice, this is something that I have not yet been able to achieve."[87]

7.34 The Master said, "How could I dare to lay claim to either sageliness or *ren*? What can be said about me is no more than this: I work at it without growing tired and encourage others without growing weary."

Gong Xihua observed, "Even this is something we disciples are unable to learn."

7.35 The Master was seriously ill, and Zilu asked permission to offer a prayer.

The Master said, "Is such a thing done?"

Zilu said, "It is. The *Eulogy*[88] reads, 'We pray for you above and below, to the spirits of Heaven and of Earth.'"

The Master said, "In that case, I have already been offering up my prayers for some time now."[89]

---

[85]Huan Tui was a minister in the state of Song who apparently wished to do Kongzi harm; cf. *Analects* 9.5 and 14.36.

[86]Cf. *Analects* 7.22.

[87]This is perhaps merely a polite demurral (cf. *Analects* 7.34), but it serves to emphasize the difficulty of obtaining in practice the proper balance between *wen*, "cultural refinement," and *zhi*, "native substance," and is no doubt meant as a warning against falling into "foppish pedantry"—the more insidious and common of the two failings described in *Analects* 6.18 above.

[88]The title of a traditional prayer text.

[89]That is, through his life's work. Any other sort of direct appeal to Heaven is unnecessary.

7.37 The Master said, "The gentleman is relaxed and at ease, while the petty man is anxious and full of worry."

7.38 The Master was tolerant while still remaining strict, impressive without being overly imposing, and respectful while still remaining at ease.

Book Eight

8.2 The Master said, "If you are respectful but lack ritual training you will become exasperating; if you are careful but lack ritual training you will become timid; if you are courageous but lack ritual training you will become unruly; and if you are upright but lack ritual training you will become inflexible.[90]

"If the gentleman is kind to his relatives, the people will be inspired toward *ren*; if he does not neglect his old acquaintances, the people will honor their obligations to others."

8.7 Zengzi said, "The *shi* 士, 'scholar,' cannot but be strong and resolute, for his burden is heavy and his Way is long. To take up *ren* as your own personal task—is this not a heavy burden? To strive without respite until death overtakes you—is this Way not long?"[91]

8.8 The Master said, "Find inspiration in the *Odes*, take your stand through ritual, and be perfected by music."

8.9 The Master said, "The people can be led along a path, but cannot be made to understand it."[92]

8.12 The Master said, "It is not easy to find someone who is able to study for even the space of three years without the inducement of an official salary."

8.13 The Master said, "If you are strong, trustworthy, and fond of learning, you can remain firm in your love of the Way even in the face of death. Do not take up residence in a state that is troubled, and leave the state that is disordered. If the Way is being realized in the world then show yourself;

---

[90]Cf. *Analects* 17.8, where *xue* 學, "study" or "learning," rather than ritual training is described as the force preventing virtue from falling into vice.

[91]Cf. *Analects* 9.11.

[92]Cf. *Analects* 16.9.

if it is not, then retire to reclusion. In a state that has the Way, to be poor and of low status is a cause for shame; in a state that is without the Way, to be wealthy and honored is equally a cause for shame."

8.19 The Master said, "How magnificent was Yao's manner of ruling! How majestic! It is only Heaven that is great, and only Yao who modeled himself after Heaven. How vast and pervasive! Among the people there were none who were able to put a name to it.[93] How majestic were his successes, how glorious his cultural splendor!"

Book Nine

9.2 A villager from Daxiang[94] remarked sarcastically, "How great is Kongzi! He is so broadly learned, and yet has failed to make a name for himself in any particular endeavor."

When the Master was told of this, he said to his disciples, "What art, then, should I take up? Charioteering? Archery? I think I shall take up charioteering."[95]

9.3 The Master said, "A cap made of hemp is prescribed by the rites, but nowadays people use silk. This is frugal, and I follow the majority. To bow before ascending the stairs[96] is what is prescribed by the rites, but nowadays people bow after ascending. This is arrogant, and—though it goes against the majority—I continue to bow before ascending."

9.5 The Master was surrounded by troops in Kuang.[97] He said, "King Wen 文 having passed away, is not *wen* 文, 'culture,' now invested here in me? If

---

[93]That is, the influence of Yao's Virtue was so subtle and pervasive that the people were transformed naturally, without being aware of what was happening. Such unself-consciousness is an important hallmark of *wuwei* behavior and Virtue-mediated influence. Cf. *Analects* 17.19, where Heaven is said to rule without the need for words.

[94]The name of a small hamlet.

[95]Kongzi's response is, of course, equally sarcastic, expressing his contempt for limited or merely technical skills. Cf. *Analects* 2.12, 9.6, and 19.7.

[96]When approaching a ruler or other superior.

[97]The most common explanation is that the target of the Kuang troops was a certain Yang Hu, who had in the past caused some trouble in the state of Kuang. Kongzi apparently physically resembled Yang Hu and—to add to the confusion—one of Kongzi's disciples was a known associate of Yang Hu's.

Heaven had intended this culture to perish, it would not have been given to those who came after the Zhou. Since Heaven does not intend that this culture should perish, what do I have to fear from the soldiers of Kuang?"

9.6 The prime minister asked Zigong, "Your Master is a sage, is he not? How is it, then, that he is skilled at so many menial tasks?"

Zigong replied, "Surely Heaven has endowed him liberally—not only intending him for sagehood, but also giving him so many other talents."

When the Master heard of this, he remarked, "How well the prime minister knows me! In my youth I was poor, and this is why I became proficient in so many menial tasks. Is the gentleman broadly skilled in trivial matters? No, he is not."[98]

9.10 Whenever the Master saw someone who was dressed in mourning, garbed in ritual cap and gown, or blind, he would immediately and without fail rise in deference, even if the person was his junior. When passing such a person, he would inevitably hasten his step."[99]

9.11 With a great sigh Yan Hui lamented, "The more I raise my head, the higher it[100] seems; the more I delve into it, the harder it becomes. Catching a glimpse of it before me, I find it suddenly at my back.

"The Master is skilled at gradually leading one on, step by step. He broadens me with culture and restrains me with the rites, and even if I wanted to rest I could not. Having exhausted all of my strength, it seems as if there is still something left, looming up ahead of me. Though I desire to follow after it, there seems to be no way through."

9.12 The Master was gravely ill, and Zilu instructed his fellow disciples to attend to Kongzi as if they were official ministers.[101]

During a remission in his illness, the Master [became aware of what was happening and] rebuked Zilu, saying, "It has been quite some time now, has it not, that you have been engaging in this charade! I have no official ministers and yet you serve me as ministers—who do you think I am going

---

[98]Cf. *Analects* 2.12, 9.2, and 19.7.

[99]As a sign of respect.

[100]The reference is clearly to the Way.

[101]That is, following the rites proper to a minister attending to a ruler—which, of course, Kongzi was not.

to fool? Am I going to fool Heaven?[102] Moreover, would I not rather die in the arms of a few of my disciples than in the arms of official ministers? Even if I am not to be accorded a grand funeral, it is not as if I am being left to die by the side of the road!"

9.13 Zigong said, "If you possessed a piece of beautiful jade, would you hide it away in a locked box, or would you try to sell it at a good price?"

The Master responded, "Oh, I would sell it! I would sell it! But I would wait for the right offer."[103]

9.14 The Master expressed a desire to go and live among the nine barbarian tribes.[104] Someone asked him, "How could you bear their *lou* 陋, 'uncouthness'?"

The Master replied, "If a gentleman were to dwell among them, what uncouthness would there be?"[105]

9.18 The Master said, "I have yet to meet a man who is as fond of Virtue as he is of sex."

9.19 The Master said, "[The task of self-cultivation] might be compared to the task of building up a mountain: if I stop even one basketful of earth short of completion, then I have stopped completely. It might also be compared to the task of leveling ground: even if I have only dumped one basketful of earth, at least I am moving forward."[106]

9.23 The Master said, "We should view the younger generation with respect, because how are we to know that those who come after us will not

---

[102]As the Jin dynasty commentator Li Chong 李充 notes, Kongzi's concern over the ritual abuses of the Ji clan—who were usurping the ritual prerogatives of the Zhou kings in an attempt to impress their contemporaries and curry favor with Heaven (see *Analects* 3.1)—no doubt accounts for some of the harshness in his rebuke of Zilu.

[103]The gentleman should surely share his Virtue with the world by taking public office. Kongzi, however, refuses to actively peddle his wares on the market, but rather waits for his Virtue to be recognized by the right ruler.

[104]A group of "barbarians" (i.e., non-Chinese) who lived along the east coast of present-day China.

[105]A testament to the transformative power of the gentleman's Virtue. Cf. *Xunzi*, chapter 2, p. 255.

[106]A bit of encouragement to balance out Yan Hui's lament in *Analects* 9.11.

prove our equals? Once, however, a man reaches the age of forty or fifty without having acquired a degree of learning, we can conclude from this fact alone that he is not worthy of commanding our respect."

9.24 The Master said, "When a man is rebuked with exemplary words after having made a mistake, he cannot help but agree with them. However, what is important is that he change himself in order to *accord* with them. When a man is praised with words of respect, he cannot help but be pleased with them. However, what is important is that he actually *live up* to them. A person who finds respectful words pleasing but does not live up to them, or agrees with others' reproaches and yet does not change—there is nothing I can do with one such as this."[107]

9.29 The Master said, "One who understands the Way is free of confusion, one who possesses *ren* is free of worries, and one who is courageous is free of fear."

Book Ten

10.2 At court, when speaking with officers of lower rank, he [Kongzi] was pleasant and affable; when speaking with officers of upper rank, he was formal and proper. When his ruler was present, he combined an attitude of reverential respect with graceful ease.

10.3 When summoned by his ruler to receive a guest, his countenance would become severe and he would quicken his steps. When he bowed to those in attendance beside him—stretching out his hands to the left or to the right, as their position required—his robes remained perfectly arrayed, both front and back. When it was time [in the ceremony] to hasten forward, he moved as though he were gliding upon wings. Once the guest had left, he invariably waited until he could report, "The guest is no longer looking back."

---

[107]Nominal assent to the Way is insufficient—one must *love* the Way and strive to embody it in one's person. The problem is what the teacher is to do with a student who intellectually understands or superficially agrees with the Way but cannot summon up the genuine commitment required of the gentleman. Cf. *Analects* 5.10, 6.12, 9.18, and 15.16.

10.10 He did not speak while eating, and ceased to converse once he had retired to bed.[108]

10.11 Even though a meal was only of coarse rice or vegetable broth, he invariably gave an offering, and did so in a grave and respectful manner.

10.12 He would not sit unless his mat was properly arranged.

10.17 One day the stables burned. Having been informed of this upon his return from court, the Master asked, "Was anyone hurt?" He did not ask about the horses.[109]

10.19 When he was sick, and his ruler came to visit him, he lay with his head to the east, draped in his court robes and with his ceremonial sash fastened about him.[110]

10.20 When summoned by his ruler, he would set off by foot, without waiting for the horses to be hitched to the carriage.[111]

10.21 Upon entering the Grand Temple, he asked questions about everything.

10.23 When receiving a gift from a friend—even something as valuable as a cart or a horse—he did not bow, unless it was a gift of sacrificial meat.[112]

10.25 When he saw someone dressed in mourning clothes, even if they were an intimate acquaintance, he invariably assumed a changed expression. When he saw someone wearing a ritual cap or a blind person, even if

---

[108]That is, he remained thoroughly focused in all of his activities.

[109]Considering that horses were quite valuable commodities and stable hands easily replaceable, Kongzi's response is both unexpected and moving.

[110]Being sick, he could not rise to greet his ruler or properly dress himself in court attire, but it would also be unseemly for him to receive his guest in civilian garb. He thus had himself arranged in bed so that he would be both ritually presentable and facing the door when the ruler entered.

[111]A sign of respect and humbleness.

[112]A gift of sacrificial meat carries with it a sort of ritual solemnity not possessed by a nonreligious gift, no matter how sumptuous it might be.

they were well-known to him he would invariably display a respectful countenance.

When passing someone dressed in funeral garb, he would bow down and grasp the crossbar of his carriage.[113] He would do the same when passing a messenger carrying official documents.

When attending a sumptuous banquet, he would invariably assume a solemn expression and rise from his seat. He would also assume a solemn expression upon hearing a sudden clap of thunder or observing a fierce wind.[114]

10.27 Startled by their arrival, the bird arose and circled several times before alighting upon a branch. [The Master] said, "This pheasant upon the mountain bridge—how timely it is! How timely it is!" Zilu bowed to the bird, and then it cried out three times before flying away.[115]

Book Eleven

11.4 The Master said, "Yan Hui is of no help to me—he is pleased with everything that I say."[116]

11.9 Yan Hui passed away. The Master lamented, "Oh! Heaven has abandoned me! Heaven has abandoned me!"

11.12 Zilu asked about serving the ghosts and spirits. The Master said, "You are not yet able to serve people—how could you be able to serve the ghosts and spirits?"

"May I inquire about death?"

"You do not yet understand life—how could you possibly understand death?"

---

[113]As a sign of respect.

[114]As a sign of respect for Heaven's power.

[115]While it is not entirely clear *why* the pheasant is being praised for timeliness (perhaps because it knows when to arise, when to alight, and when to fly off), it would seem that the ideal of timeliness—according perfectly with the demands of the situation at hand—sums up fairly well what is, on one interpretation, the general theme of Book Ten: that the Master's actions accorded perfectly with the demands of ritual propriety, no matter what the circumstances.

[116]The comment would seem to be meant ironically—cf. *Analects* 2.9.

11.17 The Ji clan was wealthier than even the Duke of Zhou ever was, and yet Ranyou collected taxes on their behalf to further increase their already excessive wealth. The Master declared, "He is no disciple of mine. If you younger disciples were to sound the war drums and attack him, I would not disapprove."

11.22 Zilu asked, "Upon learning something, should one immediately put it into practice?"

The Master replied, "As long as one's father and older brothers are still alive, how could one possibly put what one has learned immediately into practice?"[117]

[On a later occasion] Ran You asked, "Upon learning something, should one immediately put it into practice?"

The Master replied, "Upon learning something, you should immediately put it into practice."

Zihua, [having observed both exchanges], inquired, "When Zilu asked you whether or not one should immediately put into practice what one has learned, you told him one should not, as long as one's father and elder brother were still alive. When Ranyou asked the same question, however, you said that one should immediately put into practice what one has learned. I am confused, and humbly ask to have this explained to me."

The Master said, "Ranyou is overly cautious, and so I wished to urge him on. Zilu, on the other hand, is reckless, and so I sought to make him more cautious."[118]

11.26 Zilu, Zengxi, Ranyou, and Zihua were seated in attendance. The Master said to them, "I am older than any of you, but do not feel reluctant to speak your minds on that account. You are all in the habit of complaining, 'I am not appreciated.' Well, if someone *were* to appreciate your talents [and give you employment], how would you then go about things?"

Zilu spoke up immediately. "If I were given charge of a state that could field a thousand chariots—even one hemmed in between powerful states, suffering from armed invasions, and afflicted by famine—before three years were up I could infuse it with courage and a sense of what is right."

---

[117]That is, you should continue to defer to their judgment and not take the initiative.

[118]This is a paradigmatic example of how the Master's teachings were variously formulated depending upon the individual needs of his students—a Confucian version of the Buddhist practice of *upaya*, or "skillful means."

The Master smiled at him, and then turned to Ranyou. "You, Ranyou!" he said, "What would you do?"

Ranyou answered, "If I were given charge of a state sixty or seventy—or at least fifty or sixty—square *li* in area, before three years were up I would see that it was materially prosperous. As for instructing the people in ritual practice and music, this is a task that would have to await the arrival of a gentleman."

The Master then turned to Zihua. "You, Zihua! What would you do?"

Zihua answered, "It is not that I am saying that I would actually be able to do so, but my wish, at least, would be to devote myself to study. I would like, perhaps, to serve as a minor functionary—properly clad in ceremonial cap and gown—in charge of ancestral temple events or diplomatic gatherings."

The Master then turned to Zengxi. "You, Zengxi! What would you do?"

Zengxi stopped strumming upon the zither, and as the last notes faded away he set the instrument aside and rose to his feet. "I would choose to do something quite different from any of the other three."

"What harm is there in that?" the Master said. "Each of you is merely expressing your own aspirations."

Zengxi then said, "In the third month of spring, once the spring garments have been completed, I should like to assemble a company of five or six young men and six or seven boys to go bathe in the Yi River and enjoy the breeze upon the Rain Altar,[119] and then return singing to the Master's house."

The Master sighed deeply, saying, "I am with Zengxi!"

After the other three disciples had left, Zengxi stayed behind. He asked, "What did you think of what the other disciples said?"

"Each of them was merely expressing their aspirations, and nothing more."

"Why, then, did the Master smile at Zilu?"

"One governs a state by means of ritual propriety. His words failed to express the sense of deference proper to the ritual practice, and this is why I smiled at him."

"Was Ranyou, then, the only one not concerned with statecraft?"

"Since when did something sixty or seventy—even fifty or sixty—square *li* in area not constitute a state?"

---

[119]According to traditional commentators, the Yi River was near Kongzi's home, and the Rain Altar was located just above the river.

"Was Zihua, then, the only one not concerned with statecraft?"

"If ancestral temples and diplomatic gatherings are not the business of the feudal lords, what then are they? And if Zihua is able to serve in only a minor capacity, then who would be able to serve in a major one?"[120]

Book Twelve

12.1 Yan Hui asked about *ren*.

The Master said, "Restraining yourself and returning to the rites constitutes *ren*. If for one day you managed to restrain yourself and return to the rites, in this way you could lead the entire world back to *ren*. The key to achieving *ren* lies within yourself—how could it come from others?"

Yan Hui asked, "May I inquire as to the specifics?"

The Master said, "Do not look unless it is in accordance with the rites; do not listen unless it is in accordance with the rites; do not speak unless it is in accordance with the rites; do not move unless it is in accordance with the rites."

Yan Hui replied, "Although I am not quick to understand, I ask permission to devote myself to this teaching."

12.2 Zhong Gong[121] asked about *ren*.

The Master said, "When in public, comport yourself as if you were receiving an important guest; in your management of the people, behave as if you were overseeing a great sacrifice. Do not impose upon others what you yourself do not desire. In this way, you will encounter no resentment in your state or in your family."[122]

Zhong Gong replied, "Although I am not quick to understand, I ask permission to devote myself to this teaching."

---

[120]The Master is thus equally disapproving of Zilu, Ranyou, and Zihua's aspirations—all of which are overly focused upon statecraft techniques—although only Zilu's response is audacious enough to provoke a smile. The point is that true government is effected through the superior Virtue gained by ritual practice, and the task of the gentleman is thus to focus upon self-cultivation and attaining a state of joyful harmony with the Way. Such *wuwei* harmony with the Way is exemplified by Zengxi's musical bent, his reluctance to speak about his aspirations, and the sense of spontaneous joy in the cultivated life conveyed by his answer.

[121]A disciple of Kongzi.

[122]The first set of advice concerns the virtue of *zhong*, "loyalty," the second that of *shu*, "sympathetic understanding." Cf. *Analects* 4.15.

12.7 Zigong asked about governing.

The Master said, "Make sure there is sufficient food, sufficient troops, and that you have the trust of the people—that is all there is to it."

Zigong said, "If sacrificing one of these three things became unavoidable, which of them would you sacrifice first?"

The Master replied, "I would first sacrifice the troops."

Zigong said, "If sacrificing one of the two remaining things became unavoidable, which of them would you sacrifice first?"

The Master replied, "I would sacrifice the food. From ancient times there has always been death among us, but a state cannot stand once it has lost the trust of the people."

12.9 Duke Ai said to Youzi, "The harvest was poor and I cannot satisfy my needs. What should I do?"

Youzi said, "Why don't you try taxing the people one part in ten?"[123]

"I am now taxing them two parts in ten, and even so I cannot satisfy my needs. How could reducing the tax to one part in ten help?"

Youzi answered, "If the people have all that they need, how could their ruler be lacking? If the people do not have all they need, how can their ruler be satisfied?"

12.11 Duke Jing of Qi[124] asked Kongzi about governing.

Kongzi responded, "Let the ruler be a true ruler, the ministers true ministers, the fathers true fathers, and the sons true sons."[125]

The Duke replied, "Well put! Certainly if the ruler is not a true ruler, the ministers not true ministers, the fathers not true fathers, and the sons not true sons, even if there is sufficient grain, will I ever get to eat it?"

12.17 Jikangzi[126] asked Kongzi about governing.

Kongzi responded, "To *zheng* 政, 'govern,' means to *zheng* 正, 'correct.' If you set an example by being correct, who will dare to be incorrect?"

---

[123]This was a traditional Zhou practice.

[124]Reigned 547–490 B.C.E.

[125]That is, let everyone concentrate on fulfilling their role-specific duties and order will result naturally—there is no need for some special technique or theory of "governing." Cf. *Analects* 13.3.

[126]A senior minister in the state of Lu, who held power from 492–468 B.C.E.

12.18 Jikangzi was concerned about the prevalence of robbers in his state, and asked Kongzi's advice as to how to deal with this problem.

Kongzi said, "If you could just get rid of your own excessive desires, the people would not steal even if you rewarded them for it."

12.19 Jikangzi, questioning Kongzi about governing, asked, "If I were to execute those who lacked the Way in order to advance those who possessed the Way, what would you think of that?"

Kongzi responded, "In your governing what need is there for executions? If you desire good, then the people will also desire good. The Virtue of the gentleman is like the wind, and the Virtue of the petty person is like the grass—when the wind blows over the grass, the grass must bend."

12.24 Zengzi said, "The gentleman acquires friends by means of his cultivation, and then relies upon his friends for support in becoming *ren*."

Book Thirteen

13.3 Zilu asked, "If the Lord of Wei[127] were to employ you to serve in the government of his state, what would be your first priority?"

The Master answered, "It would be, of course, to assure that *ming* 名, 'names,' were being applied *zheng* 正, 'correctly!'"[128]

Zilu said, "Is this really a matter of concern? It would seem that the Master's suggestion is rather wide of the mark. Why worry about correcting names?"

The Master replied, "How boorish you are, Zilu! When it comes to matters that he does not understand, the gentleman should refrain from flaunting his ignorance. If names are not correct, speech will not be in accordance with actuality; when speech is not in accordance with actuality, things will

---

[127]This probably refers to Zhe, the grandson of Lord Ling of Wei (who appears in *Analects* 15.1 below), who took over the throne in 493 B.C.E.

[128]Cf. *Analects* 6.25, 12.11, and 12.17 as well as Xunzi's "On Correct Naming" (see *Xunzi*, chapter 22, pp. 278–84). Reading this passage in light of *Analects* 12.11 ("let the fathers be true fathers, the sons true sons"), it can be seen as a barb against the ruling family of Wei, whose disordered family relations eventually threw the state into chaos. The Duke doted upon his notorious wife, Nanzi (see *Analects* 6.28), whom his resentful son, Prince Kuai Kui, then attempted to kill. This attempt having failed, the son was forced to flee Wei, and the grandson, Zhe, subsequently took over the throne upon the Duke's death. Prince Kuai Kui then returned to Wei with the backing of a foreign army in an attempt to oust his son.

not be successfully accomplished. When things are not successfully accomplished, ritual practice and music will fail to flourish; when ritual and music fail to flourish, punishments and penalties will miss the mark. And when punishments and penalties miss the mark, the people will be at a loss as to what to do with themselves. This is why the gentleman only applies names that can be properly spoken, and assures that what he says can be properly put into action. The gentleman simply guards against arbitrariness in his speech. That is all there is to it."

13.4 Fan Chi asked to learn agricultural techniques [from Kongzi].

The Master said, "When it comes to that, any old farmer would be a better teacher than I."

He asked to learn gardening.

The Master said, "When it comes to that, any old gardener would be a better teacher than I."

Fan Chi then left. The Master remarked, "What a petty man that Fan Chi is! When the ruler loves ritual propriety, then none among the people will dare to be disrespectful. When the ruler loves rightness, then none among the people will dare not to obey. When the ruler loves trustworthiness, then none among the people will dare not to be honest. The mere existence of such a ruler would cause the people throughout the world to bundle their children on their backs and seek him out. Why, then, concern yourself with agricultural techniques?"

13.5 The Master said, "Imagine a person who can recite the three hundred odes by heart but, when delegated a governmental task, is unable to carry it out or, when sent out into the field as a diplomat, is unable to use his own initiative—no matter how many odes he might have memorized, what good are they to him?"[129]

13.6 The Master said, "When the ruler's person is *zheng* 正, 'correct,' his will is put into effect without the need for official orders. When the ruler's person is not correct, he will not be obeyed no matter how many orders he issues."

---

[129]The point of learning is not mere scholastic knowledge, but rather the ability to apply this knowledge flexibly in a situation-specific manner. Cf. *Analects* 2.11.

13.12 The Master said, "If a true king were to arise, it would certainly be a generation before we would see a return to *ren*."[130]

13.16 The Lord of She asked about governing.

The Master said, "[Act so that] those close to you are pleased, and those who are distant are drawn to you."

13.18 The Lord of She said to Kongzi, "Among my people there is one we call 'Upright Gong.' When his father stole a sheep, he reported him to the authorities."

Kongzi replied, "Among my people, those we consider 'upright' are different from this: fathers cover up for their sons, and sons cover up for their fathers. This is what it means to be 'upright.'"[131]

13.20 Zigong asked, "What does a person have to be like before he could be called a true *shi*, 'scholar?'"

The Master said, "Conducting himself with a sense of shame, and not doing dishonor to his ruler's mandate when sent abroad as a diplomat—such a person could be called a scholar."

"May I ask what the next best type of person is like?"

"His lineage and clan consider him filial, and his fellow villagers consider him deferential to his elders."

"And the next best?"

"His speech is invariably trustworthy, and his actions invariably bear fruit. What a narrow, rigid little man he is! And yet he might still be considered the next best."

"How about those who today are involved in the government?"

The Master exclaimed, "Oh! Those petty functionaries are not even worth considering."

13.21 The Master said, "If you cannot manage to find a person of perfectly balanced conduct to associate with, I suppose you must settle for the reck-

---

[130]Because a true king rules through the gradual transformative power of *de* 德, "Virtue," rather than through harsh laws and punishments, which may achieve more immediate—but short-lived—results.

[131]Cf. 17.8, where the danger of an overly rigid or strict sense of honesty or uprightness is described as being "harmful"—the harm being, presumably, to such natural relationships as that between father and son.

less and the fastidious. The reckless in their pursuit of the Way plunge right in, while the fastidious are careful not to get their hands dirty."[132]

13.24 Zigong asked, "What would you make of a person whom everyone in the village praised?"

The Master said, "I would not know what to make of him."

"What if everyone in the village reviled him?"

"I would still not know. Better if it were this way: those in the village who are good praise him, and those who are not good revile him."

Book Fourteen

14.5 Nangong Kuo[133] said to Kongzi, "Yi was a skillful archer, and Ao was strong enough to push a boat over dry land,[134] and yet neither of them met a natural death. Yu and Hou Ji, on the other hand, did nothing but personally tend to the land, and yet they both ended up with possession of the world."

The Master did not answer.

After Nangong Kuo left, the Master sighed, "What a gentlemanly person he is! How he reveres Virtue!"[135]

14.12 Zilu asked about the complete person.

The Master said, "Take a person as wise as Zang Wuzhong, as free of desire as Gongzhuo, as courageous as Zhuangzi of Bian,[136] and as accomplished in the arts as Ranyou, and then acculturate them by means of ritual and music—such a man might be called a complete person."

He then continued: "But must a complete person today be exactly like this? When seeing a chance for profit he thinks of what is right; when confronting danger he is ready to take his life into his own hands; when en-

---

[132]Cf. *Mengzi* 7B37.

[133]Most commentators identify him as an official in the state of Lu.

[134]Both Yi and Ao are legendary martial heroes.

[135]The world is won, not through martial prowess, but through careful and patient cultivation. Commentators suggest that Nangong Kuo meant to compare Kongzi himself to Yu and Hou Ji, and that Kongzi thus remained silent out of modesty.

[136]Zang Wuzhong and Meng Gongzhuo were both respected officials in Lu, and Zhuangzi of Bian was an official in the state of Bian who was legendary for his courage. The latter is no relation to the Daoist philosopher whose work is included in this volume.

during an extended period of hardship, he does not forget what he had professed in more fortunate times—such a man might also be called a complete person."

14.13 The Master asked Gongming Jia about Gongshu Wenzi,[137] saying, "Is it really true that your master did not speak, did not laugh, and did not take?"

Gongming Jia answered, "Whoever told you that was exaggerating. My master only spoke when the time was right, and so people never grew impatient listening to him. He only laughed when he was genuinely full of joy, and so people never tired of hearing him laugh. He only took what was rightfully his, and so people never resented his taking of things."

The Master said, "Was he really that good? Could he really have been that good?"

14.24 The Master said, "In ancient times scholars worked for their own improvement; nowadays they seek only to win the approval of others."

14.25 Qu Boyu[138] sent an envoy to Kongzi. Kongzi offered the envoy a seat and asked, "How is your Master doing?"

The envoy answered, "My Master wishes to reduce the number of his faults, but has not yet been able to do so."

After the envoy left, the Master said, "Now that is an envoy! That is an envoy!"[139]

14.27 The Master said, "The gentleman is ashamed to have his words exceed his actions."

14.29 Zigong was evaluating the strengths and weaknesses of others.

The Master remarked sarcastically, "What a worthy man that Zigong must be! As for me, I hardly have the time for such activities."[140]

---

[137]Gongshu Wenzi was an official in the state of Wei, and Gongming Jia presumably was his disciple.

[138]An official in the state of Wei.

[139]Kongzi is praising Qu Boyu's noble intentions and realistic evaluation of himself as well as the modesty expressed through his envoy's words. Cf. *Analects* 14.27.

[140]The Master is entirely focused upon cultivating and correcting himself; only someone who has mastered the Way has the luxury to begin evaluating others, and Zigong is hardly such a person.

14.30 The Master said, "Do not worry that you are not known to others; worry rather that you yourself lack ability."

14.34 Someone asked, "What do you think of the saying, 'Requite injury with *de* 德, "kindness"'?"[141]

The Master replied, "With what, then, would one requite kindness? Requite injury with uprightness, and kindness with kindness."

14.35 The Master sighed, "No one understands me—is that not so?"

Zigong replied, "How can you say that no one understands you, Master?"

"I am not resentful toward Heaven, nor do I cast aspersions upon other people. I study what is below in order to comprehend what is above. If there is anyone who could understand me, perhaps it is Heaven."

14.36 Gong Boliao submitted an accusation against Zilu to the head of the Ji clan, Ji Sun. Zifu Jingbo reported this to Kongzi, adding, "My Master [i.e., Ji Sun] has certainly been led astray by Gong Boliao, but my influence with him is still sufficient to see to it that Gong Boliao's corpse is displayed in the marketplace."[142]

The Master said, "Whether or not the Way is to be put into action is a matter of *ming*, 'fate.' Whether or not the Way is to be discarded is also a matter of fate. What power does Gong Boliao have to affect fate!"

14.38 Zilu spent the night at Stone Gate. The morning gatekeeper asked him, "Where have you come from?"

Zilu answered, "From the Kong clan."

"Isn't he the one who knows that what he does is impossible and yet persists anyway?"[143]

---

[141]This phrase appears in chapter 63 of the *Laozi* or *Daodejing*—and Kongzi's response to it is certainly anti-Laozian in flavor—but it was likely a traditional saying not necessarily identified with the *Daodejing* itself.

[142]Zifu Jingbo, an official in the state of Lu, is claiming here that he has enough influence with his master, the *de facto* ruler of Lu, that he can both convince him of Zilu's innocence and see to it that his fellow minister, Gong Boliao, is executed for his slander.

[143]That is, Kongzi persists in his efforts to reform the world even though it appears hopeless. Confucians embrace this derisive comment with pride; cf. 18.7.

14.39 The Master was playing the chimes in the state of Wei.

A man with a wicker basket strapped to his back passed by the door of the Kong clan residence and remarked, "Whoever is playing the chimes like that certainly had something on his mind!" After listening for a moment, he added, "How squalid! How pettily stubborn! If no one understands you, you should just stop trying to make them understand:

> If the river is deep, hike up your robes and wade across;
> If it is shallow, simply raise your hem."[144]

The Master [hearing these comments] responded, "Such resoluteness! Who could take issue with that!"[145]

14.44 Zilu asked about the gentleman.

The Master said, "He cultivates himself in order to achieve reverence."

"Is that all?"

"He cultivates himself in order to bring peace to others."

"Is that all?"

"He cultivates himself in order to bring peace to the people. Cultivating oneself and thereby bringing peace to the people is an accomplishment that even a Yao or a Shun would not disdain."

Book Fifteen

15.1 Lord Ling of Wei asked Kongzi about military formations.

Kongzi replied, "I have heard something about the use of ceremonial stands and dishes for ritual offerings, but I have never learned about the use of battalions and divisions."

He left the next day.

---

[144]From the *Odes* (*Mao* # 54).

[145]Kongzi's critic is wearing a wicker basket strapped to his back—the sign of a farmer or manual laborer—and yet has an ear for classical music and can quote from the *Odes*. No ordinary commoner, he is more likely a scholar who has gone into reclusion, whether for philosophical or political reasons. Like the gatekeeper in *Analects* 14.38, he is annoyed at Kongzi's persistence in the face of an indifferent world, and advises him to simply accord with the times—as he himself has presumably done. Kongzi's sarcastic response expresses contempt for such passivity and lack of resolution. Cf. *Analects* 8.7, 18.6 and 18.7.

15.2 In the state of Chen they had exhausted their provisions, and the disciples were so weak from hunger that they could not even stand. Zilu angrily turned to the Master and said, "Does even the gentleman find himself in such hardship?"

The Master said, "The gentleman remains firm in hardship, while the petty man is overwhelmed by it."

15.5 The Master said, "Was not Shun one who ruled by means of *wuwei*? What did he do? He made himself reverent and took his [ritual] position facing south, that is all."[146]

15.9 The Master said, "The scholar with great aspirations and the person of *ren* will not pursue life at the expense of *ren*, and they may be called upon to give up their lives in order to assure *ren*'s completion."

15.11 Yan Hui asked about running a state.

The Master said, "Put into effect the calendar of the Xia, travel in the carriages of the Shang,[147] and clothe yourself in the ceremonial caps of the Zhou. With regard to music, listen only to the *Shao* and *Wu*.[148] Rid yourself of the tunes of Zheng, and keep glib people at a distance—for the tunes of Zheng are licentious, and glib people are dangerous."

15.16 The Master said, "There is simply nothing I can do with a person who is not himself constantly asking, 'What should I do? What should I do?'"

15.18 The Master, "The gentleman takes *yi*, 'rightness,' as his *zhi*, 'substance,' and then puts this substance into practice by means of ritual, gives it expression through modesty, and perfects it by being *xin*, 'trustworthy.' Now that is a gentleman!"

15.21 The Master said, "The gentleman seeks for it in himself; the petty person seeks for it in others."[149]

---

[146]The ruler faces south, thus serving as the earthly correlate to the pole star. Cf. *Analects* 2.1.

[147]Which were said to have realized the perfect harmony of form and function without being overly ostentatious.

[148]The music of Shun and King Wu, respectively.

[149]Cf. *Analects* 14.24.

15.24 Zigong asked, "Is there one teaching that can serve as a guide for one's entire life?"

The Master answered, "Is it not *shu*, 'sympathetic understanding?' Do not impose upon others what you yourself do not desire."

15.28 The Master said, "When the multitude reviles something or someone, you must examine it and judge for yourself. The same holds true for what the multitude praises."[150]

15.29 The Master said, "Human beings can broaden the Way—it is not the Way that broadens human beings."[151]

15.30 The Master said, "To have a fault and not change your ways—this is truly to be at fault."

15.31 The Master said, "I once engaged in *si* 'thought' for an entire day without eating and an entire night without sleeping, but it did no good. It would have better for me to have spent that time in *xue*, 'study.'"[152]

15.36 The Master said, "When presented with an opportunity to exercise *ren*, defer to no one, even to your teacher."

15.37 The Master said, "The gentleman is true and correct, but is not rigid when it comes to fulfilling the details of his promises."[153]

15.41 The Master said, "Words should convey their message, and leave it at that."[154]

---

[150]Cf. *Analects* 13.24.

[151]As Cai Mo 蔡謨 (Jin dynasty) explains, "The Way is silent and without action, and requires human beings to be put into practice. Human beings are able to harmonize with the Way—this is why the text reads: 'Human beings are able to broaden the Way.' The Way does not harmonize with humans—this is why the text reads: 'It is not the Way that broadens human beings.'"

[152]Cf. *Analects* 2.15.

[153]Cf. *Analects* 19.11.

[154]Cf. *Analects* 19.14.

Book Sixteen

16.4 Kongzi said, "Beneficial types of friendship are three, as are harmful types of friendship. Befriending the upright, those who are true to their word, and those of broad learning—these are the beneficial types of friendship. Befriending clever flatterers, skillful dissemblers, and the smoothly glib—these are the harmful types of friendship."

16.5 Kongzi said, "Beneficial types of joy are three, as are harmful types of joy. Taking joy in regulating yourself through the rites and music, in speaking well of others, and in possessing many worthy friends—these are the beneficial types of joy. Taking joy in arrogant gratification, dissolute pleasure-seeking, or decadent licentiousness—these are the harmful types of joys."

16.8 The Master said, "The gentleman stands in awe of three things: *tian-ming*, 'the Heavenly Mandate,' great men, and the teachings of the sages. The petty person does not understand the Mandate of Heaven and thus does not regard it with awe; he shows disrespect to great men and ridicules the teachings of the sages."

16.9 Kongzi said, "Those who are born understanding it are the best; those who understand it through learning are second. Those who find it difficult and yet persist in their studies are still lower. The worst are the people who find it difficult but do not even try to learn."

16.13 Ziqin asked Boyu, "Have you acquired any esoteric learning?"[155]

Boyu answered, "I have not. Once my father was standing by himself in the courtyard and, as I hurried by with quickened steps, he asked, 'Have you studied the *Odes*?' I replied that I had not. He said, 'Unless you study the *Odes*, you will be unable to speak.' I retired to my room and studied the *Odes*.

"On another day my father was again standing by himself in the courtyard and, as I hurried by with quickened steps, he asked, 'Have you studied the *Rites*?' I replied that I had not. He said, 'Unless you study the *Rites*,

---

[155]Boyu is Kongzi's son, and Ziqin is wondering whether or not—as the Master's own flesh and blood—he received any special instruction withheld from the other disciples.

you will be unable to take your stand.' I retired to my room and studied the *Rites*.

"These two things are what I have been taught."

Chen Gang retired and, smiling to himself, remarked "I asked one question and learned three things: I learned about the *Odes* and about the *Rites*, and also learned that the gentleman keeps his son at a distance."

Book Seventeen

17.2 The Master said, "By *xing* 性, 'nature,' people are similar; they diverge as the result of *xi* 習, 'practice.'"

17.8 The Master said, "Zilu! Have you heard about the six virtuous teachings and the six corresponding vices?"[156]

Zilu replied, "I have not."

"Sit! I will tell you about them. Loving *ren* without balancing it with a love for learning will result in the vice of foolishness. Loving knowledge without balancing it with a love for learning will result in the vice of deviant thought. Loving trustworthiness without balancing it with a love for learning will result in the vice of harmful rigidity. Loving uprightness without balancing it with a love for learning will result in the vice of intolerance. Loving courage without balancing it with a love for learning will result in the vice of unruliness. Loving resoluteness without balancing it with a love for learning will result in the vice of willfulness."

17.9 The Master said, "Little Ones, why do you not study the *Odes*? The *Odes* can be a source of inspiration[157] and can broaden your perspective; they can be used to bring you together with others as well as to give vent to vexations and complaints. In the domestic sphere, they articulate the proper manner to serve your father, and in public life they describe the proper manner to serve your ruler. They also acquaint you with the names for a wide variety of birds and beasts, plants and trees."

---

[156]The literal meaning of *bi* 蔽—the word translated here as "vice"—is "to cover over" or "obscure." Mengzi uses it to describe how the mind can be "led astray" by things in *Mengzi* 6A15; in "Undoing Fixations," Xunzi uses it with the sense of "fixations" that can lead us to endorse inferior doctrines or ways of life (see *Xunzi*, chapter 21, pp. 272–78).

[157]Cf. *Analects* 8.8.

17.10 The Master said to Boyu, "Have you begun learning the 'South of Zhou' and the 'South of Shao' sections of the *Odes*?[158] To be a man and not apply yourself to 'South of Zhou' and 'South of Shao' would be like standing with your face to the wall, would it not?"

17.11 The Master said, "When we say, 'the rites, the rites,' are we speaking merely of jade and silk? When we say, 'music, music,' are we speaking merely of bells and drums?"[159]

17.13 The Master said, "The village worthy is the thief of Virtue."[160]

17.18 The Master said, "I hate it that purple is usurping the place of vermillion,[161] that the tunes of Zheng are being confused with classical music, and that the clever of tongue are undermining both state and clan."

17.19 The Master sighed, "Would that I did not have to speak!"

Zigong said, "If the Master did not speak, then how would we little ones receive guidance?"

The Master replied, "What does Heaven ever say? Yet the four seasons go round and find their impetus there, and the myriad creatures are born from it. What does Heaven ever say?"

17.21 Zaiwo, inquiring about the three-year mourning period, remarked, "Even one year seems already long enough. If the gentleman for three years refrains from practicing ritual, surely the rites will fall into ruin; if for three years he refrains from music, surely this will be disastrous for music. After the lapse of a year the old grain has been used up, the new grain has ripened, and the drill and tinder have been used to rekindle the fire.[162] One year is thus long enough."

---

[158]These are the first two sections of the *Odes* and are used here to refer to the *Odes* as a whole. Cf. *Analects* 16.13.

[159]Just as true music requires not merely instruments but sensitive musicians to play them, so true ritual requires not merely traditional paraphernalia but also emotionally committed, sensitive practitioners. Cf. *Analects* 2.7 and 3.12.

[160]See *Mengzi* 7B37 for an elaboration of this passage.

[161]Vermillion—the color of the Zhou—being the traditional and proper color for ceremonial clothing, and purple a more "modern" and increasingly popular variant.

[162]Apparently an annual ritual of renewal.

The Master asked, "Would you feel comfortable then eating your sweet rice and wearing your brocade gowns?"[163]

"I would."

The Master replied, "Well, if you would feel comfortable doing so, then you should do it. When the gentleman is in mourning, he finds no savor in sweet foods, finds no joy in listening to music, and finds no comfort in his place of dwelling. This is why he gives these things up. But if you would feel fine doing such things, then you should do them!"

After Zaiwo left, the Master remarked, "How lacking in *ren* is this Zaiwo! A child is completely dependent upon the care of his parents for three years—this is why the three-year mourning period is a universal custom. Did not this Zaiwo receive three years of love from his parents?"

17.23 Zilu asked, "Does the gentleman admire courage?"

The Master said, "The gentleman admires what is right most of all. A gentleman who possessed courage but lacked a sense of rightness would create great disorder, while a petty person who possessed courage but lacked a sense of rightness would become a thief or robber."

Book Eighteen

18.6 Kongzi passed Chang Ju and Jie Ni, who were yoked together pulling a plow through a field. He sent Zilu to ask them where the ford was to be found.[164]

Chang Ju inquired, "That fellow holding the reins there—who is he?"

Zilu answered, "That is Kong Qiu [Kongzi]."

---

[163]While mourning, one is restricted to a diet of plain rice and water and wearing rough hemp for clothing. One is to suspend most normal social activity, maintain particular demeanors and refrain from familiar pleasures. A child was to maintain three years (often understood as into the beginning of the third year—i.e., approximately 25 months) of mourning for a deceased parent. These rigors were thought to express respect for the dead and serve as a spiritual exercise for the living.

[164]Kongzi and his entourage were apparently attempting to cross a nearby river, but this passage is also to be read allegorically: the "ford" is the way out of the "great flood of chaos" mentioned below. The use of self-consciously primitive technology by these two figures (most plows were ox-drawn by this time), as well as their knowledge of Kongzi's identity revealed below, makes it clear that they are no ordinary commoners, but rather educated primitivist recluses who have deliberately rejected society and culture (cf. *Analects* 14.39). Like many of the figures in the *Zhuangzi*, their names appear to be allegorical ("Standing Tall in the Marsh" and "Prominent in the Mud," respectively); the appearance of this literary technique and the complex narrative quality of this passage mark it as quite late.

"Do you mean Kong Qiu of Lu?"

"The same."

"Then he knows where the ford is."[165]

Zilu then asked Jie Ni.

Jie Ni also replied with a question: "Who are you?"

"I am Zilu."

"The disciple of Kong Qiu of Lu?"

"Yes."

"We are engulfed in a great flood of chaos, and the entire world is like this—who can be relied upon to change it? This being the case, rather than follow a scholar who merely flees from one person to another,[166] wouldn't it be better to follow a scholar who flees from the age itself?" He then proceeded to cover up his seeds with dirt and did not look back.

Zilu returned and reported this conversation to Kongzi. The Master was lost in thought for a moment, and then remarked, "A person cannot flock together with the birds and the beasts.[167] If I do not seek to follow this person or the other, who then would I follow? If the Way were realized in the world, then I would not need to change anything."[168]

18.7 Zilu had fallen behind and encountered by chance an old farmer, who was carrying a wicker basket suspended from his staff. Zilu asked, "Have you seen my Master?"

> The old farmer answered,
> "Won't soil his dainty hands
> Can't tell millet from wheat[169]
> Who, then, might your master be?"

He then planted his staff in the ground and began weeding.

---

[165]The comment is sarcastic. Kongzi should know, given that he is reputed to be so wise.

[166]Referring to Kongzi's itinerant seeking after a ruler who would put his Way into practice.

[167]As these recluses seek to do.

[168]Kongzi's compassion for the suffering of the world is such that he cannot take what he views as the easy way out—simply withdrawing from society and living the life of a noble, unsullied recluse (cf. *Analects* 18.8)—although his mission as the "bell-clapper of Heaven" (*Analects* 3.24) is grueling and fraught with difficulties and frustrations.

[169]This comment is a rhyming verse in the Chinese—an indication that again we are not dealing with an ordinary, illiterate farmer.

[Not knowing how to reply], Zilu simply remained standing with his hands clasped as a sign of respect.

The old farmer subsequently invited him back to his house to stay the night. He killed a chicken and prepared some millet for Zilu to eat, and presented his two sons to him. The next day Zilu caught up to Kongzi and told him what had happened.

"He must be a scholar recluse," the Master said. He sent Zilu back to the old farmer's house to meet with him again, but by the time Zilu got there the man had already disappeared. Zilu then remarked, "To avoid public service is to be without a sense of what is right. Proper relations between elders and juniors cannot be discarded—how, then, can one discard the rightness that obtains between ruler and minister?[170] To do so is to wish to preserve one's personal purity at the expense of throwing the great social order into chaos. The gentleman takes office in order to do what is right, even though he knows that the Way will never fully be put into practice."[171]

18.8 Example of men who went into reclusion include Bo Yi, Shu Qi, Yu Zhong, Yi Yi, Zhu Zhang, Liu Xiahui, and Shao Lian.[172]

The Master said, "Not lowering their aspirations, not disgracing their persons—surely this describes Bo Yi and Shu Qi." Of Liu Xiahui and Shao Lian he remarked, "All that you can say about them is that, although they allowed their aspirations to be lowered and their persons to be disgraced, their speech was perfectly in accord with their social status and their actions perfectly considered." Of Yu Zhong and Yi Yi he said, "They lived in seclusion and freely spoke their minds, remained perfectly pure in person, and judged perfectly when it was time to resign from office."

He concluded, "I, however, am different from all of them in that I have no preconceived idea concerning what is permissible and what is not."[173]

---

[170]The point is that the old recluse recognizes the first set of relationships in requiting Zilu's expression of respect (of a younger man for an elder) with proper hospitality and in formally presenting his sons, but ignores the second by living in reclusion and avoiding any sort of official contact.

[171]Cf. *Analects* 14.38.

[172]These men were all famous recluses who withdrew from public service on moral grounds. For more on Bo Yi and Shu Qi see *Important Figures*.

[173]Cf. *Analects* 4.10.

Book Nineteen

19.6 Zixia said, "Being broadly learned and resolute of *zhi* 志, 'purpose,' incisive in one's questioning, and able to *si* 'reflect upon' what is near at hand—this is where *ren* is to be found."

19.7 Zixia said, "The myriad artisans remain in their workshops in order to perfect their crafts, just as the gentleman studies in order to realize his Way."

19.11 Zixia said, "As long as one does not cross the line when it comes to the grand principles, it is permissible to be flexible when it comes to issues of minor import."[174]

19.12 Ziyou said, "Among the disciples of Zixia, the younger ones are fairly competent when it comes to tasks such as mopping and sweeping, responding to questions, and entering and retiring from formal company, but these are all *mo* 末, 'superficialities.'[175] They are completely at a loss when it comes to mastering the *ben* 本, 'root.' Why is this?"

When Zixia heard of this, he remarked, "Ai! Ziyou seems to have missed the point. With regard to the Way of the gentleman, how are we to know who will at first seem to grasp it but then later collapse from exhaustion? It is like growing plants and trees: you differentiate the various species by observing them as sprouts.[176] When it comes to the Way of the gentleman, how can you show preference for one part over another? Starting at the beginning and working through to the end—surely this describes none other than the sage!"

19.14 Ziyou said, "Mourning should fully express grief and then stop at that."[177]

19.21 Zigong said, "A gentleman's mistake is like an eclipse of the sun or the moon: when he errs, everyone notices it, and when he makes amends, everyone looks up to him."

---

[174]Cf. *Analects* 15.37.

[175]Literally, "the branches," contrasted with the "root" below.

[176]That is, the true potential gentleman can be recognized by how he handles the small matters taught at the beginning of the course of instruction.

[177]Cf. *Analects* 15.41.

Book Twenty

20.3 Kongzi said, "One who does not understand the Heavenly Mandate lacks the means to become a gentleman. One who does not understand the rites lacks the means to take his stand. One who does not understand how to evaluate the words of others lacks the means to understand people."[178]

---

[178]Cf. *Analects* 2.4.

SELECTIVE BIBLIOGRAPHY

Translations

Ames, Roger T., and Henry Rosemont, Jr.

1998 *The Analects of Confucius: A Philosophical Translation.* New York: Ballantine Books. (Includes the Chinese text, extensive introduction, and bibliography, and notes upon recent archeological finds related to the *Analects*.)

Brooks, E. Bruce, and A. Taeko Brooks.

1998 *The Original Analects: Sayings of Confucius and His Successors.* New York: Columbia University Press. (Follows the Brookses' radical reorganization of the text and includes commentary on individual passages; the translation is at times awkward, but is perhaps the most precise and scholarly one available in English.)

Lau, D. C.

1979 *Confucius: The Analects.* New York: Penguin Books. (The classic and most commonly read translation.)

Waley, Arthur.

1989 *The Analects of Confucius.* New York: Vintage Books. (Originally published in 1938, this is perhaps the smoothest and most literary of *Analects* translations.)

Secondary Works

Eno, Robert.

1990 *The Confucian Creation of Heaven: Philosophy and the Defense of Ritual Mastery.* Albany, NY: State University of New York Press. (Portrays the early Ru-ist [Confucian] school as a tight-knit community concerned solely with the details of ritual practice.)

Fingarette, Herbert.

1972 *Confucius: The Secular as Sacred.* New York: Harper Torchbooks. (Emphasizes the communal and constitutive nature of the rites.)

Hall, David L., and Roger T. Ames.

1987 *Thinking Through Confucius*. Albany, NY: State University of New York Press. (Emphasizes the creative aspects of the Confucian tradition.)

Ivanhoe, Philip J.

1990 "Reweaving the 'One Thread' of the *Analects*." *Philosophy East & West* 40.1: 17–33. (On the relationship between the virtues of *zhong* "dutifulness," and *shu* "sympathetic understanding.")

Kupperman, Joel.

1968 "*Confucius* and the Problem of Naturalness." *Philosophy East & West* 18: 175–85. (Discusses the question of how conscious, artificial practice can ever produce "natural," spontaneous behavior.)

Lin Yu-sheng.

1924 "The Evolution of the Pre-Confucian Meaning of *Jen* 仁 and the Confucian Concept of Moral Autonomy." *Monumenta Serica* 31: 172–204. (Classic discussion of the evolution of the term *ren*.)

Nivison, David S.

1998 *The Ways of Confucianism: Investigations in Chinese Philosophy*. Bryan Van Norden, ed. Chicago and La Salle, IL: Open Court Press. (A collection of essays on Confucianism.)

Roetz, Heiner.

1993 *Confucian Ethics of the Axial Age*. Albany, NY: State University of New York Press. (Argues for the convention-transcending nature of the Confucian project and the autonomy of the Confucian moral agent.)

Shun Kwong-loi.

1993 "*Jen* and *Li* in the *Analects*." *Philosophy East & West* 43.3: 457–479. (On the relationship between the virtue of *ren* 仁 and *li* 禮, "ritual practice.")

Taylor, Rodney.

1990 *The Religious Dimensions of Confucianism*. Albany, NY: State University of New York Press. (Emphasizes the oft-overlooked religious nature of the Confucian tradition.)

Tu, Wei-ming.

1979 *Humanity and Self-Cultivation: Essays in Confucian Thought.* Berkeley, CA: Asian Humanities Press. (Includes essays on *ren* 仁 and *li* 禮, "ritual practice.")

Van Norden, Bryan W., ed.

2000 *Confucius and the Analects: New Essays.* New York: Oxford University Press. (Wide-ranging anthology on various aspects of the *Analects*.)

▪ CHAPTER TWO ▪

MOZI

Introduction

Mozi 墨子, "Master Mo," (c. 480–390 B.C.E.) founded what came to be known as the *Mojia* "Mohist School" of philosophy and is the figure around whom the text known as the *Mozi* was formed. His proper name is Mo Di 墨翟. Mozi is arguably the first true philosopher of China known to us. He developed systematic analyses and criticisms of his opponents' positions and presented an array of arguments in support of his own philosophical views. His interest and faith in argumentation led him and his later followers to study the forms and methods of philosophical debate, and their work contributed significantly to the development of early Chinese philosophy. Mozi himself was probably of quite humble origins. He may have been a member of the craft or artisan class, and his philosophy is distinctively antiaristocratic. Early in life, he may have studied with followers of Confucius. However, he went on to become a serious critic of the emerging Confucian tradition.[1]

Mozi was not just a philosopher. He led an organized utopian movement whose members engaged in direct social action, including the military defense of states and cities that he judged to be victims of wars of expansion. He was a strong and charismatic leader who inspired his followers to dedicate themselves to his unique view of social justice. This required them to lead austere and quite demanding lives under his direct control and command. Mozi could tax his followers, judge, and punish them; under certain circum-

---

[1]During Kongzi's life and after his death, people began to declare themselves followers of Kongzi and his Way. At this point, it makes sense to describe these people as constituting a "Confucian" tradition or "Confucianism."

stances he could even put them to death. The discipline that defined his movement is reflected in a number of his philosophical positions. His ideal state is highly centralized, orderly, and ideologically unified.

Mozi saw ideological differences and the factionalism they spawned as the primary source of human suffering. Therefore, he sharply criticized the family-based ethical and political system of Kongzi for its inherent partiality and advocated a strict chain of command leading up through a monarch and resting in Heaven. In place of Confucian *ren* 仁 "benevolence" he advocated a form of state consequentialism, which sought to maximize three basic goods: the wealth, order, and population of the state. As an alternative to Confucian familial love, he argued for *jian'ai* 兼愛, which is often translated as "universal love" but is better understood as "impartial care." In Mozi's view, the central ethical problem was excessive *partiality*, not a lack of *compassion*. His primary goal was to change and shape behavior— in particular the way people are treated—not to cultivate emotions, attitudes, or virtues. He showed little interest in what one would call moral psychology and embraced a simple and highly malleable view of human nature. This led him away from the widely observed Chinese concern with self-cultivation. His general lack of appreciation for psychological goods and the need to control desires and shape dispositions and attitudes also led him to reject categorically the characteristic Confucian concern with culture and ritual. These views are expressed in his arguments against elaborate funerals and musical performances, two mainstays of Confucianism.

While Mozi was not a self-cultivationist, he believed that human beings can change even apparently deeply held attitudes and dispositions quickly and easily. For a variety of reasons, he maintained that people could be induced to take up almost any form of behavior, even behavior that was suicidal. He shared a commonly held early Chinese belief in a psychological tendency to respond in kind to the treatment one receives. He further believed that in an effort to win the favor of their rulers, many people are inclined to act as their rulers desire. Those who do not respond to either of these influences can be motivated and controlled by a system of strict rewards and punishments, enforced by the state and guaranteed by the support of Heaven, ghosts, and spirits. Most important of all, Mozi believed that properly crafted rational arguments provide strong if not entirely compelling motivation to act for anyone who is able to understand them; presented with a superior argument, thinking people act accordingly.

Mozi's later followers lasted until the time of the short-lived Qin dynasty when the movement seems to have suddenly come to an end. The reasons for this are not well documented, but most likely a paramilitary group such as the Mohists would never have been tolerated by and could not survive during the centralized and militarized regime of the Qin. There is some irony in this as several prominent ideas in the *Fajia* "Legalist" thought that served as the state ideology of the Qin find clear precedents in Mozi's philosophy. The later Mohists continued Mozi's early interests and developed sophisticated systems of logical analysis, mathematics, optics, physics, defensive warfare technology and strategy, and a formal ethic based upon calculations of benefit and harm. All of these philosophical concerns can be found in the early strata of the *Mozi* that are represented in the following selections.

Chapter Eight: Honoring the Worthy[2]

Our teacher Mozi[3] says, "The kings, dukes, and great officials who now rule the various states all want their states to be wealthy, their populations great, and their administrations orderly, and yet instead of wealth they get poverty, instead of great populations they get meager ones, and instead of order they get chaos. In this way they fundamentally miss what they desire and get what they dislike."

What is the reason for this?[4]

Our teacher Mozi says, "This is because the kings, dukes, and great officials who rule the various states are not able to honor the worthy and employ the capable in carrying out their rule. And so in a state where there are many worthy men, good order will be secure, and in a state where there are few worthy men good order will be tenuous. This is why it is the proper

---

[2]There are multiple versions of many of the central chapters of the *Mozi;* these probably reflect the views of the three different sects of Mohism, which appeared after Mozi's death. I have chosen what I consider to be the most interesting version of each chapter translated here. Our chapter headings refer to the primary divisions in standard editions of the complete text.

[3]The *Mozi* is unique among early Chinese philosophical texts in the manner in which it refers to its author. Most philosophers of the period were referred to as "Master so-and-so" by adding the honorific *zi* 子 after the person's surname (see *Important Terms*). In the case of Mo Di 墨翟 this would yield "Mozi." But the Mohists refer to their master as *zimozi* 子墨子. This probably meant "Our teacher Master Mo." A similar prefixed use of *zi* is found in the *Gongyang* commentary to the *Spring and Autumn Annals*.

[4]The *Mozi* often employs the literary device of an unnamed interlocutor to carry forth the dialogue.

work of kings, dukes, and great officers to increase the number of worthy men in their states."

Since this is the case, what is the best way to go about increasing the number of worthy men?

Our teacher Mozi says, "It is analogous to the case of wanting to increase the number of good archers or charioteers in one's state. One must reward and esteem them, revere and praise them; then one can succeed in increasing the number of good archers or charioteers in one's state. How much more should this be done in the case of worthy men—those who are well versed in virtuous conduct, discriminating in discussion, and broadly knowledgeable! Such men are state treasures, guardians of the altars to the soil and grain.[5] They too must be rewarded and esteemed, revered and praised; then one can succeed in increasing the number of worthy men in one's state.

"This is why in ancient times, when the sage-kings ruled, they announced that:

> Those who are not righteous, I shall not enrich.
> Those who are not righteous, I shall not esteem.
> Those who are not righteous, I shall not regard as kin.
> Those who are not righteous, I shall not get close to.

When the wealthy and eminent in the state heard this they retired and thought to themselves, 'At first, we could rely on our wealth and eminence, but now the king promotes the righteous and does not turn away the poor and the humble. This being the case, we too must be righteous.' When the king's relatives heard this they retired and thought to themselves, 'At first, we could rely on being royal kin, but now the king promotes the righteous and does not turn away the most distant relations. This being the case, we too must be righteous.' When those close to the king heard this they retired and thought to themselves, 'At first, we could rely on being close to the king, but now the king promotes the righteous and does not turn away those far removed from him. This being the case, we too must be righteous.' When those far removed from the king heard this they too retired and thought to themselves, 'At first, we thought that being far removed from the king meant

---

[5]The site of important state sacrifices and often used as a metaphor for the foundation and stability of the state. Cf. Mozi's various references to this and other sacrificial sites in "On Ghosts." See *Mozi*, chapter 31, pp. 90–100.

we had nothing to rely upon, but now the king promotes the righteous and does not turn away those far removed from him. This being the case, we too must be righteous.' The word spread to those serving in distant cities and outlying regions, to the sons of nobles serving within the court, to all those within the capital, and on out to the common people throughout the four corners of the kingdom. Hearing this, they all strove to be righteous."

What is the reason for such success?

Our teacher Mozi says, "Because those above employed those below for only one reason and those below served those above in only one way.[6] This state of affairs can be compared to the case of a rich man who builds a high wall around his house. Once the wall is complete, he has it cut through in one place and uses this for his door. If a thief should enter, the rich man can close the door and search for the thief, knowing that he has no way to escape. Why? Because the rich man has secured what is most vital.

"This is why in ancient times, when the sage-kings ruled, they promoted the virtuous and honored the worthy. Even someone who worked as a farmer, artisan, or merchant, if they had talent they were promoted, given high rank and a handsome salary, entrusted with responsibility, and empowered to have their orders obeyed. The sage-kings said, 'If their rank is not high, the people will not revere them. If their salary is not substantial, the people will not put trust in them. If their orders are not empowered with authority, the people will not hold them in awe.' These three things were given to the worthy not as rewards but in order to help them complete their duties.

"And so, at that time, rank was awarded on the basis of virtue, work was assigned according to office, reward was distributed according to the amount of labor done, and salary allotted in proportion to the effort expended. And so officials were not guaranteed constant nobility and people did not have to perpetually remain in a humble state. Those with ability were promoted, those without ability were demoted. This is what it means to, 'Promote public righteousness and prevent private resentment.'[7]

"And so, in ancient times, Yao promoted Shun from southern Fuyang,[8] entrusted him with the administration of his kingdom, and the world was at peace. Yu promoted Yi from central Yinfang, entrusted him with the administration of his kingdom, and the nine realms were brought to perfec-

---

[6]That is, people were evaluated and served only on the basis of their righteousness.

[7]This seems to have been a recognizable political slogan of the time.

[8]A place of uncertain location.

tion.[9] Tang promoted Yi Yin from among the cooks in his kitchen, entrusted him with the administration of his kingdom, and his plans all were successful. King Wen promoted Hong Yao and Tai Yi from their work with rabbit snares, entrusted them with the administration of his kingdom, and the western territories submitted peacefully.[10] And so, at that time, even among those ministers with substantial salaries and prestigious positions, none failed to be reverent and cautious in carrying out their duties, and even among the farmers, craftsmen, and merchants, none failed to exert themselves in honoring virtue.

"And so good men should be employed as capable assistants and responsible agents. If a ruler is able to retain such men, then his plans will not be frustrated nor his body wearied with work. A ruler's fame shall be assured and his work successfully completed, his best tendencies will flourish and his worst shall not take form all because he retains the support of good men."

This is why our teacher Mozi says, "When things are going well, you must promote worthy men. When things are not going well, you must promote worthy men. And if you would reverently carry on the Way of Yao, Shun, Yu, and Tang, then you must honor the worthy. Honoring the worthy is the root and basis of good government."

Chapter Eleven: Obeying One's Superior

Our teacher Mozi says, "In ancient times, when people first came into being and before there were governments or laws, each person followed their own norm[11] for deciding what was right and wrong.[12] And so where

---

[9]Yi is Bo Yi 伯益 (not to be confused with the brother of Shu Qi—see *Important Figures*). Bo Yi assisted Yu in his flood-control work and served him as an exemplary minister. Yinfang is a place of uncertain location. According to an ancient system of territorial division, China consisted of "nine realms."

[10]Hong Yao and Tai Yi were gamekeepers for King Wen. Technically, "rabbit snares" should be rendered "rabbit nets." See selection # 177 (*Mao # 278*) in Arthur Waley, *The Book of Songs* (London: Allen and Unwin, 1952) for a poem singing the praises of such a gamekeeper, describing him as a fitting companion and confidant for a king. (Note: *The Book of Songs* is Waley's translation of the classic referred to in this volume as the *Odes*).

[11]The character *yi* 義 that I here translate as "norm" (for deciding what is right and wrong) is often rendered as "right" or "righteousness" (see *Important Terms*). The senses are clearly related, but the context here argues for "norm" as more appropriate.

[12]"Right and wrong" is the translation of the Chinese terms *shi/fei* 是非. Below, these terms are rendered verbally as "to approve" and "to condemn." Cf. *Mengzi* 2A6 and n. 27 to that passage.

there was one person there was one norm, where there were two people there were two norms, where there were ten people there were ten different norms. As many people as there were, that was how many norms were recognized. In this way people came to approve their own norms for what is right and wrong and thereby condemn the norms of others. And so they mutually condemned each other's norms. For this reason, within families, there was resentment and hatred between fathers and sons and elder and younger brothers that caused them to separate and disperse and made it impossible for them to cooperate harmoniously with one another. Throughout the world, people used water, fire, and poison to harm and injure one another, to the point where if they had strength to spare, they would not use it to help each other, if they had excess goods, they would leave them to rot away rather than distribute them to one another, and if they had helpful teachings, they would hide them away rather than teach them to one another. The chaos that ruled in the world was like what one finds among the birds and beasts.

"Those who understood the nature of this chaos saw that it arose from a lack of rulers and leaders and so they chose the best person among the most worthy and capable in the world and established him as the Son of Heaven. The Son of Heaven was established, but because his strength was not sufficient for the task of ruling the entire world, they chose among the most worthy and capable in the world and installed the best among them as the three imperial ministers. The Son of Heaven and three imperial ministers were established, but because the world is so vast it was impossible for them to know and judge in each case what would be right or wrong, beneficial or harmful for the people of distant states and different regions. And so they divided up the myriad states and established feudal lords and rulers. The feudal lords and rulers were established, but because their strength was not sufficient for the task before them, they chose among the most worthy and capable in the world and installed them as governors and leaders.

"Once the governors and leaders were in place, the Son of Heaven announced his rule to the people of the world saying, 'Whenever you hear of something good or bad, always inform your superior. Whenever your superior approves of something as right you too must approve of it. Whenever your superior condemns something as wrong you too must condemn it. Should a superior commit any transgression, one must offer proper remonstrance. Should your subordinates do anything good, one must widely recommend them. To obey one's superior and to avoid joining together with those in subordinate positions—such conduct will be rewarded by superiors and praised by subordinates. But if you hear of something good or bad and fail to inform your superior, if you are not able to approve of what your superior approves of and condemn what your superior rejects, if you do not offer proper remonstrance when a superior commits a transgression and do not widely recommend subordinates who do good, if you do not obey your superior and you join together with those in subordinate positions–such conduct will be punished by superiors and denounced by the people. This is how superiors shall determine rewards and punishments and they shall make careful examinations to ensure that their judgments are reliable.'

"And so, the leader of each village would be the most benevolent person in the village. When he announced his rule to the people of the village he would say, 'Whenever you hear of anything either good or bad, you must report it to the head of the district. Whenever the head of the district approves of something all of you must also approve of it. Whenever the head of the district condemns something all of you must also condemn it. Eliminate any bad teachings that you may have and study the good teachings of the head of the district. Eliminate any bad practices that you may have and study the good practices of the head of the district. If you do this then how could the district ever become disordered?'

"If we look into how good order was maintained in the district, what do we find? Was it not simply because the leader of the district was able to unify the norms followed within the district that he was able to maintain good order in it?

"The leader of each district would be the most benevolent person in the district. When he announced his rule to the people of the district he would say, 'Whenever you hear of anything either good or bad, you must report it to the ruler of the state. Whenever the ruler of the state approves of something all of you must also approve of it. Whenever the ruler of the state condemns something all of you must also condemn it. Eliminate any bad teachings that you may have and study the good teachings of the ruler of the state. Eliminate any bad practices that you may have and study the good practices of the ruler of the state. If you do this then how could the state ever become disordered?'

"If we look into how good order was maintained in the state, what do we find? Was it not simply because the ruler of the state was able to unify the norms followed within the state that he was able to maintain good order in it?

"The ruler of each state would be the most benevolent person in the state. When he announced his rule to the people of the state he would say,

'Whenever you hear of anything either good or bad, you must report it to the Son of Heaven. Whenever the Son of Heaven approves of something all of you must also approve of it. Whenever the Son of Heaven condemns something all of you must also condemn it. Eliminate any bad teachings that you may have and study the good teachings of the Son of Heaven. Eliminate any bad practices that you may have and study the good practices of the Son of Heaven. If you do this then how could the world ever become disordered?'

"If we look into how good order was maintained in the world, what do we find? Was it not simply because the Son of Heaven was able to unify the norms followed within the world that he was able to maintain good order in it?

"If the people of the world all obey their superiors on up to the Son of Heaven but do not obey Heaven, then Heavenly disasters still will not cease. Now, the hurricanes and torrential rains that regularly are visited upon the people is how Heaven punishes them for not obeying its will."

This is why our teacher Mozi says, "In ancient times, sage-kings created the Five Punishments[13] to facilitate good order among their people. These are like the main thread of a skein of silk or the drawstring of a net. They are how the sage-kings gathered in those in the world who refused to obey their superiors."

Chapter Sixteen: Impartial Caring

Our teacher Mozi says, "The business of a benevolent person is to promote what is beneficial to the world and eliminate what is harmful."

Granted that this is true, what are the greatest harms that are being done in the world today? Our teacher Mozi says, "It is things such as great states attacking small states, great families wreaking havoc with lesser families, the strong robbing the weak, the many doing violence to the few, the clever deceiving the ignorant, and the noble acting arrogantly toward the humble. These are some of the great harms being done in the world. In addition, there are rulers who are not kind, ministers who are not loyal, fathers who are not loving, and children who are not filial. These too are some of the great harms being done in the world. There are also those of low character

---

[13]The Five Punishments are said to be tatooing the face, cutting off the nose, cutting off the feet, castration, and death.

who use weapons, poison, water, and fire to injure and steal from one another. These too are some of the great harms done in the world."

If we try to discover the origin of these different harms, where do we find they come from? Do they come from caring for and benefiting people? This clearly must be rejected as the origin of these harms. We must recognize that they come from hating and stealing from people. If we wish to distinguish those in the world who hate and steal from people, do we refer to them as impartial or partial? We clearly must call them partial. And so it is those who are partial in their dealings with others who are the real cause of all the great harms in the world.

This is why our teacher Mozi says, "I condemn partiality."

Now those who condemn another's view must offer something in its place. If one condemns another's view without offering something in its place this is like adding water to a flood or flame to a fire. Such appeals prove to have no merit.

This is why our teacher Mozi says, "Replace partiality with impartiality."

Since this is what is correct, how then can we replace partiality with impartiality?

Our teacher Mozi says, "If people regarded other people's states in the same way that they regard their own, who then would incite their own state to attack that of another? For one would do for others as one would do for oneself. If people regarded other people's cities in the same way that they regard their own, who then would incite their own city to attack that of another? For one would do for others as one would do for oneself. If people regarded other people's families in the same way that they regard their own, who then would incite their own family to attack that of another? For one would do for others as one would do for oneself. And so if states and cities do not attack one another and families do not wreak havoc upon and steal from one another, would this be a harm to the world or a benefit? Of course one must say it is a benefit to the world."

If we try to discover the source of these different benefits, where do we find they come from? Do they come from hating and stealing from people? This clearly must be rejected as the source of these benefits. We must recognize that they come from caring for and benefitting people. If we wish to distinguish those in the world who care for and benefit people, do we refer to them as impartial or partial? We clearly must call them impartial. And so it is those who are impartial in their dealings with others who are the real cause of all the great benefits in the world.

This is why our teacher Mozi says, "I approve of impartiality. Moreover, earlier I said that, 'The business of a benevolent person is to promote what is beneficial to the world and eliminate what is harmful.' And now I have shown that impartiality gives rise to all the great benefits in the world and that partiality gives rise to all the great harms in the world."

This is why our teacher Mozi says, "I condemn partiality and approve of impartiality for the reasons given above. If one takes impartiality as the correct standard and truly seeks to promote and procure what is beneficial to the world, then those with sharp ears and keen eyes will listen and look out for others. Those with stout legs and strong arms will work for others, and those who understand the Way will educate and instruct others. And so men who reach old age without finding a wife and having children will get the support they need to live out their years. Young and helpless orphans, who are without father or mother, will find the support they need in order to reach maturity. Now such benefits can be attained only if impartiality is taken as the correct standard. And so I don't see what reason any person in the world who has heard about impartiality can give for condemning it."

Though this is so, there are still people in the world who condemn impartiality, saying, "It is surely a fine thing. Nevertheless, how can it possibly be applied?"

Our teacher Mozi says, "If it could not be applied even I would condemn it! But is there really anything that is fine that cannot be put to use? Let us consider both sides of the matter. Suppose there were two people: one who maintains partiality and one who maintains impartiality. And so the person who maintains partiality would say, 'How can I possibly regard the well-being of my friends as I do my own well-being? How can I possibly regard the parents of my friends as I do my own parents?' And so when his friends are hungry, the partial person does not feed them. When his friends are cold, he does not clothe them. When his friends are ill, he does not nurture them. And when his friends die, he does not bury them. This is what the partial person says and what he does. But this is not what the impartial person says nor is this how he acts. The impartial person says, 'I have heard that in order to be a superior person in the world, one must regard the well-being of one's friends as one regards one's own well-being; one must regard the parents of one's friends as one regards one's own parents. Only in this way can one be a superior person.' And so when the impartial person's friends are hungry, he feeds them. When his friends are cold, he clothes them. When his friends are ill, he nurtures them. And when his friends die, he buries them. This is what the impartial person says and what he does.

"Now the words of the two people that we have considered contradict each other and their actions are diametrically opposed. Let us suppose, though, that both are trustworthy in what they say and reliable in what they do. And so their words and deeds fit together like the two halves of a tally, and they always follow through and act on what they say. If we grant all of this, there is a further question I would like to ask. Suppose one must put on one's armor and helmet and go to war in a vast and open wilderness where life and death are uncertain; or suppose one was sent by one's ruler or high minister to the distant states of Ba, Yue, Qi, or Jing[14] and could not be sure of either reaching them or ever returning from one's mission. Under such conditions of uncertainty, to whom would one entrust the well-being of one's parents, wife, and children? Would one prefer that they be in the care of an impartial person or would one prefer that they be in the care of a partial person? I believe that under such circumstances, there are no fools in all the world. Even though one may not advocate impartiality, one would certainly want to entrust one's family to the person who is impartial. But this is to condemn impartiality in word but prefer it in deed, with the result that one's actions do not accord with what one says. And so I don't see what reason any person in the world who has heard about impartiality can give for condemning it."

Though this is so, there are still people in the world who condemn impartiality, saying, "It is an acceptable way for choosing reliable people but one can't use it to choose one's ruler."

Our teacher Mozi says, "Let us consider both sides of the matter. Suppose there were two rulers: one who maintains impartiality and one who maintains partiality. And so the ruler who maintains partiality would say, 'How can I possibly regard the well-being of my myriad subjects as I do my own well-being? This is profoundly at odds with the way people in the world feel. How brief is the span of a person's life upon this earth! It rushes by like a galloping team of horses glimpsed through a crack!' And so when his subjects are hungry, the partial ruler does not feed them. When his subjects are cold, he does not clothe them. When his subjects are ill, he does not nurture them. And when his subjects die, he does not bury them. This is what the partial ruler says and what he does. But this is not what the impartial ruler says nor is this how he acts. The impartial ruler says, 'I have heard that in order to be an enlightened ruler in the world, one must first worry about

---

[14]Ba, Yue, Qi, and Jing are four ancient states that were far removed from the center of Chinese civilization at the time.

the well-being of one's people and then worry about oneself. Only in this way can one be a enlightened ruler.' And so when the impartial ruler's people are hungry, he feeds them. When his people are cold, he clothes them. When his people are ill, he nurtures them. And when his people die, he buries them. This is what the impartial ruler says and what he does.

"Now the words of the two rulers that we have considered contradict each other and their actions are diametrically opposed. Let us suppose, though, that both are trustworthy in what they say and reliable in what they do. And so their words and deeds fit together like the two halves of a tally, and they always follow through and act on what they say. If we grant all of this, there is a further question I would like to ask. Suppose there were a terrible epidemic in which most of the people suffered bitterly from hunger and cold and many lay dead and unburied in the ditches and gullies.[15] Between these two rulers, which one would the people then follow? I believe that under such circumstances, there are no fools in all the world. Even though one may not advocate impartiality, one would certainly want to follow the ruler who is impartial. But this is to condemn impartiality in word but prefer it in deed with the result that one's actions do not accord with what one says. And so I don't see what reason any person in the world who has heard about impartiality can give for condemning it."

Though this is so, there are still people in the world who condemn impartiality saying, "Impartiality is benevolent and right but how can one practice it? The impossibility of practicing impartiality is like the impossibility of picking up Mount Tai and carrying it across the Chang Jiang or Huang He."[16] And so impartiality is something they want to do but feel is impossible to practice.

Our teacher Mozi says, "As for picking up Mount Tai and carrying it across the Chang Jiang or Huang He, this is something that no human being has ever done. But as for impartially caring for and benefitting one another, this is something that we know the four former sage-kings[17] themselves practiced."

---

[15]People lying unburied in the ditches and gullies was a common trope used to illustrate a state of profound misrule. Cf. for example, *Mengzi* 1B12, 2B4. (not in this volume).

[16]Picking up Mount Tai and carrying it across a vast expanse of water is a common trope for an impossible task. Cf. *Mengzi* 1A7 where the vast expanse of water is the North Sea. The Chang Jiang or "Yangtze River" and the Huang He or "Yellow River" are the largest rivers in central China.

[17]Kings Yu, Tang, Wen, and Wu.

How do we know that the four former sage-kings themselves followed these practices?

Our teacher Mozi says, "I am not of their age or time and so have not personally heard their voices or seen their faces, but I know this by what is written on bamboo and silk, etched on metal and stone, and inscribed on basins and bowls that have passed down to us through succeeding generations. For example, the *Great Oath*[18] says, 'The illumination of King Wen was like the sun and the moon. His brightness reached to the four directions and out to the western regions.' This describes the extensiveness of King Wen's impartial care for the world. It compares his impartiality to the way the sun and the moon impartially illuminate the entire world without showing any favoritism."

Though the impartiality that our teacher Mozi talks about here takes King Wen as its model, it is not just in the *Great Oath* that one finds such examples. The *Oath of Yu*[19] too offers such a model. Yu says,

> Come together all my people and heed my words! It is not that I, the little one,[20] dares to bring about such chaos; but the ruler of the Miao[21] is ever more unreasonable and deserves Heaven's punishment. This is why I now lead you, the rulers of the various states, on a campaign to rectify the ruler of the Miao.

This shows that the reason Yu launched a campaign to rectify the ruler of the Miao was not because he wanted to increase his wealth and honor, earn for himself additional favors and blessings, or because it pleased his eyes and ears, but rather because he wanted to contribute to the benefit of the world and eliminate what is harmful to it. Such was the impartiality of Yu.

---

[18]The "Great Oath" was a speech purportedly given by King Wu. The original was said to be included in the *History* but was lost. A later forgery is included in the present edition of the *History* and part of it is quite similar to what Mozi quotes here. See Legge, *The Shoo King*, pp. 296–97.

[19]The *Oath of Yu* is a lost section of the *History* that purportedly recorded the words of the sage-king Yu. Again a passage that is quite similar to what Mozi quotes can be found in the present text. See Legge, *The Shoo King*, pp. 64–65.

[20]The "little one" (literally, "small child") is a self-deprecating term of self-reference used by virtuous kings.

[21]The Miao are said to be a people who lived to the southeast in the area of present-day Hunan and Hubei.

Though the impartiality that our teacher Mozi talks about here takes Yu as its model, it is not just in the *Oath of Yu* that one finds such examples. The *Declaration of Tang*[22] too offers such a model. Tang says,

> I, the little one, Lü,[23] presume to use a dark-colored sacrifice to make my announcement to the Lord of Heaven above. I declare that Heaven's great drought is my responsibility. I do not know if I have committed some offense against those above or below. If there is any merit, I dare not conceal it. If there is any offense, I dare not excuse it. The judgment lies in your mind alone, Lord! If those within my domain have committed any offense, let the responsibility rest with me. If I have committed any offense, let the responsibility not fall upon those within my domain.

This shows that while Tang had the honor of being the Son of Heaven and possessed the wealth of the entire world, he still did not hesitate to present himself as an offering in his sacrificial declaration to the Lord on High, the ghosts, and the spirits. Such was the impartiality of Tang.

Though the impartiality that our teacher Mozi talks about here takes Tang as its model, it is not just in the *Oath of Yu* and the *Declaration of Tang* that one finds such examples. The *Odes of Zhou*[24] too offer such a model. The *Odes of Zhou* say,

> The King's Way is broad so broad;
> Without partiality or party.
> The King's Way is even so even;
> Without party or partiality.
> Straight as an arrow;

---

[22]The *Declaration of Tang* is another lost section of the *History* that purportedly recorded the words of the sage-king Tang. However, lines similar to what Mozi here quotes appear in *Analects*, chapter 20. Also similar lines can be found scattered throughout the present *Announcement of Tang* section of the History. See Legge, *The Shoo King*, pp. 184–90.

[23]On the "little one" see n. 20. Lü is the personal name of King Tang and in such a public context, this use of the personal name is another humble form of self-reference.

[24]This leads us to look in the *Odes*. However, the present text has only the last four lines quoted here (*Mao # 203*) with slight variation. The first four lines, though, are found with slight variation in the present text of the *History*. For the last four lines, see James Legge, tr., *The Chinese Classics, Volume IV, The She King*, reprint (Hong Kong: Hong Kong University Press, 1970), p. 353; for the first four, see Legge, *The Shoo King*, p. 331.

As even as a whetstone.
It is what the noble man follows;
And the common man admires.

What I have been talking about here is not just some notion or theory. In ancient times, when Kings Wen and Wu ruled, they allocated everything equitably, rewarding the worthy and punishing the wicked without showing any partiality to their relatives or brothers. Such was the impartiality of Kings Wen and Wu. And the impartiality that our teacher Mozi talks about here takes Kings Wen and Wu as its models. So I don't see what reason any person in the world who has heard about impartiality can give for condemning it.

Though this is so, there are still people in the world who condemn impartiality, saying, "It does not seek what is beneficial for one's parents, so does it not harm filial piety?"

Our teacher Mozi says, "Let us consider the case of a filial son who seeks what is beneficial for his parents. Does a filial son who seeks what is beneficial for his parents want other people to care for and benefit his parents or does he want other people to dislike and steal from his parents? According to the very meaning of filial piety, he must want other people to care for and benefit his parents. Given this, how should one act in order to bring about such a state of affairs? Should one first care for and benefit the parents of another, expecting that they in turn will respond by caring for and benefitting one's own parents? Or should one first dislike and steal from other people's parents, expecting that they in turn will respond by caring for and benefitting one's own parents? Clearly one must first care for and benefit the parents of others in order to expect that they in turn will respond by caring for and benefitting one's own parents. And so for such mutually filial sons to realize unlimited good results, must they not first care for and benefit other people's parents? Or should they let it be the case that filial sons are the exception and not the rule among the people of the world?

"Let us consider what is said in the writings of the former kings. In the *Elegies*[25] it says,

---

[25]The *Elegies* are a section in the *Odes* (see *Odes* under *Important Texts*). Only the first two lines, with slight variation, appear in the present version of the text. See Legge, *The She King*, p. 514.

There are no words that are left unanswered,
No virtue that is left without a response.
If you toss me a peach,
I respond with a plum.

According to these lines, anyone who cares for others will receive care from them while anyone who dislikes others will in turn be disliked. And so I don't see what reason any person in the world who has heard about impartiality can give for condemning it.

"Perhaps people will think that impartial care is too difficult to carry out. But things more difficult than this have been successfully carried out. In the past, King Ling of the state of Chu was fond of slender waists.[26] During his reign the people of Chu ate no more than one meal a day and became so weak that they could not raise themselves up without the support of a cane nor could they walk without leaning against a wall. Curtailing one's food is something very difficult to do, but masses of people did it in order to please King Ling. Within a single generation the people changed because they wanted to accord with the wishes of their superior.

"In the past, Gou Jian, King of the state of Yue, was fond of bravery. And so he taught his soldiers and subjects to be brave. But since he was not sure if they were really brave he had his ships set aflame and ordered that the drums signal an advance. His troops fell on top of one another in their forward charge and countless numbers of them perished in the water and flames. Even when they ceased drumming, still the troops did not retreat. We can say that the soldiers of Yue were resolute indeed! Charging into flames is something very difficult to do, but masses of people did it in order to please the King of Yue. Within a single generation the people changed because they wanted to accord with the wishes of their superior.

"In the past, Duke Wen of Jin was fond of rough and simple attire. During his reign the people of Jin wrapped themselves in sheets of cloth, wore sheepskin jackets, hats of raw silk, and hempen shoes. They would dress this way when they had an audience with the Duke and parade around in such attire at court. Getting people to wear rough and simple attire is something very difficult to do, but masses of people did it in order to please Duke Wen. Within a single generation the people changed because they wanted to accord with the wishes of their superior.

---

[26]This and the following story about the King of Yue are also cited by Han Feizi in "The Two Handles." See *Hanfeizi*, chapter 7, p. 309–10.

"Curtailing one's food, charging into flames, and wearing rough and simple attire are among the most difficult things in the world to get people to do, but masses of people did it in order to please their superiors. Within a single generation the people changed. Why? Because they wanted to accord with the wishes of their superiors.

"Now as for impartially caring for and benefitting one another, such things are incalculably beneficial and easy to practice. The only problem is that there are no superiors who take delight in them. If only there were superiors who delighted in them, who encouraged their practice through rewards and praise, and threatened those who violate them with penalties and punishments, I believe that the people would take to impartially caring for and benefitting one another just as naturally as fire rises up and water flows down. One could not stop them from being practiced anywhere in the world.

"And so impartiality is the way of the sage-kings. It offers security to kings, dukes, and great officials and provides ample food and clothing to the myriad people. So for gentlemen there is nothing better than carefully inquiring into the nature of impartiality and working to carry it out. Those who do so are sure to be kind as rulers, loyal as ministers, loving as fathers, filial as sons, good companions as older brothers, and respectful as younger brothers. And so any gentleman who wishes to be a kind ruler, loyal minister, loving father, filial son, a good companion as an elder brother, and respectful as a younger brother cannot but practice the kind of impartiality I have been describing. This is the way of the sage-kings and a great benefit to the myriad people."

Chapter Seventeen:
A Condemnation of Aggressive War

[Our teacher Mozi says,] "Now suppose someone enters another's orchard and steals their peaches and plums. When the people hear about this they will condemn such a person, and if those above who administer the government get hold of him they will punish him. Why? Because he takes from others in order to benefit himself. Stealing another's dogs, hogs, chickens, and pigs is even more wrong than entering another's orchard and stealing their peaches and plums. Why? Because more is taken from others; it is even more inhumane and a more serious crime. Entering another person's stable and stealing their horses and cattle is even more wrong than stealing their dogs, hogs, chickens and pigs. Why? Because more is taken from others. If more is taken from others, it is even more inhumane and a more serious crime. Killing an innocent person, stripping him of his clothes and taking his spear and sword is even more wrong than entering his stable and stealing his horses and cattle. Why? Because more is taken from others. If more is taken from others, it is even more inhumane and a more serious crime. Up to this point, all the gentlemen of the world know well enough to condemn such actions and declare that they are wrong. But when it comes to the great wrong of attacking another state, they do not know enough to condemn it. Rather, they praise this and declare that it is the right thing to do. Can they be said to understand the difference between right and wrong?

"Killing someone is wrong and must be punished with execution. But if we extrapolate out from this view, then killing ten people is ten times as bad and must be punished with ten executions, and killing one hundred people is one hundred times as bad and must be punished with one hundred executions. Up to this point, all the gentlemen of the world know well enough to condemn such actions and declare that they are wrong. But when it comes to the great wrong of attacking another state, they do not know enough to condemn it. Rather, they praise this and declare that it is the right thing to do. They really do not understand that this is wrong. That is why they record their praise of such activity and hand down these records to later generations. If they really understood that this is wrong, why would they record their wrongs and hand them down to later generations?

"Now suppose there is someone who does the following: when they see a little black they say that it is black but when they see a lot of black they say that it is white. We would just have to say that such a person cannot distinguish between black and white. Or suppose that when they taste a little bitterness they say that it is bitter, but when they taste a lot of bitterness they say that it is sweet. We would just have to say that such a person cannot distinguish between bitter and sweet. But now people see a small wrong and know enough to condemn it but see the great wrong of attacking another state and do not know enough to condemn it. Rather they praise this and declare that it is the right thing to do. Can they be said to understand the difference between right and wrong? This is how we know that the gentlemen of the world are confused about the difference between right and wrong."

Chapter Twenty: For Moderation in Expenditures

[Our teacher Mozi says,] "When a sage rules a state that state will be twice as well off. When a sage rules the empire the empire will be twice as well off. But they are not made twice as well off by adding territory from without. It is rather by eliminating wasteful expenditures within the state that such rulers are able to make them twice as well off. When sage-kings rule, whenever they issue orders, undertake an enterprise, employ the people or expend their resources, they never do anything that is not useful. And so they never waste their resources or overburden their people yet are able to generate great benefits.

"What is the purpose of clothes? It is to protect us from the cold of winter and the heat of summer. The proper way to make clothes is such that they keep one warm in winter and cool in summer and that is all. Whatever does not contribute to these ends should be eliminated. What is the purpose of houses? It is to protect us from the wind and cold of winter, the heat and rain of summer, and to keep out robbers and thieves. Once these ends are secured that is all. Whatever does not contribute to these ends should be eliminated. What is the purpose of armor, shields, and weapons? It is to protect us from bandits, rebels, robbers, and thieves. Should there be bandits, rebels, robbers, and thieves, those who have armor, shields, and weapons will be victorious, while those without armor, shields, and weapons will not. And so sages work to produce armor, shields, and weapons. Whenever they make armor, shields, and weapons they seek to make them as light, sharp, strong, and resilient as they can and that is all. Whatever does not contribute to these ends should be eliminated. What is the purpose of boats and vehicles? Vehicles are used to travel over land and boats are used to travel over water such that one can bring together and exchange what is beneficial throughout the world. The proper way to make boats and vehicles is such that they are as light and easy to use as possible and that is all. Whatever does not contribute to these ends should be eliminated. In making these various things, sage-kings never add anything that is not useful. And so they never waste their resources or overburden their people yet are able to generate great benefits.

"If one could eliminate the fondness that kings, dukes, and great officials have for accumulating quantities of pearls and jades, birds and beasts, and dogs and horses, and use this revenue to increase the availability of clothes, houses, armor, shields, weapons, boats, and vehicles—could one double the numbers of these? Doubling the number of such things would not be hard. What then would it be hard to double? Only the number of people. And yet one can also double the number of people. In the past, the sage-kings established a law that said, "No man of twenty can be without a family. No woman of fifteen can be without a husband." Such was the law of the sage-kings. But since the sage-kings have passed away the people have grown remiss. Those who want to start a family at an early age do so at age twenty while those who want to start a family late do so at age forty. If we combine these, it still means that men are starting families on average ten years later than the age decreed by the law of the sage-kings. If all of them have one child every three years, then two or three children should have been born during that ten-year period. And so is it not only by getting people to start families early in life that one can double the population?

"This is the only way to double the population, but those who rule the world today actually work in many ways to lessen the population. They overwork and overtax their people to the point where many lack sufficient resources, with the result that those who die of hunger and cold are more than one can count. Moreover, the great officers encourage rulers to raise armies and attack neighboring states. The longer campaigns take up to a year while the shorter ones last several months. This means that men and women don't see each other for long periods of time, and in this way the population is reduced. During these campaigns, some become ill and die because they lack a stable living arrangement with regular food and water; others die in ambushes, fiery assaults, sieges, and battles. Together, their numbers are beyond reckoning. This is because the rulers of today are finding more and more ways to lessen the population. Such things never occurred when the sages ruled. Such is not the way sages rule. They find more and more ways to increase the population."

This is why our teacher Mozi says, "To eliminate everything that is not useful is to carry out the Way of the sage-kings and offer great benefit to the world."

Chapter Twenty-Five: For Moderation in Funerals

Our teacher Mozi says, "The way benevolent people plan on behalf of the world is just like the way filial children plan on behalf of their parents."

Now how is it that filial children plan for their parents?

Our teacher Mozi says, "If their parents are poor, they do what they can to enrich them. If the members of their clan are few, they do what they can to increase their numbers. If the family is in chaos, they do what they can to make it well ordered. In pursuing these ends they may find that their strength is insufficient, their resources inadequate, or their knowledge too limited, and that they fall short. But they would never hold back any of their strength or any scheme or advantage and not apply these in their efforts to realize their parents' well-being."

These are the three benefits that filial children plan for on behalf of their parents. And this is the way they work to realize these ends. This is also the way that benevolent people plan on behalf of the world.

Our teacher Mozi says, "If the world is poor, benevolent people do what they can to enrich it. If the people are few, benevolent people do what they can to increase their numbers. If the world is in chaos, benevolent people do what they can to make it well ordered. In pursuing these ends benevolent people may find that their strength is insufficient, their resources inadequate, or their knowledge too limited, and that they fall short. But they would never hold back any of their strength or any scheme or advantage and not apply these in their efforts to realize the world's well-being."

These are the three benefits that benevolent people plan for on behalf of the world. And this is the way they work to realize these ends. But now the sage-kings of the three dynasties of old[27] have passed away and the world has lost sight of what is right. The gentlemen of later ages are divided in their opinions. Some maintain that lavish funerals and prolonged mourning [28] are benevolent and right and the proper task of filial children. Others maintain that lavish funerals and prolonged mourning are neither benevolent nor right and are not the proper task of filial children.

Our teacher Mozi says, "These two groups contradict each other in word and oppose each other in deed. Both say, 'I am dutifully following the Way of Yao, Shun, Yu, Tang, Wen, and Wu,' and yet they contradict each other in word and oppose each other in deed. And so people of later ages have become suspicious of the claims of both groups. If one doubts the claims of both groups then one should turn and consider them in regard to ruling the state and governing the people, to see whether or not lavish funerals and prolonged mourning promote the three benefits discussed earlier. If by following their words and implementing their plans concerning lavish funerals and prolonged mourning one really would enrich the poor, increase the population, bring stability to precarious situations and order to chaos, then these things clearly are benevolent and right and the proper

---

[27]The Xia, Shang, and Zhou dynasties.

[28]Almost certainly, Mozi here has in mind the Confucians who maintained elaborate and prolonged rituals of mourning. See for example, *Analects* 17.21, *Mengzi* 3A5 and 7A39, and Xunzi's "Discourse on Ritual." See *Xunzi*, chapter 19, pp. 265–71.

task of filial children. Those who offer counsel could not but encourage them. Benevolent people would work to make such practices flourish throughout the world; they would seek to establish them and bring the people to praise them and to follow them, to the end of their days. However, if by following their words and implementing their plans concerning lavish funerals and prolonged mourning one really cannot enrich the poor, increase the population, bring stability to precarious situations and order to chaos, then these things clearly are not benevolent and right or the proper task of filial children. Those who offer counsel could not but discourage them. Benevolent people would work to eradicate such practices throughout the world; they would seek to abolish them and bring the people to condemn them and to never follow them, to the end of their days. And so from ancient times until the present, it has never been the case that bringing the world to a flourishing state and eliminating what is harmful to the world has led the state and the people to disorder."

Now there are many gentlemen in the world who are still in doubt as to whether or not lavish funerals and prolonged mourning are right or wrong, beneficial or harmful. And so our teacher Mozi says, "Let us examine the case. Now if we were to implement the teachings of those who follow and uphold lavish funerals and prolonged mourning, then in mourning for a king, duke, or high official, they prescribe that there be several inner and outer coffins, a deep grave, many layers of burial clothes, elaborately and intricately embroidered funeral shrouds, and a massive burial mound. Among common men and women this would exhaust the resources of the entire family. And even a feudal lord would have to empty his entire state treasury before the appropriate amount of gold, jade, and pearls would adorn the body and the proper quantities of silk, carriages, and horses would fill up the tomb. In addition, since one is to see off the dead as if they were simply changing their abode, it is required that numerous draperies and canopies, offering vessels of various kinds, tables and chairs, pots and basins, spears and swords, feathered banners, and articles made of tooth and hide must be buried along with them. It is also said that when an emperor or feudal lord dies as many as several hundred and no fewer than several tens of retainers are to be sacrificed in order to accompany the deceased.[29] When a general or great official dies as many as several tens and no fewer than several are to be sacrificed."

---

[29]This refers to ritual sacrifice, most popular during the Shang but still practiced in Mozi's own time. Mengzi quotes Kongzi as definitively rejecting even the vestiges of such practices. See *Mengzi* 1A4 (not in this volume).

What are the rules for one who is in mourning?

Our teacher Mozi says, "Mourners are to cry and wail irregularly, at all times of the day and night, and to sound as if their sobs are choked off. They are to dress in sackcloth, allow their tears to run down without wiping them away, and live in a mourning hut made of straw, sleeping upon a rush mat and using a lump of dirt as their pillow. Moreover, they are to encourage each other to refuse food and starve themselves and to wear thin clothing in order to suffer from the cold, so that they come to have sunken faces and eyes, a sallow and darkened complexion, poor hearing and sight, and limbs too weak to function. It is also said that the most noble of people uphold the rites of mourning to the point where they cannot rise up without assistance and cannot walk without a cane and they follow these practices for three years. This is what would happen if the state took such teachings as its model and followed them as its Way. Should kings, dukes, and other great men follow such practices, they will not be able to come early to court and retire late in order to hear litigation and carry out the affairs of the government. Should officers and officials follow such practices, they would be unable to administer the Five Offices and Six Treasuries[30] in order to ensure that crops and timber are harvested and the granaries kept full. Should farmers follow such practices, they would be unable to go out to the fields early and return home late in order to carry out the ploughing, planting, and tending of crops. Should the various craftsmen follow such practices, they would be unable to work on boats and carts and fashion various vessels and utensils. Should women follow such practices, they would be unable to rise at dawn and retire at night in order to complete their work of spinning and weaving. And so lavish funerals entail burying a great deal of wealth, and prolonged mourning entails prohibiting people from pursuing their vocations for an extended period of time. The former takes wealth that has already been created and buries it, while the latter prohibits new members of society from being born for an extended period of time. To pursue wealth in this manner is like seeking a harvest while prohibiting ploughing! Such practices have nothing to offer in regard to explaining how to become wealthy. And so we now know that lavish funerals and prolonged mourning cannot enrich one's state."

---

[30]A list of these offices and their duties can be found in a later work called the *Liji* ("Book of Rites"). See the entry on the *Rites* under *Important Texts*. For a translation, see James Legge, tr. *The Li Chi: Book of Rites*, reprint, vol. 1 (New York: University Books, 1967), pp. 109–10.

But perhaps it has value for those who wish to increase population of their states?

Our teacher Mozi says, "It has nothing to offer in this regard either. Now consider what would result if lavish funerals and prolonged mourning were adopted as official policy. When one's ruler died, one would mourn him for three years. When one's mother or father died, one would mourn them for three years. When one's wife or eldest son died, one would mourn them for three years. Whenever any of these five people died, one would mourn them for three years. Next, one would mourn for one's paternal uncles, brothers, and other sons, and one's various close relatives for five months. You are to mourn for several months for fraternal aunts, sisters, first cousins, and maternal uncles. And there are set standards describing the proper levels of emaciation mourners must attain. They are to have sunken faces and eyes, a sallow and darkened complexion, poor hearing and sight, and limbs too weak to function. It is also said that the most noble of people uphold the rites of mourning to the point where they cannot rise up without assistance and cannot walk without a cane, and follow these practices for three years.

"This is what would happen if the state took such teachings as its model and followed them as its Way. If the people starve themselves in this manner then they will be unable to withstand the cold of winter or the heat of summer and countless numbers of them will grow ill and die. This greatly diminishes the chances for men and women to procreate. To seek to increase the population in this way is like seeking to increase people's longevity by getting them to fall upon their swords. Such practices have nothing to offer with regard to explaining how to increase the population. And so we now know that lavish funerals and prolonged mourning cannot increase the number of people in one's state."

But perhaps it has value for those who wish to bring good order to the government?

Our teacher Mozi says, "It has nothing to offer in this regard either. Now consider what would result if lavish funerals and prolonged mourning were adopted as official policy. The state would be poor, the people few, and the government in chaos. This is what would happen if the state took such teachings as its model and followed them as its Way. If those above were to carry out these practices, they would be unable to attend to their affairs. If those below were to carry out these practices, they would be unable to pursue their various tasks. If those above are unable to attend to their affairs, then the government will be in chaos. If those below are unable to pursue their various tasks, then food and clothing will be in short supply. If these are in short supply, then a younger brother who seeks for such things from his elder brother will be refused and will come to feel unbrotherly. In time he will come to resent his elder brother. Children who seek for such things from their parents will be refused and will come to feel unfilial. In time they will come to resent their parents. Ministers who seek for such things from their rulers will be refused and will come to feel disloyal. In time they will rebel against their superiors. This will lead unruly and depraved people who lack proper clothing and sufficient food to build up resentment and indignation in their hearts and express it in wanton violence that cannot be stopped. And so robbers and thieves will increase while decent and good people grow increasingly scarce. To seek to bring good order to one's state by increasing the number of thieves and robbers and decreasing the number of decent and good people is like asking someone who is standing in front of one to turn around three times without exposing his back to you. Such practices have nothing to offer in regard to explaining how to bring good order to the government. And so we now know that lavish funerals and prolonged mourning cannot bring good order to one's state."

But perhaps it has value for those who wish to prevent large states from attacking small states?

Our teacher Mozi says, "It has nothing to offer in this regard either. Ever since the ancient sage-kings passed away and the world lost a sense of what is right, the feudal lords have relied upon force of arms to attack one another. To the south there are the kings of Chu and Yue and to the north there are the rulers of Qi and Jin.[31] They all mercilessly drill and train their troops with the aim of attacking and absorbing one another and thereby gaining control of all the world. And so whenever a large state fails to attack a small one it is only because the small state has an abundant stock of provisions, well maintained fortifications, and harmony between its rulers and subjects. This is why great states do not want to attack it. If its provisions were not abundant, its fortifications not well maintained, or it lacked harmony between its rulers and subjects, then large states would want to attack it. Now consider what would result if lavish funerals and prolonged mourning were adopted as official policy. The state would be poor, the people few, and the government in chaos. If the state is poor, it lacks the means to accumulate abundant provisions. If its people are few, it lacks the labor

---

[31]The rulers of these particular states were jousting for preeminence in Mozi's time.

needed to maintain its walls and moats. If it is in chaos, then it will not be victorious in attack nor secure in defense. And so we now know that lavish funerals and prolonged mourning cannot prevent large states from attacking small ones."

But perhaps it has value for those who wish to win the blessings of the Lord on High, ghosts, and spirits?

Our teacher Mozi says, "It has nothing to offer in this regard either. Now consider what would result if lavish funerals and prolonged mourning were adopted as official policy. The state would be poor, the people few and the government in chaos. If the state is poor its sacrificial offerings of millet and wine will not be clean and pure. If its people are few, there will not be enough of them to serve the Lord on High, ghosts, and spirits. And if its government is in chaos, then its sacrifices will not be offered regularly and at the proper times. Now suppose this reaches the point where serving the Lord on High, ghosts, and spirits is eventually prohibited and stopped. If such a policy is implemented, the Lord on High, ghosts, and spirits would discuss this among themselves up above saying, 'Which is better? To have or to not have such people? I suppose there is no difference to us whether they exist or not!' Then were the Lord on High, ghosts, and spirits to send down calamities and punishments and abandon such a people, would this not merely be fitting?[32]

"This is why the sages of old prescribed the following methods for burial. They said that a coffin of plain wood three inches thick is enough to house the body as it decays. There should be three layers of funeral clothes, enough to cover up the unpleasantness. As for the depth of the grave, it should not be so deep as to hit water but not so shallow as to allow a stench. The burial mound should rise no higher than three feet. If one followed these methods, the deceased was properly buried. The living must not engage in prolonged mourning but should quickly go about their tasks, each person doing what they are best at in order to mutually benefit one another. These are the methods laid down by the sage-kings."

Now those who advocate lavish funerals and prolonged mourning say, "Although lavish funerals and prolonged mourning cannot enrich the poor,

---

[32]As seen clearly in the following two chapters, Mozi was a religious conservative and a fundamentalist. He insisted that a belief in and the worship of the Lord on High, ghosts, and spirits was necessary for a stable and flourishing society. He was very much opposed to the more naturalized, psychological interpretations of religious ceremony that were evolving among Confucian thinkers of the time.

increase a sparse population, stabilize a precarious situation, or bring good order to chaos, nevertheless, such is the Way of the sage-kings."

Our teacher Mozi says, "This is not the case. In ancient times, when Yao went north to instruct the eight Di barbarian tribes[33] he died en route and was buried on the northern slopes of Mount Qiong.[34] His corpse was dressed in only three layers of burial clothing and interred in a coffin of plain wood that was bound together with common vines. Mourning began only after the coffin had been lowered into the grave. The grave was then filled in and no burial mound was erected. Once the burial was complete, oxen and horses freely crossed over the grave.[35] When Shun went west to instruct the seven Rong barbarian tribes[36] he died en route and was buried in the marketplace of Nanji.[37] His corpse was dressed in only three layers of burial clothing and interred in a coffin of plain wood that was bound together with common vines. Once the burial was complete, the people in the market freely crossed over the grave. When Yu went east to instruct the nine Yi barbarian tribes[38] he died en route and was buried on Mount Huiji.[39] His corpse was dressed in only three layers of burial clothing and interred in a coffin of plain wood only three inches thick. The coffin was bound with common vines; it was not fitted tightly together nor was a ramp needed to lower it into the ground.[40] The grave was dug to a depth that did not hit water but not so shallow as to allow a stench to escape. Once he was buried, the excess dirt was piled up as a burial mound. It came to no more than three feet in height."

So if we consider the case on the basis of these three sage-kings, lavish funerals and prolonged mourning are not in fact the way of the sage-kings. These three kings each were honored as the Son of Heaven and possessed

---

[33]The name given to various non-Chinese people to the north of Chinese territory.

[34]The location of this mountain is not clear, though it obviously was located somewhere to the north of what was Chinese territory at the time.

[35]Showing that it was not accorded any special status.

[36]The name given to various non-Chinese people to the west of Chinese territory.

[37]Scholars do not agree about the location of this town. It obviously was located somewhere to the west of what was Chinese territory at the time.

[38]The name given to various non-Chinese people to the east of Chinese territory. Thus Mozi's narrative purports to report on funeral practices throughout all of China and its three land borders.

[39]A mountain located in Shanyin county of present-day Zhejiang province.

[40]This indicates that the grave was of very modest proportions for a king.

all the wealth in the world. Is it plausible to suppose that they chose to be buried in the way in which they were buried because they were worried about having enough to spend?

But the way in which kings, dukes, and high officials are buried today is very different from this. There must be outer and inner coffins and a three-layered shroud of embroidered hide. Once the jade disks and stones are prepared, there must also be spears, swords, sacrificial vessels, pots and basins, embroidery, bolts of silk, and thousands of sets of bridles. The deceased must be provided with horses and carriages along with women entertainers and their instruments. There must be ramps leading down to and connecting with the tomb and the burial mound should resemble a hill or small mountain. The extent to which such practices interfere with the work of the people and dissipate their wealth is beyond calculation. But this is the degree to which people are willing to pursue useless endeavors.

This is why our teacher Mozi says, "Earlier, I began by saying that if by following the words and implementing the plans of those who advocate lavish funerals and prolonged mourning one really would enrich the poor, increase the population, bring stability to precarious situations and order to chaos, then these things clearly are benevolent and right and the proper task of filial children. Those who offer counsel could not but encourage them. However, if by following the words and implementing the plans of those who advocate lavish funerals and prolonged mourning one really cannot enrich the poor, increase the population, bring stability to precarious situations and order to chaos, then these things clearly are not benevolent and right or the proper task of filial children. Those who offer counsel could not but discourage them.

"But we have seen that those who seek to enrich their states through these practices will actually impoverish it. Those who seek to increase the population of their states through these practices will actually decrease it. Those who seek to bring good order to their states through these practices will simply throw it into chaos. Those who seek to stop large states from attacking small states through these practices will not succeed. And those who seek to gain the blessing of the Lord on High, ghosts, and spirits through these practices will receive only disaster. If we look up to the way of Yao, Shun, Yu, Tang, Wen, and Wu we find they were opposed to such practices. If we look down to the policies of Jie, Zhou, You, and Li we find they accorded with such practices. If we consider things on this basis, then clearly lavish funerals and prolonged mourning are not the way of the sage-kings."

Now those who support lavish funerals and prolonged periods of mourning say, "If lavish funerals and prolonged mourning really are not the way of the sage-kings why is it that the gentlemen of the Middle King-dom[41] continue these practices without interruption and follow them uncritically?"

Our teacher Mozi says, "This is just a case of people 'following what they are used to and approving of what is customary.'[42] In ancient times, east of the state of Yue was the state of Kaishu.[43] When a first son was born to the people of this state they would carve him up and eat him saying it was beneficial to his future younger brothers. When their father died, they would carry their mothers off to some distant place and abandon them there saying, 'One cannot live with the wife of a ghost!' These practices were both official policy and the popular custom. They were continued without interruption and followed uncritically. But how can this be the way to realize what is benevolent and right? This is just a case of people 'following what they are used to and approving of what is customary.' South of the state of Chu was the state of the people of Yan.[44] When their parents died, they would remove and discard the flesh from their bones and then bury the bones.[45] This was the way to be a filial child. West of the state of Qin[46] was the state of Yiqu.[47] When their parents died they would gather together kindling and firewood and burn the corpse. As the smoke would rise they would say that their parents were 'ascending far off.' This was the

---

[41]That is, China.

[42]This appears to have been a common saying of the times.

[43]The precise location of this state is uncertain but its location, "east of Yue," connotes a faraway and culturally primitive area.

[44]The precise location of this state is uncertain but its location, "south of Chu," connotes a faraway and culturally primitive area.

[45]Such secondary reburial of bones, while never the dominant practice, is well attested in very early China. There is evidence for the practice in the Central Plains and Northwest as far back as the fifth millennium B.C.E. See David N. Keightley, "Early Civilization in China: Reflections on How It Became Chinese" in Paul S. Ropp, ed., *Heritage of China* (Berkeley, CA: University of California Press, 1990), p. 24.

[46]Qin was the state farthest to the West and was considered culturally backward in Mozi's time.

[47]In the basic annals section for the state of Qin in Sima Qian's *Shiji* ("Records of the Historian"), there is reference to a state by this name. Its exact location is still a matter of debate.

way to be a filial child. These practices were both official policy and the popular custom. They were continued without interruption and followed uncritically. But how can this be the way to realize what is benevolent and right? This is just a case of people 'following what they are used to and approving of what is customary.'

"If we consider the funeral practices of these three states, then clearly they are deficient. If we consider the funeral practices of gentlemen in the Middle Kingdom, then clearly they are excessive. If one were to greatly increase the deficiency of the one and greatly diminish the excess of the latter, then there would be moderation in funerals. Even though it is good to give people clothing and food when they are alive, these things still must be given in moderation. When people die, it is good to give them funerals. But how could it be that in this alone we show no moderation?"

Our teacher Mozi says that this is the proper model for a funeral: "A coffin three inches thick is adequate for the decaying bones. Three layers of clothes are adequate for the decaying flesh. The grave should be dug to a depth that does not strike water but that also does not allow fumes to escape to the surface. The burial mound should only be high enough to clearly mark the spot. There should be crying as one sees the departed off and as one comes back from the grave. But as soon as people have returned to their homes, they should resume their individual livelihoods. There should be regular sacrificial offerings made to extend filiality to one's parents."

And so I say that in this way our teacher Mozi's model neglects the good neither of the living nor of the dead. This is why our teacher Mozi says, "If gentlemen today sincerely wish to be benevolent and right and desire to become superior men, if they want to follow the way of the sage-kings of old, and work for the benefit of the people of the Middle Kingdom today, then they should make moderation in mourning their official policy and must not fail to examine this matter carefully."

Chapter Twenty-Six: Heaven's Will[48]

Our teacher Mozi says, "Gentlemen in the world today understand small matters but not those that are great. How do I know this? I know this from how they conduct themselves within their families. If one is living at

---

[48]The word translated here as "will" is *zhi,* 志, which means the settled and persisting intention of an agent. For Mozi, Heaven was less a personality with a capricious or unknowable will and more an established, observable, and predictable set of inclinations.

home[49] and commits some offense against the head of the clan, there are always the homes of neighbors to which one might flee. And yet, one's parents, brothers, and friends will unite and caution one, saying, 'You must be careful! You must be circumspect! How can you live at home and offend against the head of the clan?' This is not only how things are in the case of living at home, it is also so in the case of living in a given state. If one is living in a state and commits some offense against the ruler of the state, there are always neighboring states to which one might flee. And yet, one's parents, brothers, and friends will unite and caution one, saying, 'You must be careful! You must be circumspect! Who can live in a state and offend against its ruler?'

"Since people offer each other such strong admonitions in these cases, where there is still some place to which one might flee, should they not think it appropriate to offer even stronger warnings in a case where there is no place to which one might flee? For there is the saying, 'Committing offense in broad daylight, where can one flee to?'[50] The answer of course is that there is nowhere to flee. For Heaven will clearly see you even if you run to the forests, valleys, or hidden places where none lives. But for some reason the gentlemen of the world don't know enough to warn each other about offending Heaven. This is how I know that the gentlemen of the world understand small matters but not those that are great.

"This being the case, what is it that Heaven desires and what does it dislike? Heaven desires what is right and dislikes what is not right. This being so, if I lead the people of the world to act in accordance with what is right, then I will be doing what Heaven desires. And if I do what Heaven desires, then Heaven will do what I desire. Such being the case, what is it that I desire and what do I dislike? I desire good fortune and a substantial salary, and dislike calamities and disasters. If I do not do what Heaven desires but rather what it does not desire, then I will lead people to act in ways that lead them into disaster and calamity. But how do I know that Heaven desires what is right and dislikes what is not right? I say this is so because, throughout the world, wherever there is right there is life, and wherever there is an absence of right there is death. Wherever there is right there is wealth, wherever there is an absence of right there is poverty. Wherever there is right there is good order, wherever there is an absence of right there

---

[49]Mozi has in mind here the practice of living in a family compound, where several generations share a common courtyard but each have their separate quarters.

[50]This seems to have been a common saying of the time but its source is unknown.

is disorder. Heaven desires to have life and dislikes death, desires to have wealth and dislikes poverty, desires to have good order and dislikes disorder. This is how I know that Heaven desires what is right and dislikes what is not right.

"Moreover, what is right is what offers a standard of governing. Such a standard is not given by subordinates to govern their superiors but rather must come from superiors to govern subordinates. This is why the people devote themselves to carrying out their various tasks but do not make up their own standard. There are ministers and officials to govern them. Ministers and officials devote themselves to carrying out their various tasks but do not make up their own standard. There are the three high counselors and feudal lords to govern them. The three high counselors and feudal lords devote themselves to administering the government but they do not make up their own standard. There is the Son of Heaven to govern them. The Son of Heaven does not make up his own standard. There is Heaven to govern him. The gentlemen of the world clearly understand that the Son of Heaven governs the three high counselors and feudal lords, the ministers and officials and the people. But that Heaven governs the Son of Heaven is something that people do not yet clearly understand.

"This is why in ancient times the sage-kings of the three dynasties,[51] Yu, Tang, Wen, and Wu, wanted to make clear to the people of the world that Heaven governs the Son of Heaven. And so each of them fattened up oxen and sheep, dogs and swine, and prepared pure offerings of millet and wine as sacrifices to the Lord on High, the ghosts, and spirits and prayed for Heaven's blessings. I have never heard of a case where Heaven prayed for blessings from the Son of Heaven and this is how I know that Heaven governs the Son of Heaven."

The Son of Heaven is the most honored person in the world and the richest person in the world. And so those who desire riches and honors cannot but accord with the will of Heaven. Those who accord with Heaven's will, caring for one another impartially, and benefiting one another in their interactions, will surely be rewarded. Those who oppose Heaven's will, disliking one another out of partiality and stealing from one another in their interactions, will surely be punished. This being so, who has accorded with Heaven's will and been rewarded? Who has opposed Heaven's will and been punished?

---

[51]The Xia, Shang, and Zhou dynasties.

Our teacher Mozi says, "In ancient times the sage-kings of the three dynasties, Yu, Tang, Wen, and Wu, were among those who accorded with Heaven's will and were rewarded. In ancient times the vicious kings of the three dynasties, Jie, Zhou, You, and Li, were among those who opposed Heaven's will and were punished."

That being so, how were Yu, Tang, Wen, and Wu rewarded?

Our teacher Mozi says, "On high they honored Heaven, in the middle realm they served the ghosts and spirits, and below they cared for human beings. And so Heaven's will proclaimed, 'These men impartially care for those I care for and impartially benefit those I benefit. Their care for the people is extensive and the benefit they bring is substantial.' And so Heaven made it come to pass that they each became the Son of Heaven and were given the wealth of all the world. Their descendents have continued for a myriad of generations, their goodness has been proclaimed throughout succeeding generations and spread throughout the world. They are praised down to the present day and are known as 'sage-kings.'"

That being so, how were Jie, Zhou, You, and Li punished?

Our teacher Mozi says, "On high they maligned Heaven, in the middle realm they insulted the ghosts and spirits, and below they harmed human beings. And so Heaven's will proclaimed, 'These men through their partiality dislike those I care for and in their interactions harm those I benefit. Their dislike for the people is extensive and the harm they bring substantial.' And so Heaven made it come to pass that they did not finish out their natural span of life and their line did not even span a single full generation. They are reviled down to the present day and are known as 'vicious kings.'"

That being so, how do we know that Heaven cares for the people of the world?

Our teacher Mozi says, "Because it sheds light upon all impartially."

How do we know that Heaven sheds light upon all equally?

Our teacher Mozi says, "Because it lays claim to all impartially."

How do we know that it lays claim to all impartially?

Our teacher Mozi says, "Because it accepts sacrificial offerings from all impartially."

How do we know that it accepts sacrificial offerings from all impartially?

Our teacher Mozi says, "Within the four seas, all those who live on cultivated grain[52] fatten up oxen and sheep, dogs, and swine, and prepare pure

---

[52]The settled, civilized Chinese as opposed to nomadic, uncivilized "barbarians."

offerings of millet and wine as sacrifices to the Lord on High, the ghosts, and spirits. Since Heaven lays claim to all people, why would it not care for them? Moreover as I teach, 'Those who kill one innocent person will suffer one misfortune.'[53] Who is it that kills an innocent person? It is a human being. Who is it that bestows misfortune? It is Heaven. If Heaven did not care for the people of the world, then why would it send down misfortunes when human beings kill one another? This is how I know that Heaven cares for the people of the world."

To accord with Heaven's will is to take right as the governing standard. To oppose Heaven's will is to take force as the governing standard. But what does one do who takes right as the governing standard?

Out teacher Mozi says, "Those who control great states will not attack small states. Those who control great families will not plunder lesser families. The strong will not rob the weak. The noble will not act arrogantly toward the humble. The clever will not deceive the foolish. Such things are beneficial to Heaven above, to ghosts and spirits in the middle realm, and to human beings below. Benefiting these three, there is none that is not benefitted, and so the best of names will be accorded to such men and they will be called 'sage-kings.' Those who take force as the governing standard differ from this. They contradict this in word and oppose it in deed, like two men galloping away from one another on horseback. Those who control great states will thus attack small ones. Those who control great families will plunder lesser families. The strong will rob the weak. The noble will act arrogantly toward the humble. The clever will deceive the foolish. Such things are not beneficial to heaven above, to ghosts and spirits in the middle realm, or to human beings below. Not benefiting these three, there is none that is benefited, and so the worst of names will be accorded to such men and they will be called 'vicious kings.'"

Our teacher Mozi says, "I hold to the will of Heaven as a wheelwright holds to his compass and a carpenter his square. Wheelwrights and carpenters hold fast to their compasses and squares in order to gauge what is round and square throughout the world saying, 'What is plumb with this is true, what is not is false!' The books of all the gentlemen in the world today are so numerous that they cannot be exhaustively catalogued and their teachings and maxims are more than can be counted. Above they offer their opinions to the feudal lords and below they expound them to various

---

[53]In addition to occurring in all three versions of "Heaven's Will," this line is also found in chapter 4 (not in this volume).

men of worth. But they are far from what is benevolent and right! How do I know this? I say, 'I measure them with the clearest standard in all the world.'"

Chapter Thirty-One: On Ghosts

Our teacher Mozi says, "In the present age, since the sage-kings who ruled during the ancient three dynasties have passed away and the world has lost sight of what is right, the feudal lords all take force as their guiding standard.[54] As a result, rulers and other superiors are not kind while ministers and other subordinates are not loyal. Fathers are not loving and sons are not filial, elder brothers are not good to their younger brothers, younger brothers are not respectful of their elders, and proper conduct in general is not observed. Those in charge of the government do not exert themselves in their administrative duties, while the common people do not exert themselves in the pursuit of their various tasks. This is also why people abandon themselves to licentiousness, violence, piracy, rebellion, thievery, and robbery, and use weapons, poisons, water, and fire to stop travelers on the roads and byways, and rob their carriages, horses, coats, and furs in order to profit themselves. As a result the world is in great disorder.

"If we ask how this came about we will see that it is all because people have developed doubts concerning the existence of ghosts and spirits and do not understand that ghosts and spirits can reward the worthy and punish the wicked. Now if we could just persuade the people of the world to believe that ghosts and spirits can reward the worthy and punish the wicked, then how could the world ever become disordered?"

Now those who maintain that there are no ghosts or spirits say, "Ghosts and spirits certainly do not exist!" Day and night they preach such ideas throughout the world and sow suspicion among the masses. They cause the people of the world to develop doubts concerning the existence of ghosts and spirits and as a result the world is thrown into disorder.

This is why our teacher Mozi says, "If the kings, dukes, great officials, and gentlemen of the world today really seek to promote what is beneficial to the world and eliminate what is harmful they must inquire carefully into the issue of whether or not ghosts and spirits exist."

---

[54]The word translated as "guiding standard" is *zheng* 正, which often means "what is correct" and is related to the word *zheng* 政, which means "to rule." Mozi here is playing on these related senses.

I accept that one must inquire carefully into the issue of whether or not ghosts and spirits exist. Granted this, what is the proper method for pursuing an inquiry into this issue?[55]

Our teacher Mozi says, "You proceed in the same way as in any other case of determining whether anything exists or does not exist; you must take as your standard the evidence provided by the eyes and ears of the people. If there really are people who have heard and seen something, then you must accept that such things exist. If no one has heard or seen anything, then you must accept that such things do not exist. If you intend to proceed in this way, why not try going into a district or village and ask the people there? If, in the course of human history, from ancient times up to the present, there really are people who have seen ghostly or spiritual entities or heard the sounds of ghosts or spirits, then how could one say that ghosts and spirits do not exist? If no one has ever heard or seen them, then how could one say that ghosts and spirits exist?"

Now those who maintain that ghosts and spirits do not exist say, "Throughout the world there are innumerable reports about hearing and seeing ghostly or spiritual entities, but who really can offer testimony about having heard or seen ghostly or spiritual entities?"[56]

Our teacher Mozi says, "If we are looking for someone who has seen what so many have seen and heard what so many have heard, then in ancient times Du Bo is a good example. King Xuan of Zhou[57] killed his minister Du Bo even though he was completely innocent. Before he died Du Bo said, 'My lord is killing me even though I am completely innocent. If the dead are indeed unconscious, then that will be the end of it. But if the dead are conscious, within three years' time my lord shall know of this!' Three years later King Xuan and various feudal lords were off hunting in the wilds. There were several hundred chariots and several thousand men on foot; the hunting party filled the entire field. At high noon, Du Bo appeared in a plain chariot pulled by white horses. He was wearing vermillion clothes and a hat, holding a vermillion bow, and clasping vermillion arrows under his arm. He pur-

---

[55]Notice that in what follows, Mozi appeals to the "three gauges" discussed in " A Condemnation of Fatalism." See *Mozi*, chapter 35, p. 105–07.

[56]Mozi wants to distinguish mere hearsay and vague claims about spiritual beings from firm and clear testimony of their existence. In the examples he cites as evidence, the testimony is first hand, detailed, and corroborated by mutiple witnesses.

[57]A king who ruled during the tenth generation of the Zhou dynasty. His reign dates are 827–782 B.C.E.

sued King Xuan of Zhou and shot him as he rode in his chariot; the arrow pierced the king's heart and splintered his spine. King Xuan collapsed in his chariot and, draped over his own bow case, he died. None of the men from Zhou who were there at the time failed to witness this and none even in remote places failed to hear about it. The event was recorded in the court chronicle of Zhou. Rulers referred to it when instructing their ministers, and fathers referred to it as a warning to their sons, saying, 'Be cautious! Be watchful! Misfortune will surely befall all those who kill the innocent, and they will suffer the punishments of ghosts and spirits in this swift fashion!' And so, if we look at things in terms of what is written in the court chronicle of Zhou, then how can we doubt that ghosts and spirits exist?

"But it is not just the court chronicle of Zhou that attests to such things, in ancient times, Duke Mu of Qin [58] was once in his ancestral temple at high noon when a spirit entered through the door. It had the face of a man and the body of a bird, wore a plain white robe with dark edging, and displayed a serious and dignified expression. When Duke Mu saw it he was frightened and started to run away, but the spirit spoke to him saying, 'Do not fear! The Lord is pleased with your shining virtue[59] and has dispatched me to extend your life by nineteen years.[60] He shall ensure that your state prospers and that your descendants flourish and hold on to the state of Qin.' Clasping his hands together Duke Mu saluted the spirit several times and bowing his head asked, 'May I inquire as to your name?' The spirit replied, 'I am Gou Mang.' And so if we accept what Duke Mu of Qin saw with his own eyes, then how can we doubt that ghosts and spirits exist?

---

[58]Ruler of the state of Qin from 659–621 B.C.E.

[59]In very early Chinese texts, spirits savored the *mingde* 明德, "shining virtue," of pious worshippers in the same visceral way they were thought to enjoy the smells and flavors of the sacrifice, and the pageantry and music of the ceremony. True virtue would elicit spontaneous feelings of approval and joy while character or behavior that was *e* 惡, "vile," would give rise to disapproval and disgust. Such ideas can be seen in the later tradition. For example, in chapter 6 of the *Daxue,* "Great Learning," a cultivated person is said to be attracted to the good "as if seeing something beautiful" and repelled by the bad "as if smelling something malodorous."

[60]A span of nineteen years marked a specific astronomical and calendrical period called a *zhang* 章. Unaware of the precession of the equinoxes, ancient Chinese astronomers believed that every nineteen years the winter solstice was the first day of the first month of the year and that on that day the sun would appear at exactly the same place in the zodiac. Hence nineteen years were thought to define a significant period of time, something akin to a generation. Compare the story of the butcher in *Zhuangzi,* chapter 3, pp. 219–20, whose knife remained keen for a period of nineteen years.

"But it is not just this record that attests to such things. In ancient times, Duke Jian of Yan[61] killed his minister Zhuang Ziyi who was completely innocent. Before he died Zhuang Ziyi said, 'My lord is killing me even though I am completely innocent. If the dead are indeed unconscious, then that will be the end of it. But if the dead are conscious, within three years time my lord shall know of this!' After one year had passed Duke Jian was about to set off in his chariot to perform the great sacrifice at Zu. [62] At high noon, as Duke Jian of Yan was setting off in his chariot on the road to Zu, Zhuang Ziyi appeared bearing a vermillion colored staff and beat the Duke to death with it. There were none among the people of Yan accompanying the Duke at the time who failed to witness this and none even in remote places failed to hear about it. The event was recorded in the court chronicle of Yan. Feudal lords passed it on to succeeding generations, saying, 'Misfortune will surely befall all those who kill the innocent, and they will suffer the punishments of ghosts and spirits in this swift fashion!' And so if we look at things in terms of what is written in the court chronicle of Yan then how can we doubt that ghosts and spirits exist?

"But it is not just the court chronicle of Yan that attests to such things. In ancient times, in the time of Bao,[63] Lord Wen of Song, there was a minister, Guan Gu, who served as Chief of Sacrifice. Once while he was carrying out his duties in the temple, a shaman appeared before him holding a staff and said, 'Guan Gu! Why is it that the sacrificial jades are not of the proper size, the offerings of wine and millet not clean and pure, the animals offered not without blemish and fully fattened, and the sacrifices of each season not performed at the proper time? Is this your doing or is Bao responsible?' Guan Gu replied, 'Bao is still a babe in swaddling clothes. How could he be responsible? I, Guan Gu, the minister in charge, am the one who sees to this.' The shaman then raised his staff and clubbed him to death and Guan Gu died upon the offering platform. There were none among the people of Song

---

[61]Ruler of the state of Yan. His reign dates are 504–493 B.C.E.

[62]The name of a specific sacrificial site in the state of Yan. This adds an ironic cast to the story, for it was commonly held that a state is maintained through the spiritual power of its state sacrifices. The following lines, which are clearly a later note that became incorporated into the text, describe the locations of the state sacrifices of other contemporary states and the fact that many people witnessed these events (and hence the spiritual sighting noted in Mozi's story), "The state of Yan performed its great sacrifice at Zu, while the state of Qi offered its sacrifice at Sheji, Song at Sanglin, and Chu at Yunmeng. Large numbers of men and women would gather to observe these rituals."

[63]Bao is the personal name of the king whose posthumous name was Lord Wen. He ruled the state of Song from 610–589 B.C.E. He was also known as Duke Wen.

who were there at the time who failed to witness this and none even in remote places failed to hear about it. The event was recorded in the court chronicle of Song. Feudal lords passed it on to succeeding generations, saying, 'All those who fail to offer sacrifices with reverence and care will suffer the punishments of ghosts and spirits in this swift fashion!' And so if we look at things in terms of what is written in the court chronicle of Song, then how can we doubt that ghosts and spirits exist?

"But it is not just the court chronicle of Song that attests to such things. In ancient times, among the ministers of Lord Zhuang of Qi[64] were two named Wang Liguo and Zhong Lijiao. For three years, these two had been engaged in litigation against one another but no definitive judgment could be reached in the matter. The Lord of Qi thought of putting them both to death, but feared killing an innocent man. He thought of acquitting them both, but feared letting a guilty man go free. And so he arranged for them to provide a sheep for sacrifice and to use its blood to swear an oath of innocence upon Qi's sacred altar. The two men agreed to swear the oath, and so the ground was prepared, the sheep's throat was cut, and its blood was sprinkled about to consecrate the sacrifice. Wang Liguo's oath was read through without incident, but before they were even halfway done with Zhong Lijiao's oath, the sheep that had been sacrificed rose up and butted him, breaking his leg. Then the spirit of the altar appeared and struck Zhong Lijiao, killing him on the very place where he had sworn his oath. There were none among the people of Qi who were there at the time who failed to witness this and none even in remote places failed to hear about it. The event was recorded in the court chronicle of Qi. Feudal lords passed it on to succeeding generations, saying, 'All those who fail to be sincere when they swear an oath will suffer the punishments of ghosts and spirits in this swift fashion!' And so if we look at things in terms of what is written in the court chronicle of Qi, then how can we doubt that ghosts and spirits exist?"

This is why our teacher Mozi says, "Even in the deepest valleys or vast forests, in those hidden places where no one lives, you must always act properly. For the ghosts and spirits will see what you do!"

Now those who maintain that there are no ghosts say, "How can what the multitude claim to have seen and heard be considered adequate for settling doubts about this issue? How can one who aspires to be known as a person of high status or a gentleman throughout the world turn to and trust what the multitude claim to have seen and heard?"

---

[64]Ruler of the state of Qi. His reign dates are 553–548 B.C.E.

Our teacher Mozi says, "If what the multitude claim to have seen and heard is not enough to win your trust and settle your doubts about this issue, then I am not sure whether you will consider the sage-kings of the three dynasties, or even they together with Yao and Shun, as adequate models.[65] In this regard, from the average person to nobles alike, all say that the sage-kings of the three dynasties, or they together with Yao and Shun, are adequate models of conduct. And so if we assume that the three sage-kings of ancient times, or they together with Yao and Shun, are adequate models, then why don't we consider the actions of the former sage-kings?

"In ancient times, when King Wu had attacked the Yin and executed Zhou, he had the various feudal lords divide up the sacrifices of Yin. He entrusted the interior sacrifices to those who were closely related and the exterior sacrifices to those who were distantly related.[66] Since he did this, King Wu must have believed in the existence of ghosts and spirits. This is why, when he had attacked the Yin and executed Zhou, he had the various feudal lords divide up the sacrifices of Yin. If there were no ghosts and spirits, why would King Wen have bothered to divide up the sacrifices of Yin?

"It is not only the activities of King Wu that bear this out. Whenever the sage-kings of old rewarded anyone, they always did so at the ancestral shrine, and whenever they punished anyone, they always did so at the altar of soil. Why did they reward at the ancestral shrine? In order to announce to the spirits there that rewards were fairly apportioned. Why did they punish at the altar of soil? In order to announce to the spirits there that the cases were decided properly.

"But it is not just what can be found in books that bears this out. In the time of Emperor Shun and in the time of the sage-kings of the three dynasties Xia, Shang, and Zhou, on the very first day that they established their states and set up their capitals, they always selected the most perfectly aligned altar in the capital to serve as their ancestral shrine.[67] Also, they al-

[65]The text is slightly garbled at this point. But the sense is something like "the sage-kings of the three dynasties (i.e., Yu, Tang, Wen, and Wu) *plus* Yao and Shun.

[66]The interior sacrifices were to the Yin royal ancestors and hence needed to be carried out by their direct descendants. Mozi's point is that if there were no ghosts and spirits who received these sacrifices and were aware of who was sacrificing to them, there would have been no point in dividing up these religious duties.

[67]Mozi's point here is that the conscious effort to properly align cities to harmonize with spiritual forces also reflects a belief in the existence of ghosts and spirits. For the seminal study of this aspect of Chinese culture, see Paul Wheatley, *The Pivot of the Four Corners: A Preliminary Enquiry into the Origins and Character of the Ancient Chinese City* (Chicago, IL: Aldine Publishing Company, 1971).

ways chose the place where the trees grew most finely and luxuriantly and established it as the altar of soil. They also chose the most kind, filial, upright, and good from among the elders of their states to oversee and perform their sacrifices. They always chose the most plump, physically perfect and properly colored of the six domesticated animals as their sacrificial offerings and ensured that the proper type, quality, and number of jade tablets and insignia were used. They always chose the most fragrant and perfectly ripened of the five grains in order to make their sacrificial wine and cakes, and this is why there was seasonal variation in these offerings. In these various ways, the ancient sage-kings ruled the world by putting the ghosts and spirits ahead of the people. This is why they declared that before any of the civil officials were appointed, the sacrifical implements and robes must first be stored away in the royal treasury, those in charge of overseeing and performing the sacrifices must all be presented and invested at court, and those animals to be used as sacrifices must be separated from the rest of their flocks and herds. This is how the sage-kings of ancient times carried out their rule. In ancient times, sage-kings always showed their devotion to the ghosts and spirits in these ways and their devotion was generous and substantial. But they worried that their descendants would not understand this and so they recorded their activities in books of bamboo and silk and passed these down to succeeding generations. Still they worried that these bamboo and silk books would decay over time and become lost and that their descendants in succeeding ages would have no way to learn of this. And so they repeated this knowledge by etching it on basins and bowls and inscribing it in metal and stone. There was still some concern that their descendants in later generations would not be reverent enough to receive blessings and so in the books of the former kings and among the teachings of the sages, within each length of silk text and every book's chapter, one finds numerous and repeated references to the existence of ghosts and spritis. Why is this the case? Because the sage-kings were devoted to the ghosts and spirits. Now when those who maintain that there are no ghosts and spirits say, 'There certainly are no ghosts and spirits!' this opposes what the sage-kings were devoted to. And whatever opposes what the sage-kings were devoted to is not the way one becomes a gentleman."

Now those who maintain that there are no ghosts say, "Exactly what textual sources are there to support your claims that in the books of the former kings and among the teachings of the sages, within each length of silk text and every book's chapter, one finds numerous and repeated references to the existence of ghosts and spirits?"

Our teacher Mozi says, "Among Zhou dynasty writings, such evidence is found within the *Elegies*.[68] The *Elegies* says,

> King Wen is on high,
> How he shines in Heaven!
> Though Zhou is an ancient land,
> Its mandate was just recently granted.
> Is not Zhou illustrious!
> Is the Lord's mandate not timely!
> King Wen ascends and descends,
> He moves to the left and the right of the Lord.
> How fine, how fine is King Wen!
> His fame shall last forever!

If ghosts and spirits do not exist, then after he had died, how could King Wen move to the left and the right of the Lord? This is how I know that there are records of ghosts in the books of the Zhou.

"However, if only the books of the Zhou contained references to ghosts and one found no such references in the books of the Shang, then one could not take such stories as reliable models. But when we examine works from the Shang we find passages such as the following,

> Oh in the Xia of ancient times, before it was visited by misfortune, the various beasts and bugs below and even the soaring birds above—not one behaved in an irregular manner. How much less would one who had a human face have ventured to have a deviant heart! Even among the ghosts and spirits of the mountains and streams, none dared to be unruly.[69]

We see that by being respectful and sincere, the rulers of the Xia united Heaven and Earth and protected the earth below. And if we consider why none of the ghosts and spirits of the mountains and streams dared to be unruly, we see that it was in order to assist Yu in his work. This is how I know that there are records of ghosts in the books of the Shang.

---

[68]The quotation is from the ode "King Wen" in the *Elegies* section of the *Odes* (*Mao #* 235). For a complete translation, see Legge, *The She King*, pp. 427–31.

[69]The quoted passage is similar in content to parts of the "Instructions of Yi" section of the *History*. Cf. Legge, *The Shoo King*, pp. 193–94.

"However, if only the books of the Shang contained references to ghosts and one found no such references in the books of the Xia, then one could not take such stories as reliable models. So let us examine works from the Xia. The "Declaration of Yu"[70] says,

> A great battle was being waged at Gan and in its midst the king called for his six commanders of the left and right flanks to gather around him. He then declared to the assembled army below, 'This ruler of Hu[71] has destroyed and reviled the Five Phases[72] and has been remiss and abandoned the Three Spheres.[73] Heaven shall cut off his mandate.'
>
> Continuing he said, 'This very afternoon I shall fight the ruler of Hu to decide what this day holds for us. You ministers, high officials, and common men, know that I do this not because I desire his fields and treasures but only to respectfully carry out the punishment decreed by Heaven. If those on the left do not respectfully carry out the duties of the left and those on the right do not respectfully carry out the duties of the right, you will not be respectfully carrying out Heaven's mandate. If you charioteers do not drive your chariots straight, you will not be respectfully carrying out Heaven's mandate. [Today you are carrying out Heaven's mandate.] That is why the rewards for proper performance on this day will be conferred at the ancestral shrine and the punishments for failure will be meted out at the altar of soil.'

Why were the rewards for proper performance conferred at the ancestral shrine? In order to show the ghosts and spirits that they are fairly appor-

---

[70]In the present version of the *History* there is a passage that shares some of the language and general thrust of the text Mozi quotes. This passage is called the "Declaration at Gan" with Gan being the place named in the *Mozi* passage. For the present version, see Legge, tr. *The Shoo King,* pp. 152–55.

[71]A state ruled by relatives who shared the same surname as the Xia royal line. It was located in present-day Shanxi province.

[72]These are the basic phases that the natural and human realms are supposed to pass through in orderly succession. They are wood, fire, earth, metal, and water. While a given phase is in "ascendance," the activities and phenomena associated with that phase are thought to guide the major course of events.

[73]The realms of Heaven, earth, and human beings.

tioned. Why were the punishments for failure meted out at the altar of soil? In order to show the ghosts and spirits that the cases were decided properly. And so we see that the ancient sage-kings clearly believed that ghosts and spirits could reward the worthy and punish the wicked. This is why rewards were conferred at the ancestral shrine and punishments meted out at the altar of soil. This is how I know that there are records of ghosts in the books of the Xia."

And so, in former times, in the records of the Xia and in the following works of the Shang and the Zhou, there are numerous and repeated references to ghosts and spirits. Why is this the case? Because the sage-kings were devoted to them. How can anyone who considers what these books say still doubt the existence of ghosts and spirits? . . .

This is why our teacher Mozi says, "If the ability of ghosts and spirits to reward the worthy and punish the wicked could be firmly established as fact throughout the empire and among the common people, it would surely bring order to the state and great benefit to the people. If state officials are dishonest or corrupt in carrying out their duties or men and women engage in illicit relationships, the ghosts and spirits will see them! If the people turn to licentiousness, violence, rebellion, theft, or robbery and use weapons, poisons, water, or fire to attack travelers on the roads and byways and rob their carriages, horses, coats, and furs in order to profit themselves—there are ghosts and spirits who will see them![74] And so, state officials will not dare to be dishonest or corrupt. When they see good, they will not dare to not reward it and when they see wickedness, they will not dare to withhold punishment.[75] Thereupon, there will be an end to the common people turning to licentiousness, violence, rebellion, theft, or robbery and using weapons, poisons, water, or fire to attack travelers on the roads and byways and rob their carriages, horses, coats, and furs in order to profit themselves. And so the world will be well-ordered." . . .

Our teacher Mozi says, ". . . If it were the case that ghosts and spirits do not really exist, then in offering sacrifices, all we would be doing is expending resources of wine and millet. But though we would be expending these resources, we would not simply be pouring the wine into a ditch or gully or throwing the millet away. Primary clan members[76] and people liv-

---

[74]This line also occurs at the very beginning of the chapter.

[75]Cf. "Honoring the Worthy." See *Mozi*, chapter 8, pp. 57–60.

[76]That is, those who share the father's surname and are in line to continue his family's ancestral sacrifices.

ing out in the villages and towns all have a chance to drink the sacrificial wine and partake of the offerings. And so even if the ghosts and spirits did not exist, these offerings would still be a means for welcoming and bringing together close family and gathering together and increasing fellowship among people living out in the villages and towns."[77] . . .

Chapter Thiry-Two:
A Condemnation of Musical Performances[78]

Our teacher Mozi says, "The benevolent surely are those who devote themselves to finding ways to promote what is beneficial to the world while eliminating what is harmful; this is why they are proper models for human conduct throughout the world. If something benefits the world then they will do it. If it does not benefit the world then they will stop doing it. Moreover, when the benevolent think about the people of the world, if there is something that attracts their eyes, delights their ears, pleases their palates, and gives comfort to their bodies but this thing can only be gotten by sacrificing the people's stock of food and clothing, they will not engage in it."

And so our teacher Mozi does not condemn music because he thinks that the sounds of bells, drums, zithers, and pipes are not pleasing, nor because he thinks that inlaid and carved patterns and designs are not fine, nor because he thinks that roasts of grain- and grass-fed meat are not delicious, nor because he thinks that high towers, lofty halls, and secluded pavilions are not comfortable. Though his body knows the comfort of such places, his mouth the relish of such food, his eye the fineness of such patterns, and his ears the pleasure of such sounds, nevertheless, he sees that it does not accord with the practices of the sage-kings of old and does not promote the benefit of the people in the world today. And so our teacher Mozi says, "Musical performances are wrong!"

---

[77]Mozi shows no evidence of doubting the existence of ghosts and spirits, but the more sociological explanation for ritual sacrifice he offers here anticipates Xunzi's rich and wholly secular defense of ritual. Cf. Xunzi's "Discourse on Ritual." See *Xunzi*, chapter 19, pp. 265–71.

[78]Mozi criticizes the elaborate musical performances that were sponsored by many states in early China. These events included complex and expensive orchestras, elaborate dancing, and often were accompanied by lavish feasts. He argues that these waste vast resources of time, material, and effort without producing any tangible results. He is not directly criticizing music per se. On the other hand, he shows no sense that music serves any useful purpose in life. For a meticulous and incisive study of the production, performance, ritual, and beliefs regarding ancient Chinese chime bells, see Lothar von Falkenhausen, *Suspended Music: Chime Bells in the Culture of Bronze Age China* (Berkeley, CA: University of California Press, 1993).

Our teacher Mozi says, "These days, when kings, dukes, and other persons of high rank engage in the manufacture of musical instruments as a function of state, it is no simple matter like slicing through water or breaking apart a piece of sod. Rather, they must heavily tax the people in order to enjoy the sounds of bells, drums, zithers, and pipes. If the production of these instruments were truly analogous to the sage-kings' production of boats and carts, then I would not dare to condemn it. In ancient times, the sage-kings did indeed heavily tax the people in order to make boats and carts. But once these were completed and the people asked what they could be used for, they were told that the boats could be used for traveling over water while the carts could be used for traveling over land. By using these conveyances, gentlemen could rest their feet while common people could rest their shoulders and backs. And so why did the people give over their resources in order to produce boats and carts without considering it a burden or an imposition? Because they knew they would get something in return that benefitted them. Now if musical instruments produced a similar return that benefitted the people then I would not dare to condemn them.

"However, the present use of musical instruments imposes three hardships upon the people. Because of the expenditures involved in producing such instruments, those who are hungry are unable to get food, those who are cold are unable to obtain clothing, and those who toil are not afforded a chance to rest. These are the three greatest hardships upon the people. But what if we play the great bells, strike up the drums, sound the zithers, blow the pipes, and dance with shields and battle axes? Will this enable the people to procure food or clothing? I believe that such performances will not produce such results. But let us set aside such concerns for the moment. For now great states attack lesser states and great families assault lesser families, the strong rob the weak, the many do violence to the few, the clever deceive the simple, those of noble rank act arrogantly toward those of humble rank, and rebels and bandits flourish and cannot be stopped. But what if we play the great bells, strike up the drums, sound the zithers, blow the pipes, and dance with shields and battle axes? Will this bring order to the chaos that presently reigns in the world? I believe that such performances will not produce such results."

This is why our teacher Mozi says, "If we look to see whether heavily taxing the people to produce the sounds of great bells, drums, zithers, and pipes promotes the benefit of the people of the world and eliminates what is harmful to them, we see that it offers no such help."

This is why our teacher Mozi says, "Musical performances are wrong!"

Our teacher Mozi says, "These days, when kings, dukes, and great men sit up in their raised halls and broad pavilions and look down upon the great bells, the bells look like nothing more than inverted cauldrons. If there is no one to strike the great bells, how could they take delight in them? The bells must be struck in order to be enjoyed. But they cannot employ the very old or the very young to strike the bells. For the ears and eyes of such people are not sharp and clear, their limbs are not nimble and strong, the sounds they produce are not harmonious, and they cannot follow the complicated turns in the score. And so kings, dukes, and great men must employ people in their prime, for their ears and eyes are sharp and clear, their limbs are nimble and strong, the sounds they produce are harmonious, and they can follow the complicated turns in the performance. If they employ men to make music, then these men must abandon their work of ploughing, planting, and cultivation. If they employ women to make music then these women must abandon their work of spinning, weaving, and sewing. These days, when kings, dukes, and great men put on musical performances, they divert such vast resources that could be used to produce food and clothing for the people."

This is why our teacher Mozi says, "Musical performances are wrong!"

Our teacher Mozi says, "Now let us suppose that the great bells, drums, zithers, and lutes have all been properly prepared. What pleasure would kings, dukes, and great men find in reverently listening to them all by themselves? Their enjoyment must come from listening to them in the company of common folk or gentlemen. But if they listen in the company of gentlemen, then those gentlemen must neglect the business of governing. And if they listen in the company of common folk, then those folk must abandon their proper work. These days, when kings, dukes, and great men put on musical performances, they divert such vast resources that could be used to produce food and clothing for the people."

This is why our teacher Mozi says, "Musical performances are wrong!"

Our teacher Mozi says, "In ancient times, Duke Kang of Qi[79] found excitement and delight in the performance of the Dance of Wan.[80] The performers of the dance were not permitted to wear coarse and simple clothing nor could they eat plain or common food because it was said that, 'If their food and drink is not fine, their faces and complexion will be unworthy to

---

[79]Ruler of the state of Qi. His reign dates are 404–379 B.C.E.

[80]A choreographed performance with musical accompaniment. For a description, see Waley, *The Book of Songs*, pp. 338–40.

look at. If their clothing is not fine, their figures and movements will be unworthy of view.' And so their food had to be only the finest grains and meats and their clothing had to be only embroidered silk. They never worked to produce their own food and clothing but always were supported by the work of others."

This is why our teacher Mozi says, "These days, when kings, dukes, and great men put on musical performances, they divert such vast resources that could be used to produce food and clothing for the people."

This is why our teacher Mozi says, "Musical performances are wrong!"

Our teacher Mozi says, "Now human beings certainly are different from the various kinds of birds, beasts, and bugs that one can find in the world today. The various birds, beasts, and bugs rely upon their feathers and fur for their clothing, their hoofs and claws for their leggings and shoes, and grass and water for their food and drink. And so even if the males do not plough and cultivate the land and even if the females do not spin and weave, these creatures are still assured of having food and clothing. Human beings differ in this respect. Those who labor upon the land survive, while those who do not perish. If gentlemen do not exert themselves in pursuing their duties at court, then the laws and administration will fall into chaos. If common folk do not exert themselves in carrying out their work, there will not be enough material goods.

"Now if men of rank and gentlemen in the world today believe that what I say is not true, let us try enumerating the allotted tasks that are pursued throughout the world in order to see the harm done by musical preformances.

"Kings, dukes, and high officials begin their work at court early in the day and retire late in the evening, listening to litigation and carrying out the administration of government—these are their allotted tasks. Men of rank and gentlemen exhaust the strength of their limbs and exert every ounce of their wisdom attending to their official duties at court and collecting taxes and levies out in the passes, markets, mountains, forests, lakes, and rivers in order to fill the state's granaries and treasuries—these are their allotted tasks. Farmers go out to the fields at dawn and return at dusk, ploughing, planting, cultivating, and reaping great harvests of grain and other produce—these are their allotted tasks. Women rise at dawn and retire in the evening, spinning and weaving to produce hemp, silk, linen, and other types of cloth—these are their allotted tasks.

"Now if those who serve as kings, dukes, and high officials delight in musical performances and spend their time listening to them, they will not be able to begin their work at court early in the day and retire late in the evening, listening to litigation and carrying out the administration of government. As a result, the state will fall into chaos and the altar of grain will be in jeopardy. If men of rank and gentlemen delight in musical performances and spend their time listening to them, they will not be able to exhaust the strength of their limbs and exert every ounce of their wisdom attending to their official duties at court and collecting taxes and levies out in the passes, markets, mountains, forests, lakes, and rivers in order to fill the state's granaries and treasuries. As a result, the granaries and treasuries will not be full. If farmers delight in musical performances and spend their time listening to them, they will not be able to go out to the fields at dawn and return at dusk, ploughing, planting, cultivating, and reaping great harvests of grain and other produce. As a result, the supply of food will be insufficient. If women delight in musical performances and spend their time listening to them, they will not be able to rise at dawn and retire in the evening, spinning and weaving to produce hemp, silk, linen, and other types of cloth. As a result, there will not be an adequate supply of cloth. What is the cause of great men abandoning the administration of the government and the common people neglecting their work? It is music!"

This is why our teacher Mozi says, "Musical performances are wrong!"

Our teacher Mozi says, "How do I know that this is so? Among the works of the former kings, there is the following in Tang's *Official Punishments*,[81]

To allow constant dancing in one's hall is called *Shamen's Fancy*. If gentlemen commit this offense they are to be fined two bolts of silk. If it is a commoner, the fine is two hundred measures of yellow thread.[82]

The text goes on to say,

Alas! The dancing goes on and on! The sound of the pipes is loud and clear! The Lord on High no longer supports him. He

---

[81]There is no such section in the present *History* but in the chapter called "Instructions of Yin," there is a passage that shares much of the language and general thrust of Mozi's quotation. See Legge, *The Shoo King*, p. 196.

[82]The text of the last line is garbled and the translation is tentative.

will lose the nine realms.[83] The Lord on High no longer acco-
modates him and will send down a hundred calamities. His
family will be ruined and annihilated.

If we look into why he lost the nine realms, we see it is simply because
he promoted musical performances. The *Wu Guan*[84] says,

Qi[85] then abandoned himself to lust and music; he drank and
ate in the wilds. Qiang! Qiang! The flutes and chimes sounded
vigorously! He sank, besotted with wine! He ate gluttonously in
the wilds! The Dance of Wan was elegant and fine and its performance was heard in Heaven. But Heaven did not approve.

And so, above, Heaven and the ghosts did not approve and, below, the people were not benefitted."

This is why our teacher Mozi says, "If men of rank and the gentlemen
of the world really want to promote what is beneficial to the world and
eliminate what is harmful to it, then they will prohibit and put an end to
this thing called music!"

Chapter Thirty-Five:
A Condemnation of Fatalism

Our teacher Mozi says, "The kings, dukes, and great officials who now rule
the various states all want their states to be wealthy, their populations great,
and their administrations orderly, and yet instead of wealth they get
poverty, instead of great populations they get meager ones, and instead of
order they get chaos. In this way they fundamentally miss what they desire
and get what they dislike."[86]

---

[83]"He" refers to the tyrant Jie. The point of the passage is that Jie's personal debauchery
testifies to his low character, which makes him offensive to Heaven and unfit to rule. Thus
it justifies Tang's attack on him.

[84]An unknown text.

[85]Qi is the son of Yu, founder of the Xia dynasty. He succeeded his father to the throne.
The point of the passage is to illustrate his bad moral character that makes him offensive to
Heaven and unfit to rule.

[86]These same lines occur as the opening of "Honoring the Worthy." See *Mozi*, Chapter 8, p. 57.

What is the reason for this?

Our teacher Mozi says, "This is because, among the people, there are so many who maintain a belief in fatalism. Those who believe in fatalism say, 'If the state is fated to be rich, then it will be rich; if it is fated to be poor, then it will be poor. If the state is fated to have a large population, then the population will be large; if it is fated to have a meager population, then the population will be meager. If the state is fated to be well ordered, then it will be well ordered; if it is fated to be in chaos, then it will be in chaos. If one is fated to live a long time, then one will live a long time; if one is fated to die young, then one will die young. If something is fated to occur, then no matter how hard one tries to change this, what good will it do?' Above they use this doctrine to persuade the kings, dukes, and great officials and below they deploy it to interfere with work of the people. Therefore, those who maintain a belief in fatalism are not benevolent and their claims must be carefully examined."

Since this is the case, how are we to go about carefully examining their claims?

Our teacher Mozi says, "When one advances claims, one must first establish a standard of assessment. To make claims in the absence of such a standard is like trying to establish on the surface of a spinning potter's wheel where the sun will rise and set.[87] Without a fixed standard, one cannot clearly ascertain what is right and wrong or what is beneficial and harmful. And so, in assessing claims, one must use the three gauges."[88]

What are the "three gauges?"

Our teacher Mozi says, "The gauges of precedent, evidence, and application."

How does one assess a claim's precedents?

---

[87]This describes the practice of determining how far from true east and west the sun would rise and set. It consisted of aligning a set of gnomons (see the following note) with the rising and setting sun and using these to triangulate true east and west. It would be impossible to carry out this procedure on the surface of a spinning potter's wheel just as it would be impossible to use such a wheel as a sundial. For a description and discussion of this procedure and other uses of such gnomon, see A. C. Graham, *Later Mohist Logic, Ethics and Science* (Hong Kong: The Chinese University of Hong Kong, 1978), pp. 370–71, and Joseph Needham, *Science and Civilization in China*, vol. 3 (London: Cambridge University Press, 1959), pp. 284–302.

[88]The word I have translated as "gauge" (*biao* 表) is a gnomon used to "gauge" the direction and movement of the sun's shadow. For an illustration, see the discussion in Needham or the web site for this volume.

Our teacher Mozi says, "One looks up for precedents among the affairs and actions of the ancient sage-kings."

How does one assess a claim's evidence?

Our teacher Mozi says, "One looks down to examine evidence of what the people have heard and seen."

How does one assess a claim's application?

Our teacher Mozi says, "One implements it as state policy and sees whether or not it produces benefit for the state, families, and people. These are what are called the three gauges for assessing claims." . . .

SELECTIVE BIBLIOGRAPHY

Translations

Mei, Yi-pao.

1929   *The Ethical and Political Works of Motse.* London: Arthur Probsthain. (The most complete translation of Mozi's works available in English.)

Watson, Burton.

1963   *Mo Tzu: Basic Writings.* New York: Columbia University Press. (A readable, selective English translation of the *Mozi.* Contains all of the synoptic chapters plus the two "Against Confucians" chapters.)

Secondary Works

Graham, A. C.

1978   *Later Mohist Logic, Ethics and Science.* Hong Kong: The Chinese University Press. (A brilliant reconstruction, translation, and analysis of later Mohist philosophy and science.)

1985   *Divisions in Early Mohism Reflected in the Core Chapters of Mo-tzu.* Singapore: National University of Singapore, Institute of East Asian Philosophies. (An intriguing though speculative study that argues that the synoptic chapters can be rearranged to reveal three schools of later Mohist thought, each with a distinct political agenda and philosophical position.)

Ivanhoe, Philip J.

1998   "Mohist Philosophy." *The Routledge Encyclopedia of Philosophy,* vol. 6, pp. 451–55. London: Routledge Press. (An introduction to the philosophy of Mozi and his followers.)

Lowe, Scott.

1992   *Mo Tzu's Religious Blueprint for a Chinese Utopia.* UK: The Edwin Mellon Press, Ltd. (A general study of early Mohist religious thought. Offers brief though incisive criticisms of much of the contemporary scholarship available in English.)

Nivison, David S.

1996 "Two Roots or One?" in *The Ways of Confucianism: Investigations in Chinese Philosophy*, Bryan W. Van Norden, ed., pp. 133–48. La Salle, IL: Open Court Press. (A philosophically sophisticated discussion of the ethical thought and theory of moral action of the later Mohist, Yi Zhi.)

■ CHAPTER THREE ■

MENGZI (MENCIUS)

Introduction

Mengzi 孟子 was a Chinese Confucian philosopher who lived in the fourth century B.C.E. He was born after Kongzi died, so he never studied under Kongzi, or even met him. However, Mengzi tried to teach, practice, and defend the Way of Kongzi as he understood it. Although he is not nearly as well known in the West as Kongzi, Mengzi has long been regarded in China (and throughout East Asia) as second only to Kongzi himself in importance as a Confucian thinker.

The collection of Mengzi's sayings, dialogues, and debates with others is known simply as the *Mengzi* (or, following the Jesuit Latinization of his name, the *Mencius*). It is divided into seven "books," each of which is subdivided into two parts (called the "A" and "B" parts), which are then further divided into "chapters." So, for example, *Mengzi* 1B3 is book 1, second part, chapter 3.

Mengzi saw the main intellectual opponents of the Way of Kongzi as being the teachings of Yang Zhu and Mozi (3B9, 7A26). Mozi, as we saw in Chapter Two, advocated a kind of universalistic consequentialism. There are few, if any, texts that have survived to the present day that we can confidently identify as presenting the teachings of Yang Zhu, so we do not know exactly what his philosophy was. However, it seems clear that Yang Zhu emphasized following one's *xing* 性, "nature" (see *Important Terms*), and claimed that the teachings of both Mohism and Confucianism ask us to act contrary to our natures by making what Yang Zhu saw as excessive sacrifices for others. On this basis, Mengzi accused Yang Zhu (perhaps unfairly) of being a sort of extreme egoist.

Mengzi agrees with Yang Zhu that humans have a nature, which they should follow. Indeed, he criticizes a rival philosopher, Gaozi, for suggesting that ethical cultivation must involve violating one's nature (*Mengzi* 6A1). However, Mengzi argues against Yang Zhu that there are incipient virtuous inclinations in one's nature (*Mengzi* 6A6). He frequently describes these inclinations using a metaphor of "sprouts," and compares ethical cultivation to tending these sprouts (*Mengzi* 2A6, 2A2, 6A7–8). Mengzi presents various kinds of evidence for the existence of ethical "sprouts" in humans, including the "giveaway" actions of adults who spontaneously manifest these inclinations (such as King Xuan, whose sympathy for an ox being led to slaughter shows his nascent compassion [*Mengzi* 1A7]), and "thought experiments" (such as asking us what our intuitions are about how a normal human would react to the sight of a child about to fall into a well [*Mengzi* 2A6], or to the sight of the corpses of loved ones rotting by the roadside [*Mengzi* 3A5]).

It is important to understand that, although the presence of the sprouts guarantees the goodness of *human nature*, this does not entail that most *humans* are actually good. Mengzi stresses that a bad environment (and failure to cultivate oneself) can almost destroy one's original nature (*Mengzi* 6A8). Furthermore, our compassion for others and disdain to do what is wrong are innate, but only incipient. Thus the task of moral cultivation is to "extend" or "fill out" the reactions from the paradigmatic cases where we already have them to the relevantly similar cases where we do not yet have them, but ought to (*Mengzi* 7A15, 7A17, 7B31).

Mengzi thinks that most people will be unable to develop their nature without having their basic needs for things such as food met (*Mengzi* 7A27). Indeed, Mengzi provides specific advice about proper farm management (*Mengzi* 3A3), showing his concern with the practicalities of governing. Once their fundamental needs are met, basic—but universal—ethical education is crucial (*Mengzi* 1A7, 3A4). However, Mengzi recognizes that, while everyone has the capacity to become a sage, not everyone will realize that ability.

Advanced ethical cultivation requires education under a wise teacher. Mengzi's students pose him questions, often involving conundrums from two works that were already quite old and almost canonical by Mengzi's time: the *History* and the *Odes* (*Mengzi* 5A2, 7B3, see also *Important Texts*). It is significant that much of Mengzi's teaching is based on concrete cases, rather than abstract principles. Although he clearly thinks that there is a best Way to live, and a best choice in every situation (*Mengzi* 4B29), his approach is "particularistic" in emphasizing the context-sensitivity of virtue (*Mengzi* 4A17). Thus, he tries to cultivate in his students a skill that goes beyond any simple tool or technique (*Mengzi* 7B5). This is perhaps part of his reason for suggesting that you should "seek for in your heart" what "you do not get from doctrines" (*Mengzi* 2A2).

Mengzi uses his particular conception of human nature to provide a response to both Mohism and Yangism. As we have seen, Mengzi agrees with the Yangists that humans have a nature that they should follow, but argues that the Yangists have supplied an impoverished account of the contents of that nature. Against the Mohists, Mengzi argues that there is a natural order of development of human compassion, and that, as a matter of psychological fact, humans must learn to love members of their own family before they can learn to love strangers (*Mengzi* 7A15, 7A45). Some Mohists in Mengzi's era seem to have conceded this point, but argued that the feeling of compassion cultivated in the family should be extended outward to love everyone equally. However, Mengzi claims that, given the way in which our compassion develops out of love of kin, any effort to love everyone equally violates our naturally greater compassion for family members (*Mengzi* 3A5). Finally, Mengzi argues that the effort to base one's actions on *li* 利, "benefit" or "profit," even if it is the profit of one's kingdom as a whole, will be self-defeating (*Mengzi* 1A1).

Book One

1A1 Mengzi had an audience with King Hui of Liang. The King said, "Sir, you have come, not regarding one thousand *li* as too far. Surely you will have something to profit my state?"

Mengzi said in response, "Why must Your Majesty say, 'profit'? Let there be benevolence and righteousness and that is all. Your Majesty says, 'How can my state be profited?' The Counsellors say, 'How can my family be profited?' The scholars and commoners say, 'How can I be profited?' Those above and those below mutually compete for profit and the state is endangered.

"In a case where the ruler of a state that can field ten thousand chariots is murdered, it must be by a family that can field a thousand chariots. In a case where the ruler of a state that can field a thousand chariots is murdered, it must be by a family that can field a hundred chariots. One thousand out of ten thousand, or one hundred out of a thousand, cannot be considered to not be a lot. But if righteousness is put behind and profit is put ahead, one will not be satisfied without grasping from others.

"There have never been those who were benevolent who abandoned their parents. There have never been those who were righteous who put their ruler last. Let Your Majesty say, 'Benevolence and righteousness,' and that is all. Why must you say 'profit'?"

1A3 King Hui of Liang said, "In relation to the state, We exert our heart to the utmost. When there is a famine in the region inside the river, then We move people to the region east of the river, and move grain to the region inside the river. When there is a famine in the region east of the river, We do the converse. When We examine the government of neighboring states, there is none that exerts itself as We do. Yet the people of neighboring states do not grow fewer, and Our people do not grow more numerous. How is this?"

Mengzi responded, "Your Majesty is fond of war. Allow me to use an illustration from warfare: Thunderingly, the drums beat the soldiers forward; their swords have already clashed; casting aside their armor and trailing their weapons they run away. Some run a hundred paces and then stop; others run fifty paces and then stop. How would it be if those who ran fifty paces laughed at those who ran a hundred paces?"

He responded, "That is unacceptable. They simply did not run a hundred paces. But what they did is running away too."

Mengzi said, "If Your Majesty understands this, then you will not expect your people to be more numerous than those of neighboring states." . . .

Mencius acting as moral psychologist. Calling attention to people's "give away" actions to prove their possession of the 4 Sprouts.

1A7 King Xuan of Qi asked, "May I hear from you of the actions of the Lord Protectors Huan of Qi and Wen of Jin?"

Mengzi said in response, "The disciples of Zhongni (i.e., Kongzi) did not give accounts of the actions of Huan and Wen. Because of this, they were not passed on to later generations, and I, your servant, have not heard of them.[1] But, if you insist, then may we talk about being a genuine king?"[2]

Xuan said, "What must one's Virtue be like so that one can become a king?"

Mengzi said, "One cares for the people and becomes a king. This is something no one can stop."

Xuan said, "Can one such as I care for the people?"

---

[1]Mengzi is not being truthful here. In *Mengzi* 4B21 (not in this volume) Mengzi says there *are* historical records of Huan and Wen. See *Mengzi* 4B11 on honesty.

[2]Xuan is a king in name only. See *Important Terms*.

Mengzi said, "He can."

Xuan said, "How do you know that I can?"

Mengzi said, "I heard your attendant Hu He say,

> The King was sitting up in his hall.[3] There was an ox being led
> past below. The King saw it and said, "Where is the ox going?"
> Someone responded, "We are about to consecrate a bell with its
> blood." The King said, "Spare it. I cannot bear its frightened
> appearance, like an innocent going to the execution ground."
> Someone responded, "So should we abandon the consecrating
> of the bell?" The King said, "How can that be abandoned? Ex-
> change it for a sheep."

Mengzi continued, "I do not know if this happened."

Xuan said, "It happened."

Mengzi said, "This feeling is sufficient to be a king.[4] The commoners all
thought Your Majesty was being stingy. But I knew that Your Majesty
could not bear the frightened appearance of the ox."

The King said, "That is so. There really were commoners like that. Although Qi is a small state, how could I be stingy about one ox? It was just
that I could not bear its frightened appearance, like an innocent going to
the execution ground. Hence, I exchanged it for a sheep."

Mengzi said, "Let Your Majesty not be surprised at the commoners' taking you to be stingy. You took a small thing and exchanged it for a big
thing. How could they understand? If Your Majesty were pained at its
being innocent and going to the execution ground, then what is there to
choose between an ox and a sheep?"

The King laughed, saying, "What was this feeling really?! It's not the case
that I grudged its value and exchanged it for a sheep. But it makes sense
that the commoners would say I was stingy."

Mengzi said, "There is no harm. This is just the way benevolence works.
You saw the ox but had not seen the sheep. As for the relation of gentlemen to birds and beasts, if they see them living, they cannot bear to see

---

[3]Since ancient times in China, royal palaces have included halls raised above the ground,
often looking out onto the courtyard below. See the web site for this volume for an image
of such a hall. Cf. *Zhuangzi*, chapter 13, p. 237.

[4]"Feeling" 心, here and below, is literally "heart" (*xin*), see *Important Terms*.

them die. If they hear their cries, they cannot bear to eat their flesh. Hence, gentlemen keep their distance from the kitchen."

The King was pleased and said, "The *Odes* say,

> Another person had the heart,
> But I measured it.[5]

This describes you. I was the one who did it. I reflected and sought it out, but did not understand my heart. You spoke, and in my heart there was a feeling of compassion. In what way does this heart accord with being a king?"

Mengzi said, "Suppose there were someone who reported to your majesty, saying, 'My strength is sufficient to lift five hundred pounds, but not sufficient to lift one feather. My eyesight is sufficient to examine the tip of an autumn hair,[6] but I cannot see a wagon of firewood.' Would Your Majesty accept that?"

Xuan said, "No."

Mengzi said, "In the present case your kindness is sufficient to reach birds and beasts, but the benefits do not reach the commoners. Why is this case alone different? Hence, not lifting one feather is due to not using one's strength. Not seeing a wagon of firewood is due to not using one's eyesight. The commoners not receiving care is due to not using one's kindness. Hence, Your Majesty's not being a genuine king is due to not acting; it is not due to not being able."

Xuan said, "What is the difference between concrete cases of not doing and not being able?"

Mengzi said, " 'Pick up Mount Tai and leap over the North Sea.' If you say, 'I cannot,' this is truly not being able. 'Massage the stiff joints of an elderly person.' If you say, 'I cannot,' this is not acting; it is not a case of not being able. So Your Majesty's not being a king is not in the category of picking up Mount Tai and leaping over the North Sea. Your Majesty's not being a king is in the category of massaging the stiff joints of an elderly person.

"Treat your elders as elders, and extend it to the elders of others; treat your young ones as young ones,[7] and extend it to the young ones of others; then you can turn the whole world in the palm of your hand. The *Odes* say,

---

[5] *Mao* # 198.

[6] An animal's hair is most fine (and hence thin) during the autumn.

[7] That is, "Treat your elders and young ones as elders and young ones *should* be treated."

He set an example for his wife,
It extended to his brothers,
And so he controlled his family and state.[8]

This means that he simply took this feeling and applied it to that. Hence, if one extends one's kindness, it will be sufficient to care for all within the Four Seas. If one does not extend one's kindness, one will lack the wherewithal to care for one's wife and children. That in which the ancients greatly exceeded others was no other than this. They were simply good at extending what they did. In the present case your kindness is sufficient to reach birds and beasts, but the benefits do not reach the commoners. Why is this case alone different? Weigh, and then you will distinguish the light and the heavy. Measure, and then you will distinguish the long and the short. Things are all like this, the heart most of all. Let Your Majesty measure it.

"Perhaps Your Majesty can only be happy in his heart by rallying soldiers, endangering his scholars and ministers, and incurring the resentment of the other lords?"

Xuan said, "No. How could I be happy about these things?"

Mengzi said, "Could I hear Your Majesty's greatest desire?" The King smiled and did not speak.

Mengzi said, "Is it because your hearty and sweet foods are insufficient for your mouth? Are your light and warm clothes insufficient for your body? Or yet because the beautiful and charming sights are insufficient for your eyes to look at? The melodies are insufficient for your ears to listen to? The servants are insufficient to order about in front of you? Your Majesty's various ministers *are* sufficient to serve you. Does Your Majesty actually do what you do for these things?!"

Xuan said, "No. It is not for the sake of these things."

Mengzi said, "Then Your Majesty's greatest desire can be known. You desire to govern the land, bring to your court the states of Qin and Chu, oversee the Central Kingdom, and dominate the barbarians. By means of such things as you do, to seek such things as you desire, is like climbing a tree in search of a fish."

The King said, "Is it as extreme as that?"

Mengzi said, "The danger is greater than that! If one climbs a tree in search of a fish, although one will not get a fish, there will not be any disaster afterward. By means of such things as you do, to seek such things as

---

[8] *Mao # 240.*

you desire, if one exhausts the strength of one's heart in doing it, afterward there must be disaster."

Xuan said, "Could I hear of this?"

Mengzi said, "If the people of Zou and the people of Chu fought, who does Your Majesty think would win?"

Xuan said, "The people of Chu would win."

Mengzi said, "So the small definitely cannot match the big, the few definitely cannot match the many, the weak definitely cannot match the strong. The region within the seas is nine thousand square *li*. Qi amounts to one thousand. To take on eight with one, how is this different from Zou matching Chu?!

"Simply return to the fundamentals. Suppose Your Majesty were to bestow benevolence in governing. This would cause all under Heaven who serve others to all want to take their place in Your Majesty's court, those who plough to all want to plough in Your Majesty's uncultivated fields, merchants to all want to place their goods in Your Majesty's markets, those who travel to all wish to use Your Majesty's roads. All under Heaven who wish to complain of their rulers would all desire to report to Your Majesty. If it were like this, who could stop it?"9

The King said, "I am ignorant and unable to undertake this. But I am willing for you, Master, to redirect my resolution, enlighten, and instruct me. Although I am not clever, please let me try."

Mengzi said, "To lack a constant livelihood, yet to have a constant heart—only a *shi* 士, "scholar," is capable of this. As for the people, if they lack a constant livelihood, it follows that they will lack a constant heart. And if one simply fails to have a constant heart, dissipation and evil will not be avoided. When they thereupon sink into crime, to go and punish them is to trap the people. When there are benevolent people in positions of authority, how is it possible to trap the people? For this reason, an enlightened ruler, in regulating the people's livelihood, must ensure that it is sufficient, on the one hand, to serve one's father and mother, and on the other hand, to nurture wife and children. In good years, one is always full. In years of famine, one escapes death. Only when the people have a regulated livelihood do they rush toward the good, and thus the people follow the ruler easily.

"Nowadays, in regulating the people's livelihood, on the one hand it is insufficient to serve one's father and mother, on the other it is insufficient

---

9That is, who could stop such a ruler from eventually becoming king of all the world?

to nurture wife and children. In good years, one is always bitter. In years of famine, one cannot escape death. This is a case in which one fears not having the means to save people from death. How could one have leisure for teaching ritual and righteousness?

"If Your Majesty wishes to put benevolent government into effect, then simply return to the fundamentals. Plant every household of five *mu* with mulberry trees, and fifty-year-olds can wear silk. Let the nurturing of chickens, pigs, and dogs not be neglected, and seventy-year-olds can eat meat. If you do not disturb the seasonal work in each field of one hundred *mu*, a household with eight mouths to feed need not go hungry. If you are careful about the teachings of the schools, explaining the righteousness of filial piety and fraternal respect, then those with gray hair will not be carrying loads on the roads. For the old to wear silk and eat meat, and the black-haired people[10] to be neither hungry nor cold, yet for their ruler not to become a king—such a thing has never happened."

1B5

. . . King Xuan of Qi said, "Your teachings are excellent!"

Mengzi responded, "If Your Majesty regards them as excellent, then why do you not put them into practice?"

The King said, "We have a weakness. We are fond of wealth."

He responded, "In former times, Duke Liu was fond of wealth.[11] The *Odes* say,

> He stacked, he stored,
> He bundled up dried meat and grain,
> In bags, in sacks,
> Thinking to gather together and bring glory.
> His bows and arrows were displayed,
> With shields, spears, and battle-axes,
> He commenced his march.[12]

Hence, those who stayed at home had loaded granaries, and those who marched had full provisions. Only then could he 'commence his march.' If

---

[10]That is, the Chinese people.

[11]Duke Liu and King Tai (referred to below as Duke Danfu) are ancestors of the Zhou royal family, and are considered paradigms of virtuous rulers.

[12]*Mao # 250.*

Your Majesty is fond of wealth but allows the common folk to possess wealth, what difficulty is there in being a genuine king?"

The King responded, "We have a weakness. We are fond of sex."

He responded, "In former times, King Tai was fond of sex, and loved his wife. The *Odes* say,

> The Ancient Duke Danfu
> Came in the morning, riding his horse,
> Following the banks of the Western waters,
> He came to the foot of Mount Qi,
> With his Lady Jiang.
> They came and both settled there.[13]

At that time, there were no dissatisfied women in private, or any unmarried men in public. If Your Majesty is fond of sex but accords the common folk the same privileges, what difficulty is there in being a genuine king?"

1B6 Mengzi spoke to King Xuan of Qi, saying, "If, among Your Majesty's ministers, there were one who entrusted his wife and children to his friend, and traveled to the state of Chu, and when he returned, he discovered that his friend had let his wife and children become cold and hungry—how should one deal with this?"

The King said, "Abandon him."

Mengzi said, "If the Sergeant-at-Arms is not able to keep order among the scholars, how should one deal with this?"

The King said, "Discharge him."

Mengzi said, "If the region within the four borders is not well ordered, then how should one deal with this?" The King turned toward his attendants and changed the topic.

1B8 King Xuan of Qi asked, "Is it the case that Tang banished Jie, and that Wu struck down Zhou?"

Mengzi responded, saying, "There are such accounts in the historical records."

The King said, "Is it acceptable for subjects to kill their rulers?"

Mengzi said, "One who violates benevolence should be called a 'thief.' One who violates righteousness is called a 'mutilator.' A mutilator and thief

---

[13]*Mao # 237.*

is called a mere 'fellow.' I have heard of the execution of a mere fellow 'Zhou,' but I have not heard of the killing of one's ruler."

Book Two

2A2 Gongsun Chou asked, "Suppose that you, Master, were to be appointed to the position of high noble or prime minister in Qi and were able to put the Way into practice there. If it were so, it would not be surprising at all if the ruler of Qi were to become a lord protector or a genuine king. If it were like this, would it perturb your heart or not?"

Mengzi said, "It would not. My heart has been unperturbed since I was forty."

Gongsun Chou said, "In that case, you, Master, have far surpassed Meng Ben."[14]

Mengzi said, "This is not difficult. Gaozi had an unperturbed heart before I."[15]

Gongsun Chou said, "Is there a way of cultivating an unperturbed heart?"

Mengzi said, "There is. As for Bogong You's cultivation of courage, his body would not shrink, his eyes would not blink. He regarded the least slight from someone like being beaten in the market place. Insults he would not take off of a common fellow coarsely clad[16] he also would not take off of a ruler who could field ten thousand chariots. He looked upon running a sword through a ruler who could field ten thousand chariots as like running through a common fellow. He did not treat the various lords with deference. If an insult came his way he had to return it.

"As for Meng Shishe's cultivation of courage, he said, 'I look upon defeat the same as victory. To advance only after sizing up one's enemy, to ponder whether one will achieve victory and only then join battle, this is to be in awe of the opposing armies. How can I be certain of victory? I can only be without fear.'

---

[14]The Qing dynasty commentator Jiao Xun reports that, "Meng Ben, when traveling by water, did not avoid serpents, and, when traveling by land, did not avoid rhinoceroses and tigers."

[15]Gaozi is a rival philosopher whom Mengzi debates in *Mengzi* 6A1 ff.

[16]I borrow this well-turned phrase from D. C. Lau's translation.

"Meng Shishe resembled Zengzi. Bogong You resembled Zixia.[17] Now, as for the courage of the two, I do not really know which was better. Nonetheless, Meng Shishe preserved something important .

"Formerly, Zengzi speaking to Zixiang said, 'Are you fond of courage? I once heard about great courage from the Master,[18]

> If I examine myself and am not upright, although I am opposed by a common fellow coarsely clad, would I not be in fear? If I examine myself and am upright, although I am opposed by thousands and tens of thousands, I shall go forward.'

"Meng Shishe's preservation of his *qi* was still not as good as Zengzi's preservation of what is important."

Gongsun Chou said, "I venture to ask whether I could hear about your unperturbed heart, Master, and Gaozi's unperturbed heart?"

Mengzi answered, "Gaozi said, 'What you do not get from doctrines, do not seek for in your heart. What you do not get from your heart, do not seek for in the *qi* 氣.' 'What you do not get from your heart, do not seek for in the *qi*,' is acceptable. 'What you do not get from doctrines, do not seek for in your heart,' is unacceptable.

"Your resolution is the commander of the *qi*. *Qi* is that which fills up the body. When your resolution is fixed somewhere, the *qi* sets up camp there. Hence, it is said, 'Maintain your resolution. Do not injure the *qi*.' "[19]

Gongsun Chou asked, "Since you have already said, 'When your resolution is fixed somewhere, the *qi* sets up camp there,' why do you add, 'Maintain your resolution. Do not injure the *qi*'?"

Mengzi said, "When your resolution is unified it moves the *qi*. When the *qi* is unified it moves your resolution. Now, stumbling and running have to do with the *qi*, but nonetheless they perturb one's heart."

Gongsun Chou said, "I venture to ask wherein you excel, Master."

---

[17]On Zengzi, see *Analects* 8.7. On Zixia, see *Analects* 3.8, 6.13, and 19.12.

[18]By "the Master" he means Kongzi. What follows may be intended as a direct quotation from Kongzi, but it may also be Zengzi paraphrasing the Master's teaching.

[19]Recall that, according to Mengzi, the heart (*xin* 心, see *Important Terms*) is the seat of our ethical inclinations (*Mengzi* 2A6 and 6A6). The *zhi* 志, "resolution," is not a separate faculty, but is simply the heart directed toward a certain goal or object. Contrast what Zhuangzi suggests in "The Human Realm," about the relationship of what one hears, one's heart, and the *qi*. See *Zhuangzi*, chapter 4, pp. 221–26.

Mengzi said, "I understand words. I am good at cultivating my flood-like *qi*."

Gongsun Chou said, "I venture to ask what is meant by 'floodlike *qi*.' "

Mengzi said, "It is difficult to put into words. It is a *qi* that is supremely great and supremely unyielding. If one cultivates it with uprightness and does not harm it, it will fill up the space between Heaven and earth. It is a *qi* that unites righteousness with the Way. Without these, it starves. It is produced by accumulated righteousness. It cannot be obtained by a seizure of righteousness. If some of one's actions leave one's heart unsatisfied, it will starve. Consequently, I say that Gaozi never understood righteousness, because he regarded it as external.[20]

"One must work at it, but do not aim at it directly. Let the heart not forget, but do not help it grow. Do not be like the man from Song.[21] Among the people of the state of Song there was one who, concerned lest his grain not grow, pulled on it. Wearily, he returned home, and said to his family, 'Today I am worn out. I helped the grain to grow.' His son rushed out and looked at it. The grain was withered. Those in the world who do not help the grain to grow are few. Those who abandon it, thinking it will not help, are those who do not weed their grain. Those who help it grow are those who pull on the grain. Not only does this not help, but it even harms it."

Gongsun Chou said, "What is meant by 'understanding words' ?"[22]

Mengzi said, "If someone's expressions are one-sided, I know that by which they are deluded.[23] If someone's expressions are excessive, I know that by which they are entangled. If someone's expressions are heretical, I know that by which they are separated from the Way. If someone's expressions are evasive, I know that by which they are exhausted. When these states grow in the heart, they are harmful in governing. When they are manifested in governing, they are harmful in one's activities. When sages arise again, they will surely follow what I have said."

---

[20]On the externality of righteousness, see *Mengzi* 6A4–5.

[21]The people of Song were the butt of many jokes. Cf. *Zhuangzi*, chapter 1, p. 207, and *Hanfeizi*, chapter 49, p. 324.

[22]Cf. *Analects* 20.3.

[23]The notion that people can be deluded (or "fixated") by seeing only part of the Way also appears in *Analects* 17.8, and becomes a central notion in Xunzi's thought. See *Xunzi*, chapter 21, "Undoing Fixation," pp. 272–278.

Gongsun Chou said, "Zai Wo and Zigong were good at rhetoric. Ran Niu, Minzi, and Yan Yuan were good at discussing virtuous actions.[24] Kongzi combined all these excellences, but said, 'When it comes to rhetoric, I am incapable.' In that case, are you, Master, already a sage?!"

Mengzi said, "Oh, what kind of talk is that?! Long ago, Zigong asked Kongzi, 'Are you, Master, really a sage?' Kongzi replied, 'As for being a sage, I am incapable of that. I study without tiring and teach without wearying.'[25] Zigong said, 'To study without tiring is wisdom; to teach without wearying is benevolence. Being benevolent and wise, the Master is certainly already a sage!' So, to be a sage is not something Kongzi was comfortable with. What kind of talk was what you just said?!"

Gongsun Chou said, "Formerly, I heard the following: Zigong, Ziyou, and Zizhang all had one aspect of a sage. Ran Niu, Minzi, and Yan Yuan had all aspects of a sage, but in miniature. I venture to ask in which group you would be comfortable?"

Mengzi said, "Leave this topic for now."

Gongsun Chou said, "What about Bo Yi and Yi Yin?"

Mengzi said, "Their Ways were different. If he was not his ruler, he would not serve him; if they were not his subjects, he would not direct them; if things were orderly, he would advance; if they were chaotic, he would retreat. This was Bo Yi. Whom do I serve who is not my ruler? Whom do I direct who are not my subjects? If things were orderly, he would advance, and if they were chaotic he would also advance. This was Yi Yin. When one should take office, he would take office; when one should stop, he would stop; when one should take a long time, he would take a long time; when one should hurry, he would hurry. This was Kongzi. All were sages of ancient times. I have never been able to act like them, but my wish is to learn from Kongzi."

Gongsun Chou asked, "Were Bo Yi and Yi Yin at the same level as Kongzi?"

Mengzi said, "No. Since humans were first born there has never been another Kongzi."

Gongsun Chou said, "In that case, were there any similarities?"

Mengzi said, "There were. If any became ruler of a territory of a hundred *li*, he would be able to possess all under Heaven by bringing the various lords to his court. And if any could obtain all under Heaven by

---

[24]These people are disciples of Kongzi, as are the additional people in the next list below.

[25]Similar comments are attributed to Kongzi in *Analects* 7.2 and 7.34.

performing one unrighteous deed, or killing one innocent person, he would not do it. In these things they are the same."

Gongsun Chou asked, "I venture to ask wherein they differed?"

Mengzi said, "Zai Wo, Zigong, and You Ruo had wisdom sufficient to recognize a sage. Even if they exaggerated, they would not have done so to the extent of flattering someone they were fond of. Zai Wo said, 'In my view of Kongzi, he is far more noble than Yao and Shun!' Zigong said, 'He sees their rituals and appreciates their government; he hears their music and appreciates their Virtue; from a hundred generations later, through the succession of a hundred kings, nothing gets away from him. Since humans were first born, there has never been another like the Master.' You Ruo said, 'Is it only true of people? The unicorn among beasts, the phoenix among birds, Mount Tai among hills, and rivers and seas among flowing waters, are all of a kind. The sage among people is also of the same kind. Some stand out from this kind; some stick up from the row; since humans were first born, there has never been one who does this more so than Kongzi.' "

2A6 Mengzi said, "Humans all have hearts that are not unfeeling toward others. The former kings[26] had hearts that were not unfeeling toward others, so they had governments that were not unfeeling toward others. If one puts into practice a government that is not unfeeling toward others by means of a heart that is not unfeeling toward others, bringing order to the whole world is in the palm of your hand.

"The reason why I say that humans all have hearts that are not unfeeling toward others is this. Suppose someone suddenly saw a child about to fall into a well: everyone in such a situation would have a feeling of alarm and compassion—not because one sought to get in good with the child's parents, not because one wanted fame among their neighbors and friends, and not because one would dislike the sound of the child's cries.

"From this we can see that if one is without the heart of compassion, one is not a human. If one is without the heart of disdain, one is not a human. If one is without the heart of deference, one is not a human. If one is without the heart of approval and disapproval,[27] one is not a human. The heart of compassion is the sprout of benevolence. The heart of disdain is the

---

[26]That is, the sage-kings of antiquity, such as Yao and Shun.

[27]The words here rendered "approval" and "disapproval" are *shi* 是 and *fei* 非, respectively. A common meaning of these terms is "right" and "wrong" but in this context Mengzi intends not only knowledge but approval of what is right and disapproval of what is wrong.

sprout of righteousness. The heart of deference is the sprout of propriety. The heart of approval and disapproval is the sprout of wisdom.[28]

"People having these four sprouts is like their having four limbs. To have these four sprouts but to say of oneself that one is unable to be virtuous is to steal from oneself. To say that one's ruler is unable to be virtuous is to steal from one's ruler. In general, having these four sprouts within oneself, if one knows to fill them all out, it will be like a fire starting up, a spring breaking through! If one can merely fill them out, they will be sufficient to care for all within the Four Seas. If one merely fails to fill them out, they will be insufficient to serve one's parents."

2B13 Mengzi left the state of Qi.[29] While on the road, Chongyu asked, "It seems that you, Master, have an unhappy countenance. The other day, I heard it from you, Master, that [Kongzi said], 'The gentleman does not resent Heaven for his troubles, nor does he cast aspersions upon other people.' "[30]

Mengzi said, "That time [in which Kongzi spoke] is the same as this time. Every five hundred years, there must arise a sage-king. Between them, there must be those whose names are known to a generation for their accomplishments. From the founding of the Zhou dynasty, it has already been more than seven hundred years. Numerically, this is excessive. And if one examines it in terms of the conditions of the world, then it is possible that a new sage-king will arise. Now, Heaven does not yet desire to pacify the world. If it desired to pacify the world, who besides me in the present time is there to help do it? Why would I be unhappy?!"

---

[28]Mengzi also discusses these four cardinal virtues in *Mengzi* 4A27 and 6A6. For more on *ren* 仁, "benevolence," see *Mengzi* 1A7. For more on *yi* 義, "righteousness," see *Mengzi* 6A10. For more on *zhi* 智, "wisdom," see *Mengzi* 5A9. On Mengzi's general view of self-cultivation, see *Mengzi* 7A17 and 7B31.

[29]Mengzi left the state of Qi because his efforts to persuade the ruler to implement the "benevolent government" policies he advocated had failed. See *Mengzi* 1A7, 1B5, 1B6, and 1B8.

[30]Cf. *Analects* 14.35.

Book Three

3A3

. . . Mengzi said, "The well-field system takes a one *li* square piece of land, amounting to 900 *mu*.[31] At its center is the public field. Eight families each keep privately 100 *mu*, and jointly cultivate the public field. Only after the public work is completed do they dare do their private work. This is the distinctive role of the rural people." . . .

3A4 There was a certain Xu Xing who, on account of the doctrines of Shennong, went from the state of Chu to Teng, and, going in person to his gate, told Duke Wen, "People from distant parts have heard that you, My Lord, practice benevolent government. I wish to receive a homestead and become one of your subjects." Duke Wen gave him a place. His followers were a few dozen people, all of whom wore coarse clothing and made sandals and mats for a living.

Chen Liang's disciple Chen Xiang and his younger brother Xin carried their ploughs on their backs and went from Song to Teng, saying, "We have heard that you, My Lord, practice the government of a sage. This is to be a sage. I wish to become the subject of a sage."

Chen Xiang met Xu Xing and was delighted. He completely abandoned his former studies and studied with him instead. Chen Xiang met Mengzi and discoursed on the doctrines of Xu Xing, saying, "The ruler of Teng is truly a worthy ruler. Nonetheless, he has not yet heard the Way. The worthy plough with their subjects and then eat, eating breakfast and dinner with them and then governing. In the present case, Teng has granaries and treasuries; this is to harm the people in order to nurture oneself. How can this be worthy?"

Mengzi said, "Xuzi must plant his grain first and only then eat?"

Chen said, "That is so."

Mengzi said, "Xuzi must weave his cloth and only then wear clothes?"

Chen said, "No. Xuzi wears hemp."

Mengzi said, "Does Xuzi wear a cap?"

Chen said, "He does."

Mengzi said, "What sort does he wear?"

---

[31]The "well-field system" begins with the idea of taking a square region of land and subdividing it into nine equal fields. The boundaries between these regions would then look something like this: 井. This happens to be the character for "well" in Chinese, hence the expression "well-field."

Chen said, "He wears plain silk."

Mengzi said, "Does he weave it himself?"

Chen said, "No. He exchanges millet for it."

Mengzi said, "Why does Xuzi not weave it himself?"

Chen said, "That would interfere with farming."

Mengzi said, "Does Xuzi use clay pots for cooking, and an iron plough?"

Chen said, "That is so."

Mengzi said, "Does he make them himself?"

Chen said, "No. He exchanges millet for them."

Mengzi said, "Exchanging millet for tools does not harm the blacksmith. And when the blacksmith exchanges tools for millet, does this really hurt the farmer?! Why does Xuzi not become a blacksmith, and only get everything from his own household to use? Why does he exchange things in such confusion with the various artisans? Why does Xuzi not avoid all this trouble?"

Chen said, "The activities of the various artisans inherently cannot be done along with farming."

Mengzi said, "In that case, can governing the world alone be done along with farming? There are the affairs of great people, and the affairs of lesser people. Furthermore, the products of the various artisans are available to each person. If one can make use of them only after one has made them oneself, this will lead the whole world to exhaustion. Hence it is said, 'Some labor with their hearts; some labor with their physical strength.' Those who labor with their hearts govern others; those who labor with their physical strength are governed by others. Those who are governed by others feed those others; those who govern others are fed by those others. This is righteousness throughout the world.[32] . . .

"It is the way of people that if they are full of food, have warm clothes, and live in comfort, but are without instruction, then they come close to being animals. Sage-king Shun was anxious about this too, so he instructed Xie to be Minister of Instruction, and instruct them about human relations: the relation of father and children is one of love, ruler and minister is one of righteousness, husband and wife is one of distinction, elder and younger is one of precedence, and that between friends is one of trust. Yao said, 'Encourage them, draw them forward, straighten them, rectify them, help them, make them practice, assist them, make them get it themselves,

---

[32]What follows in the original text is a historical narrative (similar to that in *Mengzi* 3B9) that explains the achievements of the sage-rulers of old in making civilization possible.

and then benefit them.' Since the sage's anxiousness for his subjects was like this, could he have the free time to farm?" . . .

[Chen said,] "If we follow the Way of Xuzi, market prices will never vary, and there will be no artifice in the state. Even if one sends a child to go to the market, no one will cheat him. Cotton cloth or silk cloth of the same length will be of equal price. Bundles of hemp or silk of the same weight will be of equal price. The same amount of any of the five grains will be the same price. Shoes of the same size will be of equal price."

Mengzi said, "It is the essence of things to be unequal.[33] One thing is twice or five times more than another, another ten or a hundred times more, another a thousand or ten thousand times more. If you line them up and identify them, this will bring chaos to the world. If a great shoe and a shoddy shoe are the same price, will anyone make the former? If we follow the Way of Xuzi, we will lead each other into artifice. How can this bring order to the state?"

3A5 The Mohist Yi Zhi sought to see Mengzi through the help of Xu Bi.[34] Mengzi said, "I am definitely willing to see him, but today I am still ill. When my illness improves, I will go and see him. Yi Zhi does not have to come again." The next day, he again sought to see Mengzi. Mengzi said, "Today I [still] can [not] see him. [But] if one is not upright, the Way will not be manifest. I will make him upright.[35]

"I have heard that Yizi is a Mohist. Mohists, in regulating mourning, take frugality as their Way. Yizi longs to change the world to the Mohist Way. Could it be that he honors the Mohist practice, while regarding it as not right? Nonetheless, Yizi buried his parents lavishly, so he served his parents by means of what he demeans."

Xuzi told Yizi this. Yizi said, "As for the Way of the Confucians, the ancients tended the people 'like caring for a baby.'[36] What does this saying mean? I take it to mean that love is without distinctions, but it is bestowed beginning with one's parents."

---

[33]Zhuangzi may be implicitly criticizing this passage in "On Equalizing Things." See *Zhuangzi*, chapter 2, pp. 209–19.

[34]For more on Mohism, see *Mengzi* 3B9 and 7A26, as well as chapter 2 of this volume, p. 55–109.

[35]Notice that the conversation between Mengzi and Yi Zhi—who is referred to below as Yizi ("Master Yi")—is conducted using Xu Bi as an intermediary (presumably because Mengzi is ill). Cf. *Analects* 10.19.

[36]This is a line from the *History*. See Legge, *The Shoo King*, p. 389.

Xuzi told Mengzi this. Mengzi said, "Does Yizi truly hold that one's affection for one's elder brother's son is like one's affection for one's neighbor's baby? There is only one thing to be gleaned from that saying: when a crawling baby is about to fall into a well, it is not the baby's fault. Furthermore, Heaven, in producing the things in the world, causes them to have one source, but Yizi gives them two sources.[37]

"Now, in past ages, there were those who did not bury their parents. When their parents died, they took them and abandoned them in a ditch. The next day they passed by them, and foxes were eating them, bugs were sucking on them. Sweat broke out on the survivors' foreheads. They turned away and did not look. Now, it was not for the sake of others that they sweated. What was inside their hearts broke through to their countenances. So they went home and, returning with baskets and shovels, covered them. If covering them was really right, then when filial children and benevolent people cover their parents, it must also be part of the Way."

Xuzi told Yizi this. Yizi looked thoughtful for a moment and said, "He has taught me."

3B2

. . . Mengzi said, "When a daughter marries, her mother instructs her. Sending her off at the gate, she cautions her, saying, 'When you go to your family, you must be respectful, and you must be cautious. Do not disobey your husband.' To regard obedience as proper is the Way of a wife or concubine."[38] . . .

3B9 Gongduzi said, "Outsiders all say that you are fond of disputation, Master. I venture to ask why?"

Mengzi said, "How could I be fond of disputation? I simply have no choice. The people of the world were born long ago, and have alternated between being orderly and chaotic. In the time of Yao, the waters overflowed their courses, innundating the central states. Serpents occupied the land, and the people were unsettled. In low-lying regions, they made nests

---

[37]Nivison ("Two Roots or One?" in his 1996) argues that the two sources (*ben* 本, literally "roots") Yizi accepts are (1) our innate sense of benevolence, which is first directed at our parents (cf. *Mengzi* 7A15), and (2) a doctrine of universalization that instructs us to extend this innate feeling so that it applies to everyone equally.

[38]On the ethical status of women, see also *Mengzi* 4B33.

in trees. On the high ground, they lived in caves. The *History* says, 'The deluge warned us.'[39] 'The deluge' refers to the flooding water. Yu was directed to regulate the waters. Yu dredged out the earth and guided the water into the sea, chasing the reptiles into the marshes. The waters flowed out through the channels, and these became the Jiang, Huai, He, and Han rivers. The dangers to people having been eliminated, birds and beasts harmful to humans were destroyed, and only then were humans able to live on the plains.

"After Yao and Shun passed away, the Way of the sages decayed. Cruel rulers arose one after another, destroying homes to make ponds, so that the people had nowhere they could rest.[40] They made people abandon the fields so that they could be made into parks, so that the people could not get clothes and food. Evil doctrines and cruel practices also arose. As parks, ponds, and marshes became more numerous, the birds and beasts returned. By the time of Zhou, the world was again in great disorder. The Duke of Zhou assisted King Wu in punishing Zhou; he attacked the state of Yan, and after three years executed its ruler; he drove Feilian to a corner by the sea and terminated him; he eliminated fifty states; he drove tigers, leopards, rhinoceroses, and elephants far off, and the whole world rejoiced. The *History* says, 'Splendid indeed were the plans of King Wen! Great indeed were the achievements of King Wu! They assist and instruct us descendants. In all things they are correct, and lack nothing.'[41]

"With the decay of the Way, evil doctrines, and cruel actions again arose. Ministers murdering their rulers—this happened. Sons murdering their fathers—this happened. Kongzi was afraid, and composed the *Spring and Autumn Annals*. The *Spring and Autumn Annals* is the activity of the Son of Heaven.[42] For this reason, Kongzi said, 'Those who appreciate me, will it not be because of the *Spring and Autumn Annals*? Those who blame me, will it not be because of the *Spring and Autumn Annals*?'

"Once again, a sage-king has not arisen; the various lords are dissipated; pundits engage in contrary wrangling; the doctrines of Yang Zhu and Mo

---

[39]See Legge, *The Shoo King*, p. 60.

[40]The ponds referred to in this line, and the parks referred to in the next, were for the use of the ruler only, and not for the benefit of the people.

[41]See Legge, *The Shoo King*, p. 581.

[42]The Chinese line here is ambiguous. It could mean that the *Spring and Autumn Annals* contains accounts of the activities of the ruler, or that composing it is the prerogative of the ruler.

Di fill the world.[43] If a doctrine does not lean toward Yang, then it leans toward Mo. Yang is 'egoism.' This is to not have a ruler. Mo is 'universal love.' This is to not have a father. To not have a father and to not have a ruler is to be an animal. Gongming Yi said, 'In your kitchens there is fat meat, and in your stables there are fat horses. Your people look gaunt, and in the wilds are the bodies of those dead of starvation. This is to lead animals to devour people.'

"If the Ways of Yang and Mo do not cease, and the Way of Kongzi is not made evident, then evil doctrines will dupe the people, and obstruct benevolence and righteousness. If benevolence and righteousness are obstructed, that leads animals to devour people. I am afraid that people will begin to devour one another! If we defend the Way of the former sages, fend off Yang and Mo, and get rid of specious words, then evil doctrines will be unable to arise. If they arise in one's heart, they are harmful in one's activities. If they arise in one's activities, they are harmful in governing. When sages arise again, they will certainly not differ with what I have said.

"Formerly, Yu supressed the flood, and the world was settled. The Duke of Zhou incorporated the barbarians, drove away ferocious animals, and the common people were at peace. Kongzi completed the *Spring and Autumn Annals*, and disorderly ministers and brutal sons were afraid. The *Odes* say,

> The barbarians of the west and north, these he chastised.
> Jing and Shu, these he punished.
> Thus no one dared to take us on.[44]

Those who have no father and no ruler, these the Duke of Zhou chastised. I, too, desire to rectify people's hearts, to bring to an end evil doctrines, to fend off bad conduct, to get rid of specious words, so as to carry on the work of these three sages. How could I be fond of disputation? I simply have no choice. Anyone who can with words fend off Yang and Mo is a disciple of the sages."

---

[43]On the philosophy of Mo Di (Mozi), see also *Mengzi* 3A5 and 7A26, as well as chapter 2 of this volume pp. 55–109. On the philosophy of Yang Zhu, see *Mengzi* 7A26.

[44]*Mao* # 300. Jing is another name for the state of Chu. Shu was a small state located in what is now Anhui province.

3B10 Kuang Zhang said, "Wasn't Cheng Zhongzi an uncorruptible scholar?![45] While living in Wuling, he did not eat for three days, until his ears did not hear, and his eyes did not see. Above a well there was a plum tree whose fruit had been half-eaten by worms. Crawling, he went over to eat from it, and only after three bites could his ears hear and his eyes see."

Mengzi said, "Among the scholars of the state of Qi, Zhongzi is someone I would have to regard as standing out like a thumb among the fingers. Nonetheless, how could Zhongzi be uncorruptible? To fill out what Zhongzi attempts, one would have to be an earthworm.[46] Now, an earthworm eats dry earth above and drinks muddy water below. The house in which Zhongzi lives, was it built by Bo Yi, or was it in fact built by Robber Zhi? Was the millet that he eats planted by Bo Yi, or was it in fact planted by Robber Zhi? This cannot be known."

Kuang said, "Why is that a problem? He himself weaves sandles of hemp, his wife spinning the hemp, in exchange for these other things."

Mengzi said, "Zhongzi comes from a great family of Qi. His elder brother Dai received a salary of ten thousand bushels of grain from estates at Ge. He regarded his brother's salary as an unrighteous salary, and would not live off of it. He regarded his brother's dwelling as an unrighteous dwelling, and would not live in it. He left his elder brother, distancing himself from his mother, and lived in Wuling. On a later day, he visited home, and someone had given a live goose to his elder brother as a gift. He knitted his brow and said, 'What will you use this cackling thing for?!' After that, his mother killed the goose, and gave it to him to eat. His elder brother came home and said, 'This is the meat of that "cackling thing." ' He went out and threw it up. If it comes from his mother, he doesn't eat, but if it comes from his wife, then he eats it. If it's his elder brother's dwelling, then he won't live in it; if it's in Wuling, then he lives in it. Is this really being able to fill out the category of action that he considers righteous?! Someone like Zhongzi must be an earthworm in order to fill out what he attempts."

Book Four

4A10 Mengzi said, "One cannot have a discussion with those who are destroying themselves. One cannot act with those who throw themselves

---

[45]Cheng Zhongzi may be another follower of Xu Xing (see *Mengzi* 3A4).

[46]Compare the notion of "filling out" the sprouts in *Mengzi* 2A6.

away. Those whose words are opposed to propriety and righteousness are who I mean by 'those who are destroying themselves.' Those who say, 'I myself am unable to dwell in benevolence and follow righteousness' are who I mean by 'those who throw themselves away.' Benevolence is people's peaceful abode. Righteousness is people's proper path. For one to vacate one's peaceful abode and not dwell in it, or for one to set aside one's proper path and not follow it—how sad!"

4A11 Mengzi said, "The Way lies in what is near, but people seek it in what is distant; one's task lies in what is easy, but people seek it in what is difficult. If everyone would treat their kin as kin, and their elders as elders, the world would be at peace."

4A15 Mengzi said, "Of what is present within a person, nothing is more ingenuous than the pupils of the eyes. The pupils cannot hide one's evil. If, in one's bosom, one is upright, the pupils will be bright. If, in one's bosom, one is not upright, the pupils will be shady. If one listens to people's words and looks at their pupils, how can they hide?!"

4A17 Chunyu Kun said, "That men and women should not touch in handing something to one another—is this the ritual?"[47]

Mengzi said, "It is the ritual."

Chunyu Kun said, "If your sister-in-law were drowning, would you pull her out with your hand?"

Mengzi said, "To not pull your sister-in-law out when she is drowning is to be a beast. That men and women should not touch in handing something to one another is the ritual, but if your sister-in-law is drowning, to pull her out with your hand is discretion."[48]

Chunyu Kun said, "Currently, the world is drowning! Why is it that you, sir, do not pull it out?"

Mengzi said, "When the world is drowning, one pulls it out with the Way; when one's sister-in-law is drowning, one pulls her out with one's hand. Do you want me save the world with a pull of my hand?"

---

[47]Chunyu Kun was a rival philosopher.

[48]*Quan* 權, "discretion," literally means "weighing," as on a balance. On "discretion," see also *Mengzi* 7A26.

4A27 Mengzi said, "The core of benevolence is serving one's parents. The core of righteousness is obeying one's elder brother. The core of wisdom is knowing these two and not abandoning them. The core of ritual is to regulate and adorn these two. The core of music is to delight in these two.

"If one delights in them then they grow. If they grow then how can they be stopped? If they cannot be stopped, then without realizing it one's feet begin to step in time to them and one's hands dance according to their rythms."[49]

4B2 When Zichan was in charge of the government of the state of Zheng, he used his own carriage to carry people across the Zhen and the Wei rivers. Mengzi said, "He was kind, but did not understand how to govern. By September, the foot bridges are to be repaired, and by October, the carriage bridges are to be repaired, so the people no longer face the difficulty of wading across the rivers.[50] If gentlemen are equitable in governing, it is acceptable even to order people out of their way while they travel. How can they carry every single person across? Hence, there will simply not be enough days if, in governing, one tries to make everyone happy."

4B6 Mengzi said, "The propriety that is not propriety, the righteousness that is not righteousness—the great person will not practice these."[51]

4B8 Mengzi said, "People must have some things that they do not do, and only then can they really do anything."

4B11 Mengzi said, "As for great people, their words do not have to be trustworthy,[52] and their actions do not have to bear fruit. They rest only in righteousness."

4B18 Xuzi said, "Zhongni several times spoke of water, saying, 'Ah water! Ah water!'[53] What did he find so worthy about water?" Mengzi said, "It

---

[49]I owe the translation of these last lines to Philip J. Ivanhoe.

[50]The rivers have fords that are shallow enough to wade across on foot, or drive through on a carriage. The bridges are damaged each year by the heavy rains in the spring and summer. Consequently, they must be repaired in the autumn.

[51]Cf. *Mengzi* 7B37.

[52]To illustrate a case in which a great person's words do not have to be trustworthy, the Han dynasty commentator Zhao Qi refers to *Analects* 13.18 in which upright "sons cover up for their fathers." Compare also *Mengzi* 1A7, n. 1 and *Analects* 13.20.

[53]Cf. *Analects* 6.23.

gushes from the spring, not letting up day or night, only advancing after filling up the hollows, and going on to the four seas. Things that have a source are like this.[54] It was simply this that he found so worthy. If it merely fails to have a source, the rain collects during the spring months, and the drainage ditches are all full. However, you can just stand and wait and it will become dry. Hence, gentlemen are ashamed to have their reputation exceed what they genuinely are."

4B19 Mengzi said, "That by which humans differ from birds and beasts is slight. The people abandon it. The gentleman preserves it. The sage-king Shun was insightful about things. He was perceptive about human relationships. He acted out of benevolence and righteousness. He did not act out benevolence and righteousness."

4B24

. . . Mengzi said, "The people of the state of Zheng sent Zizhuo Ruzi to invade the state of Wei. Wei sent Si of Yugong to pursue him. Zizhuo Ruzi said, 'Today my illness is acting up. I am unable to hold my bow. I suppose I shall die.' He asked his chariot driver, 'Who is it that chases me?' His driver said, 'It is Si of Yugong.' He said, 'I shall live!' His driver said, 'Si of Yugong is the best archer of the state of Wei. What do you mean, Master, when you say, "I shall live"?' He said, 'Si of Yugong studied archery under Tuo of Yingong. Tuo of Yingong studied archery under me. Now, Tuo of Yingong is an upright person. Those whom he chooses for friends must be upright.' Si of Yugong arrived and said, 'Why do you not hold your bow, Master?' He said, 'Today my illness is acting up. I am unable to hold my bow.' He replied, 'I, petty person that I am, studied archery under Tuo of Yingong. Tuo of Yingong studied archery under you, Master. I cannot bear to take your Way and turn it against you, Master. Nonetheless, what I do today is my ruler's business. I dare not cast it aside.' He pulled out some arrows and hit them against the wheel of his chariot, breaking off their tips. He then shot off a set of four arrows and only then returned."

4B28 Mengzi said, "That by means of which gentlemen differ from others is that they preserve their hearts. Gentlemen preserve their hearts through benevolence and through propriety. The benevolent love others, and those

---

[54]On the notion of one's *ben* 本 ("source," or what is "fundamental"), see also *Mengzi* 3A5 and 6A10.

who have propriety respect others. Those who love others are generally loved by others. Those who respect others are generally respected by others.

"Here is a person who is harsh to me. A gentleman in this situation will invariably examine himself, saying, 'I must not be benevolent. I must be lacking in propriety. How else could this situation have come upon me?!' If he examines himself and *is* benevolent, and if he examines himself and *has* propriety, yet the other person is still harsh, a gentleman will invariably examine himself, saying, 'I must not be loyal.' If he examines himself and *is* loyal, yet the other person is still harsh, a gentleman says, 'This person is simply incorrigible! What difference is there between a person like this and an animal?! What point is there in rebuking an animal?'" . . .

4B29 Yu and Hou Ji were in a peaceful era, yet they were so busy governing that they passed the doors of their homes three times without entering. Kongzi deemed them worthy. Yan Hui was in a chaotic era, lived in a narrow alleyway, subsisting upon meager bits of rice and water—other people could not have borne such hardship, and yet it never spoiled Yan Hui's joy. Kongzi deemed him worthy.[55]

Mengzi said, "Yu, Hou Ji, and Yan Hui had the same Way. Yu thought that, if there were anyone in the world who drowned, it was as if he had drowned them himself. Hou Ji thought that, if there were anyone in the world who was starving, it was as if he had starved them himself. Hence, their urgency was like this. If Yu, Hou Ji, and Yan Hui had exchanged places, they all would have done as the others.

"Now, suppose there is someone from your household involved in an altercation outside. It is acceptable to go and help even though you are disheveled and not fully dressed. But if there is someone from your village involved in an altercation outside, it is foolish to go and help when you are disheveled and not fully dressed. Even bolting your door is acceptable in this case."

4B33 There was a man of the state of Qi who lived in a home with his wife and concubine. When the husband went out, he would always return full of wine and meat. His wife asked whom he ate with, and they were those of the highest wealth and rank. His wife told his concubine, "When our husband goes out, he always returns full of wine and meat. When I ask whom he ate

---

[55]Cf. *Analects* 6.11.

with, it is always those of the highest wealth and rank. Yet no one noteworthy ever comes here. I shall go and spy on where our husband goes."

Arising early, she discreetly followed where her husband went. Throughout the city, there was no one who stopped to chat with him. In the end, he approached those performing sacrifices among the graves beyond the East Wall of the city, and begged for their leftovers. If this was not enough, he would then look around and approach others. This was his way of getting his fill.

His wife returned home and told his concubine, saying, "A husband is someone whom we look toward till the ends of our lives. And he's like this!" And with the concubine she cursed her husband, and they cried together in the middle of the courtyard. But their husband did not know this, and came happily home, strutting before his wife and concubine.

From the perspective of a gentleman, it is rare indeed that the means by which people seek wealth, rank, profit, and success would not make their wives and concubines cry together in shame![56]

Book Five

5A2 Wan Zhang asked, "The *Odes* say,

> How should one proceed in taking a wife?
> One must inform one's parents.[57]

If this saying is trustworthy, it seems that no one would follow it more than the sage Shun. How is it that Shun took a wife without informing them?"

Mengzi said, "If he had informed them he would have been unable to take a wife. For a man and a woman to dwell together in one home is the greatest of human relations.[58] If he had informed them, he would be abandoning the greatest of human relations, which would have caused resentment toward his parents. Because of this he did not inform them."

Wang Zhang said, "I have now received your instruction regarding Shun's taking a wife without informing his parents. But how is it that the Emperor gave his daughter to Shun as a wife and did not inform them?"

---

[56]A sense of shame is probably related to the "sprout of disdain" (see *Mengzi* 7A7). Consequently, this passage suggests that women, too, have the sprouts or hearts of virtue (see *Mengzi* 2A6). On the ethical status of women, see also *Mengzi* 3B2.

[57]*Mao # 101.*

[58]On the "human relations," see also *Mengzi* 3A4 and 4B19.

Mengzi said, "The Emperor knew too that if he informed them he would not be able to give his daughter to him as a wife."

Wang Zhang said, "His parents made Shun repair the grain silo, and then they took the ladder away and his father set fire to the silo, but Shun escaped. Then they made him dig a well. He left the well, but, not knowing this, they covered up the well. His brother Xiang said, 'The credit for the plot to kill this ruler is all mine! His oxen and sheep, his granaries and silos shall be my parents', but his spear and shield, his lute, and his bow are mine! And I shall make my two sisters-in-law service me in bed!' So Xiang went into Shun's room, but Shun was on his bed playing his lute. Xiang, looking embarrassed, said, 'I was worried and thinking of you!' Shun said, 'The various ministers of mine—help me to direct them.' But surely Shun did not fail to understand that Xiang planned to murder him?"

Mengzi said, "How could he not understand? But when Xiang was anxious, he was also anxious; when Xiang was happy, he was also happy."

Wan Zhang asked, "In that case, did Shun feign happiness?"

Mengzi said, "No. Formerly, someone made a gift of a live fish to Zichan of the state of Zheng. Zichan had the pondkeeper take care of it in the pond. But the pondkeeper cooked it, and reported back to Zichan, 'When I first let it go, it seemed sickly, but in a little while it perked up, and went off happily.' Zichan said, 'It's where it should be! It's where it should be!' The pondkeeper left and said, 'Whoever said that Zichan was wise! I have already cooked and eaten it, and he says, "It's where it should be! It's where it should be!"' Hence, gentlemen can be tricked by what is in accordance with their practices, but it is hard to ensnare them with what is not the Way. Xiang came in accordance with the Way of one who loves his elder brother. Hence, Shun genuinely trusted him and was happy about him. How could he have feigned it?"

5A9 Wan Zhang asked, "Someone said that the sage Boli Xi sold himself to a herder in the state of Qin for five ramskins, and fed cattle, because he sought to meet Duke Mu of Qin. Is this story trustworthy?"

Mengzi said, "It is not. That is not the case. This was fabricated by those obsessed with taking office. Boli Xi was a person of the state of Yu.[59] The people of the state of Jin, in exchange for jade from Chui Ji and a team of horses

---

[59]A small state in which the ancestors of Shun were said to be enfeoffed. It was located in what is now the northeast part of Pinglu county in modern Shanxi province.

from Qu, gained right of passage through Yu to attack the state of Guo.[60] Qi of Gong remonstrated against this, but Boli Xi did not remonstrate against it. He knew that the Duke of Yu could not be remonstrated with, so he left and went to Qin. He was already seventy years old. If he did not yet know that it would be base to feed oxen in order to seek to meet Duke Mu of Qin, could he have been called wise? He knew that the Duke of Yu could not be remonstrated with so he did not remonstrate with him. Can this be called unwise? He knew that the Duke of Yu was about to perish, so he abandoned him first. This cannot be called unwise. When he was, in good time, raised to prominence in Qin, he knew that Duke Mu was someone with whom he could work, so he became his minister. Can this be called unwise? He was a minister in Qin and made his ruler distinguished throughout the world, so that he is an example for later ages. Is this something he would be capable of if he were not a worthy person? To sell oneself so as to accomplish things for one's lord—even a villager who cared for himself would not do this. Can one say that a worthy person would do it?"

Book Six

6A1 Gaozi said, "Human nature is like a willow tree; righteousness is like cups and bowls. To make human nature benevolent and righteous is like making a willow tree into cups and bowls."[61]

Mengzi said, "Can you, sir, following the nature of the willow tree, make it into cups and bowls? You must violate and rob the willow tree, and only then can you make it into cups and bowls. If you must violate and rob the willow tree in order to make it into cups and bowls, must you also violate and rob people in order to make them benevolent and righteous? If there is something that leads people to regard benevolence and righteousness as misfortunes for them, it will surely be your doctrine, will it not?"

6A2 Gaozi said, "Human nature is like swirling water. Make an opening for it on the eastern side, then it flows east. Make an opening for it on the western side, then it flows west. Human nature's not distinguishing be-

---

[60]A small state ruled by the descendants of King Wen's younger brother. It was located in what is now Pinglu county in modern Shanxi province.

[61]Gaozi was a rival philosopher (see also *Mengzi* 2A2). Compare his comment here (as well as his statement in 6A4 below that the desires for food and sex are nature) with Xunzi's comments in "An Exhortation to Learning" and "Human Nature Is Bad." See *Xunzi*, chapter 1, pp. 248–52 and chapter 23, pp. 284–91, respectively.

tween good and not good is like water's not distinguishing between eastern and western."

Mengzi said, "Water surely does not distinguish between east and west. But does it not distinguish between upward and downward? Human nature's being good is like water's tending downward. There is no human who does not tend toward goodness. There is no water that does not tend downward.

"Now, by striking water and making it leap up, you can cause it to go past your forehead. If you guide it by damming it, you can cause it to remain on a mountaintop. But is this the nature of water?! It is that way because of the circumstances. That humans can be caused to not be good is due to their natures also being like this."

6A3 Gaozi said, "Life is what is meant by 'nature.' "[62]

Mengzi said, "Is *life is what is meant by 'nature'* the same as *white is what is meant by 'white'* ?"[63]

Gaozi said, "It is."

Mengzi said, "Is the white of a white feather the same as the white of white snow, and is the white of white snow the same as the white of white jade?"

Gaozi said, "It is."

Mengzi said, "Then is the nature of a dog the same as the nature of an ox, and is the nature of an ox the same as the nature of a human?"

6A4 Gaozi said, "The desires for food and sex are nature. Benevolence is internal; it is not external. Righteousness is external; it is not internal."[64]

Mengzi said, "Why do you say that benevolence is internal and righteousness is external?"

Gaozi said, "They are elderly, and we treat them as elderly. It is not that they are elderly because of us. Similarly, that is white, and we treat it as white, according to its being white externally to us. Hence, I say it is external."

---

[62]The Song dynasty commentator Zhu Xi remarks, " 'Life' refers to that by means of which humans and animals perceive and move." The Han dynasty commentator Zhao Qi suggests that Gaozi's comment means that, "In general, things that are the same in being alive will all be the same in nature."

[63]In ancient Chinese dialectic, "white" was the stock example of a term that functions the same way regardless of the context of its occurence. See Graham (1989), pp. 150–55.

[64]Cf. Gongduzi's explanation in *Mengzi* 6A5 of what it means for a virtue to be "internal."

Mengzi said, "[Elderliness] is different from whiteness. The whiteness of a [white] horse is no different from the whiteness of a gray-haired person. But surely we do not regard the elderliness of an old horse as being no different from the elderliness of an old person?[65] Furthermore, do you say that the one who is elderly is righteous, or that the one who treats another as elderly is righteous?"

Gaozi said, "My younger brother I love; the younger brother of a person from Qin I do not love. In this case, it is I who feel happy [because of my love for my brother]. Hence, I say that it is internal. I treat as elderly an elderly person from Chu, and I also treat as elderly my own elderly. In this case, it is the elderly person who feels happy. Hence I say that it is external."[66]

Mengzi said, "Savoring the roast of a person from Qin is no different from savoring my roast. So what you describe is also the case with objects. Is savoring a roast, then, also external?"

6A5 Meng Jizi asked Gonduzi, "Why do you say that righteousness is internal?"[67]

Gongduzi said, "I act out of my respect, hence I say that it is internal."

Meng Jizi said, "If a fellow villager is older than your eldest brother by a year, then whom do you respect?"

Gongduzi said, "I respect my brother."

Meng Jizi said, "When you are pouring wine, then whom do you serve first?"

Gongduzi said, "I first pour wine for the fellow villager."[68]

Meng Jizi said, "The one whom you respect is the former, but the one whom you treat as elder is the latter. Hence, it really is external. It does not come from [how you feel] internally."

Gongduzi was not able to answer. He told Mengzi about it. Mengzi said, "Next time, ask him, 'Do you respect your uncle? or do you respect your younger brother?' He will say, 'I respect my uncle.' Then you say,

---

[65]Because an elderly person deserves to be treated with deference and respect, while an elderly horse is, in Mengzi or Gaozi's view, almost worthless.

[66]The Song Dynasty commentator Zhu Xi explains, "He means that the love is determined by me, hence benevolence is internal; respect is determined by elderliness, hence righteousness is external."

[67]Meng Jizi is a follower of Gaozi. Gongduzi is a follower of Mengzi.

[68]Because ritual dictates that the elder person be served first.

'When your younger brother is playing the part of the deceased in the sacrifice, then whom do you respect?' He will say, 'I respect my younger brother.' Then you say, 'What happened to the respect for your uncle?' He will say, 'The reason [why my respect changes] has to do with the role my younger brother occupies.' Then you also say, 'In the case you asked about in our previous discussion, the reason why my respect changes has to do with the role the fellow villager occupies. Ordinary respect is directed toward my brother, but temporary respect is directed toward the fellow villager.' "

Meng Jizi, upon hearing all this, said, "If you respect your uncle, then it is respect. If you respect your younger brother, then it is respect. So it really is external. It does not come from [how you feel] internally."

Gongduzi said, "On a winter day, one drinks broth. On a summer day, one drinks water. Are drinking and eating also, then, external?"

6A6 Gongduzi said, "Gaozi says, 'Human nature is neither good nor not good.' Some say, 'Human nature can become good, and it can become not good.' Therefore, when Wen and Wu arose, the people were fond of goodness. When You and Li arose, the people were fond of destructiveness. Some say, 'There are natures that are good, and there are natures that are not good.' Therefore, with Yao as ruler, there was Xiang. With the Blind Man as a father, there was Shun.[69] And with Zhou as their nephew, and as their ruler besides, there were Viscount Qi of Wei and Prince Bi Gan. Now, you say that human nature is good. Are all those others, then, wrong?"

Mengzi said, "As for their *qing* 情, "what they genuinely are," they can become good. This is what I mean by calling their natures good. As for their becoming not good, this is not the fault of their potential. Humans all have the heart of compassion. Humans all have the heart of disdain. Humans all have the heart of respect. Humans all have the heart of approval and disapproval. The heart of compassion is benevolence. The heart of disdain is righteousness. The heart of respect is propriety. The heart of approval and disapproval is wisdom. Benevolence, righteousness, propriety, and wisdom are not welded to us externally. We inherently have them. It is

---

[69]See *Mengzi* 5A2 for a story illustrative of the evil of Shun's brother Xiang and his father, the so-called "Blind Man."

simply that we do not concentrate upon them.[70] Hence, it is said, 'Seek it and you will get it. Abandon it and you will lose it.' Some differ from others by two, five, or countless times—this is because they cannot exhaust their potentials. The *Odes* say,

> Heaven gives birth to the teeming people.
> If there is a thing, there is a norm.
> This is the constant people cleave to.
> They are fond of this beautiful Virtue.[71]

Kongzi said, 'The one who composed this ode understood the Way!'[72] Hence, if there is a thing, there must be a norm. It is this that is the constant people cleave to. Hence, they are fond of this beautiful Virtue."

6A7 Mengzi said, "In years of plenty, most young men are gentle; in years of poverty, most young men are cruel. It is not that the potential that Heaven confers on them varies like this. They are like this because of that by which their hearts are sunk and drowned.

"Consider barley. Sow the seeds and cover them. The soil is the same and the time of planting is also the same. They grow rapidly, and by the time of the summer solstice they have all ripened. Although there are some differences, these are due to the richness of the soil, and to unevenness in the rain and in human effort. Hence, in general, things of the same kind are all similar. Why would one have any doubt about this when it comes to humans alone? We and the sage are of the same kind. Hence, Longzi said, 'When one makes a shoe for a foot one has not seen, we know that one will not make a basket.' The similarity of all the shoes in the world is due to the fact that the feet of the world are the same.

"Mouths have the same preferences in flavors. Yi Ya was the first to discover that which our mouths prefer. If it were the case that the natures of mouths regarding flavors varied among people—just as dogs and horses are different species from us—then why is it that throughout the world all preferences follow Yi Ya in flavors? The fact that, when it comes to flavors, the

---

[70]Mengzi also discusses these virtues in *Mengzi* 2A6 and 4A27. For more on *ren* 仁, "benevolence," see *Mengzi* 1A7. For more on *yi* 義, "righteousness," see *Mengzi* 6A10. For more on *zhi* 智, "wisdom," see *Mengzi* 5A9. For more on *si* 思, "concentration," see *Mengzi* 6A15. For all four terms, also consult the appropriate entries under *Important Terms*. On Mengzi's general view of self-cultivation, see *Mengzi* 7A17 and 7B31.

[71]*Mao # 260.*

[72]No quotation such as this is found in the received text of the *Analects*.

whole world looks to Yi Ya is due to the fact that mouths throughout the world are similar.

"Ears are like this too. When it comes to sounds, the whole world looks to Shi Kuang. This is due to the fact that ears throughout the word are similar. Eyes are like this too. When it comes to a handsome man like Zidu, no one in the world does not appreciate his beauty. Anyone who does not appreciate the beauty of Zidu has no eyes. Hence, I say that mouths have the same preferences in flavors, ears have the same preferences in sounds, eyes have the same preferences in attractiveness. When it comes to hearts, are they alone without preferences in common?

"What is it that hearts prefer in common? I say that it is fine patterns and righteousness. The sages first discovered what our hearts prefer in common. Hence, fine patterns and righteousness delight our hearts like meat delights our mouths."

6A8 Mengzi said, "The trees of Ox Mountain were once beautiful. But because it bordered on a large state, hatchets and axes besieged it. Could it remain verdant? Due to the rest it got during the day or night, and the moisture of rain and dew, it was not that there were no sprouts or shoots growing there. But oxen and sheep then came and grazed on them. Hence, it was as if it were barren. People, seeing it barren, believed that there had never been any timber there. Could this be the nature of the mountain?!

"When we consider what is present in people, could they truly lack the hearts of benevolence and righteousness?![73] That by which they discard their good heart is simply like the hatchets and axes in relation to the trees.[74] With them besieging it day by day, can it remain beautiful? With the rest it gets during the day or night, and the restorative effects of the morning qi 氣, their likes and dislikes are sometimes close to those of others. But then what they do during the day again fetters and destroys it. If the fettering is repeated, then the evening qi is insufficient to preserve it. If the evening qi is insufficient to preserve it, then one is not far from a bird or beast. Others see that he is a bird or beast, and think that there was never any capacity there. Is this what a human truly is?!

"Hence, if it merely gets nourishment, there is nothing that will not grow. If it merely loses its nourishment, there is nothing that will not van-

---

[73]On "the hearts of benevolence and righteousness," compare *Mengzi* 2A6 and 6A6.

[74]The phrase *liang xin* 良心, "good heart," is reminiscent of the *liang zhi* 良知, "best knowledge," and *liang neng* 良能, "best capability," mentioned in *Mengzi* 7A15.

ish. Kongzi said, 'Grasped then preserved; abandoned then lost. Its goings and comings have no fixed time. No one knows its home.'[75] Was it not the heart of which he spoke?"

6A10 Mengzi said, "Fish is something I desire; bear's paw[76] is also something I desire. If I cannot have both, I will forsake fish and select bear's paw. Life is something I desire; righteousness is also something I desire. If I cannot have both, I will forsake life and select righteousness. Life is something I desire, but there is something I desire more than life. Hence, I will not do just anything to obtain it. Death is something I hate, but there is something I hate more than death. Hence, there are calamities I do not avoid. If it were the case that someone desired nothing more than life, then what means that could obtain life would that person not use? If it were the case that someone hated nothing more than death, then what would that person not do that would avoid calamity? From this we can see that there are means of obtaining life that one will not employ. From this we can also see that there are things that would avoid calamity that one will not do. Therefore, there are things one desires more than life and there are also things one hates more than death. It is not the case that only the worthy person has this heart. All humans have it. The worthy person simply never loses it.[77]

"A basket of food and a bowl of soup—if one gets them then one will live; if one doesn't get them then one will die. But if they're given with contempt, then even a homeless person will not accept them. If they're trampled upon, then even a beggar won't take them. However, when it comes to a salary of ten thousand bushels of grain, then one doesn't notice propriety and righteousness and accepts them. What do ten thousand bushels add to me? Do I accept them for the sake of a beautiful mansion? for the obedience of a wife and concubines? to have poor acquaintances be indebted to me? In the previous case, for the sake of one's own life one did not accept what was offered. In the current case, for the sake of a beautiful mansion one does it. In the previous case, for the sake of one's own life one did not accept what was offered. In the current case, for the obedience of a wife and concubine one does it. In the previous case, for the sake of one's own life one did not accept what was offered. In the current case, in order to have poor acquaintances be indebted to oneself one does it. Is this in-

---

[75]No quotation like this is found in the received text of the *Analects*.

[76]A culinary delicacy.

[77]Cf. Xunzi's "On Correct Naming." See *Xunzi*, chapter 22, pp. 278–84.

deed something that one can't stop doing? This is what is called losing one's fundamental heart."[78]

6A12 Mengzi said, "Suppose someone has a ring finger that is bent and will not straighten, and it is not the case that it hurts or that it interferes with one's activities. But if there is something that can straighten it, one will not consider the road from one end of the world to the other too far, because one's finger is not as good as other people's. If one's finger is not as good as other people's, one knows to dislike it. But if one's heart is not as good as other people's, one does not know to dislike it. This is what is called not appreciating the categories of importance."

6A15 Gongduzi asked, "We are the same in being humans. Yet some become great humans and some become petty humans. Why?"

Mengzi said, "Those who follow their greater part become great humans. Those who follow their petty part become petty humans."

Gonduzi said, "We are the same in being humans. Why is it that some follow their greater part and some follow their petty part?"

Mengzi said, "It is not the office of the ears and eyes to concentrate, and they are misled by things. Things interact with things and simply lead them along. But the office of the heart is to concentrate. If it concentrates then it will get [Virtue]. If it does not concentrate, then it will not get it.[79] This is what Heaven has given us. If one first takes one's stand on what is greater, then what is lesser will not be able to snatch it away. This is how to become a great human."

The xin ("heart") is the natural ruler of the self, the highest part of the self. It controls/tempers the animalistic qi ("vital energy") within humans. One should accept this hierarchy as a religious worldview. Rejecting it would be immoral and inauspicious.

Book Seven

7A1 Mengzi said, "To fully apply one's heart is to understand one's nature.[80] If one understands one's nature, then one understands Heaven. To preserve one's mind and nourish one's nature is the means to serve Heaven. To not become conflicted over the length of one's life, and to cultivate oneself to await it is the means to stand and await one's fate."

---

[78]"Fundamental" is literally *ben* 本, "root." Cf. *Mengzi* 3A5.

[79]On *si* 思, "concentration," see also *Mengzi* 6A6 and *Important Terms*.

[80]This should be read in the light of *Mengzi* 6A6.

7A3 Mengzi said, " 'If one seeks, one will get it; if one abandons it, one will lose it.'[81] In this case, seeking helps in getting, because the seeking is in oneself. 'There is a way to seek it, and getting it depends on fate.' In this case, seeking does not help in getting, because the seeking is external."[82]

7A4 Mengzi said, "The ten thousand things are all brought to completion by us. To turn toward oneself and discover integrity—there is no greater delight than this. To firmly act out of sympathetic understanding[83]—there is nothing closer to benevolence than this."

7A7 Mengzi said, "A sense of shame is indeed important for people! Those who are crafty in their contrivances and schemes have no use for shame. If one is not ashamed of not being as good as others, how will one ever be as good as others?"[84]

7A15 Mengzi said, "That which people are capable of without studying is their best capability. That which they know without pondering is their best knowledge.

"Among babes in arms there is none that does not know to love its parents. When they grow older, there is none that does not know to respect its elder brother. Treating one's parents as parents[85] is benevolence. Respecting one's elders is righteousness. There is nothing else to do but extend these to the world."[86]

7A17 Mengzi said, "Do not do that which you would not do; do not desire that which you would not desire. Simply be like this."[87]

---

[81]Cf. *Mengzi* 6A6.

[82]The Song dynasty commentator Zhu Xi says, " 'In oneself' means that benevolence, righteousness, propriety, and wisdom are all things that my nature has. . . . 'Is external' means that riches, honor, profit, and success are all external things."

[83]See *Analects* 15.24 on "sympathetic understanding."

[84]The Song dynasty commentator Zhu Xi says, "A sense of shame is the heart of disdain that we have inherently" (cf. *Mengzi* 6A6 and 2A6).

[85]That is, as parents should be treated (including having the proper feelings toward them).

[86]Cf. *Mengzi* 7A17 and 7B31.

[87]This passage should be read in the light of *Mengzi* 7B31.

7A26 Mengzi said, "Yangzi chose egoism. If plucking out one hair from his body would have benefitted the whole world, he would not do it. Mozi loved universally. If scraping himself bare from head to heels would benefit the whole world, he would do it. Zimo held to the middle.[88] Holding to the middle is close to it. But if one holds to the middle without discretion,[89] that is the same as holding to one extreme. What I dislike about those who hold to one extreme is that they detract from the Way. They elevate one thing and leave aside a hundred others."

7A27 Mengzi said, "Those who are starving find their food delicious; those who are parched find their drink delicious. They have no standard for food and drink because their hunger and thirst injure it. Is it only the mouth and belly that hunger and thirst injure?! Human hearts too are subject to injury. If one can prevent the injury of hunger and thirst from being an injury to one's heart, then there will be no concern about not being as good as other people."

7A35 Tao Ying asked, "When Shun was Son of Heaven, and Gao Yao was his Minister of Crime, if 'the Blind Man' had murdered someone, what would they have done?"[90]

Mengzi said, "Gao Yao would simply have arrested him!"

Tao Ying asked, "So Shun would not have forbidden it?"

Mengzi said, "How could Shun have forbidden it? Gao Yao had a sanction for his actions."

Tao Ying asked, "So what would Shun have done?"

Mengzi said, "Shun looked at casting aside the whole world like casting aside a worn sandal. He would have secretly carried him on his back and fled, to live in the coastland, happy to the end of his days, joyfully forgetting the world."

7A39 King Xuan of Qi wanted to shorten the period of mourning. Gongsun Chou said, "Isn't mourning for a year better than stopping completely?"

---

[88]On Mozi, see *Mengzi* 3A5 and 3B9, as well as chapter 2 of this volume. On Yangzi (Yang Zhu), see *Mengzi* 3B9. We know nothing about Zimo beyond what this passage tells us.

[89]On "discretion," see *Mengzi* 4A17 and the note to that passage.

[90]Tao Ying is a follower of Mengzi. On Shun's father, the "Blind Man," see *Mengzi* 5A2.

Mengzi said, "This is like if someone were twisting his elder brother's arm, and you simply said to him, 'How about doing it more gently?' Simply instruct him in filial piety and brotherly respect."

One of the imperial sons had a mother who died. His tutor asked on his behalf to let him mourn for a few months.[91] Gongsun Chou said, "How about this case?"

Mengzi said, "In this case, he desires to mourn the full period but he cannot. Even doing it one extra day would be better than stopping completely. What I had been talking about before was a case in which he did not do it, even though nothing prevented it."

7A45 Mengzi said, "Gentlemen, in relation to animals, are sparing of them, but are not benevolent toward them. In relation to the people, they are benevolent toward them, but do not treat them as kin. They treat their kin as kin, and then are benevolent toward the people. They are benevolent toward the people, and then are sparing of animals."[92]

7B3 Mengzi said, "It would be better to not have the *History* than to completely believe it. I accept only two or three passages in the 'Completion of the War' chapter. A benevolent person has no enemies in the world. When the one who was supremely benevolent [King Wu] attacked the one who was supremely unbenevolent [Tyrant Zhou], how could the blood have flowed till it floated the grain-pounding sticks?"[93]

7B5 Mengzi said, "A carpenter or a wheelwright can give another his compass or T-square, but he cannot make another skillful."

7B11 Mengzi said, "If one is fond of making a name for oneself, one may be able to relinquish a state that can field a thousand chariots. But if one is just not that kind of person, relinquishing a basket of rice or a bowl of soup would show in one's face."

---

[91]Chinese commentators explain that the son's mother was a secondary wife of the king, and the king's primary wife opposed letting him mourn for the full three-year period. On the three-year mourning period, see *Analects* 17.21.

[92]Cf. *Mengzi* 3A5 and 1A7.

[93]See Legge, *The Shoo King*, p. 315.

7B16 Mengzi said, "Benevolence is being a human. To bring them into harmony and put it into words is the Way."[94]

7B24 Mengzi said, "The mouth in relation to flavors, the eyes in relation to sights, the ears in relation to tones, the nose in relation to odors, the four limbs in relation to comfort—these are matters of human nature, but they are mandated.[95] A gentleman does not refer to them as 'human nature.' Benevolence in relation to father and son, righteousness in relation to ruler and minister, propriety in relation to guest and host, wisdom in relation to value, the sage in relation to the Way of Heaven—these are mandated, but they involve human nature. A gentleman does not refer to them as 'mandated.' "

7B31 Mengzi said, "People all have things that they will not bear. To extend this reaction to that which they will bear is benevolence. People all have things that they will not do. To extend this reaction to that which they will do is righteousness. If people can fill out the heart that does not desire to harm others, their benevolence will be inexhaustible. If people can fill out the heart that will not trespass, their righteousness will be inexhaustible. If people can fill out the core reaction[96] of not accepting being addressed disrespectfully, there will be nowhere they go where they do not do what is righteous. If a scholar may not speak and speaks, this is flattering by speaking. If one should speak but does not speak, this is flattering by not speaking. These are both in the category of trespassing."

7B37 Wan Zhang asked, "When in the state of Chen, Kongzi said, 'Perhaps I should return home. The scholars of my school are wild and hasty, advancing and grasping, but do not forget their early behavior.'[97] When in Chen, why did Kongzi think of the wild scholars of his home state of Lu?"

Mengzi said, "Kongzi said, 'If I do not get to associate with those who attain the Way, then must it not be those who are wild or squeamish? Those who are wild advance and grasp. Those who are squeamish have some things that they will not do.'[98] Did Kongzi not want those who attained the

---

[94]Alternative translation: "To bring them into harmony is called the Way."

[95]That is, they are mandated (or required) by Heaven.

[96]Compare *Mengzi* 4A27 on the notion of a "core" reaction.

[97]Compare *Analects* 5.22.

[98]Compare *Analects* 13.21.

Way?! He could not be sure of getting them. Hence, he thought of the next best."

Wan Zhang said, "I venture to ask what one must be like, such that one can be called 'wild.'"

Mengzi said, "Those like Qin Zhang, Zeng Xi, and Mu Pi are the ones Kongzi called 'wild.'"[99]

Wan Zhang said, "Why did he call them 'wild'?"

Mengzi said, "Their resolutions were grand. They said, 'The ancients! The ancients!' But if one calmly examines their conduct, it does not match their resolutions and words. If he also failed to get those who are wild, he desired to get to associate with those who disdain to do what is not pure. These are the squeamish. They are the next best.

"Kongzi said, 'The only ones who pass by my door without entering my home whom I do not regret getting as associates are the village worthies. The village worthies are the thieves of virtue.'"[100]

Wan Zhang said, "What must one be like, such that one can be called a 'village worthy'?"

Mengzi said, "The village worthies are those who say,

> Why are [the resolutions of the wild scholars] so grand? Their words take no notice of their actions, and their actions take no notice of their words. Then they say, "The ancients! The ancients!" And why are the actions [of the squeamish] so solitary and aloof? Born in this era, we should be for this era. To be good is enough.

Eunuch-like, pandering to their eras—these are the village worthies."

Wan Zhang said, "If the whole village declares them worthy people, there is nowhere they will go where they will not be worthy people. Why did Kongzi regard them as thieves of virtue?"

Mengzi said, "If you try to condemn them, there is nothing you can point to; if you try to censure them, there is nothing to censure. They are in agreement with the current customs; they are in harmony with the sordid era in which they live. That in which they dwell seems to be loyalty and trustworthiness; that which they do seems to be blameless and pure. The

---

[99]Unfortunately, we know almost nothing about these three individuals. However, there is an interesting and revealing anecdote involving Zeng Xi in *Analects* 11.26.

[100]Cf. *Analects* 17.13.

multitude delight in them; they regard themselves as right. But you cannot enter into the Way of Yao and Shun with them. Hence, Kongzi said they are 'thieves of virtue.'

"Kongzi said, 'I hate that which seems but is not. I hate weeds out of fear that they will be confused with grain.[101] I hate cleverness out of fear that it will be confused with righteousness. I hate glibness out of fear that it will be confused with trustworthiness. I hate the tunes of the state of Zheng out of fear that they will be confused with genuine music. I hate purple out of fear that it will be confused with vermillion.[102] I hate the village worthies, out of fear that they will be confused with those who have Virtue.'

"The gentleman simply returns to the standard. If the standard is correct, then the multitudinous people will be inspired. When the people are inspired, then there will be no evil or wickedness."

---

[101] Note that "grain" is also used in *Mengzi* 2A2 as a metaphor for one's incipient, natural virtues. Compare also the use of "sprouts" in *Mengzi* 2A6.

[102] Cf. *Analects* 17.18 and 15.11.

SELECTIVE BIBLIOGRAPHY

Translations

Lau, D. C., tr.

1970   *Mencius.* New York: Penguin Books. (This is still the best complete English translation, and includes several helpful appendices. Lau published a revised, two-volume translation in Hong Kong in 1984 but it is not widely available in the United States.)

Legge, James, tr.

1970   *The Works of Mencius.* New York: Dover Books. (This is a reprint of Legge's revised 1895 translation, which includes the Chinese text and extensive notes. It is still one of the best, although Legge's English is sometimes dated.)

Secondary Works

Graham, Angus C.

1990   "The Background of the Mencian Theory of Human Nature," in his *Studies in Chinese Philosophy and Philosophical Literature*, pp. 7–66. Albany, NY: SUNY Press. (Originally published in 1967. This is an excellent overview of the context for Mengzi's use of *xing* 性, "nature.")

Ihara, Craig.

1991   "David Wong on Emotions in Mencius," *Philosophy East and West* 41.1 (January): 45–54. (A critique of Wong [1991], cited below.)

Ivanhoe, Philip J.

1990   *Ethics in the Confucian Tradition: The Thought of Mencius and Wang Yang-ming.* Atlanta, GA: Scholars Press. (A good examination of Mengzi and how he differs from one of his Neo-Confucian interpreters.)

Lau, D. C.

1970   "On Mencius' Use of the Method of Analogy in Argument." Appendix 5 in Lau, tr., *Mencius* (cited above). (On *Mengzi* 6A1 ff.)

Nivison, David S.

1996   *The Ways of Confucianism*. Chicago, IL: Open Court Press. (Essays on a variety of passages and topics relating to Mengzi.)

Shun, Kwong-loi.

1997   *Mencius and Early Chinese Thought*. Stanford, CA: Stanford University Press. (Provides a survey of the secondary literature on many passages and problems in the *Mengzi*.)

Van Norden, Bryan W.

1997   "Mengzi on Courage," in Peter A. French, Theodore E. Uehling, and Howard K. Wettstein, eds., *Midwest Studies in Philosophy*, vol. XXI, pp. 237–56. Notre Dame, IN: University of Notre Dame Press. (On the virtue of courage in the *Mengzi*, particularly as dealt with in passage 2A2.)

2000   "Mengzi and Xunzi: Two Views of Human Agency." in T. C. Kline, III, and Philip J. Ivanhoe, eds., pp. 103–134. Indianapolis, IN: Hackett Publishing. (Discussion of the role of desires and other motivations in Mengzi and some other early philosophers.)

Wong, David.

1991   "Is There a Distinction between Reason and Emotion in Mencius?" *Philosophy East and West* 41.1 (January): 31–44. (Discusses some of the issues raised by *Mengzi* 1A7. See also Ihara [1991], cited above.)

Yearley, Lee H.

1990   *Mencius and Aquinas: Theories of Virtue and Conceptions of Courage*. Albany, NY: SUNY Press. (A comparative study with many insights into Mengzi's conception of the virtues.)

▪ CHAPTER FOUR ▪

LAOZI

("The Daodejing")

Introduction

Traditionally, Laozi 老子 is said to have been an older contemporary of Confucius and the author of the *Laozi* or *Daodejing* 道德經. But most contemporary scholars regard Laozi (literally "Old Master") as a mythical character and the *Laozi* to be composite work. The present version of the text consists of short passages, from a variety of sources, over half of which are rhymed. These were collected together into a single volume of eighty-one chapters that were then divided into two books. Book I consists of chapters one through thirty-seven, the *dao* 道, "Way," half of the text; Book II consists of chapters thirty-eight through eighty-one, the *de* 德, "Virtue," half. On the basis of this organization, this version of the text came to be known as the *Daodejing*, which means simply "The Classic of *Dao* and *De*." This division in no way reflects the contents of the chapters themselves, except that the first chapter begins with the word *dao* and the thirty-eighth chapter begins by describing the highest *de*. The text may have reached its present form sometime during the third or perhaps second century B.C.E. Another version of the text, named after its place of discovery, *Mawangdui* 馬王堆, is similar in content and firmly dated to the middle of the second century B.C.E. But in the *Mawangdui* version, the order of the Books is reversed, giving us the *Dedaojing*.

Though it was probably cobbled together from different sources, the *Laozi* may well have been assembled during a relatively short period of time and perhaps by a single editor. When it was put together, China was near the end of a prolonged era of fierce interstate rivalry known as the Warring States Period (see *Important Periods*). The text can be understood, at least in part, as a reaction to this troubled age. In it we hear the lament of a time tired of war and chaos, one yearning for a bygone age of innocence, security, and peace. The text denounces wars of expansion and government corruption, and traces both complaints to the unbounded greed and ambition of those in power. These ideas are connected to the view that excessive desire per se is bad and the related belief that our "real" or "natural" desires are actually quite modest and limited. The text claims that it is unnatural to have excessive desires and having them will not only not lead to a satisfying life but paradoxically to destitution, want, alienation, and self-destruction.

The *Laozi* appeals to an earlier golden age in human history, before people made sharp distinctions among things. This was a time when values and qualities were not clearly distinguished, when things simply were as they were and people acted out of pre-reflective spontaneity. Chapter thirty-eight describes the history of the decline of the Way from an earlier golden age to its present debased state. The *dao* declined as civilization and human self-consciousness arose. The *Laozi* urges us to return to the earlier, natural state when the Way was fully realized in the world. We are to "untangle," "blunt" and "round off" the sharp corners of our present life and let our "wheels move only along old (and presumably more comfortable) ruts."

According to the *Laozi*, the *dao* is the source, sustenance, and ideal state of all things in the world. It is "hidden" and it contains within it the patterns of all that we see, but it is not ontologically transcendent. In the apt metaphor of the text, it is the "root" of all things. The *dao* is *ziran* 自然, "so of itself" or "spontaneous," and its unencumbered activity brings about various natural states of affairs through *wuwei* 無為, "nonaction" (see *Important Terms*). Human beings have a place in the *dao* but are not particularly exalted. They are simply things among things (a view well represented by the marvelous landscape paintings inspired by Daoism).[1] Because of their unbridled desires and their unique capacity to think, act intentionally, and alter their nature–thus acting contrary to *wuwei* and bringing about states that are not *ziran*–humans tend to forsake their proper place and upset the natural harmony of the Way. The *Laozi* seeks to undo the consequences of such misguided human views and practices and lead us to "return" to the earlier ideal. The text is more a form of philosophical therapy than the presentation of a theory. We are to be challenged by its paradoxes and moved by its images and poetic cadence more than by any arguments it presents.

---

[1]For an example, see the web site for this volume.

Book One

Chapter One

A Way that can be followed is not a constant Way.[2]
A name that can be named is not a constant name.
Nameless, it is the beginning of Heaven and earth;[3]
Named, it is the mother of the myriad creatures.
And so,
> Always eliminate desires in order to observe its mysteries;
> Always have desires in order to observe its manifestations.

These two come forth in unity but diverge in name.
Their unity is known as an enigma.[4]
Within this enigma is yet a deeper enigma.
The gate of all mysteries!

Chapter Two

Everyone in the world knows that when the beautiful strives to be
> beautiful, it is repulsive.

Everyone knows that when the good strives to be good, it is no good.[5]
And so,
> To have and to lack generate each other.[6]
> Difficult and easy give form to each other.
> Long and short off-set each other.
> High and low incline into each other.
> Note and rhythm harmonize with each other.
> Before and after follow each other.

---

[2]Unlike the case of the following line, which has a similar basic structure, there is no way to reproduce in English the alternating nominal and verbal uses of the word *dao* 道, "Way." More literally, the first line reads, *dao* 道 [a] "Way," "path," or "teaching," *kedao* 可道 [which] "can be talked about" or "followed," *fei changdao* 非常道, "is not a constant Way." Cf. the grammar and sense of the poem "The Thorny Bush Upon the Wall" in the *Odes* (*Mao # 46*). For other passages that discuss the Way and names, see chapters 32, 34.

[3]On the idea of being "nameless" see chapters 32, 37, and 41.

[4]Cf. the reference to *xuantong* 玄同, "Enigmatic Unity," in chapter 56.

[5]The point is the common theme that self-conscious effort to be excellent in any way fatally undermines itself. Cf. for example, chapters 38, 81.

[6]Cf. chapter 40.

This is why sages abide in the business of nonaction,[7]
and practice the teaching that is without words.[8]
They work with the myriad creatures and turn none away.[9]
They produce without possessing.[10]
They act with no expectation of reward.[11]
When their work is done, they do not linger.[12]
And, by not lingering, merit never deserts them.

Chapter Three

Not paying honor to the worthy leads the people to avoid contention.
Not showing reverence for precious goods[13] leads them to not steal.
Not making a display of what is desirable leads their hearts away from
chaos.[14]
This is why sages bring things to order by opening people's hearts [15] and
filling their bellies.
They weaken the people's commitments and strengthen their bones;
They make sure that the people are without zhi, "knowledge,"[16] or
desires;
And that those with knowledge do not dare to act.
Sages enact nonaction and everything becomes well ordered.

---

[7]For wuwei 無為, "nonaction," see *Important Terms*. The seminal study of this idea, which explores the notion across different schools of early Chinese philosophy, is Edward G. Slingerland's Ph.D. dissertation, *Effortless Action: Wuwei as a Spiritual Ideal in Early China*, (Stanford University, 1998).

[8]Cf. a similar line in chapter 43.

[9]Cf. chapter 34.

[10]This line also occurs in chapters 10 and 51.

[11]This line also appears in chapters, 10, 51, and 77.

[12]Recognizing that the credit for their success lies with the Way and not with themselves is a characteristic attitude of Daoist sages. For similar ideas, see chapters 9, 17, 34, and 77. This and the previous line occur together in chapter 77.

[13]For other passages discussing "precious goods," see chapters 12 and 64.

[14]Cf. *Analects* 12.18.

[15]See xin 心, "heart," under *Important Terms*.

[16]See zhi 智, "wisdom," under *Important Terms*.

Chapter Four

The Way is like an empty vessel;
No use could ever fill it up.
Vast and deep!
It seems to be the ancestor of the myriad creatures.
It blunts their sharpness;[17]
Untangles their tangles;
Softens their glare;
Merges with their dust.
Deep and clear!
It seems to be there.
I do not know whose child it is;
It is the image of what was before the Lord himself![18]

Chapter Five

Heaven and earth are not benevolent;
They treat the myriad creatures as straw dogs.[19]
Sages are not benevolent;
They treat the people as straw dogs.
Is not the space between Heaven and earth like a bellows?
Empty yet inexhaustible!
Work it and more will come forth.
An excess of speech will lead to exhaustion,[20]
It is better to hold on to the mean.

---

[17]The following four lines, preceeded by two lines from chapter 52, appear in chapter 56.

[18]This is the only occurence in the text of the character *di* 帝, "Lord," a name for the high god or supreme ancestral spirit of ancient China. For other passages concerning *xiang* 象, "image," see chapters 14, 21, 35, and 41.

[19]"Straw dogs" were used as ceremonial offerings. Before and during the ceremony, they were protected and cherished, but as soon as the ceremony ended, they were discarded and defiled. Others interpret the characters in this expression as "straw and dogs." The point is the same.

[20]Cf. the opening lines of chapter 23.

Chapter Six

The spirit of the valley never dies;
She is called the "Enigmatic Female."
The portal of the Enigmatic Female;
Is called the root of Heaven and earth.
An unbroken, gossamer thread;
It seems to be there.
But use will not unsettle it.

Chapter Seven

Heaven is long lasting;
Earth endures.
Heaven is able to be long lasting and earth is able to endure, because they
   do not live for themselves.
And so, they are able to be long lasting and to endure.
This is why sages put themselves last and yet come first;
Treat themselves as unimportant and yet are preserved.
Is it not because they have no thought of themselves, that they are able to
   perfect themselves?

Chapter Eight

The highest good is like water.
Water is good at benefiting the myriad creatures, while not contending
   with them.
It resides in the places that people find repellent, and so comes close to
   the Way.
   In a residence, the good lies in location.
   In hearts, the good lies in depth.
   In interactions with others, the good lies in benevolence.
   In words, the good lies in trustworthiness.
   In government, the good lies in orderliness.
   In carrying out one's business, the good lies in ability.
   In actions, the good lies in timeliness.
Only by avoiding contention can one avoid blame.

Chapter Nine

To hold the vessel upright in order to fill it[21] is not as good as to stop in
   time.
If you make your blade too keen it will not hold its edge.
When gold and jade fill the hall none can hold on to them.
To be haughty when wealth and honor come your way is to bring disaster
   upon yourself.
To withdraw when the work is done is the Way of Heaven.[22]

Chapter Ten

Embracing your soul and holding on to the One, can you keep them
   from departing?[23]
Concentrating your *qi* 氣 "vital energies"[24] and attaining the utmost
   suppleness, can you be a child?
Cleaning and purifying your enigmatic mirror, can you erase every flaw?
Caring for the people and ordering the state, can you eliminate all
   knowledge?
When the portal of Heaven opens and closes, can you play the part of the
   feminine?
Comprehending all within the four directions, can you reside in nonaction?
To produce them!
To nurture them!
To produce without possessing;[25]
To act with no expectation of reward;[26]
To lead without lording over;
Such is Enigmatic Virtue![27]

---

[21]The reference is to a "tilting vessel" that would fall over and pour out its contents if
filled to the top.

[22]For similar lines, see chapters 2, 17, 34, and 77.

[23]For other examples of "the One," see chapters 22, 39, and 42.

[24]See *qi* under *Important Terms*.

[25]This line also appears in chapters 2 and 51.

[26]This line also appears in chapters 2, 51, and 77.

[27]Chapter 51 concludes with the same four lines. For another passage concerning *xuande*
玄德, "Enigmatic Virtue," see chapter 65.

Chapter Eleven

Thirty spokes are joined in the hub of a wheel.
But only by relying on what is not there,[28] do we have the use of the
    carriage.
By adding and removing clay we form a vessel.
But only by relying on what is not there, do we have use of the vessel.
By carving out doors and windows we make a room.
But only by relying on what is not there, do we have use of the room.
And so, what is there is the basis for profit;
What is not there is the basis for use.

Chapter Twelve

The five colors blind our eyes.[29]
The five notes deafen our ears.
The five flavors deaden our palates.
The chase and the hunt madden our hearts.
Precious goods impede our activities.
This is why sages are for the belly and not for the eye;
And so they cast off the one and take up the other.[30]

Chapter Thirteen

Be apprehensive about favor or disgrace.
Revere calamity as you revere your own body.
What does it mean to be apprehensive about favor and disgrace?
To receive favor is to be in the position of a subordinate.
When you get it be apprehensive;
When you lose it be apprehensive.

---

[28]Literally, only by relying on "nothing" (i.e., the empty space of the hub) can the wheel
turn and the carriage roll.

[29]These sets of five refer to conventional standards of evaluation in regard to the different sensory faculties. The passage is not a rejection of the pleasures of the senses nor does it
express skepticism regarding the senses per se. Rather, like the view one finds in *Zhuangzi*,
chapter 2 (see pp. 209–19), it expresses a profound distrust of covential categories and
values and advocates moderation of sensual pleasures.

[30]This line also appears in chapters 38 and 72.

This is what it means to be apprehensive about favor and disgrace.
What does it mean to revere calamity as you revere your own body?
I can suffer calamity only because I have a body.
When I no longer have a body, what calamity could I possibly have?
And so,
> Those who revere their bodies as if they were the entire world
> can be given custody of the world.
> Those who care for their bodies as if they were the entire world
> can be entrusted with the world.

Chapter Fourteen

Looked for but not seen, its name is "minute."
Listened for but not heard, its name is "rarified."
Grabbed for but not gotten, its name is "subtle."[31]
These three cannot be perfectly explained, and so are confused and
  regarded as one.
Its top is not clear or bright,
Its bottom is not obscure or dark.
Trailing off without end, it cannot be named.
It returns to its home, back before there were things.[32]
This is called the formless form, the image of no thing.[33]
This is called the confused and indistinct.
Greet it and you will not see its head;
Follow it and you will not see its tail.
Hold fast to the Way of old, in order to control what is here today.
The ability to know the ancient beginnings, this is called the thread of
  the Way.

Chapter Fifteen

In ancients times, the best and most accomplished scholars;
Were subtle, mysterious, enigmatic, and far-reaching.
Their profundity was beyond understanding.

---

[31]Cf. the thought expressed in these lines to what one finds in chapter 35.

[32]Returning to an ideal past state is a common theme in the text. For other examples see chapters 16, 25, 28, 30, and 52.

[33]For other passages that concern *xiang*, "image," see chapters 4, 21, 35, and 41.

Because they were beyond understanding, only with difficulty can we try
  to describe them:
  Poised, like one who must ford a stream in winter.
  Cautious, like one who fears his neighbors on every side.
  Reserved, like a visitor.
  Opening up, like ice about to break.
  Honest, like unhewn wood.[34]
  Broad, like a valley.
  Turbid, like muddy water.
Who can, through stillness, gradually make muddied water clear?
Who can, through movement, gradually stir to life what has long been still?
Those who preserve this Way do not desire fullness.
And, because they are not full, they have no need for renewal.

Chapter Sixteen

Attain extreme tenuousness;
Preserve quiet integrity.
The myriad creatures are all in motion!
I watch as they turn back.
The teeming multitude of things, each returns home to its root;
And returning to one's root is called stillness.
This is known as returning to one's destiny;
And returning to one's destiny is known as constancy.
To know constancy is called "enlightenment."
Those who do not know constancy wantonly produce misfortune.
To know constancy is to be accommodating.
To be accommodating is to work for the good of all.
To work for the good of all is to be a true king.
To be a true king is to be Heavenly.
To be Heavenly is to embody the Way.
To embody the Way is to be long lived,
And one will avoid danger to the end of one's days.[35]

---

[34]*Pu* 朴, "unhewn wood," is a symbol for anything in its unadulterated natural state. In other contexts I will translate it as "simplicity," but here and in certain later passages the metaphor is an important part of the passage's sense. For other examples, see chapters 19, 28, 32, 37, and 57.

[35]This line also appears in chapter 52.

Chapter Seventeen

The greatest of rulers is but a shadowy presence;
Next is the ruler who is loved and praised;
Next is the one who is feared;
Next is the one who is reviled.
Those lacking in trust are not trusted.[36]
But [the greatest rulers] are cautious and honor words.[37]
When their task is done and work complete,[38]
Their people all say, "This is just how we are."[39]

Chapter Eighteen

When the great Way is abandoned, there are benevolence and righteousness.
When wisdom and intelligence come forth, there is great hypocrisy.
When the six familial relationships are out of balance, there are kind parents and filial children.
When the state is in turmoil and chaos, there are loyal ministers.[40]

Chapter Nineteen

Cut off sageliness, abandon wisdom, and the people will benefit one-hundred-fold.
Cut off benevolence, abandon righteousness, and the people will return to being filial and kind.
Cut off cleverness, abandon profit, and robbers and thieves will be no more.
This might leave the people lacking in culture;

---

[36]This line appears again in chapter 23. I interpret it as an expression of the *Daodejing's* characteristic view on *de* 德, "Virtue." For a discussion of the idea of "Virtue" in the *Daodejing* and how it differs from related Confucian conceptions of "Virtue" or "moral charisma" see my "The Concept of *de* ('Virtue') in the *Laozi*," in Csikszentmihalyi and Ivanhoe (1998), pp. 239–57. For other passages concerning the concept of trust, see chapters 49 and 63.

[37]Sages are reluctant and slow to speak, but their words are worthy of complete trust.

[38]Cf. chapters 2, 9, 34, and 77.

[39]Literally, "We are this way *ziran*, 自然." See *ziran* under *Important Terms*. For other examples, see chapters 23, 25, 51, and 64.

[40]The idea that more can lead to less and its implication that less can yield more is a theme that appears in several places in the text. For examples see chapters 19 and 38.

So give them something with which to identify:
Manifest plainness.
Embrace simplicity.[41]
Do not think just of yourself.
Make few your desires.

Chapter Twenty

Cut off learning and be without worry!
How much distance is there really between agreement and flattery?
How much difference is there between the fair and the foul?
What other people fear one cannot but fear.
Immense!
Yet still not at its limit!
The multitude are bright and merry;
As if enjoying a grand festival;
As if ascending a terrace in springtime.
I alone am still and inactive, revealing no sign;[42]
Like a child who has not yet learned to smile.
Weak and weary, I seem to have nowhere to go.
The multitude all have more than enough.
I alone seem to be at a loss.
I have the mind of a fool!
Listless and blank!
The common folk are bright and brilliant.
I alone am muddled and confused.
The common folk are careful and discriminating.
I alone am dull and inattentive.
Vast!
Like the ocean!
Blown about!
As if it would never end!
The multitude all have something to do.
I alone remain obstinate and immobile, like some old rustic.
I alone differ from others, and value being nourished by mother.

---

[41]Literally, "unhewn wood." See n. 34.

[42]In this passage, the author enters into an autobiographical mode. See also chapters 69 and 70.

Chapter Twenty-One

The outward appearance of great Virtue comes forth from the Way alone.
As for the Way, it is vague and elusive.
Vague and elusive!
Within is an image.[43]
Vague and elusive!
Within is a thing.
Withdrawn and dark!
Within is an essence.
This essence is genuine and authentic.
Within there is trust.
From ancient times until the present day, its name has never left it.
It is how we know the origin of all things.
How do I know what the origin of all things is like?
Through this!

Chapter Twenty-Two

Those who are crooked will be perfected.
Those who are bent will be straight.
Those who are empty will be full.
Those who are worn will be renewed.
Those who have little will gain.
Those who have plenty will be confounded.
This is why sages embrace the One and serve as models for the whole
world.[44]
They do not make a display of themselves and so are illustrious.
They do not affirm their own views and so are well known.
They do not brag about themselves and so are accorded merit.
They do not boast about themselves and so are heard of for a long
time.[45]
Because they do not contend, no one in the world can contend with
them.[46]

---

[43]For other passges concerning *xiang*, "image," see 4, 14, 35, and 41.

[44]For other examples of "the One," see chapters 10, 39, and 42.

[45]See chapter 24 for a set of lines similar to the preceeding four.

[46]The same line appears in chapter 66.

The ancient saying, "Those who are crooked will be perfected" is not
    without substance![47]
Truly the sages are and remain perfect.

Chapter Twenty-Three

To be sparing with words is what comes naturally.
And so,
    A blustery wind does not last all morning;
    A heavy downpour does not last all day.
Who produces these?
Heaven and earth!
If not even Heaven and earth can keep things going for a long time,
How much less can human beings?
This is why one should follow the Way in all that one does.
One who follows the Way identifies with the Way.
One who follows Virtue identifies with Virtue.
One who follows loss identifies with loss.
The Way is pleased to have those who identify with the Way.
Virtue is pleased to have those who identify with Virtue.
Loss is pleased to have those who identify with loss.
Those lacking in trust are not trusted.[48]

Chapter Twenty-Four

Those who stand on tiptoe cannot stand firm.
Those who stride cannot go far.
Those who make a display of themselves are not illustrious.
Those who affirm their own views are not well known.
Those who brag about themselves are not accorded merit.
Those who boast about themselves are not heard of for long.[49]
From the point of view of the Way, such things are known as "excess
    provisions and pointless activities."

---

[47]While the *Daodejing* does not cite ancient sages or texts by name, here and elsewhere
it clearly does quote ancient sources. For other examples see chapters 42, 62, and 69.

[48]The same line appears in chapter 17. See n. 36.

[49]See chapter 22 for a set of lines similar to the preceeding four.

All creatures find these repulsive;
And so one who has the Way does not abide in them.[50]

Chapter Twenty-Five

There is a thing confused yet perfect, which arose before Heaven and
   earth.
Still and indistinct, it stands alone and unchanging.
It goes everywhere yet is never at a loss.
One can regard it as the mother of Heaven and earth.
I do not know its proper name;
I have given it the style "the Way."[51]
Forced to give it a proper name, I would call it "Great."
The Great passes on;
What passes on extends into the distance;
What extends into the distance returns to its source.[52]
And so the Way is great;
Heaven is great;
Earth is great;
And a true king too is great.
In the universe are four things that are great and the true king is first
   among them.
People model themselves on the earth.
The earth models itself on Heaven.
Heaven models itself on the Way.
The Way models itself on what is natural.[53]

---

[50]This line appears again in chapter 31.

[51]There is a play here on the difference between one's *ming* 名, "proper name," and one's *zi* 字, "style." In traditional Chinese society one does not use the former, personal name in public. And so the author can be understood as saying he is not intimately familiar with the Dao and so knows only its style, or perhaps that it would be unseemly to speak its true and proper name to unfamiliars.

[52]Cf. The description of the Way found in the *Zhuangzi*, chapter 6, pp. 230–35.

[53]"Natural" is *ziran*.

Chapter Twenty-Six

The heavy is the root of the light.
The still rules over the agitated.[54]
This is why sages travel all day without leaving their baggage wagons.
No matter how magnificent the view or lovely the place, they remain
    aloof and unaffected.
How can a lord who can field ten thousand chariots take lightly his role
    in the world!
If he is light, he loses the root;
If he is agitated, he loses his rule.

Chapter Twenty-Seven

One who is good at traveling leaves no tracks or traces.
One who is good at speaking is free of slips or flaws.
One who is good at numbers need not count or reckon.
One who is good at closing up needs no bolts or locks,
    yet what they have secured cannot be opened.
One who is good at binding needs no rope or string,
    yet what they have tied cannot be undone.
This is why sages are good at saving people and so never abandon
    people,[55]
Are good at saving things and so never abandon things.
This is called inheriting enlightenment.[56]
And so the good person is teacher of the bad;
The bad person is material for the good.
Those who do not honor their teachers or who fail to care for their
    material,
    though knowledgeable are profoundly deluded.
This is a fundamental mystery.

---

[54]Cf. chapter 45.

[55]Cf. chapter 62.

[56]The expression *ximing* 襲明, "inheriting enlightenment," is open to numerous interpretations. I take it as describing the good that bad people inherit from those who already
are enlightened.

Chapter Twenty-Eight

Know the male but preserve the female, and be a canyon for all the
world.
If you are a canyon for all the world, constant Virtue will never leave you,
and you can return home to be a child.
Know the white but preserve the black, and be a model for all the world.
If you are a model for all the world, constant Virtue will never err,
and you can return home to the infinite.
Know glory but preserve disgrace, and be a valley for all the world.
If you are a valley for all the world, constant Virtue will always be
sufficient, and you can return to being unhewn wood.[57]
When unhewn wood is broken up, it becomes vessels.[58]
Sages put these to use and become leaders of the officials.
And so the greatest carving cuts nothing off.

Chapter Twenty-Nine

Those who would gain the world and do something with it, I see that
they will fail.[59]
For the world is a spiritual vessel and one cannot put it to use.
Those who use it ruin it.
Those who grab hold of it lose it.[60]
And so,
Sometimes things lead and sometimes they follow;
Sometimes they breathe gently and sometimes they pant;
Sometimes they are strong and sometimes they are weak;
Sometimes they fight and sometimes they fall;
This is why sages cast off whatever is extreme, extravagant, or excessive.

---

[57]Or "simplicity." See n. 34.

[58]*Qi* 器, "vessel," or "implement" is a common metaphor for a government official. Playing on this image, it carries the slightly negative connotation of someone with limited "capacity." Cf. *Analects* 2.12 and the note to that passage.

[59]For *qu tianxia* 取天下, "gaining the world," see chapters 48 and 57.

[60]These two lines also appear in chapter 64.

Chapter Thirty

One who serves a ruler with the Way will never take the world by force of
arms.
For such actions tend to come back in kind.
Wherever an army resides, thorns and thistles grow.
In the wake of a large campaign, bad harvests are sure to follow.
Those who are good at military action achieve their goal and then stop.
They do not dare to rely on force of arms.
They achieve their goal but do not brag.
They achieve their goal but do not boast.
They achieve their goal but are not arrogant.
They achieve their goal but only because they have no choice.
They achieve their goal but do not force the issue.
For after a period of vigor there is old age.
To rely on such practices is said to be contrary to the Way.
And what is contrary to the Way will come to an early end.[61]

Chapter Thirty-One

Fine weapons are inauspicious instruments;
All creatures find them repulsive.
And so one who has the Way does not rely upon them.
At home, a cultivated person gives precedence to the left;
At war, a cultivated person gives precedence to the right.[62]
Weapons are inauspicious instruments, not the instruments of a
cultivated person.
But if given no choice, the cultivated person will use them.
Peace and quiet are the highest ideals;
A military victory is not a thing of beauty.
To beautify victory is to delight in the slaughter of human beings.
One who delights in the slaughter of human beings will not realize his
ambitions in the world.
On auspicious occasions, precedence is given to the left;
On inauspicious occasions, precedence is given to the right.

---

[61]The final three lines also appear at the end of chapter 55.

[62]The left side being associated with happy and auspicious events and the right side with
sad and inauspicious events.

The lieutenant commander is stationed on the left;
The supreme commander is stationed on the right.
This shows that the supreme commander is associated with the rites of
  mourning.
When great numbers of people have been killed, one weeps for them in
  grief and sorrow.
Military victory is associated with the rites of mourning.

Chapter Thirty-Two

The Way is forever nameless.[63]
Unhewn wood[64] is insignificant, yet no one in the world can master it.
If barons and kings could preserve it, the myriad creatures would all
  defer to them of their own accord;
Heaven and earth would unite and sweet dew would fall;
And the people would be peaceful and just, though no one so decrees.
When unhewn wood is carved up, then there are names.
Now that there are names, know enough to stop!
To know when to stop is how to stay out of danger.[65]
Streams and torrents flow into rivers and oceans,
Just as the world flows into the Way.

Chapter Thirty-Three

Those who know others are knowledgeable;
Those who know themselves are enlightened.
Those who conquer others have power;
Those who conquer themselves are strong;
Those who know contentment are rich.[66]
Those who persevere have firm commitments.
Those who do not lose their place will endure.
Those who die a natural death are long-lived.[67]

---

[63]On the idea of being "nameless," see chapters 1, 37, and 41.

[64]Or "simplicity." See n. 34.

[65]Cf. the similar line in chapter 44.

[66]For the value of *zu* 足, "contentment," see chapters 44 and 46.

[67]Cf. the teaching quoted in chapter 42.

Chapter Thirty-Four

How expansive is the great Way!
Flowing to the left and to the right.
The myriad creatures rely upon it for life, and it turns none of them
    away.[68]
When its work is done it claims no merit.[69]
It clothes and nourishes the myriad creatures, but does not lord it over
    them.
Because it is always without desires, one could consider it insignificant.[70]
Because the myriad creatures all turn to it and yet it does not lord it over
    them,
    one could consider it great.
Because it never considers itself great, it is able to perfect its greatness.

Chapter Thirty-Five

Hold on to the great image and the whole world will come to you.[71]
They will come and suffer no harm;
They will be peaceful, secure, and prosperous.
Music and fine food will induce the passerby to stop.
But talk about the Way—how insipid and without relish it is!
Look for it and it cannot be seen;
Listen for it and it cannot be heard;
But use it and it will never run dry!

Chapter Thirty-Six

What you intend to shrink, you first must stretch.
What you intend to weaken, you first must strengthen.
What you intend to abandon, you first must make flourish.
What you intend to steal from, you first must provide for.
This is called subtle enlightenment.

---

[68]Cf. chapter 2.

[69]Cf. chapters 2, 9, 17, and 77.

[70]Literally, one could *ming* 名, "name," it or classify it among the small.

[71]For other passages that concern *xiang*, "image," see chapters 4, 14, 21, and 41.

The supple and weak overcome the hard and the strong.
Fish should not be taken out of the deep pools.
The sharp implements of the state should not be shown to the people.[72]

Chapter Thirty-Seven

The Way does nothing yet nothing is left undone.[73]
Should barons and kings be able to preserve it, the myriad creatures will
    transform themselves.[74]
After they are transformed, should some still desire to act,
I shall press them down with the weight of nameless unhewn wood.[75]
Nameless unhewn wood is but freedom from desire.
Without desire and still, the world will settle itself.

Book Two

Chapter Thirty-Eight

Those of highest Virtue do not strive for Virtue and so they have it.
Those of lowest Virtue never stray from Virtue and so they lack it.
Those of highest Virtue practice nonaction and never act for ulterior
    motives.
Those of lowest Virtue act and always have some ulterior motive.
Those of highest benevolence act, but without ulterior motives.
Those of highest righteousness act, but with ulterior motives.
Those who are ritually correct[76] act, but if others do not respond,
    they roll up their sleeves and resort to force.

---

[72]The proper sense of *liqi* 利器, "sharp implements," is a matter of considerable controversy. Whether it refers to the weapons of the state, its ministers, labor-saving tools, the
Daoist sage, or something else is hard to say, so I have left it ambiguous. Cf. the use in chapter 57.

[73]Cf. the similar line in chapter 48.

[74]For *zihua* 自化, "transform themselves," see chapter 57.

[75]Or "nameless simplicity." See n. 34. On the idea of being "nameless," see chapters 1,
32, and 41.

[76]The word rendered here as "ritually correct" is *li* 禮, which in other contexts is translated as "having propriety."

And so,
>When the Way was lost there was Virtue;
>When Virtue was lost there was benevolence;
>When benevolence was lost there was righteousness;
>When righteousness was lost there were the rites.

The rites are the wearing thin of loyalty and trust, and the beginning of chaos.

The ability to predict what is to come is an embellishment of the Way, and the beginning of ignorance.

This is why the most accomplished reside in what is thick, not in what is thin.

They reside in what is most substantial, not in mere embellishment.

And so they cast off the one and take up the other.[77]

Chapter Thirty-Nine

In the past, among those who attained the One were these:[78]
>Heaven attained the One and became pure;
>Earth attained the One and became settled;
>The spirits attained the One and became numinous;
>The valley attained the One and became full;
>The myriad creatures attained the One and flourished;
>Barons and kings attained the One and became mainstays of the state.

All of this came about through the One.

If Heaven lacked what made it pure it might rip apart.

If earth lacked what made it settled it might open up.

If the spirits lacked what made them numinous they might cease their activity.

If the valley lacked what made it full it might run dry.

If the myriad creatures lacked what made them flourish they might become extinct.

If barons and kings lacked what made them honored and lofty they might fall.

And so what is honored has its root in what is base;

What is lofty has its foundation in what is lowly.

---

[77]This line also appears in chapters 12 and 72.

[78]For other examples of "the One," see chapters 10, 22, and 42.

This is why barons and kings refer to themselves as,
   "The Orphan," "The Desolate," or "The Forlorn." [79]
Is this not a case where what is base serves as the foundation!
Is it not?
And so the greatest of praise is without praise.
Do not desire what jingles like jade,
   but what rumbles like rock!

Chapter Forty

Turning back is how the Way moves.
Weakness is how the Way operates.
The world and all its creatures arise from what is there;
What is there arises from what is not there.

Chapter Forty-One

When the best scholars hear about the Way,
They assiduously put it into practice.
When average scholars hear about the Way,
They sometimes uphold it and sometimes forsake it.
When the worst scholars hear about the Way,
They laugh at it!
If they did not laugh at it, it would not really be the Way.
And so the common saying has it:
   The clearest Way seems obscure;
   The Way ahead seems to lead backward;
   The most level Way seems uneven;
   Highest Virtue seems like a valley;
   Great purity seems sullied,
   Ample Virtue seems insufficient;
   Solid Virtue seems unstable;
   The simple and genuine seems fickle;
   The great square has no corners;
   The great vessel takes long to perfect;
   The great note sounds faint;

---

[79]The same expressions occur in chapter 42.

The great image is without shape;[80]
The Way is hidden and without name.[81]
Only the Way is good at providing and completing.

Chapter Forty-Two

The Way produces the One.
The One produces two.
Two produces three.
Three produces the myriad creatures.[82]
The myriad creatures shoulder *yin* and embrace *yang*,
    and by blending these *qi* "vital energies" they attain harmony.
People most despise being orphaned, desolate or forlorn,
    and yet barons and kings take these as their personal appellations.[83]
And so sometimes diminishing a thing adds to it;
Sometimes adding to a thing diminishes it.
What others teach, I too teach: "The violent and overbearing will not die
    a natural death."
I shall take this as the father of all my teachings.

Chapter Forty-Three

The most supple things in the world ride roughshod over the most rigid.
That which is not there can enter even where there is no space.
This is how I know the advantages of nonaction!

---

[80]For other passages that concern *xiang* 象, "image," see chapters 4, 14, 21, and 35.

[81]On the idea of being "nameless" see chapters 1, 32, and 37.

[82]The precise referents of these terms are hard to determine. I take the Way to be the most inclusive term designating the hidden, underlying source of things. The "one" would then be its *xiang* 象, "image," the closest thing we can have to a picture or representation of the Way. (For other examples see chapters 10, 22, and 39.) The "two" would then be the fundamental *qi* 氣, "vital energies," *yin* and *yang* (see *qi, yin* and *yang* under *Important Terms*). These, together with our image of the Way as a unified whole, give rise to everything in the world. A similar scheme is described in the appendices to the *Changes*. This process, whatever its particulars, was understood as a natural progression. There was no creator and the "nothing" out of which things arose is a primal state of undifferentiated vital energy, the state of no things but not absolute Nothingness. See Slingerland's note on these lines in *Effortless Action*, page 145, note 28.

[83]See chapter 39.

The teaching that is without words,[84]
The advantages of nonaction,
Few in the world attain these.

Chapter Forty-Four

Your name or your body, which do you hold more dear?
Your body or your property, which is of greater value?
Gain or loss, which is the greater calamity?
And so, deep affections give rise to great expenditures.
Excessive hoarding results in great loss.
Know contentment and avoid disgrace;[85]
Know when to stop and avoid danger;[86]
And you will long endure.

Chapter Forty-Five

Great perfection seems wanting but use will not wear it out.
Great fullness seems empty but use will not drain it.
Great straightness seems crooked;
Great skillfulness seems clumsy;
Great speech seems to stammer.
Agitation overcomes cold.
Stillness overcomes heat.
Purity and stillness rectify Heaven and earth.

Chapter Forty-Six

When the world has the Way, fleet-footed horses are used to haul dung.
When the world is without the Way, war horses are raised in the
    suburbs.[87]
The greatest misfortune is not to know contentment.[88]

---

[84]Cf. the similar line in chapter 2.

[85]For the value of "contentment" see chapters 33 and 46.

[86]Cf. the similar line in chapter 32.

[87]Very close to the city, thus showing a heightened state of mobilization.

[88]For the value of "contentment" see chapters 33 and 44.

The worst calamity is the desire to acquire.
And so those who know the contentment of contentment are always
    content.

Chapter Forty-Seven

Without going out the door, one can know the whole world.
Without looking out the window, one can see the Way of Heaven.
The further one goes, the less one knows.
This is why sages
    Know without going abroad,
    Name without having to see,
    Perfect through nonaction.

Chapter Forty-Eight

In the pursuit of learning, one does more each day;
In the pursuit of the Way, one does less each day;
One does less and less until one does nothing;[89]
One does nothing yet nothing is left undone.[90]
Gaining the world always is accomplished by following no activity.[91]
As soon as one actively tries, one will fall short of gaining the world.

Chapter Forty-Nine

Sages do not have constant hearts of their own;
They take the people's hearts as their hearts.
    I am good to those who are good;
    I also am good to those who are not good;
    This is to be good out of Virtue.[92]

---

[89]Until one reaches the state of *wuwei,* "nonaction."

[90]Cf. the similar lines in chapter 37.

[91]For *wushi* 無事, "no activity," see chapters 57 and 63. For *qu tianxia,* "gaining the world," see chapters 29 and 57.

[92]I read this line, and the line three lines below it, as playing on the etymological and semantic relationship between *de* 德, "virtue," and *de* 得, "to get." Since those with virtue naturally are good to and trust others, they accrue ("get") Virtue; this enables them to gain ("get") the support of others and realize ("get") their greater ends. Cf. chapters 17, 23, 27, and 38.

I trust the trustworthy;

I also trust the untrustworthy.

This is to trust out of Virtue.

Sages blend into the world and accord with the people's hearts.

The people all pay attention to their eyes and ears;

The sages regard them as children.

Chapter Fifty

Between life and death,

Three out of ten are the disciples of life;[93]

Three out of ten are the disciples of death;

Three out of ten create a place for death.[94]

Why is this?

Because of their profound desire to live.[95]

I have heard that those good at nurturing life,

On land do not meet with rhinoceroses or tigers,

And in battle do not encounter armored warriors.

Rhinoceroses find no place to thrust their horns;

Tigers find no place to sink their claws;

Soldiers find no place to drive in their blades.

Why is this?

Because such people have no place for death.

Chapter Fifty-One

The Way produces them;

Virtue rears them;

Things shape them;

Circumstances perfect them.

This is why the myriad creatures all revere the Way and honor Virtue.

---

[93]Cf. chapter 76.

[94]This passage has been interpreted in a wide variety of ways. I take its general theme to be the preservation of one's natural span of life, here connected to the idea that wanting something too badly often leads to its opposite. Some are fated to live long and others to die young. But about one in three bring misfortune on themselves. The missing person in ten is of course the sage. By not doing, sages avoid creating a place for death to enter.

[95]Cf. chapter 75.

The Way is revered and Virtue honored not because this is decreed,
 but because it is natural.
And so the Way produces them and Virtue rears them;
 Raises and nurtures them;
 Settles and confirms them;
 Nourishes and shelters them.
To produce without possessing;[96]
To act with no expectation of reward;[97]
To lead without lording over;
Such is Enigmatic Virtue![98]

Chapter Fifty-Two

The world had a beginning;
This can be considered the mother of the world.
Knowing the mother, return and know her children;
Knowing her children, return and preserve their mother;
And one will avoid danger to the end of one's days.[99]
Stop up the openings;
Close the gates;[100]
To the end of one's life one will remain unperturbed.
Unstop the openings;
Multiply your activities;
And to the end of one's life one will be beyond salvation.
To discern the minute is called "enlightenment."
To preserve the weak is called "strength."
Use this light and return home to this enlightenment.
Do not bring disaster upon yourself.
This is called "practicing the constant."

---

[96]This line also appears in chapters 2 and 10.

[97]This line also appears in chapters 2, 10, and 77.

[98]Chapter 10 concludes with these same four lines. For *xuande* 玄德, "Enigmatic Virtue,"
see chapter 65.

[99]This line also appears in chapter 16.

[100]This and the preceeding line also appear in chapter 56.

Chapter Fifty-Three

If I know anything at all, I know that in following the great Way, there is
but one concern:
The great Way is smooth and easy;
Yet people love to take shortcuts![101]
The court is resplendent;
Yet the fields are overgrown.
The granaries are empty;
Yet some wear elegant clothes;
Fine swords dangle at their sides;
They are stuffed with food and drink;
And possess wealth in gross abundance.
This is known as taking pride in robbery.
Far is this from the Way!

Chapter Fifty-Four

What is firmly grounded will not be pulled out.
What is firmly embraced will not be lost.
Through the sacrifices of one's descendants, it will never cease.
Cultivate it in oneself and its Virtue will be genuine.[102]
Cultivate it in one's family and its Virtue will be more than enough.
Cultivate it in one's village and its Virtue will be long lasting.
Cultivate it in one's state and its Virtue will be abundant.
Cultivate it throughout the world and its Virtue will be everywhere.[103]
And so, take stock of the self by looking at the self;
Take stock of the family by looking at the family;

---

[101]See *Analects* 6.12 (not in this volume) for a related use of the word *jing* 徑, "shortcut."

[102]"It" refers to the Way. Note that in this and the following lines the word translated as
"Virtue" also clearly has the sense of a kind of "power."

[103]The progression from cultivating the Way in oneself to cultivating it throughout the
empire is reminiscent of the progression one sees in chapter 4 of the *Daxue* 大學, "Great
Learning," a work not included in this volume. There we are told that those who wish to
"make bright their shining Virtue throughout the world" must first "order their states."
Those who wish to order their states must first "regulate their families," Those who wish to
regulate their families must first "cultivate themselves" and so on. Wing-tsit Chan (p. 196)
points out that Mencius identifies this basic idea as a "common saying" in *Mengzi* 4A5 (not
in this volume).

Take stock of the village by looking at the village;
Take stock of the state by looking at the state;
Take stock of the world by looking at the world;
How do I know that the world is this way?
Through this!

Chapter Fifty-Five

Those who are steeped in Virtue are like new-born children;[104]
Poisonous creatures will not strike them;
Fierce beasts will not seize them;
Birds of prey will not snatch them away.
Their bones are weak and sinews yielding and yet their grip is firm.
They do not yet know the union of male and female, but their potency is
   at its height.
This is because they are perfectly pure;
They can wail all day without growing hoarse.
This is because they are perfectly balanced.
Knowing balance is called "constancy."
Knowing constancy is called "enlightenment."
What helps life along is called "inauspicious."[105]
When the heart and mind is used to guide the *qi* 氣, "vital energies," this
   is called "forcing things."[106]
For after a period of vigor there is old age.
To rely on such practices is said to be contrary to the Way.
And what is contrary to the Way will come to an early end.[107]

---

[104]The early Confucian Mengzi also uses the newborn as an image for his ideal state of mind. See his discussion of the *chizi zhi xin* 赤子之心, "a child's heart," in *Mengzi* 4B12, not in this volume.

[105]Cf. the closing lines of *Zhuangzi*, chapter 5 (see p. 229), where Zhuangzi says, "Follow the natural and do not *yisheng* 益生, 'help life along.'"

[106]Early Daoists tended to advocate allowing one's *qi* to find their natural course. For example, see the "fasting of the heart and mind" passage in chapter 4 of the *Zhuangzi*, p. 223. They were opposed to those such as the early Confucian Mengzi, who argued that the mind should guide the vital energies. See Mengzi's discussion of nourishing the "floodlike *qi*" in *Mengzi* 2A2.

[107]The final three lines also appear at the end of chapter 30.

Chapter Fifty-Six

Those who know do not talk about it;
Those who talk about it do not know.
Stop up the openings;
Close the gates;[108]
Blunt the sharpness;
Untangle the tangles;
Soften the glare;
Merge with the dust.[109]
This is known as Enigmatic Unity.[110]
And so one can neither be too familiar with nor too distant from them;
One can neither benefit nor harm them;
One can neither honor nor demean them,
And so they are honored by the whole world.[111]

Chapter Fifty-Seven

Follow what is correct and regular in ordering your state;
Follow what is strange and perverse in deploying your troops;
Follow no activity and gain the world. [112]
How do I know that things are this way?
Through this!
The more taboos and prohibitions there are in the world, the poorer the
    people.
The more sharp implements the people have, the more benighted the
    state.[113]
The more clever and skillful the people, the more strange and perverse
    things arise.
The more clear the laws and edicts, the more thieves and robbers.

---

[108]This and the preceding line also appear together in chapter 52.

[109]This and the preceding three lines also appear together in chapter 4.

[110]Cf. chapter 1, "Their unity is known as an enigma."

[111]This line also appears in chapter 62.

[112]For *wushi*, "no activity," see chapters 48 and 63. For *qu tianxia*, "gaining the world,"
see chapters 29 and 48.

[113]For the expression "sharp implements" see chapter 36.

And so sages say,
> "I do nothing and the people transform themselves;
> I prefer stillness and the people correct and regulate themselves;
> I engage in no activity and the people prosper on their own;
> I am without desires and the people simplify[114] their own lives."

Chapter Fifty-Eight

The more dull and depressed the government, the more honest and
    agreeable the people.
The more active and searching the government, the more deformed and
    deficient the people.
Good fortune rests upon disaster;
Disaster lies hidden within good fortune.
Who knows the highest standards?
Perhaps there is nothing that is truly correct and regular!
What is correct and regular turns strange and perverse;
What is good turns monstrous.
Long indeed have the people been deluded.
And so sages are,
> Square but do not cut,
> Cornered but do not clip,
> Upright but not imposing,
> Shining but not dazzling.

Chapter Fifty-Nine

In bringing order to the people or in serving Heaven, nothing is as good
    as frugality.
To be frugal is called submitting early on.
Submitting early on is known as deeply accumulating Virtue.
If you deeply accumulate Virtue, nothing can stand in your way.
If nothing can stand in your way, no one will know your limits.
If no one knows your limits, you can possess the state.
If you possess the mother of the state, you can long endure.
This is known as deep roots and strong stems.
This is the Way of long life and far-reaching vision.

---

[114]Literally, "unhewn wood." See n. 34.

Chapter Sixty

Ruling a great state is like cooking a small fish.[115]
When one manages the world through the Way, ghosts lose their
    numinous qualities.
It's not that ghosts really lose their numinous qualities,
    but that their numinous qualities do not injure human beings.[116]
Not only do their numinous qualities not injure human beings,
    sages too do not injure human beings.[117]
Since neither of these two injures human beings, Virtue gathers and
    accrues to both.

Chapter Sixty-One

A great state is like the delta of a mighty river;[118]
It is where the whole world gathers.
It is the female of the whole world.[119]
The female always gets the better of the male through stillness.
Through stillness, she places herself below the male.
And so, a great state, by placing itself below a lesser state, can take the
    lesser state.
A lesser state, by placing itself below a great state, can be taken by the
    greater state.
And so, one places itself below in order to take;
The other places itself below in order to be taken.

---

[115]The idea is that too much attention and meddling will make either fall apart.

[116]Laozi seems here to be arguing against the idea, seen in thinkers like Mozi et al., that the ideal state requires the active participation of ghosts and other spirits in meting out rewards or punishments. Laozi does not deny the existence of such beings but, like Kongzi, sees a direct appeal to them as inappropriate. Cf. Kongzi's advice concerning ghosts and spirits in *Analects* 6.22.

[117]They do not disturb the people through too much attention and meddling.

[118]Literally, *xialiu* 下流, "low flow." Cf. the use of the same term in *Analects* 19.20 (not in this volume) ". . . the gentleman dislikes living in low places (*xialiu*) where all the foul things of the world collect." The Daoist of course inverts Confucian values, esteeming what the world regards as lowly.

[119]In the sense that the ideal great state places itself below and attracts the whole world. Also, like a valley or the delta of a river, the great state is like a woman in being fertile and having the ability to feed the whole world. Consider the common metaphor of the Nile as the "cradle of civilization." Cf. chapter 66.

The great state wants no more than to provide for all people alike.

The lesser state wants no more than to find someone to serve.

Since both can get what they want, it is fitting that the great state place itself in the lower position.

Chapter Sixty-Two

The Way is the inner sanctum of the myriad creatures. [120]

It is the treasure of the good man and the savior of the bad.

Fine words can sell things;[121] ·

Noble deeds can promote someone;

But can one cast away the bad in people?[122]

And so, when setting up the Son of Heaven or appointing the Three Ministers,[123]

Those who offer up precious jades and present fine steeds are not as good as those who stay in their seats and promote this Way.

Why was this Way so honored in ancient times?

Did they not say that through it,

"One could get what one seeks and escape punishment for one's crimes?"

And so, this is why it is honored by the whole world. [124]

Chapter Sixty-Three

Act, but through nonaction.

Be active, but have no activities.[125]

Taste, but have no tastes.[126]

No matter how great or small, many or few,

---

[120]"Inner sanctum" is the translation of *ao* 奥, the southwest corner of one's house where the household gods are lodged and worshipped.

[121]Cf. chapter 81.

[122]Cf. chapter 27.

[123]Cf. Mozi's discussion of how the Son of Heaven and Three Ministers are to be appointed, in *Mozi*, chapter 2, "Obeying One's Superiors," pp. 60–63.

[124]This line also appears in chapter 56.

[125]For *wushi*, "no activities," see chapters 48 and 57.

[126]The idea in each case is that one should do what one does in unpremeditated and spontaneous response to the situation at hand. One should do away with set schemes, categories, standards and plans, and follow one's natural inclinations and tendencies. And so, for example, one should taste and savor what one finds pleasing, not what others might enjoy or what accords with some socially sanctioned view about good taste. Cf. chapter 12.

Repay resentment with Virtue.[127]
Plan for what is difficult while it is easy.
Work at what is great while it is small.
The difficult undertakings in the world all start with what is easy.
The great undertakings in the world all begin with what is small.
This is why sages never work at great things and are able to achieve
    greatness.
Those who easily enter into promises always prove unworthy of trust.
Those who often think that things are easy regularly encounter
    difficulties.
And so sages consider things difficult and in the end are without
    difficulties.

Chapter Sixty-Four

What is at peace is easy to secure.
What has yet to begin is easy to plan for.
What is brittle is easy to scatter.
What is faint is easy to disperse.
Work at things before they come to be;
Regulate things before they become disordered.
A tree whose girth fills one's embrace sprang from a downy sprout;
A terrace nine stories high arose from a layer of dirt;
A journey of a thousand leagues began with a single step.
    Those who use it ruin it.
    Those who grab hold of it lose it.[128]
This is why sages practice nonaction and so do not ruin;
They do not lay hold and so do not lose.
People often ruin things just when they are on the verge of success.
Be as careful at the end as you are at the beginning and you will not ruin
    things.
This is why sages desire to be without desires and show no regard for
    precious goods.[129]

---

[127]Here we see a clear contrast with the view of early Confucians. See *Analects* 14.34. Cf. chapter 49.

[128]These two lines also appear in chapter 29.

[129]Cf. *Mengzi* 7B35 (not in this volume), "For cultivating the heart and mind nothing is better than to make few one's desires."

They study what is not studied and return to what the multitude
   pass by.[130]
They work to support the myriad creatures in their natural condition and
   never dare to act.

Chapter Sixty-Five

In ancient times, those good at practicing the Way did not use it to
   enlighten the people,
      but rather to keep them in the dark.[131]
The people are hard to govern because they know too much.
And so to rule a state with knowledge is to be a detriment to the state.
Not to rule a state through knowledge is to be a blessing to the state.
Know that these two provide the standard.
Always to know this standard is called Enigmatic Virtue.[132]
How profound and far-reaching is Enigmatic Virtue!
It turns back with things;
And only then is there the Great Compliance.[133]

---

[130]Daoist sages take Nature as their model. In philosophical discussions of the time, there was a debate about whether the proper content of learning is part of or opposed to what is naturally so. This debate in turn was a reflection of a larger debate about the character of human nature. Mengzi endorses only particular natural tendencies—those that incline us toward morality—and on this basis claims that human nature is good. Xunzi argues that our untutored nature inclines us toward bad states of affairs. On this basis he concludes our nature is bad and must be reformed through protracted study and practice. We can see Laozi, Mengzi, and Xunzi as representing a spectrum of views about the proper content of learning that reflects their different views about the goodness of our pre-reflective nature, running from greatest to least confidence in our raw natural state.

[131]The idea that the best of actions flow forth without reflection or knowledge was not uncommon in early China. In his note on this line, Wing-tsit Chan cites a passage from the *Odes* in which the Lord on High commends King Wen for his behavior, "Without reflection or knowledge, you comply with my principles" (*Mao #* 241). See Chan, p. 216. Cf. *Analects* 15.5.

[132]For *xuande*, "Enigmatic Virtue," see chapters 10 and 51.

[133]This is the only occurrence of the expression *dashun* 大順, "Great Compliance," in the text. However, as Arthur Waley (p. 223) points out in his note to this chapter, it does occur in *Zhuangzi*, chapter 12 (not in this volume). Note too that the same word *shun* appears in *Mao #* 241 quoted in n. 131 above.

Chapter Sixty-Six

The rivers and ocean are able to rule over a hundred valleys,
  because they are good at placing themselves in the lower position.[134]
And so they are able to rule over a hundred valleys.
This is why if you want to be above the people you must proclaim that
  you are below them.
If you want to lead the people, you must put yourself behind them.
This is how sages are able to reside above the people without being
  considered a burden,
How they are able to be out in front of the people without being
  regarded as a harm.
This is why the whole world delights in supporting them and never
  wearies.
Because they do not contend, no one in the world can contend with
  them. [135]

Chapter Sixty-Seven

The whole world agrees in saying that my Way is great but appears
  unworthy.
It is only because it is great that it appears to be unworthy.
If it appeared worthy, it would have become small long ago.
Isn't that so!
I have three treasures that I hold on to and preserve:
    The first I call loving kindness;
    The second I call frugality;
    The third I call never daring to put oneself first in the world.
The kind can be courageous;
The frugal can be generous;
Those who never dare to put themselves first in the world
  can become leaders of the various officials.
Now to be courageous without loving kindness,
To be generous without frugality,
To put oneself first without putting oneself behind others,

---

[134]Cf. chapter 61.

[135]The same line appears in chapter 22.

These will lead to death.[136]
If one has loving kindness, in attack one will be victorious,
In defense one will be secure.
For Heaven will save you and protect you with loving kindness.

Chapter Sixty-Eight

Those good at fighting are never warlike.[137]
Those good at attack are never enraged.
Those good at conquering their enemies never confront them.
Those good at using others put themselves in a lower position.
This is called the Virtue of noncontention;
This is called the power of using others;
This is called matching up with Heaven, the highest achievement of the
    ancients.

Chapter Sixty-Nine

Military strategists have a saying,
    "I never dare to play host but prefer to play guest.[138]
    I never dare to advance an inch but retreat a foot."
This is called a formation without form,
Rolling up one's sleeve but having no arm,
Forcing the issue but lacking an enemy.[139]
Who can avoid misfortune in war?
But there is none greater than underestimating the enemy!
Underestimating the enemy almost cost me my three treasures.[140]
And so when swords are crossed and troops clash, the side that grieves
    shall be victorious.

---

[136]The idea that true virtue lies in a harmony within a tension, that it requires a balance between extremes, is seen in many traditions. Early Confucians too held a version of this view. For example, see *Analects* 8.2.

[137]That is, they are not overly aggressive and pugnacious.

[138]They avoid initiating the action, the first move being the prerogative of the host.

[139]Cf. the last two lines with a similar line in chapter 38.

[140]See chapter 67 for a possible reference.

Chapter Seventy

My teachings are easy to understand and easy to implement;
But no one in the whole world has been able to understand or implement
    them.
My teachings have an ancestor and my activities have a lord;
But people fail to understand these and so I am not understood.
Those who understand me are rare;[141]
Those who take me as a model are honored.
This is why sages wear coarse cloth while cherishing precious jade.[142]

Chapter Seventy-One

To know that one does not know is best;
Not to know but to believe that one knows is a disease.[143]
Only by seeing this disease as a disease can one be free of it.
Sages are free of this disease;
Because they see this disease as a disease, they are free of it.

Chapter Seventy-Two

When the people do not fear what warrants awe,
Something truly awful will come to them.
Do not constrain their homes or villages.
Do not oppress their lives.
Because you do not oppress them, you will not be oppressed.
This is why sages know themselves but do not make a display of
    themselves;
They care for themselves but do not revere themselves.
And so they cast off the one and take up the other.[144]

---

[141]Cf. this complaint with Kongzi's remark in *Analects* 14.35.

[142]They appear common and unworthy on the outside but possess a secret treasure within. In *Analects* 17.1 (not in this volume) a man named Yang Huo criticizes Kongzi's reluctance to take office by asking him, "Can one who cherishes his treasure within and allows his state to go astray be considered benevolent?" Cf. *Analects* 9.13.

[143]This passage is similar in thought to *Analects* 2.17 (not in this volume) "If you know something realize that you know it. If you do not know something realize that you do not. This is what knowing is."

[144]This line also appears in chapters 12 and 38.

Chapter Seventy-Three

To be courageous in daring leads to death;
To be courageous in not daring leads to life.
These two bring benefit to some and loss to others.
Who knows why Heaven dislikes what it does?
Even sages regard this as a difficult question.
The Way does not contend but is good at victory;
Does not speak but is good at responding;
Does not call but things come of their own accord;
Is not anxious but is good at laying plans.
Heaven's net is vast;
Its mesh is loose but misses nothing.

Chapter Seventy-Four

If the people are not afraid of death, why threaten them with death?
  "But what if I could keep the people always afraid of death and seize and
  put to death those who dare to act in strange or perverse ways?
  Who then would dare to act in such a manner?"[145]
There is always the killing done by the Chief Executioner.[146]
The Chief Executioner is the greatest carver among carpenters.
Those who would do the work of the greatest carver among carpenters,
  rarely avoid wounding their own hands.

Chapter Seventy-Five

The people are hungry because those above eat up too much in taxes;
This is why the people are hungry.
The people are difficult to govern because those above engage in action;
This is why the people are difficult to govern.
People look upon death lightly because those above are obsessed with
  their own lives;[147]
This is why the people look upon death lightly.
Those who do not strive to live are more worthy than those who cherish life.

---

[145]These two lines introduce a question and mark a dialogue within the text. Cf. *Analects* 12.19.

[146]The death that Heaven brings to each person.

[147]Cf. chapter 50.

Chapter Seventy-Six

When alive human beings are supple and weak;
When dead they are stiff and strong.
When alive the myriad creatures, plants and trees are supple and weak;
When dead they are withered and dry.
And so the stiff and the strong are the disciples of death;[148]
The supple and weak are the disciples of life.
This is why,
    A weapon that is too strong will not prove victorious;
    A tree that is too strong will break.
The strong and the mighty reside down below;
The soft and the supple reside on top.[149]

Chapter Seventy-Seven

The Way of Heaven, is it not like the stretching of a bow?
What is high it presses down;
What is low it lifts up.
It takes from what has excess;
It augments what is deficient.
The Way of Heaven takes from what has excess and augments what is
    deficient.
The Way of human beings is not like this.
It takes from the deficient and offers it up to those with excess.
Who is able to offer what they have in excess to the world?
Only one who has the Way!
This is why sages act with no expectation of reward.[150]
When their work is done, they do not linger.[151]
They do not desire to make a display of their worthiness.

---

[148]Cf. chapter 50.

[149]The Han dynasty commentator Wang Bi illustrates the point of these last two lines with the examples of the roots of a tree and its twigs.

[150]This line also appears in chapters 2, 10, and 51.

[151]Cf. chapters 2, 9, 17, and 34. This and the previous line also appear together in chapter 2.

Chapter Seventy-Eight

In all the world, nothing is more supple or weak than water;
Yet nothing can surpass it for attacking what is stiff and strong.
And so nothing can take its place.
That the weak overcomes the strong and the supple overcomes the hard,
These are things everyone in the world knows but none can practice.
This is why sages say,
　　Those who can take on the disgrace of the state
　　Are called lords of the altar to the soil and grain.[152]
　　Those who can take on the misfortune of the state,
　　Are called kings of all the world.[153]
Straightforward words seem paradoxical.

Chapter Seventy-Nine

In cases of great resentment, even when resolution is reached, some
　　resentment remains.
How can this be considered good?
This is why sages maintain the left-hand portion of the tally,[154]
But do not hold people accountable.
Those with Virtue oversee the tally;
Those without Virtue oversee collection.[155]
The Way of Heaven plays no favorites;
It is always on the side of the good.

---

[152]These were the main altars of the state and a common metaphor for its independence and well-being.

[153]The idea that the most worthy rulers are willing to offer themselves to Heaven as surrogates on behalf of the people and in the name of the state is a motif seen in writings of this period and earlier. See King Tang's pronouncement to the spirits in the *Analects* 20.1 (not in this volume) and Nivison, *The Ways of Confucianism*, especially pp. 20–24.

[154]The left-hand portion of a contract of obligation, the part that was held by the creditor.

[155]The central idea of this chapter, which is seen throughout the text, is that one cannot force others to be good. If one resorts to force, one's actions will eventually rebound in kind upon oneself. The only way to affect others and turn them to the good is through the power of one's *de,* "Virtue."

Chapter Eighty

Reduce the size of the state;
Lessen the population.
Make sure that even though there are labor saving tools, they are never used.
Make sure that the people look upon death as a weighty matter and never move to distant places.
Even though they have ships and carts, they will have no use for them.
Even though they have armor and weapons, they will have no reason to deploy them.
Make sure that the people return to the use of the knotted cord.[156]
Make their food savory,
Their clothes fine,
Their houses comfortable,
Their lives happy.
Then even though neighboring states are within sight of each other,
Even though they can hear the sounds of each other's dogs and chickens,
Their people will grow old and die without ever having visited one another.

Chapter Eighty-One

Words worthy of trust are not refined;
Refined words are not worthy of trust.[157]
The good do not engage in disputation;
Those who engage in disputation are not good.[158]

---

[156]That is, let them abandon writing. The use of the knotted cord to keep track of records is mentioned in the Great Appendix to the *Changes* and *Zhuangzi*, chapter 10 (not in this volume), as well as elsewhere in the early literature. The details are unclear but the practice probably entailed making a knot in a cord for every ten or twenty units counted. Thus it resembles the western practice of notching or "scoring" a piece of wood for every twenty units counted, each notch representing a "score" or twenty.

[157]In *Analects* 14.6 (not in this volume) Kongzi says, "Those who have *de*, 'Virtue,' will always speak well. Those who speak well will not always have Virtue." Cf. chapter 62.

[158]Confucians too had a general mistrust of glib talkers and disputation. This reflects their similar, though distinct, beliefs about the power of a good person's *de*, "Virtue," to sway others. For examples, see *Analects* 1.3 and Mengzi's explanation of why he must engage in disputation, though not being fond of it, found in *Mengzi* 3B9.

Those who know are not full of knowledge;
Those full of knowledge do not know.
Sages do not accumulate.
The more they do for others, they more they have;
The more they give to others the more they possess.
The Way of Heaven is to benefit and not harm.
The Way of the sage is to act but not contend.

SELECTIVE BIBLIOGRAPHY

Translations

Chan, Alan K. L.

1991 *Two Visions of the Way*. Albany, NY: SUNY Press. (A translation and study of the Heshanggong and Wang Bi commentaries on the *Laozi*.)

Chan, Wing-tsit.

1963 *The Way of Lao Tzu (Tao te ching)*. Chicago, IL: University of Chicago Press. (An accurate and scholarly translation that makes revealing use of the commentarial tradition.)

Hendricks, Robert G.

1989 *Lao-Tzu Te-Tao Ching*. New York: Ballantine, 1989. (A fine translation and introduction to the *Mawangdui* version of the text.)

Lau, D. C.

1963 *Tao Te Ching*. Baltimore: Penguin Books. (An elegantly terse translation with informative introduction and appendices.)

Waley, Arthur.

1963 *The Way and Its Power*. New York: Grove Press. (A thoughtful translation with a substantial introduction.)

Secondary Works

Creel, Herrlee G.

1970 *What Is Taoism? And Other Studies in Chinese Cultural History*. Chicago, IL: The University of Chicago Press. (Contains several seminal essays on the thought and history of the text.)

Csikszentmihalyi, Mark, and Philip J. Ivanhoe, eds.

1999 *Essays on Religious and Philosophical Aspects of the Laozi*. Albany, NY: SUNY Press. (An anthology of essays on the thought of the text.)

Kohn, Livia, and Michael LaFargue, eds.

1998 *Lao-tzu and the Tao-te-ching*. Albany, NY: SUNY Press. (A broad range of essays on the text, its reception, and interpretation.)

Lau, D. C.

1958 "The Treatment of Opposites in Lao Tzu 老子." *Bulletin of the School of Oriental and African Studies* 21, pp. 344–60. (An intriguing exploration of one of the more paradoxical aspects of the text.)

▪ CHAPTER FIVE ▪

ZHUANGZI

Introduction

Little is known of Zhuangzi 莊子 beyond what we can gather from the book named after him. Much of the book, however, is unapologetically fictional, so the stories it tells about him provide us more insight into his persona than into the historical facts of his life. We know from external sources that his friend Huizi served in the court of King Hui of Liang (390–319 B.C.E.), which places Zhuangzi in the end of the fourth century B.C.E. The version of the text we have was assembled around 300 C.E. and is widely agreed to be the work of multiple authors. Though some passages seem to have been written by Zhuangzi, the book must initially have been compiled by his students and then supplemented by later contributors and editors. The following selections are drawn primarily from what scholars generally recognize as the earliest portions of the text, which were either written or inspired by Zhuangzi himself.

Zhuangzi has a huge vocabulary, draws freely from history and mythology, and is equally at home writing poetry, logical analyses, dialogue, and narrative. His references to Kongzi, Laozi, and the Mohists demonstrate that he was familiar with their ideas, though the absence of quotations leaves uncertain whether he had access to the same texts we do. Huizi, who argued against the possibility of distinguishing one thing from another, is known to have debated one of Mengzi's students. So Zhuangzi must at least have heard about Mengzi's ideas, though he never mentions him by name.

Zhuangzi does not present his ideas systematically or define his central terms. But he regularly speaks of *tian* 天, "Heaven," as the highest ideal for all things. He contrasts *tian,* which could also be translated as "nature," to *ren* 人, "people," or "humanity." The human, for Zhuangzi, includes everything from concrete activities that interfere with nature, such as the mutilation of criminals, to abstract ideas, such as *shi/fei* 是非, "right and wrong," that people project onto the world. Zhuangzi also speaks of *dao* 道, "the Way," which encompasses both the Way the world is and the way for people to live in it. Though he believes there is a way, he is skeptical of our ability to learn much about it through words or thinking. In fact, he attacks thinking in order to make room, instead, for experience and intuition. Sometimes his attacks are direct, with arguments illustrating the limitations of language, sometimes indirect, with strange stories having no obvious moral or hero. Rather than delivering a message, the *Zhuangzi* seems to go out of its way to defy understanding. In this sense, though the stories are often fantastic, the book is meant to offer a realistic lesson in the uselessness of trying to figure out life. Thinking and talking have a place: Zhuangzi does a lot of both of them. The challenge is to harmonize thinking and talking with the other, incomprehensible aspects life.

In the second century B.C.E., the historian Sima Qian classified Zhuangzi as a founding member of the Daoist school, rather than as a Confucian or a Mohist. This is an oversimplification. There was no "Daoist school" in his time, and, as readers will soon see, he would have resisted any classification of this sort. He knew and thought a lot about the other philosophers presented in this book, particularly Kongzi. But his relationships to them were too complex to be summarized as simple agreement or disagreement. The influence of these other thinkers on Zhuangzi and the implications of his arguments for their ideas are complex and difficult questions that readers will have to sort out for themselves, with the help of some of the secondary literature that is listed following the translation.

Chapter One: Wandering Round and About

In the northern darkness there is a fish named Minnow. No one knows how many thousand *li* around he is. He transforms himself into a bird named Breeze.[1] No one knows how many thousand *li* across she is. She ruffles and flies, and her wings are like clouds hanging from Heaven. As the seas turn, she thinks to migrate to the southern darkness. The southern darkness is Heaven's pool.[2]

---

[1]The exact meaning of the bird's name is unclear, but it was pronounced similarly to the word for wind.

[2]The word translated as "Heaven" also means both sky and Nature.

The *Tales of Qi*[3] records wonders. It says, "In her migration to the southern darkness, Breeze flaps along the water for three thousand *li,* spirals up on a whirlwind to ninety thousand *li,* and goes six months at a stretch."

Horse-shaped clouds, motes of dust, living things blowing breath at each other—is the blue-green of Heaven its proper color or just its being so endlessly far away? It looks just the same to her gazing down from above.

If water isn't deep it can't support big boats. Spill a cup of water on the floor and crumbs will be its boats. But put the cup there and it will stick—because the water is too shallow and the boat too big. If wind isn't deep it can't support big wings. This is why Breeze rises ninety thousand *li* with the wind there beneath her. Only then can she rest on the wind, carrying blue Heaven on her back, and nothing can stop her. Only then does she set her sights to the south.

The cicada and the student-dove laugh at her, saying, "When we start up and fly, we struggle for the elm or the sandalwood. Sometimes we don't even make it but just plunk to the ground. What is she doing rising ninety thousand *li* and heading south?" People going to the green meadows can bring three meals and return with their bellies still full. People going a hundred *li* need to grind grain for an overnight. People going a thousand *li* need to gather grain for three months. What do these two little bugs know? Little knowledge does not measure up to big knowledge, or few years to many. How do I know this is so? The morning mushroom does not know the waxing and waning of the moon, and the Hui-cricket does not know spring and fall. This is because they are short lived. South of Chu there is a turtle called Dark Genius, which counts five hundred years as a single spring and five hundred years as a single fall. In high antiquity there was a tree called Big Spring, which counted eight thousand years as a single spring and eight thousand years as a single fall. Nowadays, only eight-hundred-year-old Peng Zu is famous, and everyone compares themselves to him. Isn't it sad?

This was the subject of King Tang's questions to his teacher, Cramped.[4]

---

[3] We have no knowledge of this text and, judging from its name, it appears to be fictitious. Here and elsewhere, Zhuangzi may be parodying appeals to textual authority by appealing to fanciful "classics."

[4] Tang's teacher is named "Ji 棘," which commentators explain means narrow—as opposed to "Tang 湯," which means broad. Chapter Five of the book *Liezi* is entitled "The Questions of Tang" and contains an expanded version of what might have been their conversation. For a translation, see A. C. Graham, *The Book of Lieh Tzu,* reprint (London: John Murray, 1973), pp. 92–117. For more on King Tang, see *Important Figures.*

In the bald north there is a dark sea, Heaven's pool. There is a fish there whose breadth is several tens of thousands of *li*. No one knows his length. His name is Minnow. There is a bird there, whose name is Breeze. Her back is as huge as Mount Tai, and her wings are like clouds hanging from Heaven. Circling on the whirlwind, she spirals upward ninety thousand *li,* bursts through the clouds and mist, carrying the blue sky. Afterward she heads south, traveling to the southern darkness.

The accusing quail laughs at her, saying, "Where is *she* going? I rear up and don't go more than a few yards before coming down, soaring and roaming amid brambles and briars—this indeed is the perfection of flying! Where is she going?" This is the debate between little and big.

People who know how to do one job, handle a small town, or impress a ruler to get put in charge of a state see themselves like this. Songzi would still laugh at them. The whole world could praise him and he would not be encouraged. The whole world could condemn him and he would not be upset. He has fixed the difference between inner and outer and distinguished the limits of glory and disgrace. Yet he stops there. He is unconventional, but there is still something left unplanted.

Liezi [5] rides about on the wind. It's wonderful! He's gone two weeks at a time. His attitude toward wealth is unconventional. But, though he manages to avoid walking, he still relies on something. If he could chariot the norms of Heaven and earth and ride the changes in the six mists[6] to wander the inexhaustible, then what would there be to rely on? Hence it is said that perfect people have no self, spiritual people have no accomplishment, and sagely people have no name.

The sage-king Yao offered his empire to the hermit Whence. "To keep the torches burning when the sun and moon are shining is troubling too much for light. Irrigating the fields when the spring rains are falling is working too hard for water. You are here, my teacher, and the empire is in order. With me still presiding over it, I feel defective. Please take it."

---

[5] Little is known of Liezi. The book that bears his name contains scant biographical information. He may have been a practitioner of magic, or an ascetic who achieved freedom by withdrawing from the world. Either way, Zhuangzi's highly metaphoric criticism of him here suggests that he would have been better off accepting the world as it is.

[6] "Mists," here and below, is *qi* 氣. See *Important Terms*.

Whence said, "With you ordering it, the empire is well ordered. If I were to go ahead and replace you, would it be for the name? But name is only the guest of reality. Do I want to be the guest? The tailor bird nesting in the deep forest takes no more than a branch. The mole drinking at the river takes no more than a bellyful. Give it up, my lord. I have no use for the empire. Though the cook at the sacrifice fails to order the kitchen, the presiding priest does not leap over the goblets and platters to replace him."

[margin note: Language and labels are secondary to, or even obscure, the basic reality.]

Shoulder Dig said to Step Brother,[7] "I heard what Jie Yu said.[8] It was big but didn't stand for anything. It went on and on without coming back. I was frightened by what he said. It was as endless as the Milky Way, full of inconsistencies, and didn't approach the human situation."

Step Brother asked, "What did he say?"

"He said there are spiritual people living in the distant Maiden Mountains. Their skin is like frost, and they are gentle and restrained as virgins. They don't eat the five grains but sip wind and drink dew. They chariot the cloudy mists, ride the flying dragons, and wander beyond the four seas. By concentrating their spirit, they keep things from harm and ripen the harvests. I thought he was crazy and didn't believe him."

[margin note: "qi"]

Step Brother said, "Yes. The blind can't appreciate beautiful patterns or the deaf bells and drums. But are blindness and deafness confined to the physical form? Your knowledge has them, too. His talk is like a fertile woman.[9] Those people he describes, with that Virtue of theirs, will align with the ten thousand things and make them one. The world longs for chaos, but why should they fret and make the world their business? Nothing can harm these people. Though a great flood should knock against Heaven, they would not drown. Though a heat wave should melt stone and scorch the earth, they would not burn. From their dust and chaff you could mold the sages Yao and Shun. Why would they want to make things their business? A man of Song[10] invested in ceremonial caps and took them to Yue. But the Yue people cut their hair and tattoo their bodies and had no use for them. Yao brought order

---

[7]This character's name, Lian Shu, may also suggest a connection to the Shu clan, one of the Three Families that ruled Kongzi's native state of Lu for most of his lifetime.

[8]In *Analects* 18.5 (not in this volume), Jie Yu, known as The Madman of Chu, criticizes Kongzi for wasting his efforts on a lost cause. When Kongzi tries to speak with him, he runs away.

[9]Jie Yu's words are "like a fertile woman" in the sense that they await the right kind of person in order to bear fruit.

[10]The people of Song were the butt of many jokes. Cf. *Mengzi* 2A2 and *Hanfeizi*, chapter 49, p. 324.

His notions were preconceived and rigidly applied, as opposed to relatively
(ultimately of rightness, "yi")   understood.

to the people of the empire and stabilized the government within the seas. But when he went to see the four masters of the distant Maiden Mountains, north of the Fen River, he lost the world in a daze."[11]

The man only understood the small world he rendered with his own
culture-specific knowledge (little knowledge), in his own society.

Huizi said to Zhuangzi, "The king of Wei[12] left me the seeds of a big gourd. I planted them, and when they grew, the fruit was a yard across. I filled them with water but they weren't sturdy enough to hold it. I split them into ladles but they were too big to dip into anything. It wasn't that they weren't wonderfully big, but they were useless. So I smashed them."[13]

Zhuangzi said, "You, sir, are certainly clumsy about using big things. There were some people in Song who were good at making ointment to prevent chapped hands. Year after year, they used it in their business bleaching silk. A traveler heard about it and asked to buy the formula for a hundred pieces of gold. The clan assembled and consulted, saying, 'For years we've bleached silk and never made more than a few pieces of gold. Today in a single morning we can sell the trick for a hundred pieces. Let's give it to him!'

"The traveler got it and recommended it to the king of Wu, who was having trouble with the state of Yue. The king of Wu put him in command, and that winter he met the men of Yue in a naval battle. Using the ointment to keep his soldiers' hands from chapping, he defeated Yue badly and was rewarded with a portion of the conquered territory. The ability to prevent chapped hands was the same in either case. But one gained territory while the others never escaped bleaching silk because what they used it for was different.[14] Now you had these gigantic gourds. Why not lash them to-

---

[11]Earlier in Chinese history, the Fen River had been the northwestern border separating the Chinese from the non-Chinese world (i.e., the "barbarians"). By Zhuangzi's time, however, military expansion and cultural assimilation had moved the boundary back, so the Fen was closer to the center.

[12]Wei is another name for the state of Liang. Hence this is King Hui of Liang, the same ruler who employed Huizi in his administration.

[13]It is clear from the beginning of the next anecdote that Huizi's story here is meant as a criticism of Zhuangzi.

[14]Wu and Yue were two non-Chinese states to the south that were gradually incorporated into the Chinese world during the Spring and Autumn and Warring States periods. When hostilities broke out between them in 510 B.C.E., Wu dominated initially, which was presumably when Zhuangzi's story was meant to take place. Yue rallied its forces, however, and destroyed Wu in 473, which probably meant execution for the traveler or his descendants. The history of Wu, which would have been familiar to Zhuangzi's contemporary readers, makes the moral of the parable uncertain.

gether like big buoys and go floating on the rivers and lakes instead of worrying that they were too big to dip into anything? Your mind is full of underbrush, my friend." [15]

Huizi said to Zhuangzi, "I have a big tree, the kind people call Spring. Its trunk is so gnarled it won't take a chalk line, and its branches are so twisted they won't fit a compass or square. It stands by the road but no builder looks twice at it. Your talk is similarly big and useless, and everyone alike rejects it."

Zhuangzi said, "Haven't you seen a weasel? It bends down then rises up. It springs east and west, not worrying about heights or depths—and lands in a snare or dies in a net. Now the yak is so big he looks like clouds hanging from Heaven. He sure can be big, but he can't catch mice. You have a big tree and are upset that you can't use it. Why not plant it by a nothing-at-all village in a wide empty waste? You could do nothing, dilly-dallying by its side, or nap, ho-hum, beneath it. It won't fall to any axe's chop and nothing will harm it. Since it isn't any use, what bad can happen to it?"

Chapter Two: On Equalizing Things

Master Dapple of the South Wall sat leaning on his armrest. He looked up and sighed, vacant, as though he'd lost his counterpart. Yancheng Ziyou[16] stood before him in attendance. "What's this?" he said. "Can the body really be turned into dried wood? Can the mind really be turned into dead ashes? The one leaning on the armrest now is not the one who leaned on it before!"

Master Dapple said, "My, isn't that a good question you've asked, Ziyou! Just now I lost myself. Do you know? You've heard the pipes of people, but not the pipes of earth. Or if you've heard the pipes of earth, you haven't heard the pipes of Heaven."

"May I ask what you mean?"

"The Big Lump belches breath and it's called wind. If only it wouldn't start! When it starts, the ten thousand holes begin to hiss. Don't you hear the

---

[15]*Xin* 心 can be translated as either "heart" or "mind," though the latter is usually more appropriate for Zhuangzi. The description of Huizi's mind as full of underbrush may be a reference to Mengzi's metaphor of moral sprouts. See also *xin* under *Important Terms*.

[16]This is evidently Kongzi's disciple, Ziyou, who is described in *Analects* 17.4 (not in this volume) as using music to instruct people in the Way.

shsh-shsh? In the mountain vales there are great trees a hundred spans around with knots like noses, like mouths, like ears, like sockets, like rings, like mortars, like ditches, like gullies. Gurgling, humming, hooting, whistling, shouting, shrieking, moaning, gnashing! The leaders sing 'Eeeeeeh!' The followers sing 'Ooooooh!' In a light breeze it's a little chorus, but in a gusty wind it's a huge orchestra. And when the violent winds are over, the ten thousand holes are empty. Haven't you witnessed the brouhaha?"

Ziyou said, "So the pipes of earth are those holes, and the pipes of people are bamboo flutes. May I ask about the pipes of Heaven?"

Master Dapple said, "Blowing the ten thousand differences, making each be itself and all choose themselves—who provokes it? Does Heaven turn? Does earth stay still? Do the sun and moon vie for position? Who is in charge here? Who pulls the strings? Who sits with nothing to do, gives it a push and sets it in motion? Do you think it's locked in motion and can't be stopped? Or do you think it's spinning out of control and can't slow itself down? Do the clouds make the rain? Or does the rain make the clouds? Who rumbles all this out? Who sits there with nothing to do and takes perverse delight in egging it on? The wind rises in the north—now west, now east, now dilly-dallying up above. Who huffs and puffs it? Who sits with nothing to do and blows it? May I ask the cause?"[17]

> Big knowledge is unbounded,
> Little knowledge is unbound.
> Big talk is unstoppable,
> Little talk doesn't stop.

> In sound sleep, spirits mingle,
> On waking, bodies open out.
> They greet and grapple,
> And use their minds all day to struggle.

The humble ones, the high ones, the hidden ones: the little fears panic, the big fears calm.

> They fly like an arrow from a bow—
> that's the way they guard their rights and wrongs.

---

[17]I follow Graham in importing the final lines of this passage, from "Does Heaven turn?" to the end, from a later chapter.

They stick like they'd sworn an oath—
that's the way they hold to victory.

They die like fall and winter—
that describes their daily deterioration.

They drown—
and what makes it happen can't bring them back.

They're sated as though sealed—
that describes their stagnation.

As the mind nears death, nothing can bring it back to vitality.

Happiness, anger, despair, joy, planning, sighing,
bending, freezing, elegance, ease, candor, posturing—

It's music out of emptiness!
Mist condensing into mushrooms!

Day and night they alternate in front of us without our knowing where they sprout from. Enough! Enough! Morning and evening we've got them, wherever they come from.

Without them there would not be me,
Without me there would be nothing to choose.

This is close. But no one knows what makes it like this. It seems as though there is a true master, but you can't get a glimpse of it. In our actions we take the self on faith, but we can't see its form. There is essence but no form.

The hundred bones, the nine orifices, the six organs all exist together. Which do I think of as closest to me? Do you like them all? Or do you have a favorite? If so, are the rest its servants and concubines? Can't servants and concubines rule among themselves? Can they take turns being lord and servant? But if there is a true lord among them, whether I find its *qing* 情, "essence," or not makes no difference to its truth.

Once you take a complete form, you don't forget it until the end. Clashing with things and rubbing against them, the race is run at a gallop and nothing can stop it. Isn't it sad? Your whole life slaving away and never seeing the completion of your labors. Exhausted, you drudge and slave away without knowing where to turn for rest. Can you not mourn? People say they are not dead, but what difference does it make? Your form changes and your mind goes with it. Can you tell me that's not mournful? Is everyone's life really this confused? Or am I the only one confused and not other people?

If a made-up mind counts as a teacher, then who doesn't have a teacher? Why should it just be the self-chosen experts on the order of things who have them? Stupid people would have them, too. But to have right and wrong before you've made up your mind—that's like leaving for Yue today and getting there yesterday! That's like saying what isn't is. What isn't is? Even the spiritual sage Yu couldn't make sense of that. How could I?

Saying is not just blowing. Saying says something. But if what it says is not fixed, then does it really say anything? Or does it say nothing? We think it is different from the peeping of fledglings. But is there really any difference or isn't there? How is the Way obscured that there are true and false? How are words obscured that there are *shi* 是, "right," and *fei* 非, "wrong"? Where can you go that the Way does not exist? How can words exist and not be okay? The Way is obscured by small completions. Words are obscured by glory and show. So we have the rights and wrongs of the Confucians and the Mohists. Each calls right what the other calls wrong and each calls wrong what the other calls right. But if you want to right their wrongs and wrong their rights, it's better to throw them open to the light.

> There is nothing that cannot be looked at that way.
> There is nothing that cannot be looked at this way.
> But that is not the way I see things;
> Only as I know things myself do I know them.

Hence it is said, "*Bi* 彼, 'that,' comes from *shi* 是, 'this,' and this follows from that." This is the doctrine of the parallel birth of "this" and "that." Even so, born together they die together. Dying together they are born together. If they are both okay, they are both not okay. If they are both not okay, they are both okay. If they are right in a way, they are wrong in a way. If they are wrong in a way, they are right in a way. For this reason the sage does not follow this route but illuminates things with Heaven's light.[18] He

---

[18] Translating the word for "Heaven" as "nature," this line could be read, "lets them shine by their natural light."

just goes along with things. What is this is also that, and what is that is also this. That is both right and wrong. This is also both right and wrong. So is there really a this and a that? Or isn't there any this or that? The place where neither this nor that finds its counterpart is called the pivot of the Way. Once the pivot finds its socket it can respond endlessly. What's right is endless. And what's wrong is endless, too. This is why I say it's better to throw them open to the light.

Making a point to show that a point is not a point is not as good as making a nonpoint to show that a point is not a point. Using a horse to show that a horse is not a horse is not as good as using a nonhorse to show that a horse is not a horse.[19] Heaven and earth are one point, the ten thousand things are one horse. *using language to undermine language*

Okay? Okay. Not okay? Not okay. A way is made by walking it. A thing is so by calling it. How is it so? In so-ing it, it is so. How is it not so? In not-so-ing it, it is not so. There is always a way in which things are so. There is always a way in which things are okay. There is nothing that is not so, nothing that is not okay. You can insist that it is a twig or a pillar, a freak or the beautiful Xi Shi.[20] No matter how diverse or strange, the Way comprehends them as one. Their division is their completion and their completion is their ruin. But nothing is completed or injured when they are again comprehended as one. Only the penetrating person knows to comprehend them as one. Don't insist but lodge in the usual. The usual is useful. You can use it to penetrate. When you penetrate, you get it. Get it and you're almost there. Just go along with things. Doing that without knowing how things are is what I call the Way.

But exhausting the spirit trying to illuminate the unity of things without knowing that they are all the same is called "three in the morning." What do I mean by "three in the morning"? When the monkey trainer was passing out nuts he said, "You get three in the morning and four at night." The monkeys were all angry. "All right," he said, "you get four in the morning and three at night." The monkeys were all pleased. With no loss in name or substance, he made use of their joy and anger because he went along with them. So the sage harmonizes people with right and wrong and rests them on Heaven's wheel. This is called walking two roads.

---

[19]A reference to the "School of Names" thinker Gongsun Long. For more, see *Important Figures* and *Important Terms*.

[20]Xi Shi was a legendary beauty sent by the king of Yue to marry the king of Wu, spy on him, and help overthrow his kingdom.

In olden days, people's knowledge got somewhere. Where did it get? There were those who thought there had never been anything. Perfect! Done! There was nothing to add. Next were those who thought there were things but never any boundaries. Next were those who thought there were boundaries but never any right or wrong. The Way is lost in the glorification of right and wrong. The Way is lost in the completion of love. But are there such things as loss and completion? Or are there no such things as loss and completion? Loss and completion—that's Master Bright Works playing his lute. No loss and no completion—that's Master Bright Works not playing his lute. Bright Works playing his lute, Shi Kuang holding his baton, Huizi leaning on his desk: the knowledge of these three masters was almost perfect, and they passed their successes on to later years. What they liked they tried to set apart from other things. What they liked they tried to illuminate. But they only succeeded in illuminating the other things and so ended in a paradoxical gloom. Their followers ended up tangled in the string of works and were incomplete their whole lives. If this counts as completion, then we are all complete, too. If this doesn't count as completion, then none of us have ever been complete. So the torch of slippery doubt is what the sage steers by. Don't insist, but lodge in the usual: this is what I mean by throwing things open to the light.

Now suppose I say something here. I don't know whether it fits into your category or not. But in terms of the category that includes both things that fit and things that don't, it's no different from anything else. Nonetheless, let me try saying it:

> There is a beginning. There is a not-yet beginning to be a beginning. There is a not-yet beginning to be a not-yet beginning to be a beginning.

> There is something. There is nothing. There is a not-yet beginning to be nothing. There is a not-yet beginning to be a not-yet beginning to be nothing. Suddenly there is nothing. But then I don't know whether nothing is or isn't.

Now I've said something, but I don't know if what I've said meant anything or not.

> Nothing in the world is bigger than the tip of an autumn hair[21] but Grand Mountain is small. No one lives longer than a dead

---

[21]An animals' hair is most fine (and hence thin) during the autumn.

child and Peng Zu died young. Heaven and earth were born alongside me, and the ten thousand things and I are one.

If we're already one, can I say it? But since I've just said we're one, can I not say it? The unity and my saying it make two. The two and their unity make three. Starting from here, even a clever mathematician couldn't get it, much less an ordinary person! If going from nothing to something you get three, what about going from something to something? Don't do it! Just go along with things.

The Way has never been bounded, words have never been constant. Insist on it and there are boundary-paths. Let me describe these paths. There is left. There is right. There are relations. There is righteousness. There are divisions. There are debates. There is competition. There is contention. These are called the eight Virtues. The sage acknowledges what is beyond the six dimensions but does not discuss it. He discusses what is within the six dimensions but does not deliberate on it. He deliberates on the springs and autumns of successive generations and the records of former kings but does not debate about them. Divisions have something they do not divide. Debates have something they do not debate. "What?" you ask. The sage clasps it to his bosom while ordinary people debate to show it off. Hence it is said, "Debate leaves something undiscriminated."

The great Way is not announced.
The great debate is not spoken.
Great benevolence is not benevolent.
Great modesty is not reserved.
Great courage is not aggressive.

A way that shines does not lead.
Words in debate do not reach.
Benevolence that is constant is not complete.
Modesty that is pure is not trustworthy.
Courage that is aggressive is not complete.

These five are round but almost square. Therefore knowledge that stops at what it does not know is perfect. Who knows the unspoken distinction, the unled Way? If you could know it, it would be called the store of Heaven. Pour into it and it does not fill up, draw from it and it does not run dry. Not knowing where it comes from, it is called the shaded glow.

Once Yao said to Shun, "I want to attack Zong, Guai, and Xu-ao. I sit on my throne and it bothers me. Why is this?"[22]

Shun said, "These three small states still dwell among the underbrush. Why are you bothered? Once ten suns came out together and the ten thousand things were all illuminated. Shouldn't Virtue be better than ten suns?"[23]

Gaptooth asked Royal Relativity,[24] "Do you know what all things agree upon as right?"

Royal Relativity said, "How could I know that?"

"Do you know that you don't know it?"

"How could I know that?"

"Doesn't anyone know anything?!"

"How could I know that? But even so, suppose I tried saying something. How could I possibly know that when I say I know something, I don't not know it? How could I possibly know that when I say I don't know something, I don't know it?[25] Let me try asking you something. If people sleep in the damp, their backs hurt and they wake half paralyzed. But is this true of an eel? If they live in trees they shudder with fear. But is this true of a monkey? Of these three, then, which knows the right place to live? People eat the flesh of cattle, deer eat fodder, maggots like snakes, and hawks enjoy mice. Of these four, which knows the right taste? Monkeys take baboons as partners, deer befriend elk, and eels consort with fish. People say that Mao-qiang and Lady Li are beautiful. But if fish saw them they would dive deep, if birds saw them they would fly high, and if deer saw them they would cut and run. Of these four, which knows beauty rightly? From where I see it,

[22]Three backward states that resisted Yao's authority. To see why this bothered him, consider *Analects* 2.1 and 12.19.

[23]The *Huainanzi* tells us that the ten suns were too bright, so nine had to be shot down by the archer Yi. Shun's point is that, rather than insist on enlightening these backward states himself, the Virtuous path would be to allow them to find their own way naturally. He is advocating "the shaded glow," "illuminating things with Heaven's light" rather than one's own.

[24]The second character in this name, Ni, means end or extreme. Elsewhere, in a portion of the text not translated here, Zhuangzi argues that extremes are extreme only relative to one another: the small is small only in comparison to the large, etc., hence the current translation. Later on, Zhuangzi will speak of "harmonizing things by means of Heaven's relativity," that is, taking advantage of their sameness in difference, like the monkey trainer.

[25]Cf. *Analects* 2.17 (not in this volume): "To say that you know when you do know and that you don't when you don't is knowledge."

the sprouts of benevolence and righteousness and the pathways of right and wrong are all snarled and jumbled.[26] How would I know the difference between them?"

Gaptooth said, "If you don't know gain from loss, do perfected people know?"[27]

Royal Relativity said, "Perfected people are spiritual. Though the lowlands burn, they are not hot. Though the He and the Han rivers freeze, they are not cold. When furious lightning splits the mountains and winds thrash the sea, they are not scared. People like this mount the clouds and mists, straddle the sun and moon, and roam beyond the four seas. Death and life make no difference to them, how much less the sprouts of benefit and harm!"

Master Nervous Magpie asked Master Long Desk, "I heard from my teacher, Kongzi, that the sage does not make it his business to attend to affairs. He does not seek gain or avoid loss. He does not enjoy being sought out and does not follow any Way. Saying nothing he says something, saying something he says nothing, and he wanders outside the floating dust. My teacher thought this was wild talk, but I thought it captured the mysterious Way. What do you think about it?"

Master Long Desk said, "This would make Huang Di's ears ring. How could Kongzi understand it? But you're getting ahead of yourself. You see an egg and listen for the rooster's crow. You see a bow and expect roast owl. I'm going to try saying some crazy things to you, and you listen crazily— how about it? Flank the sun and moon, embrace space and time, and meet like lips, settling in the slippery murk where servants exalt each other. Ordinary people slave away, while the sage is stupid and simple, participating in ten thousand ages and unifying them in complete simplicity. The ten thousand things are as they are, and so are jumbled together.

"How do I know that loving life is not a mistake? How do I know that hating death is not like a lost child forgetting its way home? Lady Li was the daughter of the border guard of Ai. When the duke of Jin got her, her tears fell until they soaked her collar. But once she reached the royal palace,

---

[26] Cf. "sprouts of benevolence and righteousness" (*ren yi zhi duan* 仁義之端) with *Mengzi* 2A6.

[27] "Gain" (利 *li*) and "loss" (害 *hai*) are important terms for Mozi—who thinks of them as "benefit" and "harm," respectively—and Mengzi, who contrasts *li*, in the sense of "profit," with *yi* 義, "righteousness."

slept in the king's bed, and ate the meats of his table, she regretted her tears. How do I know that the dead don't regret that they ever longed for life?[28]

"One who dreams of drinking wine may weep in the morning. One who dreams of weeping may go for a hunt the next day. In the dream, you don't know it's a dream. In the middle of a dream, you may interpret a dream within it. Only after waking do you know it was a dream. Still, there may be an even greater awakening after which you know that this, too, was just a greater dream. But the stupid ones think they are awake and confidently claim to know it. Are they rulers? Are they herdsmen? Really?! Kongzi and you are both dreaming. And in saying you are dreaming, I am dreaming, too. These words might be called a puzzle. But if after ten thousand generations we encounter a single sage who knows the solution, it would be no different from what we encounter every morning and evening."

Once you and I have started arguing, if you win and I lose, then are you really right and am I really wrong? If I win and you lose, then am I really right and are you really wrong? Is one of us right and the other one wrong? Or are both of us right and both of us wrong? If you and I can't understand one another, then other people will certainly be even more in the dark. Whom shall we get to set us right? Shall we get someone who agrees with you to set us right? But if they already agree with you how can they set us right? Shall we get someone who agrees with me to set us right? But if they already agree with me, how can they set us right? Shall we get someone who disagrees with both of us to set us right? But if they already disagree with both of us, how can they set us right? Shall we get someone who agrees with both of us to set us right? But if they already agree with both of us, how can they set us right? If you and I and they all can't understand each other, should we wait for someone else?

Shifting voices waiting on one another may just as well not wait on one another. Harmonize them by means of Heaven's relativity, orient them with the flowing flood, and so live out your years. Forget the years, forget righteousness, but be stirred by the limitless and lodge within it. What do I mean by "harmonize them by means of Heaven's relativity"? I mean right is not right, so is not so. If right were really right, it would be so different from not-

---

[28]Lady Li, a legendary beauty and villain, was born a member of the non-Chinese Rong people living to the north and west of China. She was given as a hostage to Duke Xian of Jin (r. 676–651 B.C.E.), became his concubine, estranged him from his wife and legitimate heirs, and wreaked havoc in the kingdom. She is an ambiguous figure: a barbarian in China, beautiful yet dangerous. Zhuangzi compounds the ambiguity by retelling the story from her perspective.

right that there would be no room for argument. If so were really so, then it would be so different from not-so that there would be no room for argument.

Penumbra said to Shadow, "First you walk and then you stop. First you sit and then you rise. Why are you so restless?"

Shadow said, "Do I depend on something to be the way I am? Does what I depend on also depend on something to be the way it is? Does a snake depend on its scales to move or a cicada on its wings to fly? How should I know why I am this way? How should I know why I'm not otherwise?"

One night, Zhuangzi dreamed of being a butterfly—a happy butterfly, showing off and doing as he pleased, unaware of being Zhuangzi. Suddenly he awoke, drowsily, Zhuangzi again. And he could not tell whether it was Zhuangzi who had dreamt the butterfly or the butterfly dreaming Zhuangzi. But there must be some difference between them! This is called "the transformation of things."

Chapter Three: The Key to Nourishing Life

Life is bounded. Knowledge is unbounded. Using the bounded to follow the unbounded is dangerous. And if you take that as knowledge, that's really dangerous! If you do good, avoid fame. If you do bad, avoid punishment. Follow the middle line and you can protect yourself, complete your life, raise your family, and finish your years.

A butcher was cutting up an ox for Lord Wenhui.[29] Wherever his hand touched, wherever his shoulder leaned, wherever his foot stepped, wherever his knee pushed—with a zip! with a whoosh!—he handled his chopper with aplomb, and never skipped a beat. He moved in time to the *Dance of the Mulberry Forest,* and harmonized with the *Head of the Line Symphony.*[30] Lord Wenhui said, "Ah, excellent, that technique can reach such heights!"

---

[29]This is the same King Hui who gave Huizi the seeds to the giant gourds in *Zhuangzi*, chapter 1, p. 208, and who speaks with Mengzi in *Mengzi* 1A1 and 1A3. This story may be a parody of *Mengzi* 1A7, substituting a lesson on butchery for one on compassion.

[30]The *Dance of the Mulberry Forest* celebrates Tang's victory over Jie and the founding of the Shang dynasty. The *Head of the Line Symphony* is part of a larger corpus known as the *Whole Pond Music* commemorating the reign of Yao. The spontaneous harmony of the butcher's movements with traditional music may suggest the inner compatibility of Zhuangzi's Daoism with Confucianism. Cf. *Mengzi* 4A27.

The butcher sheathed his chopper and responded, "What your servant values is the Way, which goes beyond technique. When I first began cutting up oxen, I did not see anything but oxen. Three years later, I couldn't see the whole ox. And now, I encounter them with spirit and don't look with my eyes. Sensible knowledge stops and spiritual desires proceed. I rely on the Heavenly patterns, strike in the big gaps, am guided by the large fissures, and follow what is inherently so. I never touch a ligament or tendon, much less do any heavy wrenching! A good butcher changes his chopper every year because he chips it. An average butcher changes it every month because he breaks it. There are spaces between those joints, and the edge of the blade has no thickness. If you use what has no thickness to go where there is space—oh! there's plenty of extra room to play about in. That's why after nineteen years[31] the blade of my chopper is still as though fresh from the grindstone.

"Still, when I get to a hard place, I see the difficulty and take breathless care. My gaze settles! My movements slow! I move the chopper slightly, and in a twinkling it's come apart, crumbling to the ground like a clod of earth! I stand holding my chopper and glance all around, dwelling on my accomplishment. Then I clean my chopper and put it away."

Lord Wenhui said, "Excellent! I have heard the words of a butcher and learned how to care for life!"

Gongwen Xuan[32] was startled when he saw the Commander of the Right,[33] and he asked "What kind of man is this? What happened to you? Was it Heaven, or was it human?"

The Commander said, "It was Heaven, not human. Heaven makes each thing unique.[34] People try to look alike. That's how I know it was Heaven, not human. The marsh pheasant has to go ten steps for a peck, a hundred

---

[31]For the significance of this period of time, see the *Mozi*, chapter 31, p. 92, n. 60.

[32]Nothing is known about this person, though the name does not appear to be fictional.

[33]The Comander of the Right indicates the supreme military commander.

[34]The word for "unique" can also mean "one-footed," so the suggestion is that the Commander is missing a foot. Gongwen's question asks whether he was born that way or lost it later. Amputations, tattoos, and death were common punishments not just for crimes but for bad political advice, and even for good advice that the ruler did not want to hear, and hence were considered indicative of moral as well as physical deformity. Zhuangzi's stories of criminals, cripples, and outcasts, therefore, address the same theme as the abstract discussions of perfection, completion, and wholeness.

steps for a drink. But it doesn't want to be pampered in a cage. It does the spirit no good even to be king."

When Laozi died, Qin Shih[35] went to mourn him, cried three times, and left. A student asked, "Weren't you our teacher's friend?"

"Yes."

"Then is it okay for you to mourn him this way?"

"Yes. At first I thought these were his people, but now I see they are not. When I went in earlier, there were old ones crying as though for a child, and young ones as though for their mothers. The one who gathered them here did not want them to talk, but they talk. He did not want them to cry, but they cry. They've run from Heaven, denied their essence, forgotten what they received, and hence suffer what used to be called 'the punishment for running from Heaven.'[36] Our teacher came because it was time and left when it had passed. If you are content with the time and abide by the passing, there's no room for sorrow or joy. This is what they used to call 'the divine release.' You can point to the exhausted fuel. But the flame has passed on, and no one knows where it will end."

Chapter Four: The Human Realm

Yan Hui asked Kongzi for permission to make a trip.[37]

"Where are you going?" he said.

"To Wei."

"What will you do there?"

"I have heard that the lord of Wei is young and willful. He trifles with his state and does not acknowledge his mistakes. He is so careless with people's lives that the dead fill the state like falling leaves in a swamp.[38] The people have nowhere to turn. I have heard my teacher say, 'Leave the well-governed state and go to the chaotic one. There are plenty of sick people at the doctor's door.' I want to use what I have learned to think of a way the state may be saved."

---

[35]Nothing is known about this person, though the name does not appear to be fictional.

[36]Cf. *Analects* 3.13 (not in this volume): "When you commit a crime against Heaven, there is nowhere you can turn."

[37]Yan Hui, also known as Yan Yuan, was Kongzi's favorite and most promising student; he died young. See *Analects* 5.9, 6.3, 6.7, and 6.11.

[38]This is probably Duke Chu, who first ruled in Wei from 492 to 481 B.C.E.

Kongzi said, "Sheesh! You're just going to get yourself hurt. The Way does not like complexity. Complexity quickly becomes too much. Too much leads to agitation, agitation leads to worry, and worry never solved anything. The perfect people of olden times first found it in themselves before looking for it in others. If what you've found in yourself isn't settled yet, what leisure can you spare for this bully's behavior?

"Do you know how Virtue is squandered and where knowledge comes from? Virtue is squandered in fame, and knowledge arises from struggle. People use fame to trample each other and knowledge as a weapon. Both of them are tools of ill-fortune, not the means of finishing your mission.

"Though your Virtue is deep and your faith strong, you have not comprehended the man's *qi* 氣. You've got a reputation for not being contentious, but you have not comprehended the man's mind. If you insist on parading standards of benevolence and righteousness before this bully, you will just make him look bad in comparison to you. That's antagonism, and one who antagonizes others is sure to be antagonized in return. You don't want to antagonize him!

"Or suppose he likes worthy people and dislikes the depraved, then what use is there in changing him? Better not to speak! Kings and dukes love to dominate people and force their submission. He'll want to dazzle you, intimidate you, tongue-tie you, cue you, and persuade you. Trying to reform this kind of person is like piling fire on fire or water on water. It's called 'adding to the excessive.' Your initial compliance will know no end until he no longer trusts your good word. You will surely die at this bully's hands. . . .

"Even so, you must have a plan. Come, tell me about it!"

Yan Hui said, "Suppose I am upright but dispassionate, energetic but not divisive. Would that work?"

"No! How could that work?" said Kongzi. "You'd use all your energy to sustain the performance, and your face would be unsettled. Other people can't stand that, so they have to resist what you suggest in order to ease their own minds. If gradual Virtue wouldn't work, how much less such a great show of force! He'll dig in his heels and resist change. Though he may seem well disposed on the outside, on the inside he'll never consider it. How could that work?"

Yan Hui said, "Then how about being inwardly straight and outwardly bending, having integrity but conforming to my superiors? By being inwardly straight, I could follow Heaven. As a follower of Heaven, I would know that even the Son of Heaven and I are both children of Heaven. If I speak only for myself, why worry about the approval or disapproval of other people? I could be what people call childlike, which is what I mean by being a follower of Heaven.

"By being outwardly bending, I could follow other people. Lifting the ceremonial tablets, kneeling, bending, bowing—this is the etiquette of a minister. Others do it, why shouldn't I? As long as I do what other people do, who can complain? This is what I mean by following people.

"Having integrity and conforming to superiors, one follows olden times. My words, whether they are in fact instructions or even criticisms, belong to antiquity; they are not my own. This way one can be straightforward without causing injury. This is what I mean by following olden times. Would that work?"

Kongzi said, "No! How could that work? You have too many policies. You are planning without reconnaissance. Even if you succeeded in avoiding blame, it would stop there. How could you hope to change him? You're still making the mind your teacher."

Yan Hui said, "I have nothing else to offer. May I ask what to do?"

Kongzi said, "You must fast! Let me explain. Is it easy to do anything with your mind? If you think it is, bright Heaven will not approve."

Yan Hui said, "My family is poor. Indeed, I have not drunk wine or eaten any meat for months. Can this be considered fasting?"

Kongzi said, "That is the fasting one does before a sacrifice, not the fasting of the mind."

"May I ask about fasting of the mind?"

"Unify your *zhi* 志, 'plans.' Do not listen with your ears but listen with your mind. Do not listen with your mind but listen with your *qi*. Listening stops with the ear. The mind stops with signs. *Qi* is empty and waits on external things. Only the Way gathers in emptiness. Emptiness is the fasting of the mind."[39]

Yan Hui said, "Prior to receiving this instruction, I was full of thoughts of Hui. But having applied it, it's as though Hui never existed. Is this what you mean by emptiness?"

The Master said, "Perfect. Let me tell you. You can go wander in his cage without being moved by his fame. If you're getting through, sing. If not,

---

[39]In *Mengzi* 2A2, Mengzi criticizes Gaozi for suggesting that the mind must conform itself to words, i.e., doctrine. Here Zhuangzi has Kongzi disagreeing with both of them by saying that both the mind and words must be guided by *qi*.

stop. No schools. No prescriptions. Dwell in unity and lodge in what cannot be helped, and you're almost there.

"To stop leaving tracks is easy. Not to walk upon the ground is hard.[40] It's easy to fake what people do. Faking what Heaven does is hard. You've heard of using wings to fly, but not of using no wings to fly. You've heard of using knowledge to know, but not of using no knowledge to know. Look up at the hole in the wall that fills the empty room with light. The blessed stop stopping. Not stopping means galloping while you sit. If you let the ears and the eyes communicate with the inside and banish knowledge outside the mind, then even ghosts and spirits will come to dwell. Why not men? This is the transformation of ten thousand things, the secret of the ancient sages, not to mention ordinary people!"

Zigao, the Duke of She,[41] was sent to Qi. He said to Kongzi, "The king is putting me on a high-priority mission. Qi treats emissaries very well, but never hurries. You can't budge an ordinary person along, much less a feudal lord! I'm already shaking. You've always told me, 'Few tasks of whatever size are completed happily except by means of the Way. If you don't complete it, you'll be in trouble with other people. If you do complete it, you'll have trouble with your own *yin* and *yang*.[42] Only someone of Virtue can avoid trouble in success and failure alike.' I'm the kind of person who eats simply and sparingly so my diet doesn't give me indigestion. But I received my orders in the morning and by evening I was drinking ice-water. I'm burning up inside! I haven't even started on the actual job yet and I'm already having trouble with *yin* and *yang*; if the mission doesn't succeed, then I'll also be in trouble with other people. I lose both ways! I can't handle the responsibility of taking on this assignment. Do you have anything you can tell me?"

---

[40]Cf. Zhuangzi's criticism of Liezi in *Zhuangzi*, chapter 1, p. 206, "though he manages to avoid walking, he still relies on something."

[41]The Duke of She was an influential politician in the state of Chu in the early fifth century B.C.E. The *Zuozhuan* describes him as an advocate of the Confucian principle of government by Virtue instead of force who later made good on his word by returning power to the rightful ruler when he was in a position to take over militarily. He and Kongzi spoke about politics and disagreed politely over the priority of obligations to the family and to the state. See *Analects* 7.19, 13.16, and 13.18.

[42]Success achieved in the wrong way harms a person internally. Good health requires a balanced harmony between the *yin* and *yang*. See *yin* and *yang* under *Important Terms*.

Kongzi said, "In this world, there are two great concerns. One is destiny. One is righteousness. Children's love for their family is destiny:[43] you can't undo it in your mind. The service of subjects for their rulers is righteousness: there is nowhere you can go and not have rulers, nowhere you can escape between Heaven and earth. These are great concerns. To serve your family, wherever they go, is the perfection of filial piety. To serve your rulers, whatever they ask, is the height of loyalty. To serve your own mind, so that sorrow and joy aren't constantly revolving in front of you, knowing what you can't do anything about and accepting it as though it were destiny, is the perfection of Virtue. As a subject or a child, there will certainly be things you can't avoid. As long as you stick to the actual job and forget about yourself, what leisure do you have to love life or hate death? You'll be able to do it.

"Let me tell you something else I've heard. In relationships, when people are close together, they generate trust through regular contact. When they are far apart, they have to establish loyalty with words, and words require communication. Communicating the words of two happy or two angry people is the hardest thing in the world. Two happy people inevitably exaggerate the good. Two angry people inevitably exaggerate the bad. But any exaggeration is false, and falsehood destroys trust. That's when communication becomes dangerous. So the *Model Sayings*[44] have it, 'Communicate the real essence; don't communicate exaggerated words.' Then you might come out whole.

"When people pit their strength in games of skill, they start out bright like *yang* but usually end dark as *yin*. They get up to more strange tricks the longer they go. People drinking wine at a ceremony start out orderly enough but usually end in chaos. The party gets stranger the longer it lasts. Everything is like this. What starts out clean usually ends up dirty. What starts out simple inevitably turns unsupportable.

"Words are like wind and waves. Actions fulfill or disappoint them. Wind and waves are easily moved, and fulfillment and disappointment easily lead to danger. Rage has no other source but clever words and one-sided language.[45] As the hunt draws to a close, the dying animal doesn't choose its sounds but snorts its breath furiously, breeding a similar madness in the

---

[43]The word translated here as "destiny" is translated as "orders" in the previous paragraph. In both cases, the character in question is *ming* 命 ("fate" or "mandate"). See *ming* under *Important Terms*.

[44]Another probably fanciful "classical source."

[45]That is, what matters most is not what people do, but what they say, since it is the words that give the actions meaning.

minds of its hunters. Pushing hard toward the conclusion makes people vicious without their knowing it. And if they don't know it, who knows how it will end? So the *Model Sayings* have it, 'Don't change your orders. Don't strive for completion. Anything over the line is too much.' Changing your orders and striving for completion are dangerous business. A fine completion takes a long time, and a bad one cannot be changed. Can you afford not to be careful?

"Harness things so your heart can wander. Nourish your middle by accepting what cannot be avoided: that's perfection. What is there for you to do in return? Nothing is as good as fulfilling your destiny.[46] That's as hard as it gets." . . .

Splay-limb Shu's chin is sunk in his belly. His shoulders are above his head, pinched together so they point at the sky. His five organs are on top, his thighs tight against his ribs. Plying a needle and taking in laundry he makes enough to fill his mouth. Winnowing leftover grain he gets enough to feed ten people. When the people in charge are calling out troops, Splay-limb wanders among them waving goodbye. When they are press-ganging workers he is exempted as a chronic invalid. When they dole out grain to the sick, he gets three measures, and ten bundles of firewood. With splayed limbs, he is still able to keep himself alive and to live out the years Heaven gave him. What if he had splayed Virtue? . . .

Chapter Five: Signs of Abundant Virtue

In Lu there was an amputee named Royal Nag who had as many followers as Kongzi. Chang Ji[47] asked Kongzi, "Royal Nag is an amputee, yet you and he divide Lu for students. He doesn't stand and teach or sit and discuss, yet they go to him empty and come home full. Can there be teaching without words or a developed mind in a deformed body? What kind of person is he?"

Kongzi said, "He is a sage. I'm just running late and haven't been to see him yet. And if I intend to make him my teacher, is it surprising that others do? Forget about Lu; I'm going to lead the whole world to follow him."

---

[46]"Fulfilling destiny" could also be translated "following orders."

[47]Nothing is known about this person, though the name does not appear to be fictional. He may be connected to the Ji clan, the most powerful of the Three Families that ruled Lu for most of Kongzi's lifetime, reducing the Duke of Lu to little more than a figurehead.

Chang Ji said, "If that amputee can lord it over you, he must be far from ordinary. Someone like that must have a special way of thinking."

Kongzi said, "Death and life are big, but they make no difference to him. Heaven and earth could flip over, and it would not matter to him. He peers into the falseless and does not shift with things. He considers it destiny that they should change and holds on to their ancestor."

Chang Ji said, "What does that mean?"

Kongzi said, "Looked at from their differences, liver and gall are as far apart as the states of Chu and Yue. Looked at from their sameness, the ten thousand things are all one. Someone like him does not know what is appropriate for his ears and eyes but lets his mind wander in the harmony of Virtue. He looks at the way things are one and does not see what they're missing. He looks at losing a foot like shaking off dust."

Chang Ji said, "For his own sake he uses knowledge to gain control of his mind and uses control of his mind to achieve a constant mind. But why should others make so much of him?"

Kongzi said, "People don't mirror themselves in moving water, they mirror themselves in still water.[48] Only the still can still the crowd's stillness. Of those that receive their destiny on earth, only the pine and cypress are green winter and summer. Of those that receive their destiny from Heaven, only the sages Yao and Shun are proper. Those fortunate enough to correct their own lives can correct the lives of the crowd. The proof of guarding the beginning is the fact of not being nervous. A brave soldier will boldly go against the nine armies. If someone can risk his life like this for fame, how much more so one whose palace is Heaven and earth and whose treasure is the ten thousand things, one who only lodges in the form, treats hearing and sight as images, unifies what knowledge knows, and whose mind never tastes death? He will pick his day to transcend the falseness, which is why people follow him. Why would he be willing to make mere things his business?" . . .

Duke Ai of Lu[49] asked Kongzi, "There was an ugly man in Wei named Sad Nag. Men hung around with him. They thought about him all the time and couldn't tear themselves away. Women saw him and by the dozen they vowed to their parents that they'd rather be his concubine than another man's wife. No one ever heard him sing the lead, all he ever did was harmonize with oth-

[48]Cf. *Xunzi*, chapter 21, p. 277.

[49]Duke Ai (r. 494–468 B.C.E.) is depicted asking questions of Kongzi and his disciples in several passages in the *Analects*. For example, see *Analects* 6.3 and 12.9.

ers. He had no lordly status to save people from death, no piles of wealth to fill their bellies, and he was ugly enough to shock the world. He harmonized without singing and knew nothing beyond his own borders, but cocks and hens coupled in his presence. There had to be something special about him! So We summoned him for an audience, and he really was ugly enough to shock the world. He stayed with Us, and before a month was out We took an interest in his personality. By the time a year passed, We trusted him. Since the state had no minister, We put him in charge. He looked glum and faltered, as though he might even decline. We were embarrassed but eventually got him to take it. Before long, however, he abandoned Us. We were crushed, as though We'd lost a loved one, as though there was no one to enjoy the state with. What kind of man was this?"

Kongzi said, "I was once sent to Chu. On the way I saw piglets feeding at their dead mother. After a while, they all blinked and ran off. They didn't see themselves in her, didn't find their kind. What they loved was their mother—not her form, but what moved her form. When someone dies in battle, his people don't bother with medals at his burial. An amputee's old shoes mean nothing to him. Both have lost the root. Women of the imperial retinue don't pare their nails or pierce their ears. A married man is sent on no more outside missions. When we do this to keep the form whole, how much more should we do to keep Virtue whole! Now this Sad Nag was trusted before he spoke and was loved though he accomplished nothing. He got people to give him their own states and worry he wouldn't take them! He must have completed the potential, though his Virtue took no form."

Duke Ai asked, "What do you mean by completing the potential?"

Kongzi said, "Death, life, survival, loss, failure, success, poverty, wealth, worth, depravity, slander, praise, hunger, thirst, winter, summer—their change is the process of destiny. Day and night they alternate in front of us, but knowledge cannot measure their beginning. Don't let them slip out of harmony or penetrate the spirit store. Indulge them harmoniously. Let them circulate without leaking away. Day and night, without a break, make it springtime with things. As you greet each new circumstance, generate the season in your own mind. This is what I mean by completing the potential."

"What do you mean by Virtue taking no form?"

"Levelness is the height of still water, so it can be used as a standard.[50] Hold it from within and it will not be disturbed from without. Virtue is

---

[50]Cf. the opening section of chapter 13, p. 237 below.

the cultivation of complete harmony. When Virtue takes no form, things cannot leave it."

Later, Duke Ai told Minzi,[51] "At first when I ruled the empire, I held the reins of the people and worried about their welfare. I thought I had perfected it. Now that I've heard this explanation of the perfect person, I worry that I lacked the real substance and that I damaged the state by neglecting myself. Kongzi and I are not subject and lord, but friends in Virtue." . . .

Where sages wander, knowledge is a curse, restrictions are paste, favors are a patch, and effort is for trade. Sages do not plan, so why do they need knowledge? They do not cut, so why do they need paste? They have nothing to lose, so why do they need favors? They're not buying, so why do they need trade? In these four ways they feed at Heaven. Feeding at Heaven, they are nourished by Heaven. Once they are nourished by Heaven, why do they need other people? They have human form but not human *qing* 情 "essence." Since they have human form, they flock with people. Since they lack human essence, right and wrong do not get to them. Infinitesimally small, they flock with people. Indescribably large, they complete their Heaven alone.

Huizi asked Zhuangzi, "Can people really have no essence?"

Zhuangzi said, "Yes, they can."

Huizi said, "But if they have no essence, how can you call them 'people'?"

Zhuangzi said, "The Way gave them a face. Heaven gave them a form. How can you not call them 'people'?"

Huizi said, "But if you call them 'people,' how can they have no essence?" "human essence" as the censurable human capacity/tendency to make distinctions"

Zhuangzi said, "Rights and wrongs (*shi/fei* 是 非) are what I mean by 'essence.' By 'no essence,' I mean people not letting in good and bad to hurt them. Follow the natural and do not help life along."[52]

Huizi said, "How can people exist without helping life?"

Zhuangzi said, "The Way gave them a face, Heaven gave them a form— by not letting likes and dislikes in to do harm, that's how. But you shut out your spirit, and tire your energies, leaning on a podium ranting, slumping

---

[51]Min Ziqian is a disciple of Kongzi praised in several passages in the *Analects* that are not included in this volume.

[52]Cf. *Laozi*, chapter 55.

at your desk and napping. Heaven chose a form for you, and you use it to sing disputations![53]

Chapter Six: The Great Ancestral Teacher

To know what Heaven does and to know what humans do is to have reached perfection. Those who know what Heaven does are born of Heaven.[54] Those who know what humans do use what they know they know to nurture what they know they don't know, living out their Heavenly years and not dying along the way. This is the flourishing of knowledge.

Even so, there is a problem. Knowledge depends on something before it can be fitting. But what it depends on has not yet been fixed. So how do I know that what I call "Heaven" is not really human and what I call "human" is not really Heaven? Only when there are true people can we have true knowledge. What do I mean by true people? The true people of olden times did not resist poverty. They did not glory in success. They did not plan their affairs. They could miss without regretting it and hit without being pleased. Such people could climb high without shuddering. They could enter water without getting wet and fire without getting burned. Such is the knowledge that is able to climb up to the Way. . . .

The true people of the olden days knew nothing of loving life and nothing of hating death. They emerged without delight and returned without resistance. They came and went briskly, nothing more. They neither forgot their beginning nor sought their end. They enjoyed what they received, forgot it, and handed it back. This is called not using the mind to block the Way, not using the human to help Heaven. These are called true people. . . .

Hence what they liked was one and what they didn't like was one. Their being one was one and their not being one was one. Seeing it as one, they were followers of Heaven. Seeing it as not one, they were followers of hu-

---

[53]The *qing* 情, "essence," is the underlying truth or fact about a thing, as opposed to its reputation or the opinions people have of it. The "human essence" is understood here as the basic emotions or commitments that give rise to judgments of right and wrong. Cf. *Mengzi* 6A6 and 6A8. Someone without essence would not have no emotions, but would lack preconceptions about what those emotions are.

[54]Translating the word for "Heaven" as "nature," the phrase "born of Heaven" could also be read "live naturally."

manity. When neither Heaven nor humanity wins out over the other, this is called being a true person. . . .

When the springs dry up, the fish are stuck together on the land. They douse each other with spit and spray each other with drool, but it is not as good as forgetting each other in the rivers and lakes. Praising Yao and condemning Jie is not as good as forgetting them both and transforming with the Way. The Big Lump burdens me with a form, labors me with life, eases me with old age, and rests me with death. So if I like my life, for the same reason I must also like my death.

You hide your boat in a gully or your net in a swamp and call them secure. But in the middle of the night a strong man could still take them on his back and leave, and you would be asleep and not know. Hiding the small in the large seems fitting, but still you lose. But if you hid the world in the world, you would have nothing to lose. This is the essence of what lasts. You trespass on human form and still delight in it. As a human, you can change ten thousand times without ever reaching the limit. Can you count the different things that have made you happy? So the sage wanders in what exists everywhere and can't be lost. He likes growing old and he likes dying young. He likes the beginning and he likes the end. People model themselves on the sage. But why not on that to which the ten thousand things are tied and on which every change depends?

The Way has an essence and can be trusted. But it takes no action and has no form. It can be passed on but not received, gotten but not seen. It is its own trunk, its own root. Before Heaven and earth existed, it spiritualized the ghosts and gods, and gave birth to Heaven and earth. It is above the supreme ultimate but not high, below the six limits but not deep. It was born before Heaven and earth but does not age. It is more venerable than high antiquity but is not old.[55] . . .

South Lord Master Flower said to Out-of-step Woman, "You are old in years but have the look of a child. How do you do it?"

She said, "I've heard the Way."

South Lord Master Flower asked, "May I study the Way?"

She said, "How? How could you? You're not the person for it. Buliang Yi had the stuff of a sage but not the way of a sage. I have the way of a sage but not the stuff of a sage. I wanted to teach him, to see if maybe he really could become a sagely person. If not, at least it would be easier to explain

---

[55]Cf. *Laozi*, chapter 25.

the way of a sage to someone with the stuff of a sage. So I stuck with it, explaining it to him for three days, after which he could put the world outside of himself. Once he'd put the world outside, I kept at it. After seven days he could put things outside. Once he'd put things outside, I kept at it. After nine days he could put life outside himself. Once he'd put life outside himself, the light dawned. After the light had dawned, he could see he was alone. Having seen he was alone, he could have no past or present. With no past or present, he was able to enter no living or dying. What kills life does not die; what lives life is not alive. The kind of thing it is—there is nothing it does not see off, nothing it does not greet, nothing it does not ruin, nothing it does not bring to completion. Its name is Disturbing Peace. The Disturbing Peace completes things only after disturbing them."

South Lord Master Flower asked, "Where did you hear it?"

She said, "I heard it from Ink-Aid's son. Ink-Aid's son heard it from Faltering Recitation's grandson. Faltering Recitation's grandson heard it from Looking-up-at-the-light. Looking-up-at-the-light heard it from Whispered Promise. Whispered Promise heard it from Needs Work. Needs Work heard it from Sing "Ooh!" Sing "Ooh!" heard it from Mysterious Darkness. Mysterious Darkness heard it from Present-in-vacancy. Present-in-vacancy heard it from Dubious Beginning."

Master Sacrifice, Master Chariot,[56] Master Plow, and Master Arrive all four spoke together, saying, "Who can take nothing as the head, life as the spine, and death as the tail? Who knows death, life, existence, and annihilation as all the same thing? I'll be that person's friend." All four looked at each other and smiled. There was no resistance in their hearts, and so they became friends.

Suddenly, Master Chariot got sick. Master Sacrifice went to ask after him. "How extraordinary of the maker of things to knot me up like this. My back is hunched out. My organs are all out of order. My chin is hidden in my navel. My shoulders are peaked. And my neck bones point to Heaven." But though his *yin* and *yang qi* were fouled, in his mind there was nothing the matter. He hobbled over to look at his reflection in the well. "Sheesh! The maker of things really is knotting me up."

Master Sacrifice said, "Do you dislike it?"

---

[56] Zi Yu, "Master Chariot," is also the name of Kongzi's disciple Zengzi. Since none of the other names refer to real people, however, it is probably not significant.

He said, "Not at all. What is there to dislike? If, in time, he turns my left arm into rooster, I'll use it to crow the day. If he turns my right arm into a bow, I'll shoot down a dove for roasting. If he turns my buttocks into wheels and my spirit into a horse, I'll climb aboard. What better carriage? You get something when it's time. You lose it when it's passed. If you are content with the time and abide by the passing, there's no room for sorrow or joy. This is what the ancients called 'loosing the bonds.' If you don't loose yourself, things will bind you. Nothing has ever beaten Heaven. What is there to dislike?"

Suddenly Master Arrive got sick. Gasping, he was on the point of death. His wife and children circled around him weeping. Master Plow came to ask after him and said to them, "Stop! Get back! Don't be afraid of the change." Leaning on the door frame he said, "How extraordinary, the one who makes these changes! What will he do with you next? Where will he send you? Will he make you a rat's liver? Will he make you a bug's arm?"

Master Arrive said, "A child goes wherever its parents say—east, west, north, or south. How much more are *yin* and *yang* to a person than parents! If they bring me to the point of death and I refuse to obey, I would only be being stubborn. What fault is it of theirs? The Big Lump burdens me with a form, labors me with life, eases me with old age, and rests me with death. So if I like my life, for the same reason I must also like my death. Suppose a great smith were casting metal. If the metal were to rear up and say 'I insist on being a *Moye*!'[57] the great smith would certainly take it as inauspicious material. If, having once trespassed on the human form, I were to say 'Only a human! Only a human!' then the maker of changes would certainly take me as an inauspicious person. If you take Heaven and earth as a great furnace and the maker of changes as a great smith, then where can you go that will not be all right? I will doze off whole and, drowsily, wake up." . . .

Yan Hui questioned Kongzi, "When Mengsun Cai's mother died he cried without tears.[58] In his inner heart he did not mourn. And conducting the funeral, he did not grieve. With these three lapses, his reputation as a mourner still covers Lu. Is it really possible to gain the name while lacking the substance? I was shocked."

---

[57]*Moye* was the famous sword of King Helü of Wu (514–496 B.C.E.), the smelting of which was said to have required human sacrifices in order to fuse the alloys. The art of metallurgy was endowed with mystical significance, partly because it was dimly understood, and partly also because of the enormous military advantages it conferred upon its possessors.

[58]The Mengsun clan was one of the Three Families that ruled Lu during Kongzi's lifetime, though nothing specific is known of Mengsun Cai.

Kongzi said, "Mengsun is done. He is beyond knowing. He would make it even simpler, but he can't. Still, he did simplify it some. Mengsun does not know why he lives. He does not know why he dies. He's not aware of moving forward. He's not aware of falling back. If he changes into something, he lets the unknown change finish it. When he changes, how does he know he isn't not changing? When he doesn't change, how does he know he hasn't changed already? Take you and me—we're dreaming and haven't woken up! But something can shock his body without harming his mind. He stays here only for a day but feels no death. Mengsun is awake. People cry, so he cries; this is why.

"We say 'I.' But how do I know what I mean by 'I'? You dream you're a bird crossing Heaven or a fish sunk in the depths. There's no telling if the one who speaks now is awake or dreaming. Directing the trip doesn't measure up to smiling, and laughing doesn't measure up to stepping aside. Step aside and leave the changes. Then you will enter the oneness of the vacant sky."

Master Thinker went to see Whence. Whence asked him, "How has Yao rewarded you?"

Master Thinker said, "Yao told me, 'You must submit to benevolence and righteousness to speak clearly about right and wrong.'"

Whence said, "So what did you come here for? Yao's already tattooed your face with benevolence and righteousness and cut off your nose with right and wrong. How can you expect to wander distant, unrestrained, and rolling paths?"

Master Thinker said, "But still, I'd like to wander along the edge."

Whence said, "It's not like that. The blind can't share in the loveliness of faces or the near-sighted in far-off vistas."

Master Thinker said, "But beauties lose their looks and strong men lose their strength. Even Huang Di forgot his knowledge—all in the process of being recast. How do you know the maker of things won't erase my tattoos, replace my nose, and make me whole so I can follow you, sir?"

Whence said, "Ah, you never know! I'll give you the main outlines.

My teacher! My teacher! He orders ten thousand things but is not righteous. He's kind to ten thousand generations but is not benevolent. He's more venerable than high antiquity but is not old. He roofs Heaven, floors earth, and fashions everything between but is not handy. That's how you wander."

Yan Hui said, "I'm improving."

Kongzi said, "How so?"

"I've forgotten benevolence and righteousness."

"Good, but there's more."

Yan Hui saw him again the next day and said, "I'm improving."

"How so?"

"I've forgotten rites and music."

"Good, but there's more."

Yan Hui saw him again the next day and said, "I'm improving."

"How so?"

"I sit and forget."

Kongzi started and said, "What do you mean by 'sit and forget'?"

Yan Hui said, "I cast off my limbs, dismiss hearing and sight, leave my form, abandon knowledge, and unify them in the great comprehension. That's what I mean by 'sit and forget.' "

Kongzi said, "If you've unified them then you have no preferences. If you've changed then you have no constancy. You really are worthy! I would like to ask to be your follower!"[59] . . .

Chapter Seven: The Proper Way for Emperors and Kings

Gaptooth asked Royal Relativity four times and got four "I-don't-know's" in response.[60] Gaptooth jumped up and down, he was so happy, and went to tell Master Reed Coat.

Master Reed Coat said, "You're just learning that now? Shun didn't measure up to the really ancient sages. Shun still stockpiled benevolence in order to win people. He got people, but he never escaped from not-people. Now the really ancient sages—they slept calmly and woke blankly. Sometimes they took themselves for horses. Sometimes they took themselves for cows. Their knowledge of the essence was trustworthy, and their Virtue was exceptionally true. They never entered into not-people." . . .

Don't make a name for yourself or follow a plan. Don't take responsibility or claim knowledge. Thoroughly embody what can't be exhausted and wander where you can't be seen. Take everything you get from Heaven but don't consider it gain. Just be empty. Perfected people use their minds like

---

[59]Cf. Kongzi's remarks in *Analects* 5.9 and 6.11.

[60]See *Zhuangzi*, chapter 2, p. 216.

mirrors, not welcoming things as they come or escorting them as they go. They respond without keeping, so they can conquer without harm.

The emperor of the north sea was Whish. The emperor of the south sea was Whoosh. The emperor of the center was All-full. Whish and Whoosh sometimes lodged together at All-full's place and he treated them exceptionally well. Whish and Whoosh decided to return All-full's kindness. "Everyone has seven holes to see, hear, eat and breathe, but he alone has none. Let's try drilling him some!" Each day they drilled a hole. And in seven days, All-full died.[61]

impressing more knowledge, categories, fabricated qualities onto All-full destroyed his nature and killed him (he was already "All-full" before tampered with!)

Chapter Twelve:
Heaven and Earth

. . . Kongzi's student Zigong[62] wandered south to Chu and was returning through Jin. As he passed the south bank of the Han River, he saw an old man gardening a small plot. He'd dug a tunnel for a well and was coming out carrying a jug to water his fields. He was huffing and puffing, working hard for little reward.

Zigong said, "There's a machine now that can water a hundred gardens in one day. You get a big reward for easy work. Wouldn't you like one, sir?"

The gardener raised his head to look at him. "How does it work?"

"You carve the contraption[63] out of a piece of wood. The back is heavy and the front is light. You can lift the water with one hand, until it's practically bubbling over. It's called a well sweep."[64]

The gardener flushed angrily and laughed, "I heard from my teacher that where there are mechanical contraptions there will be mechanical business, and where there is mechanical business there are mechanical minds. With a mechanical mind, you cannot preserve your simplicity. When you cannot preserve your simplicity, your spiritual life is unsettled, and the Way

---

[61]This marks the end of the "Inner Chapters," which many regard as the earliest strata within the *Zhuangzi* and possibly the work of the man Zhuangzi.

[62]Zigong was arguably Kongzi's most successful student. He was held in high esteem both by the Master and also by influential politicians. Kongzi sometimes seemed to worry that things came too easily to him. See *Analects* 1.15, 5.9, 5.12 etc.

[63]This word can also mean "shackle."

[64]For an image of a well sweep, see the web site for this volume.

will not support an unsettled spiritual life. I'm not ignorant of your contraption. I would be embarrassed to use it!" . . .

When the freak gives birth in the middle of the night, she reaches frantically for a torch, gasping, worrying only whether the child looks like her. . . .

Chapter Thirteen: Heaven's Way

. . . The sage is calm, but not because he declares calmness good. None of the ten thousand things are enough to rattle his mind, so he is calm. When water is calm, you can see the wispy hair on your temples in it. Its surface is level and sets the standard for great builders. If water is so clear when calm, how much more so the spirit! The calm mind of the sage is a mirror to Heaven and earth and a looking glass for the ten thousand things. . . .

Duke Huan[65] was reading a book up in his hall. Wheelwright Slab was chiseling a wheel [in the courtyard] below.[66] He put down his hammer and chisel and ascended, asking Duke Huan, "Excuse me. What are you reading?"

The Duke said, "The words of the sages."

"Are the sages still around?"

The Duke said, "They're dead."

"Then what M'Lord is reading is nothing more than the leavings of the ancients."

Duke Huan said, "How dare a wheelwright criticize what We read? If you have an explanation, okay. If not, you die!"

Wheelwright Slab said, "Your servant looks at it from the point of view of his own business. When I chisel a wheel, if I hit too softly, it slips and won't bite. If I hit too hard, it jams and won't move. Neither too soft nor too hard—I get it in my hand and respond with my mind. But my mouth cannot put it into words. There is an art to it. But your servant can't show it to his own son, and he can't get it from me. I've done it this way seventy years and am growing old chiseling wheels. The ancients died with what they could not pass down. So what M'Lord is reading can only be their leavings."

---

[65]For Duke Huan of Qi, see the entry for Guan Zhong under *Important Figures*.

[66]The scene in this passage is similar to what we see in *Mengzi* 1A7. See *Mengzi*, 1A7; see especially n. 3.

Chapter Fourteen:
Heaven's Turning

. . . For traveling on water there's nothing like a boat. For traveling on land, there's nothing like a cart. But though a boat can go on water, if you try pushing it on land, you can push until you die and not go an inch. Aren't past and present like water and land? Aren't the states of Zhou and Lu like boats and carts? Those who insist on using the ways of Zhou in Lu might as well be pushing a boat on land. They exhaust themselves without success and bring certain misfortune on their heads. They do not know the directionless revolution that responds to things without tiring. . . .

The beautiful Xi Shi had a stomach ache and glowered at the villagers. When her ugly neighbor saw how good she looked that way, he went home clasping his stomach and glowering at his neighbors, too, until the wealthy people slammed their windows and doors and the poor grabbed their children and ran. . . .

Chapter Seventeen:
Autumn Floods

. . . The *kui*[67] said to the millipede, "I go hippety-flopping on one foot, and there's nothing like it! How do you manage those ten thousand feet of yours?"

The millipede said, "It's not like that. Haven't you seen a man spit? He just hawks and—drops big as pearls! fine as mist! mixing and falling! You can't count them all! I just put my heavenly mechanism into motion. I don't know how it works!"

The millipede said to the snake, "I use this mob of legs to walk but still don't match up to you with none at all. How do you do it?"

The snake said, "The heavenly mechanism does it. What could be easier? What use would I have for legs?"

The snake said to the wind, "I move with just my ribs and spine. But I still seem to exist. You bluster up from the north sea and bluster off to the south sea, but you don't seem to be anything at all. How do you do it?"

The wind said, "Yes, I bluster up from the north sea and off to the south sea. But a finger raised against me can stop me. A screen can beat me. Even

---

[67]A mythical one-legged beast.

so, only I can snap huge trees and lift great buildings, because I turn all those little defeats into a great victory. Only the sage is capable of the great victory."

Did you hear about the frog in the collapsed well? He said to the turtle of the eastern sea, "Aren't I happy! I come out and spring on the railing, or I go in and rest in the hollow of a missing brick. When I float in the water, it hugs me under the arms and supports my chin. When I stomp in the mud, my feet sink in until it covers my ankles. Look around at the larvae and shrimp and polliwogs. None of them can match me! To control the water of an entire gully and straddle the happiness of a whole collapsed well—this is really getting somewhere! Why don't you come in some time and see?"

Before the turtle of the eastern sea could get his left foot in, his right knee was already stuck. He teetered and fell back, and then began to tell of the sea. "A thousand *li* wouldn't measure its breadth. A thousand fathoms wouldn't plumb its depths. In Yu's time there were floods nine years in ten, but its waters never rose. In Tang's time there were droughts seven years in eight, but its shores never receded. Not to change or shift for an instant or ever, not to advance or retreat a little or a lot—that's the happiness of the eastern sea."

When the frog in the caved in well heard this, he spluttered in surprise and forgot who he was. . . . *like the proud quail and the great bird in Chapter One, p. 206*

Did you hear about the toddler from Shouling who studied walking in Handan? Before he learned the local walk, he'd lost his native gait and had to shuffle home on his hands and knees.[68] . . .

Zhuangzi was angling by the Pu River when the king of Chu sent two officers to him, saying, "We would like to trouble you with administering Our kingdom."

Without looking up from his pole, Zhuangzi said, "I've heard Chu has a sacred turtle. It's been dead three thousand years and the king keeps it wrapped and boxed and stored up in his ancestral hall. Now, would that turtle rather have its bones treasured in death, or be alive dragging its tail in the mud?"

---

[68]Shouling was not actually a city but a tomb, construction of which was begun in 335 B.C.E. and probably continued throughout Zhuangzi's lifetime. Handan was the walled capital of Zhao and was also famous for its funerary parks. Assuming that the project at Shouling was to some extent modeled on the one at Handan, Zhuangzi's story may imply a sly criticism of people who follow the past to make sepulchers for themselves in the present.

The two officers said, "It would rather be alive dragging its tail in the mud." *He prefers to maintain his simple life.*

Zhuangzi said, "Go! I'll keep my tail in the mud, too." . . .

Zhuangzi considers being caught in the administration of a kingdom destructive and confining (blinding people against the Way)

Zhuangzi and Huizi were wandering on a bridge over the Hao River. Zhuangzi said, "Look at those mottled fish out wandering at ease. That's what fish like!"

Huizi said, "You are not a fish. How do you know what fish like?"

Zhuangzi said, "You are not me. How do you know I don't know what fish like?"

Huizi said, "I'm not you, so I certainly don't know what you know. And since you're not a fish, you don't know what fish like. There, perfect!"

Zhuangzi said, "Let's go back to the beginning. When you asked how I knew what fish like, you had to know I knew already in order to ask. I know it by the Hao River—that's how."[69]

Chapter Eighteen:
Perfect Happiness

. . . When Zhuangzi's wife died, Huizi came to mourn her. At that moment, Zhuangzi was squatting down, beating on a tub, and singing.

Huizi said, "You lived with this person, raised children, and grew old together. Not to cry when she died would be bad enough. But to beat on a tub singing! Isn't that too much?"

Zhuangzi said, "No. When she first died, don't you think I was like everyone else? But then I considered her beginning, before she was alive. Not only before she had life, but before she had form. Not only before she had form, but before she had *qi*.

In all the mixed up bustle and confusion, something changed and there was *qi*. The *qi* changed and there was form. The form changed and she had life. Today there was another change and she died. It's just like the round of the four seasons: spring, summer, fall, and winter. She was resting quietly, perfectly at home, and I followed her crying 'Wah-hah!' It seemed like I hadn't comprehended fate. So I stopped." . . .

---

[69]The word translated as "how" can also mean "where."

Chapter Nineteen: Penetrating Life

. . . Yan Hui said to Kongzi, "I once crossed the depths at Goblet Gulf. The ferryman handled the boat like a spiritual being. I asked him, 'Can a person learn to handle a boat like that?' He said, 'A good swimmer can master the ability. And a diver can handle it easily even if he's never seen a boat before.' I asked him for more but he wouldn't tell me. May I ask you what he meant?"

Kongzi said, "A good swimmer can master it because he forgets the water. A diver can handle it easily without ever seeing a boat before because he views the depths like a hillside and a flipped boat like a slipping cart. The ten thousand things could all flip and slip in front of him and they wouldn't get in his front door. Where could he go and not be at ease? Betting for tiles, you're good. Betting for buckles, you worry. Betting for gold, you panic. Your skill is the same, but you care, so you value what is on the outside. Those who value what is on the outside are clumsy on the inside." . . .

Chapter Twenty: The Mountain Tree

. . . Zhuangzi was wandering by the edge of the Diaoling preserve when he saw a strange magpie flying up from the south. Her wings were seven feet across and her eyes were an inch around. She bumped into his forehead and then crashed in a chestnut grove. He said, "What kind of bird is this, with such magnificent wings that don't get it anywhere and such big eyes that can't see?"[70] Hitching up his robes and tiptoeing forward, he pursued it, bow in hand. He saw a cicada forgetting itself in a pretty bit of shade. A praying mantis took advantage of the cover to grab for it, forgetting its own body at the sight of gain. The strange magpie was right behind, eyeing the prize and forgetting its truth. Zhuangzi shuddered. "Eeeee! Things certainly entangle one another, each one dragging in the next!" He threw down his bow and ran back the way he came—but then the warden of the grove saw and pursued him, cursing.

Zhuangzi went home and didn't come out for three days. His attendant, Straw, asked, "Sir, why haven't you left the house recently?"

Zhuangzi said, "I was guarding my body but forgot myself. I looked at muddy water and mistook it for clear depths. I've heard my teacher say,

---

[70]The strange magpie could be Breeze on her return journey. See *Zhuangzi*, chapter 1, pp. 204–09.

'Out in the world, follow its rules.' Now I was wandering by Diaoling and forgot myself. A strange magpie bumped my forehead, wandered into the chestnut grove, and forgot its truth. And the grove warden took me for a poacher! That's why I haven't been out." ...

Chapter Twenty-Two: Knowledge Wandered North

... Master East Wall asked Zhuangzi, "Where is this so-called Way?"

Zhuangzi said, "There's nowhere it isn't."

Master East Wall said "You must be more specific."

Zhuangzi said, "It's in an ant."

"How about even lower?"

"It's in the grass."

"How about lower still?"

"In tiles."

"How about even lower than that?"

"It's in dung and urine."

When Master East Wall did not reply, Zhuangzi said, "Your questions don't reach the substance. When the inspector of the hunt asked the superintendent of the market about poking pigs for fatness, he was told the lower the better. But you shouldn't insist on that. Don't reject anything. The perfect Way is like this and so are great words. 'Whole,' 'everywhere,' and 'all' are three different names for the same thing, making a single point." ...

Criticizes the endless stubborn debates over the right and wrong ways to reach the Way. The true Way transcends distinctions and embodies all ambiguity.

Chapter Twenty-Three: Mister Gengsang Chu

... People who have had their feet cut off forsake jewelry, because they are beyond praise and blame. Chained convicts are not afraid of heights because they have left life and death behind them. They have given up. They do not care. They have forgotten other people, and by forgetting other people they have become people of Heaven. You can honor them and they won't be pleased. You can despise them and they won't be mad. Only those who have identified with Heaven's harmony are like this. ...

Chapter Twenty-Four: Mister Ghostless Slow

... Zhuangzi was accompanying a funeral when he passed by Huizi's grave. Turning to his attendants, he said, "When plasterer Ying got a speck of mud on his nose as thick as a fly's wing, he would ask Builder Stone to slice it off. Builder Stone would twirl his axe like the wind and chop away obediently, getting all the mud and leaving the nose unharmed, while the plasterer stood there without changing his expression. Years later, when Ying had passed away, Lord Yuan of Song[71] heard about the trick and summoned Builder Stone.

"'Do it for Us!' he commanded.

"Builder Stone replied, 'I was able to do it once, but the material I worked with died long ago.'

"Since my own teacher died," Zhuangzi continued, "I have been without material. I have no one to talk to." . . .

Kongzi said, "I have heard the unspoken speech but I've never tried to speak it . . . I wish I had a beak a yard long!"[72] . . .

Chapter Twenty-Six: Outside Things

. . . A trap is for fish: when you've got the fish, you can forget the trap. A snare is for rabbits: when you've got the rabbit, you can forget the snare. Words are for meaning: when you've got the meaning, you can forget the words. Where can I find someone who's forgotten words so I can have a word with him? . . .

Chapter Thirty-Two: Mister Clampdown Lie

. . . When Zhuangzi was about to die, his students wanted to bury him lavishly. He said to them, "I'll have Heaven and earth for a casket, the sun and moon for ornaments, the constellations as pall-bearers, and the ten thousand things as mourners. Isn't everything prepared for the funeral? What could you add?"

"We're afraid the crows and kites will eat you."

"Above ground I'll feed the crows and kites. Below I'll feed the crickets and ants." Zhuangzi said. "Stealing from one to feed the other would be awfully unfair."[73]

---

[71]Reigned 531–517 B.C.E.

[72]Cf. *Zhuangzi*, chapter 2, p. 212, "We think [human speech] is different from the peeping of fledglings. But is there really any difference or isn't there?"

[73]Cf. *Analects* 9.12.

SELECTIVE BIBLIOGRAPHY

Translations

Fung, Yu-lan.

1989   *A Taoist Classic: Chuang Tzu.* Beijing: Foreign Languages Press. (An insightful translation, which I have borrowed from at points. The inclusion of Guo Xiang's [d. 312 C.E.] comments gives readers a rare and valuable insight into the commentarial tradition.)

Graham, Angus Charles.

1981   *Chuang Tzu: The Inner Chapters.* London: George Allen and Unwin. (A philosophically oriented translation, especially useful when read in conjunction with Graham's other works explaining his reading.)

Watson, Burton.

1968   *The Complete Works of Chuang Tzu.* New York: Columbia University Press. (An exquisite translation that I have often made the basis of my own. The standard.)

Mair, Victor.

1998   *Wandering on the Way: Early Taoist Tales and Parables of Chuang Tzu.* Honolulu: University of Hawaii Press. (A fine recent translation.)

Secondary Works:

Ames, Roger T., ed.

1998   *Wandering at Ease in the Zhuangzi.* Albany, NY: State University of New York Press. (An anthology of historical and textual as well as philosophical analyses and reflections on Zhuangzi.)

Chinn, Ewing.

1997   "Zhuangzi and Relativistic Skepticism." *Asian Philosophy* 7: 207–20. (A response to Chad Hansen's argument that Zhuangzi's skepticism commits him to relativistic skepticism, defending instead a perspectival realist position.)

Fox, Alan.

1996   "Reflex and Reflectivity: *Wuwei* in the *Zhuangzi.*" *Asian Philosophy* 6: 59–73. (An interpretation of the idea of *wuwei* based on the image of the hinge of the Way, as productive of a well-adjusted person.)

Graham, Angus Charles.

1969–70 "Chuang-tzu's 'Essay on Seeing Things as Equal.' " *History of Religions* 9.2–3: 137–59. (A groundbreaking study of technical terms in the second chapter.)

1990 *Studies in Chinese Philosophy and Philosophical Literature.* Albany: State University of New York Press. (The chapter "How Much of Chuang Tzu Did Chuang Tzu Write?" differentiates the text's various contributors and editors.)

Ivanhoe, Philip J.

1991 "Zhuangzi's Conversion Experience." *Journal of Chinese Religions* 19: 13–25. (A useful study of the various interpretations of Zhuangzi's experience at Diaoling. [See *Zhuangzi*, chapter 20.]).

1993 "Zhuangzi on Skepticism, Skill, and the Ineffable Dao." *Journal of the American Academy of Religions* 61: 639–54. (An important analysis of the status of skill.)

Kjellberg, Paul, and Philip J. Ivanhoe, eds.

1996 *Essays on Skepticism, Relativism, and Ethics in the Zhuangzi.* Albany, NY: State University of New York Press. (An anthology of essays on the relation between Zhuangzi's skepticism and his positive philosophical project.)

Mair, Victor, ed.

1983 *Experimental Essays on Chuang-tzu.* Honolulu, HI: University of Hawaii Press. (The earliest of several good anthologies on Zhuangzi. The essays by Graham, Hansen, and Yearley have been especially influential.)

Van Norden, Bryan W.

1996 "Competing Interpretations of the Inner Chapters of the Zhuangzi." *Philosophy East & West* 46: 247–68. (An analysis of the tensions within the first seven chapters that give rise to conflicting interpretations, along with an interpretation of sagehood that reconciles them.)

■ CHAPTER SIX ■

XUNZI

Introduction

Before the unification of China by the Qin state in 221 B.C.E., which brought to a close the classical period of Chinese philosophy, Confucianism had one last great exponent, Xunzi 荀子, whose work represents the highest development of the school in the Warring States period. Whereas the views of Kongzi and Mengzi are preserved only in piecemeal sayings, Xunzi's thought has come down to the present in the form of tightly constructed essays that give sustained discussion of various topics and together constitute a remarkably coherent system of arguments. Although his writing is not quite as colorful as that of Zhuangzi, his style is extremely elegant and forceful, occasionally bursting into poetry that movingly conveys his passion for the Confucian way of life.

Much of Xunzi's effort is devoted to ardently defending Confucianism against various challenges. For example, he vehemently condemns Mozi's rejection of ritual and music and argues vigorously that these cultural forms are absolutely necessary. He also attacks Laozi and Zhuangzi for advocating that people adopt the perspective of Heaven and abandon conventional values in favor of yielding to the natural flow of things. Xunzi instead stresses the distinctive importance of the human point of view, and in stark contrast to their emphasis on *wu-wei* 無為, "non-action" or "non-striving action," he claims that good things are achieved only through *wei* 偽, "deliberate effort." Yet even as he repudiates rival philosophers, Xunzi also learns from them and incorporates their insights. The influence of Zhuangzi on his thought is particularly evident in his characterization of the heart as mirror-like and in his description of how it comes to know the Way, though the substance of Xunzi's views differs considerably from that of Zhuangzi.

For Xunzi, the threats to Confucianism come not only from outside the tradition, but also from *within* it, in the form of Mengzi's doctrine that human nature is good. In Xunzi's opinion, such a claim undermines the authority of ritual as a guide to behavior, destroys the necessity of learning, and simply flies in the face of the facts. Xunzi makes the opposite declaration that human nature is bad, but this should not be read as saying that people naturally delight in evil. Rather, his point is that people lack any inborn guide to right conduct, and that without the external restraint of ritual they will fall into wrongdoing and be reduced to a chaotic, impoverished state strongly reminiscent of the "state of nature" depicted by Thomas Hobbes. Nevertheless, Xunzi shares Mengzi's belief that everyone has the potential to achieve moral perfection. However, since we are not inclined to virtue by nature, the process of self-transformation will be slow and difficult, and this idea is reflected in Xunzi's repeated comparison of learning with the harsh processes involved in bending wood.

In his own day, Xunzi was a well-known scholar and was even given high office at one point. Among his students were Han Feizi and Li Si, who was instrumental in bringing about the Qin state's domination of China. Xunzi may even have lived to witness this event. Other students of his were responsible for preserving classic Chinese texts, including the *Odes*. Despite Xunzi's important position in early Chinese intellectual history, when Mengzi's views later came to be favored, Xunzi was rejected for claiming that human nature is bad, and his works were largely neglected for centuries. Recently, however, there has been a renewal of scholarly interest in Xunzi, and he is once again receiving the attention he deserves.

Chapter One: An Exhortation to Learning

The gentleman says: Learning must never stop. Blue dye is gotten from the indigo plant, and yet it is bluer than the plant. Ice comes from water, and yet it is colder than water. Through steaming and bending, you can make wood straight as a plumb line into a wheel. And after its curve conforms to the compass, even when parched under the sun it will not become straight again, because the steaming and bending have made it a certain way. Likewise, when wood comes under the ink-line, it becomes straight, and when metal is brought to the whetstone, it becomes sharp.[1] The gentleman learns broadly and examines himself thrice daily,[2] and then his knowledge is clear and his conduct is without fault.

---

[1] Cf. Gaozi's metaphors for self cultivation in *Mengzi* 6A1–2, and *Xunzi*, ch. 23, p. 284.

[2] Cf. *Analects* 1.4 (not in this volume).

And so if you do not climb a high mountain, you will not know the height of Heaven. If you do not approach a deep ravine, you will not know the depth of the earth. If you do not hear the words passed down from the former kings, you will not know the magnificence of learning. The children of the Han, Yue, Yi, and Mo[3] peoples all cry with the same sound at birth, but when grown they have different customs, because teaching makes them be this way. . . .

I once spent the whole day pondering, but it wasn't as good as a moment's worth of learning.[4] I once stood on my toes to look far away, but it wasn't as good as the broad view from a high place. If you climb to a high place and wave, you have not lengthened your arms, but you can be seen from farther away. If you shout from upwind, you have not made your voice stronger, but you can be heard more clearly. One who makes use of a chariot and horses has not thereby improved his feet, but he can now go a thousand *li*. One who makes use of a boat and oars has not thereby become able to swim, but he can now cross rivers and streams. The gentleman is not different from others by birth. Rather, he is good at making use of things. . . .

If you accumulate enough earth to form a mountain, then wind and rain will arise from it. If you accumulate enough water to form a deep pool, then dragons will come to live in it. If you accumulate enough goodness to achieve Virtue, then you will naturally attain to spiritlike powers and enlightenment, and the heart of a sage is complete therein.

And so,

> If you do not accumulate little steps,
> You will have no way to go a thousand *li*.
> If you do not accumulate small streams,
> You will no way to form river or sea.[5]

Even the famous horse Qi Ji[6] could not go more than ten paces in a single leap, but with ten days of riding even an old nag can equal him, because accomplishment rests in not giving up.[7] If you start carving and give up,

---

[3]These are the names of "barbarian" states and tribes.

[4]Cf. *Analects* 15.31.

[5]In the present translation, passages which rhymed in the original have been translated with rhyming English (though not always exactly according to the Chinese rhyme scheme), or, where this has not been feasible, they have been pointed out in the footnotes.

[6]The horse Qi Ji was famous for his ability to go a thousand *li* in a single day.

[7]This line was also rhymed in the original.

you won't even be able to break rotten wood, but if you start carving and don't give up, then you can engrave even metal and stone. The earthworm does not have sharp teeth and claws, nor does it have strong bones and muscles. Yet, above, it eats of the earth, and below, it drinks from the Yellow Springs,[8] because it acts with single-mindedness. In contrast, the crab has six legs and two pincers. Yet were it not for the abandoned holes of water-snakes and eels, it would have no place to lodge, because it is frenetic-minded.

For this reason,

> Without Somber intention,
> No brilliant understanding can there be.
> Without determined effort,
> No glorious achievements will one see. . . .

Where does learning begin? Where does learning end? I say: Its order begins with reciting the classics, and ends with studying ritual. Its purpose begins with becoming a noble man, and ends with becoming a sage. If you truly accumulate effort for a long time, then you will advance. Learning proceeds until death and only then does it stop. And so the order of learning has a stopping point, but its purpose cannot be given up for even a moment. To pursue it is to be human, to give it up is to be a beast. The *History* is the record of government affairs. The *Odes* is the repository of temperate sounds. Rituals are the great divisions in the proper model for things; they are the outlines of the proper classes of things. And so learning comes to ritual and then stops, for this is called the ultimate point in pursuit of the Way and Virtue. In the reverence and refinement of ritual, the balance and harmony of music, the broad content of the *Odes* and *History*, the subtleties of the *Spring and Autumn Annals*, all things between Heaven and Earth are complete.

The learning of the gentleman enters through his ears, fastens to his heart, spreads through his four limbs, and manifests itself in his actions. His slightest word, his most subtle movement, all can serve as a model for others. The learning of the petty person enters through his ears and passes out his mouth. From mouth to ears is only four inches—how could it be enough to improve a whole body much larger than that? Students in an-

---

[8]The Yellow Springs were believed to be deep underground and were thought of as the abode of the spirits of the dead.

cient times learned for their own sake, but the students of today learn for the sake of impressing others.[9] Thus the learning of the gentleman is used to improve his own person, while the learning of the petty man is used like gift-oxen.[10] To speak without being asked is what people call being presumptuous, and to speak two things when asked only one is what people call being wordy. Being presumptuous is wrong, and being wordy is wrong. The gentleman is simply like an echo.

In learning, nothing is more expedient than to draw near to the right person. Rituals and music provide proper models but give no precepts. The *Odes* and *History* contain ancient stories but no explanation of their present application. The *Spring and Autumn Annals* is terse and cannot be quickly understood. However, if you imitate the right person in his practice of the precepts of the gentleman, then you will come to honor these things for their comprehensiveness, and see them as encompassing the whole world. Thus, in learning there is nothing more expedient than to draw near to the right person.

Of the paths to learning, none is quicker than to like the right person, and exalting ritual comes second. If at best you cannot like the right person, and at worst you cannot exalt ritual, then you will simply be learning haphazard knowledge and focusing your intentions on blindly following the *Odes* and *History*. If so, then to the end of your days you cannot avoid being nothing more than a vulgar scholar.[11] If you are going to take the former kings as your fount and make benevolence and righteousness[12] your root, then rituals are exactly the highways and byways for you. It will be like the action of turning up your fur collar by simply curling your five fin-

---

[9]Cf. *Analects* 14.24.

[10]In ancient China, animals were given as gifts to superiors or honored guests. Xunzi's point is that the petty man likewise shows off his learning to ingratiate himself to others and win official position.

[11]The last word here is *ru* 儒, which later came to mean simply "Confucian" (see *Important Terms*). In Xunzi's time it did not yet have such a specific denotation but instead referred more generally to a "scholar."

[12]The word here is *yi* 義, an extremely important term for Xunzi. In his writings, it can refer both to a specific set of social standards created by the sages, and to the virtue of abiding by those standards. In the former usage, it is frequently paired with ritual, and the standards to which it refers appear to be higher-order standards for structuring society (e.g., by defining various social roles), from which are derived the more particular directives for behavior contained in ritual. For those contexts, in order to mark that Xunzi is referring to an external set of standards, rather than an internal disposition, it is rendered in this translation as "the standards of righteousness." See *yi* under *Important Terms*.

gers and pulling on it—it goes smoothly numberless times. If you do not take the regulations of ritual as your way, but instead go at it with just the *Odes* and *History*, then it will be like trying to measure the depth of a river with your finger, or trying to pound millet with a halberd, or trying to eat out of a pot with an awl—you simply will not succeed at it. And so if you exalt ritual, then even if you are not brilliant, you will still be a man of the proper model. If you do not exalt ritual, then even if you are an acute debater, you will be only a dissolute scholar. . . .

One who misses a single shot out of a hundred does not deserve to be called good at archery. One who falls short of going a thousand *li* by a half-step does not deserve to be called good at chariot-driving. One who does not fully comprehend the proper kinds and classes of things, or who is not single-minded in pursuit of benevolence and righteousness does not deserve to be called good at learning. Learning is precisely learning to pursue them single-mindedly. To depart from it in one affair and enter into it in another is the way of common people. The good men among them are few. The bad men among them are many. Such were Jie and Zhou and Robber Zhi. Make it perfect and complete, and only then is it truly learning.

The gentleman knows that whatever is imperfect and unrefined does not deserve praise. And so he repeatedly recites his learning in order to master it, ponders it over in order to comprehend it, makes his person so as to dwell in it, and eliminates things harmful to it in order to nourish it. He makes his eyes not want to see what is not right, makes his ears not want to hear what is not right, makes his mouth not want to speak what is not right, and makes his heart not want to deliberate over what is not right.[13] He comes to the point where he loves it, and then his eyes love it more than the five colors, his ears love it more than the five tones, his mouth loves it more than the five flavors, and his heart considers it more profitable than possessing the whole world. For this reason, power and profit cannot sway him, the masses cannot shift him, and nothing in the world can shake him.[14] He lives by this, and he dies by this. This is called grasping Virtue. When one has grasped Virtue, then one can achieve fixity. When one can achieve fixity, then one can respond to things. To be capable both of fixity and of responding to things—such a one is called the perfected person. Heaven shows off its brilliance, earth shows off its breadth, and the gentleman values his perfection.

---

[13]Cf. *Analects* 12.1.

[14]Compare *Mengzi* 3B2 (not in this volume).

Chapter Two:
Cultivating Oneself

When you observe goodness in others, then inspect yourself, desirous of studying it. When you observe badness in others, then examine yourself, fearful of discovering it.[15] If you find goodness in your person, then approve of yourself, desirous of holding firm to it. If you find badness in your person, then reproach yourself, regarding it as calamity. And so, he who rightly criticizes me is my teacher, and he who rightly supports me is my friend, while he who flatters and toadies to me is someone who would do me villainy. Accordingly, the gentleman exalts his teachers and loves his friends, so as to utterly hate those who would do him villainy. He loves goodness tirelessly, and can receive admonitions and take heed. Even if he desired not to improve, how could he avoid it?

The petty man is the opposite. He is utterly disorderly, but hates for people to criticize him. He is utterly unworthy, but wishes for people to consider him worthy. His heart is like that of a tiger or wolf, and his conduct like that of beasts, but he hates for people to consider him a villain. To those who flatter and toady to him he shows favor, while those who would admonish him he keeps at a distance. Those who try to be correct he considers laughable, and those truly loyal to him he considers villains. Even though he wishes not to perish, how could he avoid it? The *Odes* says,

> They conspire and slander. How greatly lamentable!
> Plans worth adopting, they wholly reject.
> Plans worth dismissing, they wholly accept.[16]

This expresses my meaning.

The measure for goodness in all things is this:

> Use it to control your *qi* 氣 and nourish your life,
> Then you will live longer than Peng Zu.
> Use it to cultivate yourself and establish your fame,
> Then you will equal Yao and Yu.
> It is fitting in times of prosperity.
> It is useful in facing adversity

---

[15]Cf. *Analects* 4.17.

[16]*Mao # 195.*

—truly such is ritual. If your exertions of blood, *qi*, intention, and thought accord with ritual, they will be ordered and effective. If they do not accord with ritual, they will be disorderly and unproductive. If your meals, clothing, dwelling, and activities accord with ritual, they will be congenial and well regulated. If they do not accord with ritual, then you will encounter dangers and illnesses. If your countenance, bearing, movements, and stride accord with ritual, they will be graceful. If they do not accord with ritual, they will be barbaric, obtuse, perverse, vulgar, and unruly. Hence,

> In lives without ritual people cannot survive;
> In affairs without ritual success does not thrive;
> To states without ritual peace does not arrive.

The *Odes* says, "Their rituals and ceremonies completely follow the proper measure. Their laughter and speech are completely appropriate."[17] This expresses my meaning.

To lead others along in what is good is called "teaching." To harmonize with others in what is good is called "proper compliance." To lead others along in what is bad is called "flattery." To harmonize with others in what is bad is called "toadying." To approve of what is right and condemn what is wrong is called "wisdom." To approve of what is wrong and condemn what is right is called "stupidity." To attack a good person is called "slander." To injure a good person is called "villainy." To call the right as right and the wrong as wrong is called "uprightness." To steal goods is called "thievery." To conceal one's actions is called "deceptiveness." To speak too easily of things is called "boastfulness." To be without fixity in one's likes and dislikes is called "lacking constancy." To abandon righteousness in favor of profit is called "utmost villainy." To have heard many things is called "broadness." To have heard few things is called "shallowness." To have seen many things is called "being learned." To have seen few things is called "boorishness."[18] To have difficulty in progressing is called "indolence." To forget things easily is called "being leaky." For one's actions to be few and well ordered is called "being controlled." For one's actions to be many and disorderly is called "being wasteful."

---

[17] *Mao* # 209. This same poem is quoted again in the "Discourse on Ritual" chapter. See *Xunzi*, chapter 19, p. 268.

[18] "Boorishness," *lou* 陋, is an important term for Xunzi. It is the uncultivated state in which a person has not yet been shown the greatest goods in life (that is, the way of the sages), and so does not properly appreciate them. Cf. *Analects* 9.14.

These are the methods for controlling the *qi* and nourishing the heart: For unyielding *qi*, soften it with harmoniousness. For overly deep thinking, simplify it with easy goodness. For overly ferocious courage, reform it with proper compliance. For expedience-seeking hastiness, restrain it with regulated movements. For small-minded narrowness, broaden it with expansiveness. For excessive humility, sluggishness, or greed for profit, resist it with lofty intentions. For vulgarness or dissoluteness, expunge it with teachers and friends. For indolence or profligacy, illuminate it with the prospect of disasters. For simple-minded rectitude or honest integrity, make it suitable with ritual and music, and enlighten it with reflection. In each method of controlling the *qi* and nourishing the heart, nothing is more direct than following ritual, nothing is more important than having a good teacher, and nothing works with greater spiritlike efficacy than to like it with single-minded devotion. These are called the methods for controlling the *qi* and nourishing the heart.

One whose intentions and thoughts are cultivated will disregard wealth and nobility. One whose greatest concern is for the Way and righteousness will take lightly kings and dukes. It is simply that when one examines oneself on the inside, external goods carry little weight. A saying goes, "The gentleman makes things his servants. The petty man is servant to things." This expresses my meaning. If an action tires your body but puts your heart at ease, do it. If it involves little profit but much righteousness, do it. Being successful in the service of a ruler who creates chaos is not as good as simply being compliant in the service of an impoverished ruler. And so, a good farmer does not fail to plant because of drought, a good merchant does not fail to open shop because of losses, and the noble man and the gentleman are not lax in their pursuit of the Way because of poverty.

If your bearing is reverent and respectful and your heart is loyal and faithful, if your method is ritual and the standards of righteousness and your disposition is concern for others, then you may wander across the whole world, and even if you become trapped among barbarians, no one will not value you. If you are eager to take the lead in laborious matters, if you can give way in pleasant matters, and if you show integrity, honesty, reliability, faithfulness, self-control, and meticulousness, then you may wander across the whole world, and even if you become trapped among barbarians, no one will not employ you. If your bearing is arrogant and obtuse and your heart is stubborn and deceitful, if your method is to follow Mozi[19] and your truest essence is polluted and corrupt, then you may wan-

---

[19]That is, to reject ritual.

der across the whole world, and even if you reach every corner of it, no one will not consider you base. If you try to put off or wriggle out of laborious matters, if you are grasping and will not yield in pleasant matters, if you are perverse and dishonest, if you are not meticulous in work, then you may wander across the whole world, and even if you reach every corner of it, no one will not reject you. . . .

He who likes the right model and carries it out is a man of good breeding. He who focuses his intentions upon it and embodies it is a gentleman. He who completely understands it and practices it without tiring is a sage. If a person lacks the proper model, then he will act recklessly. If he has the proper model but does not fix his intentions on its true meaning, then he will act too rigidly. If he relies on the proper model and also deeply understands its categories, only then will he act with comfortable mastery of it.

Ritual is that by which to correct your person. The teacher is that by which to correct your practice of ritual.[20] If you are without ritual, then how will you correct your person? If you are without a teacher, how will you know that your practice of ritual is right? When ritual dictates thus-and-so, and you are thus-and-so, then this means your disposition accords with ritual. When the teacher explains thus-and-so, and you also explain thus-and-so, then this means your understanding is just like your teacher's understanding. If your disposition accords with ritual, and your understanding is just like your teacher's understanding, then this is to be a sage. And so, to contradict ritual is to be without a proper model, and to contradict your teacher is to be without a teacher. If you do not concur with your teacher and the proper model but instead like to use your own judgment, then this is like relying on a blind person to distinguish colors, or like relying on a deaf person to distinguish sounds. You will accomplish nothing but chaos and recklessness. And so, in learning, ritual is your proper model, and the teacher is one whom you take as the correct standard and whom you aspire to accord with. The *Odes* says, "While not knowing, not understanding, he follows the principles of the Lord on High." [21] This expresses my meaning. . . .

In seeking profit, the gentleman acts with restraint. In averting harms, he acts early. In avoiding disgrace, he acts fearfully. In carrying out the Way, he acts courageously. Even if he lives in poverty, the gentleman's intentions are still grand. Even if he is wealthy and honored, his demeanor is reverent.

---

[20]That is, the teacher shows one both the right rituals to practice and how to practice them rightly.

[21]*Mao* # 241.

Even if he lives at ease, his *qi* is not lazy. Even if he is weary from toil, his countenance is not disagreeable. When angry he is not excessively harsh, and when happy he is not excessively indulgent. The gentlemen retains grand intentions even in poverty, because he exalts benevolence. He maintains a reverent demeanor even when wealthy and honored, because he takes lightly contingent fortune. His *qi* does not become lazy when he is at ease, because he is heedful of good order. His countenance is not disagreeable even when weary from toil, because he is fond of good relations. He is neither excessively harsh when angry nor excessively indulgent when happy, because his adherence to the proper model overcomes any personal capriciousness. The *History* says, "Do not innovate in your fondnesses; follow the Way of the kings. Do not innovate in your aversions; follow the road of the kings."[22] This is saying that through his avoidance of prejudice[23] and adherence to righteousness the gentleman overcomes capricious personal desires.

Chapter Five: Against Physiognomy

. . . What is that by which humans are human? I say: It is because they have distinctions. Desiring food when hungry, desiring warmth when cold, desiring rest when tired, liking the beneficial and hating the harmful—these are things people have from birth. These one does not have to await, but are already so. These are what Yu and Jie both share. However, that by which humans are human is not that they are special in having two legs and no feathers, but that they have distinctions. Now the ape's form is such that it also has two legs and no feathers. However, the gentleman sips ape soup and eats ape meat. Thus, that by which humans are human is not that they are special in having two legs and no feathers, but that they have distinctions. The birds and beasts have fathers and sons but not the intimate relationship of father and son. They have the male sex and the female sex but no differentiation between male and female. And so among human ways, none is without distinctions. Of distinctions, none are greater than social

---

[22]Cf. Legge, *The Shoo King*, p. 331. These same lines are quoted again in the "Discourse on Heaven" chapter. See *Xunzi*, chapter 17, p. 264.

[23]"Avoidance of prejudice" is my translation for *gong* 公. It is a virtue opposite both to prejudice in favor of oneself, that is, selfishness, and to prejudice in favor of certain people or certain views, that is, unfair bias. Stated more positively, it combines both public-spiritedness and impartiality. Cf. *Hanfeizi*, chapter 49, p. 328, n. 39.

divisions, and of social divisions, none are greater than rituals, and of rituals, none are greater than those of the sage-kings.[24]

But there are a hundred sage-kings—which of them shall one take as one's model? And so I say: Culture persists for a long time and then expires, regulations persist for a long time and then cease. The authorities in charge of preserving models and arrangements do their utmost in carrying out ritual but lose their grasp. And so I say: If you wish to observe the tracks of the sage-kings, then look to the most clear among them. Such are the later kings. The later kings were rulers of the whole world. To reject the later kings and take one's way from furthest antiquity is like rejecting one's own ruler and serving another's ruler. And so I say: If you wish to observe a thousand years time, then reckon upon today's events. If you wish to understand ten thousand or one hundred thousand, then examine one and two. If you wish to understand the ancient ages, then examine the way of the Zhou. If you wish to understand the way of the Zhou, then examine the gentlemen that their people valued. Thus it is said: Use the near to know the far; use the one to know the ten thousand; use the subtle to know the brilliant. This expresses my meaning. . . .

Chapter Nine: The Regulations of a True King

. . . Water and fire have *qi* but are without life. Grasses and trees have life but are without awareness. Birds and beasts have awareness but are without standards of righteousness. Humans have *qi* and life and awareness, and moreover they have *yi* 義, "standards of righteousness." And so they are the most precious things under Heaven. They are not as strong as oxen or as fast as horses, but oxen and horses are used by them. How is this so? I say: It is because humans are able to form communities while the animals cannot. Why are humans able to form communities? I say: It is because of social divisions. How can social divisions be put into practice? I say: It is because of standards of righteousness. And so if they use standards of righteousness in order to make social divisions, then they will be harmonized. If they are harmonized, then they will be unified. If they are unified, then they will have more force. If they have more force, then they will be strong. If they are strong, then they will be able to overcome the animals. And so

---

[24]Zhuangzi also argues that making normative distinctions sets humans apart from animals, but claims that this tendency is the greatest source of trouble and should be avoided. Here Xunzi turns Zhuangzi's point on its head and glorifies such distinctions as the source of all good. See *Zhuangzi*, chapter 2, pp. 209–19.

they can get to live in homes and palaces. Thus, that people can order themselves with the four seasons, control the ten thousand things, and bring benefit to all under Heaven is for no other reason than that they get these things from social divisions and standards of righteousness. And so human life cannot be without community. If they form communities but are without social divisions, then they will struggle. If they struggle, then there will be chaos. If there is chaos then they will disband. If they disband then they will be weak. If they are weak then they cannot overcome the animals. And so they will not get to live in homes and palaces. This is the meaning of saying that "one must not let go of ritual and the standards of righteousness for even a moment."

One who can use these to serve his parents is called filial. One who can use these to serve his elder brother is called a proper younger brother. One who can use these to serve his superiors is called properly compliant. One who can use these to employ his subordinates is called a proper ruler. The true ruler is one who is good at forming a community.[25] When the way of forming community is properly practiced, then the ten thousand things will each obtain what is appropriate for them, the six domestic animals will each obtain their proper growth, and all the various living things will obtain their proper lifespans. And so, when nurturing accords with the proper times, then the six domestic animals will multiply. When reaping accords with the proper times, then the grasses and trees will flourish. If government commands accord with the proper times, then the common people will be united, and good and worthy men will gladly follow.

These are the regulations of a sage-king: When the grasses and trees are flowering and abundant, then axes and hatchets are not to enter the mountains and forests, so as not to cut short their life, and not to break off their growth. When the turtles and crocodiles, fish and eels are pregnant and giving birth, then nets and drugs are not to enter the marshes, so as not to cut short their life, and not to break off their growth. Plow in the spring, weed in the summer, harvest in the fall, and store in the winter. These four activities are not to miss their proper times, and then the five grains will not be depleted, and the common people will have a surplus to eat. Be vigilant in the seasonal prohibitions concerning ponds, rivers, and marshes, and then turtles and fish will be fine and plentiful, and the common people will

---

[25]Here Xunzi is playing upon the close similarity between the words "ruler," 君 *jun*, and "community," 群 *qun*, in both pronunciation and written form. (At the time Xunzi was writing, the two may in fact have had the very same sound).

have a surplus to use. Cutting and nurturing are not to miss their proper times, and then the mountains and forests will not be barren, and the common people will have surplus materials.

This is the way a sage-king operates: He observes Heaven above, and applies this knowledge on earth below. He arranges completely everything between Heaven and earth and spreads beneficence over the ten thousand things. His actions are subtle but illustrious, brief but of long-lasting consequence, narrowly confined but of wide-ranging impact. He has spiritlike powers of intelligence that are broad and vast, yet work by the utmost restraint. Thus it is said: The person who by even the slightest movements always does what is right is called a sage.[26] . . .

Chapter Seventeen: Discourse on Heaven

The activities of Heaven are constant. They do not persist because of Yao. They do not perish because of Jie. If you respond to them with order, then you will have good fortune. If you respond to them with chaos, then you will have misfortune. If you strengthen the fundamental works[27] and moderate expenditures, then Heaven cannot make you poor. If your means of nurture are prepared and your actions are timely, then Heaven cannot make you ill. If you cultivate the Way and do not deviate from it, then Heaven cannot ruin you. Thus, floods and drought cannot make you go hungry or thirsty, cold and heat cannot make you sick, and aberrations and anomalies cannot cause you misfortune.

If the fundamental works are neglected and expenditures are extravagant, then Heaven cannot make you wealthy. If your means of nurture are sparse and your actions are infrequent, then Heaven cannot make you sound in body. If you turn your back on the Way and act recklessly, then Heaven cannot make you fortunate. And so, although floods and drought have not yet come, you still will go hungry. Although heat and cold are not yet pressing, you still will become sick. Although aberrations and anomalies have not yet come, you still will have misfortune. Receiving the benefit of the seasons comes along with having an ordered age, but calamities and disasters are incompatible with there being an ordered age. You must not complain against Heaven; its way is simply thus. And so, one who understands

---

[26]The text of this paragraph is very difficult, and the translation is tentative.

[27]The "fundamental works" are agriculture and textile production.

clearly the respective allotments of Heaven and humans can be called a person of utmost achievement.

That which is accomplished without your doing it and which is obtained without your seeking it is called the work of Heaven. With respect to what is so, even though he thinks deeply, a proper person does not try to ponder it. Even though he is mighty, he does not try to augment it by his own abilities. Even though he is expertly refined, he does not try to make it more keenly honed. This is called not competing with Heaven's work. When Heaven has its proper seasons, earth has its proper resources, and humans have their proper order, this is called being able to form a triad. To neglect that whereby we form a triad and wish instead for those things to which we stand as the third is a state of confusion. The arrayed stars follow each other in their revolutions, the sun and the moon take turns shining, the four seasons proceed in succession, *yin* and *yang* undergo their great transformations, and winds and rain are broadly bestowed. From harmony of these, the ten thousand things are made alive. Through nurturing by these, they come to thrive. That which one does not see the workings of but sees only its accomplishments—such is called spiritlike power. That which everyone knows how it comes about but no one understands it in its formless state—such is called the accomplishment of Heaven. Only the sage does not seek to understand Heaven.

When the work of Heaven has been established and the accomplishments of Heaven have been completed, then the body is set and spirit arises. Liking, disliking, happiness, anger, sorrow, and joy are contained therein—these are called one's "Heavenly dispositions." The abilities of eyes, ears, nose, mouth, and body each have their respective objects and are not able to assume each other's abilities—these are called one's "Heavenly faculties." The heart dwells in the central cavity so as to control the five faculties—this is called one's "Heavenly ruler."[28] Using what is not of one's kind as a resource for nourishing what is of one's kind—this is called one's "Heavenly nourishment." To be in accordance with what is proper for one's kind is called "happiness," and to go against what is proper for one's kind is called "disaster"—this is called one's "Heavenly government." To becloud your Heavenly ruler, disorder your Heavenly faculties, abandon your Heavenly nourishment, go against your Heavenly government, and turn your back on your Heavenly dispositions, so that you lose the accomplishments

---

[28]Xunzi is playing on the fact that the character 官 *guan* (here translated as "faculty") means both "organ" and "official."

of Heaven—this is called the "greatest misfortune." The sage keeps clear his Heavenly ruler, sets straight his Heavenly faculties, makes complete his Heavenly nourishment, accords with his Heavenly government, and nurtures his Heavenly dispositions, so as to keep whole the accomplishment of Heaven. A person who is thus is someone who knows what he is to do and what he is not to do. Then Heaven and earth will have their proper positions and the ten thousand things will all be servants to him. His conduct will be completely ordered, his nourishment will be completely appropriate, and his life will suffer no harm—this is called "knowing Heaven."

Thus, the greatest cleverness lies in not doing certain things, and the greatest wisdom lies in not pondering certain things. With respect to Heaven, focus only on those manifest phenomena to which you can align yourself. With respect to earth, focus only on those manifest places which are suitable for growing. With respect to the four seasons, focus only on that manifest order by which work is to be arranged. With respect to *yin* and *yang*, focus only on those manifest harmonies that can be used to order things. Let the officials keep watch over Heaven and you keep watch over the Way. . . .

If stars fall or trees cry out, the people of the state are filled with fear and say, "What is this?" I say: It is nothing. These are simply rarely occurring things among the changes in Heaven and earth and the transformations of *yin* and *yang*. To marvel at them is alright, but to fear them is not. Eclipses of the sun and moon, unseasonable winds and rain, unexpected appearances of strange stars—there is no age in which such things do not occur. If the superiors are enlightened and the government is stable, then even if all these things come about in the same age, there is no harm done. If the superiors are benighted and the government is unstable, then even if none of these things comes to pass, it is of no benefit. The falling of stars and the crying out of trees are simply rarely occurring things among the changes in Heaven and earth and the transformations of *yin* and *yang*. To marvel at them is alright, but to fear them is not.

Of things that come to pass, it is human ill-omens that are to be feared. When poor plowing harms the planting, when the hoeing loses control over the weeds, when the government is unstable and loses control over the people, such that the fields are overgrown with weeds and the planting is bad, buying grain is expensive and the people face famine, and there are corpses lying in the roads—these are called "human ill-omens." When government orders are not clear, when policies are not timely, when the fundamental tasks are not well ordered—these are called "human ill-omens."

When ritual and the standards of righteousness are not cultivated, when insiders and outsiders are not properly differentiated, when men and women engage in perverse, disorderly conduct, then father and son will be suspicious of one another, superiors and inferiors will desert one another, and bandits and other difficulties will arrive together—these are called "human ill-omens." Ill-omens thus arise from disorder. . . .

One performs the rain sacrifice and it rains. Why? I say: There is no special reason why. It is the same as when one does not perform the rain sacrifice and it rains anyway. When the sun and moon suffer eclipse, one tries to save them. When Heaven sends drought, one performs the rain sacrifice. One performs divination and only then decides on important affairs. But this is not for the sake of getting what one seeks, but rather to give things proper form. Thus, the gentleman looks upon this as proper form, but the common people look upon it as connecting with spirits. If one looks upon it as proper form, then one will have good fortune. If one looks upon it as connecting with spirits, then one will have ill fortune. . . .

> To exalt Heaven and long for it—[29]
>> How can this compare to nourishing things and overseeing them?
> To obey Heaven and praise it—
>> How can this compare to overseeing what Heaven has mandated and using it?
> To observe the seasons and wait upon them—
>> How can this compare to responding to the seasons and employing them?
> To follow along with things and increase them—
>> How can this compare to developing their powers and transforming them?
> To long for things and appraise them—
>> How can this compare to ordering things and never losing them?
> To desire that from which things arise—
>> How can this compare to taking hold of that by which things are completed?

---

[29]From here down to the word "confusion" in the next paragraph, the original text is rhymed.

Thus, if one rejects what lies with man and instead longs for what lies with Heaven, then one will have lost grasp of the true disposition of things.

The unchanging element among the reigns of the hundred kings can serve as the thread of the Way. As one thing passes by and another arises, respond to them with this thread. If one has mastered the thread, there will be no chaos. If one does not know the thread, one will not know how to respond to changes. The major substance of the thread has never perished, but chaos arises from falling short of it, whereas order arises from adhering to it meticulously. And so as for what is counted good in light of the Way, courses of action conforming to it may be followed, but those veering from it may not be followed. Those that obscure it will create great confusion. Those who cross waters mark out the deep places, but if the markers are not clear, then people will fall in. Those who order the people mark out the Way, but if the markers are not clear, then there will be chaos. The rituals are those markers. To reject ritual is to bemuddle the world, and to bemuddle the world is to create great chaos. And so, when the Way is in no part unclear, and that which is within the bounds and outside the bounds have different markers, and that which is inglorious and that which is illustrious have constant measures, then the pitfalls of the people will be eliminated.

The ten thousand things are but one facet of the Way. A single thing is but one facet of the ten thousand things. Those who are foolish take a single facet of a single thing and think themselves to know the Way—this is to be without knowledge. Shenzi saw the value of hanging back, but did not see the value of being in the lead.[30] Laozi saw the value of yielding, but did not see the value of exerting oneself. Mozi saw the value of making things uniform, but did not see the value of establishing differences. Songzi saw the value of having few desires, but did not see the value of having many desires. If there is only hanging back and no being in the lead, then the masses will have no gateway to advancing. If there is only yielding and no exerting oneself, then the noble and the lowly will not be distinguished. If there is only uniformity and no difference, then governmental orders cannot be promulgated. If there are only few desires and not many desires, then the masses cannot be transformed. The *History* says, "Do not innovate in your fondnesses; follow the Way of the kings. Do not innovate in your aversions; follow the road of the kings." [31] This expresses my meaning. . . .

---

[30]From here down to the quote from the *History*, the original text is rhymed.

[31]Quoted earlier in the "Cultivating Oneself" chapter. See *Xunzi*, chapter 2, p. 257.

Chapter Nineteen: Discourse on Ritual

From what did ritual arise? I say: Humans are born having desires. When they have desires but do not get the objects of their desires, then they cannot but seek some means of satisfaction. If there is no measure or limit to their seeking, then they cannot help but struggle with each other. If they struggle with each other then there will be chaos, and if there is chaos then they will be impoverished. The former kings hated such chaos, and so they established rituals and the standards of righteousness in order to allot things to people, to nurture their desires, and to satisfy their seeking. They caused desires never to exhaust material goods, and material goods never to be depleted by desires, so that the two support each other and prosper. This is how ritual arose.[32]

Thus, ritual is a means of nurture. Meats and grains, the five flavors and the various spices are means to nurture the mouth. Fragrances and perfumes are means to nurture the nose. Carving and inlay, insignias and patterns are means to nurture the eyes. Bells and drums, pipes and chimes, lutes and zithers are means to nurture the ears. Homes and palaces, cushions and beds, tables and mats are means to nurture the body. Thus, ritual is a means of nurture. The gentleman not only obtains its nurturing, but also loves its differentiations. What is meant by "differentiations"? I say: It is for noble and lowly to have their proper ranking, for elder and youth to have their proper distance, and for poor and rich, humble and eminent each to have their proper weights. And so, in the Grand Chariot of the Emperor there are cushions, as a means to nurture his body. On the sides are carried sweet-smelling angelica, as a means to nurture his nose. In front there is a patterned yoke, as a means to nurture his eyes. The sounds of the attached bells match the tunes *Wu* and *Xiang*[33] when proceeding slowly, and they match the tunes *Shao* and *Hu*[34] when proceeding quickly, as a means to nurture his ears. There is a dragon pennant with nine tassels, as a means to nurture his ability to inspire trust. There are insignias of a crouching rhinoceros and kneeling tiger, serpent-decorated coverings for the horses, silk curtains, and dragon patterns on the chariot hooks, as a means to nurture his awe-inspiring authority. And so, the horses of the Grand

---

[32]Cf. *Mozi*, chapter 11, pp. 60–61.

[33]The *Wu* and the *Xiang* were pieces of music associated with King Wu.

[34]The *Shao* and *Hu* were pieces of music associated with Shun and Tang, respectively.

Chariot are repeatedly given training to be obedient, and only then will they be harnessed, as a means to nurture his safety.

Know well that to abide by the proper measure even at risk of death is the means to nurture one's life. Know well that to make expenditures is the way to nurture wealth. Know well that reverence, respect, and deference are the way to nurture safety. Know well that ritual, the standards of righteousness, good form and proper order are the way to nurture one's dispositions. And so, if a person has his eyes only on living, such a one is sure to die. If a person has his eyes only on benefiting himself, such a one is sure to be harmed. If a person takes comfort only in laziness and sluggishness, such a one is sure to be endangered. If a person takes pleasure only in delighting his inborn dispositions, such a one is sure to be destroyed. And so, if a person puts even one measure of effort into following ritual and the standards of righteousness, he will get back twice as much. If he puts even one measure of effort into following his nature and inborn dispositions, he will lose twice as much. And so, the Confucians are those who will cause people to gain twice as much, and the Mohists are those who will cause people to lose twice as much. This is the difference between the Confucians and the Mohists.

Ritual has three roots. Heaven and earth are the root of life. Forefathers and ancestors are the root of one's kind. Rulers and teachers are the root of order. Without Heaven and earth, how would one live? Without forefathers and ancestors, how would one have come forth? Without rulers and teachers, how would there be order? Of these three, if even one is neglected there will be no one safe. And so, ritual serves Heaven above and earth below, it honors forefathers and ancestors, and it exalts rulers and teachers. These are the three roots of ritual. . . .

In every case, ritual begins in that which must be released, reaches full development in giving it proper form, and finishes in providing it satisfaction. And so when ritual is at its most perfect, the requirements of inner dispositions and proper form are both completely fulfilled. At its next best, the dispositions and outer form overcome one another in succession. Its lowest manner is to revert to the dispositions alone so as to subsume everything in this grand unity.

> By ritual, Heaven and earth harmoniously combine;
> By ritual, the sun and the moon radiantly shine;
> By ritual, the four seasons in progression arise;
> By ritual, the stars move orderly across the skies;

By ritual, the great rivers through their courses flow;
By ritual, the ten thousand things all thrive and grow;
By ritual, for love and hate proper measure is made;
By ritual, on joy and anger fit limits are laid.
By ritual, compliant subordinates are created,
By ritual, enlightened leaders are generated;
With ritual, all things can change yet not bring chaos,
But deviate from ritual and you face only loss.

Is not ritual perfect indeed! It establishes a lofty standard that is the ultimate of its kind, and none under Heaven can add to or subtract from it. In it, the fundamental and the secondary accord with each other, and beginning and end match each other. In its differentiations of things, it is the utmost in patterning. In its explanations, it is the utmost in keen discernment. Those under Heaven who follow it will have good order. Those who do not follow it will have chaos. Those who follow it will have safety. Those who do not follow it will be endangered. Those who follow it will be preserved. Those who do not follow it will perish. The petty man cannot fathom it. Deep indeed is the principle of ritual! Investigations into the hard and the white, the same and the different drown when they try to enter into it.[35] Vast indeed is the principle of ritual! Those expert in creating institutions and the purveyors of perverse, vulgar doctrines are lost when they try to enter it. High indeed is the principle of ritual! Those who take violent arrogance, haughty indulgence, and contempt of custom for loftiness fall when they try to enter it.

And so, when the ink-line is reliably laid out, then one cannot be deceived by the curved and the straight. When the scale is reliably hung, then one cannot be deceived by the light and the heavy. When the compass and carpenter's square are reliably set out, then one cannot be deceived by the circular and the rectangular. The gentleman examines ritual carefully, and then he cannot be deceived by trickery and artifice. Thus, the ink-line is the ultimate in straightness, the scale is the ultimate in balance, the compass and carpenter's square are the ultimate in circular and rectangular, and ritual is the ultimate in the human way. Those who nevertheless do not take ritual as their model nor find sufficiency in it are called "standardless commoners." Those who take ritual as their model and find sufficiency in it are called "men of standards." To be able to reflect and ponder what is

---

[35]This refers to debates among members of the so-called *Mingjia*. See *Important Terms*.

central to ritual is called "being able to deliberate." To be able not to diverge from what is central to ritual is called "being able to be firm." When one can deliberate and be firm, and adds to this fondness for it, then this is to be a sage. Thus, Heaven is the ultimate in height, earth is the ultimate in depth, the boundless is the ultimate in breadth, and the sage is the ultimate in the Way. And so, learning is precisely learning to be a sage—one does not learn solely so as to become a standardless commoner.

Ritual takes resources and goods as its implements. It takes noble and lowly as its patterns. It takes abundance and scarcity as its differentiations. It takes elevating some and lowering others as its essentials. When patterning and order are made bountiful, and the dispositions and implements are limited, this is the most elevated state of ritual. When the dispositions and implements are made bountiful, but the patterning and order are limited, this is the lowest state of ritual. When patterning and order, dispositions and implements are in turn central and peripheral, so that they proceed together and are mixed evenly, this is the intermediate course of ritual. And so at his greatest, the gentleman achieves the most elevated state of ritual, and at the least he fulfills completely its lowest form, and when in intermediate circumstances, he dwells in its intermediate form. Whether going slowly, quickly, or at full gallop, he never departs from this, for this is the gentleman's home and palace. If a person grasps this, he is a man of good breeding or a gentleman. If he departs from this, he is but a commoner. Thus, to be able to travel everywhere in its midst and in every case obtain its proper arrangement is to be a sage. And so, being generous is due to the accumulated richness of ritual. Being great is due to the vastness of ritual. Being lofty is due to the elevated nature of ritual. Being enlightened is due to the exhaustive nature of ritual. The *Odes* says, "Their rituals and ceremonies completely follow the proper measure. Their laughter and speech are completely appropriate."[36] This expresses my meaning.

Ritual is that which takes care to order living and dying. Birth is the beginning of people, and death is the end of people. When beginning and end are both good, then the human way is complete. Thus, the gentleman is respectful of the beginning and careful about the end. When end and beginning are treated alike, this is the way of the gentleman, and the proper form contained in ritual and the standards of righteousness. To treat people generously while alive but stingily when dead is to show respect to those with

---

[36]*Mao* # 209. These same lines are quoted earlier in the "Cultivating Oneself" chapter. See *Xunzi*, chapter 2, p. 254.

awareness and show arrogance to those without awareness. This is the way of a vile person and is an attitude of betrayal. The gentleman considers it shameful to use such a betraying attitude in dealing with servants and children—how much more so in the case of those he exalts and those he loves! . . .

Ritual cuts off what is too long and extends what is too short. It subtracts from what is excessive and adds to what is insufficient. It achieves proper form for love and respect, and it brings to perfection the beauty of carrying out the standards of righteousness. Thus, fine ornaments and coarse materials, music and weeping, happiness and sorrow—these things are opposites, but ritual makes use of them all, employing them and alternating them at the appropriate times. And so, fine ornaments, music, and happiness are that by which one responds to peaceful events and that by which one pays homage to good fortune. Coarse mourning garments, weeping, and sorrow are that by which one responds to threatening events and that by which one pays homage to ill fortune. Thus, the way ritual makes use of fine ornaments is such as not to lead to exorbitance and indulgence. The way it makes use of coarse mourning garments is such as not to lead to infirmity or despondency. The way it makes use of music and happiness is such as not to lead to perversity or laziness. The way it makes use of weeping and sorrow is such as not to lead to dejection or self-harm. This is the mid-way course of ritual.

Thus, when the changes in disposition and appearance are sufficient to differentiate good fortune and ill fortune and to make clear the proper measures for noble and lowly, close relations and distant relations, then ritual stops. To go beyond this is vile, and even should it be a feat of amazing difficulty, the gentleman will still consider it base. And so, to measure one's food and then eat it, to measure one's waist and then tie the mourning sash, to show off to those in high positions one's emaciation and infirmity—this is the way of a vile person. It is not the proper patterning of ritual and the standards of righteousness; it is not the true disposition of a filial son. It is rather the behavior of one acting for ulterior purposes.

And so, a joyful glow and a shining face, a sorrowful look and a haggard appearance—these are the ways in which the dispositions in good fortune and ill fortune, happiness and sorrow are expressed in one's countenance. Singing and laughing, weeping and sobbing—these are the ways in which the dispositions in good fortune and ill fortune, happiness and sorrow are expressed in one's voice. Fine meats and grains and wine and fish, gruel and roughage and plain water—these are the ways in which the dispositions in good fortune and ill fortune, happiness and sorrow are expressed in one's food and drink. Ceremonial caps and embroidered insignias and woven patterns, coarse cloth and a mourning headband and thin garments and hempen sandals—these are the ways in which the dispositions in good fortune and ill fortune, happiness and sorrow are expressed in one's dress. Homes and palaces and cushions and beds and tables and mats, a thatched roof and mourning lean-to and rough mat and earthen pillow—these are the ways in which the dispositions in good fortune and ill fortune, happiness and sorrow are expressed in one's dwelling.

In people's lives originally there are the beginnings of these two dispositions. If you cut them short and extend them, broaden them and narrow them, add to them and subtract from them, make them conform to their proper classes and fully express them, make them abundant and beautify them, cause root and branch, beginning and end all to go smoothly and fit together, then they can serve as the model for ten thousand ages—and just such is what ritual does! None but a devotedly and thoroughly cultivated gentleman can understand it.

Thus, I say that human nature is the original beginning and the raw material, and *wei* 偽, "deliberate effort," is to pattern and order it and make it exalted. If there were no human nature, then there would be nothing for deliberate effort to be applied to. If there were no deliberate effort, then human nature would not be able to beautify itself. Human nature and deliberate effort must unite, and then the reputation of the sage and the work of unifying all under Heaven is thereupon brought to completion. And so I say, when Heaven and earth unite, then the myriad creatures are born. When *yin* and *yang* interact, then changes and transformations arise. When human nature and deliberate effort unite, then all under Heaven is ordered. For Heaven can give birth to creatures, but it cannot enforce distinctions among creatures. Earth can support people, but it cannot order people. In the world, the ten thousand things and human beings all must await the sage, and only then will they be appropriately divided up. The *Odes* says, "He mollifies the hundred spirits, and extends this to the rivers and towering peaks."[37] This expresses my meaning.[38] . . .

Among all the living things between Heaven and earth, those that have blood and *qi* are sure to have awareness, and of those that have awareness,

---

[37] *Mao* # 273.

[38] This paragraph does not fit well with the context. Burton Watson (1963) suggests that it may have fallen out of place from chapter 23. Nonetheless, it expresses very important ideas relating to Xunzi's view of human nature.

none does not love its own kind. Now if one of the great birds or beasts loses its group of companions, then after a month or a season has passed, it is sure to retrace its former path and go by its old home. When it does, it is sure to pace back and forth, cry out, stomp the ground, pause hesitatingly, and only then is it able to leave the place. Even among smaller creatures such as swallows and sparrows, they will still screech for a moment before being able to leave. Thus, among the creatures that have blood and *qi*, none has greater awareness than man, and so man's feeling for his parents knows no limit until the day they die. Will we follow foolish, ignorant, perverse men? Those who have died that morning they forget by that evening. If one gives way to this, then one will not even be as good as the birds and beasts. How could such people come together and live in groups without there being chaos? Will we follow cultivated gentlemen? For them the twenty-five months of the three year mourning period passes by as quickly as a galloping horse glimpsed though a crack. If one simply acquiesces in this, then mourning would continue without end. Therefore, the former kings and sages accordingly established a middle way and fixed a proper measure for it, such that once mourning is made sufficient to achieve good form and proper order, then one stops it.

Chapter Twenty: Discourse on Music

Music is joy, an unavoidable human disposition. So, people cannot be without music; if they feel joy, they must express it in sound and give it shape in movement. The way of human beings is that changes in the motions of their nature are completely contained in these sounds and movements. So, people cannot be without joy, and their joy cannot be without shape, but if it takes shape and does not accord with the Way, then there will inevitably be chaos. The former kings hated such chaos, and therefore they established the sounds of the *Ya* and the *Song*[39] in order to guide them. They caused the sounds to be enjoyable without becoming excessive.[40] They caused the patterns to be recognizable without becoming degenerate. They caused the progression, complexity, intensity, and rhythm of the music to be sufficient to move the goodness in people's hearts. They caused perverse and corrupt *qi* to have no place to attach itself to them. This is the

---

[39]The names of parts of the *Odes*. See the entry for the *Odes* in *Important Texts*.

[40]Cf. *Analects* 3.20.

manner in which the former kings created music, and so why is Mozi denouncing it?[41]

And so, when music is performed in the ancestral temple and the ruler and ministers, superiors and inferiors, listen to it together, there are none who do not become harmoniously respectful. When it is performed within the home and father and sons, elder and younger brothers listen to it together, there are none who do not become harmoniously affectionate. And when it is performed in the village, and old and young people listen to it together, there are none who do not become harmoniously cooperative. Thus, music observes a single standard in order to fix its harmony, it brings together different instruments in order to ornament its rhythm, and it combines their playing in order to achieve a beautiful pattern. It is sufficient to lead people in a single, unified way, and is sufficient to bring order to the myriad changes within them. This is the method by which the former kings created music, and so why is Mozi denouncing it?[42] . . .

Chapter Twenty-One: Undoing Fixation

Almost always, the problem with people is that they become fixated on one angle and are deluded about the greater order of things. If they are brought under control, then they will return to the right standards. If they are of two minds, then they will be hesitant and confused. There are not two Ways for the world, and the sage is not of two minds. Nowadays the feudal lords have different governments, and the hundred schools have different teachings, so that necessarily some are right and some are wrong, and some lead to order and some lead to chaos. The rulers of chaotic states and the followers of pernicious schools all sincerely seek what they consider correct and put themselves into achieving it. They hate what they consider erroneous views of the Way, and others are seduced into following their same path. They selfishly favor the approach in which they have accumulated effort and only fear to hear it disparaged. They rely on it when regarding other approaches and only fear to hear those others praised. Therefore, they depart further and further from getting under control and think they are right not to stop. Is this not because they have become fixated on one angle and missed the true object of their search? If the heart does not apply itself to the eyes, then black and white can be right in front of you and the eyes will not see them. If the heart does not apply itself to the ears, then drums

---

[41]Cf. *Mozi*, chapter 32, pp. 100–05.

[42]The repetition of this sentence may be meant to mock Mozi's own repetitive style.

and thunder can be right at your side and the ears will not hear them. How much more so in the case of that which is applying itself in the first place![43] The person of true Virtue and the true Way is denounced from above by the rulers of chaotic states, and denounced from below by the followers of pernicious schools. Is this not lamentable?

Thus, among the cases of fixation, one can be fixated on desires, or one can be fixated on dislikes. One can be fixated on origins, or one can be fixated on ends. One can be fixated on what is far away, or one can be fixated on what is nearby. One can be fixated by broad learning, or one can be fixated by narrowness. One can be fixated on the ancient past, or one can be fixated on the present. In whatever respect the ten thousand things are different, they can become objects of fixation to the exclusion of each other. This is the common problem in the ways of human hearts. . . .

Mozi was fixated on the useful and did not understand the value of good form. Songzi was fixated on having few desires and did not understand the value of achieving the objects of desires. Shenzi was fixated on laws and did not understand the value of having worthy people. Shen Buhai was fixated on power and did not understand the value of having wise people. Huizi was fixated on words and did not understand the value of their corresponding objects. Zhuangzi was fixated on the Heavenly and did not understand the value of the human.

Thus, if one speaks of it in terms of usefulness, then the Way will consist completely in seeking what is profitable. If one speaks of it in terms of desires, then the Way will consist completely in learning to be satisfied. If one speaks of it in terms of laws, then the Way will consist completely in making arrangements. If one speaks of it in terms of power, then the Way will consist completely in finding what is expedient. If one speaks of it in terms of wording, then the Way will consist completely in discoursing on matters. If one speaks of it in terms of the Heavenly, then the Way will consist completely in following along with things. These various approaches are all merely one aspect of the Way. As for the Way itself, its substance is constant, yet it covers all changes. No one aspect is sufficient to exhibit it fully.

People of biased understanding observe just a single aspect of the Way and are unable to recognize it as such. So, they think it sufficient and proceed to embellish it. On the inside, they use it to disorder their own lives. On the outside, they use it to confuse other people. As superiors, they use

---

[43]That is, just as the heart must apply itself to the sense organs in order for them to perceive correctly, so it must watch over itself in order to avoid obsession and apprehend the truth.

it to transfix their subordinates. As subordinates, they use it to transfix their superiors. This is the disaster of being fixated and blocked up in one's thinking. Kongzi was benevolent, wise, and was not fixated, and so through his study of various methods, he was worthy of being one of the former kings. His one line alone grasped the way of the Zhou and upheld and used it, because he was not fixated by accumulated efforts in any area. Thus, his Virtue equals that of the Duke of Zhou, and his name ranks with those of the three kings. This is the good fortune that comes from not being fixated.

The sage knows the problems in the ways of men's hearts, and sees the disaster of being fixated and blocked up in one's thinking. So, he is neither for desires, nor for dislikes, is neither for the origins, nor for the end results, is neither for what is near, nor for what is far away, is neither for what is broad, nor for what is shallow, is neither for the ancient past, nor for the present. He lays out all the ten thousand things and in their midst hangs his scales over them. For this reason, the various different things are unable to become fixating and so disorder the proper categories of things.

What am I calling his "scales"? I say: It is the Way. Thus, one's heart must not be ignorant of the Way. If the heart does not know the Way, then it will not approve of the Way, but will rather approve what is not the Way. For what person would wish to be so dissolute as to keep to what they disapprove and reject what they approve? If one chooses people using a heart that does not approve of the Way, then one is sure to accord with people who do not follow the Way, and one will not know to accord with people who *do* follow the Way. To use a heart that does not approve of the Way and to join together with people who do not follow the Way when judging people who do follow the Way—this is the root of chaos.

How will one know [which are the people who follow the Way]? I say: The heart must know the Way, and only then will it approve of the Way. Only after it approves of the Way will it be able to keep to the Way and reject what is not the Way. If one chooses people using a heart that approves of the Way, then one will accord with people who follow the Way, and one will not accord with people who do not follow the Way. To use a heart that approves of the Way and to join together with people who follow the Way when judging what is not the Way—this is the essential thing for good order. What problem of not knowing [which people follow the Way] could there be? Thus, the essential thing for good order rests in knowing the Way.

How do people know the Way? I say: It is with the heart. How does the heart know the Way? I say: It is through emptiness, single-mindedness, and stillness. The heart is never not holding something. Yet, there is a state called being "empty." The heart is never not two-fold. Yet, there is a state called being "single-minded." The heart is never not moving. Yet, there is a state called being "still." Humans are born and have awareness. With awareness, they have focus.[44] To focus is to be holding something. Yet, there is a state called being "empty." Not to let what one is already holding harm what one is about to receive is called being "empty."[45] The heart is born and has awareness. With awareness, there come awareness of differences. These differences are known at the same time, and when they are known at the same time, this is to be two-fold. Yet, there is a state called being "single-minded." Not to let one idea harm another idea is called being "single-minded." When the heart sleeps, then it dreams. When it relaxes, then it goes about on its own. When one puts it to use, then it forms plans. Thus, the heart is never not moving. Yet, there is a state called being "still." Not to let dreams and worries disorder one's understanding is called being "still."

For those who have not yet grasped the Way but are seeking the Way, I say: Emptiness, single-mindedness, and stillness—make these be your principles. If one who would search for the Way achieves emptiness, then he may enter upon it. If one who would work at the Way achieves single-mindedness, then he will exhaustively obtain it. If one who would ponder the Way achieves stillness, then he will discern it keenly. One who knows the Way and observes things by it, who knows the Way and puts it into practice, is one who embodies the Way. To be empty, single-minded, and still—this is called great clarity and brilliance. For such a one, none of the ten thousand things takes form and is not seen. None is seen and not judged. None is judged and loses its proper position. He sits in his chamber yet sees all within the four seas.[46] He dwells in today yet judges what is long ago and far away in time. He comprehensively observes the ten thousand things and knows their true dispositions. He inspects and examines order and disorder and discerns their measures. He sets straight Heaven and earth, and arranges and makes useful the ten thousand things. He institutes great order, and the whole world is en-

---

[44]Reading 志 as it appears in the text. Most commentators and translators read it as 誌, "memory." Cf. Mengzi 2A2; especially n. 19.

[45]From this explanation, it is clear that what Xunzi means by "emptiness" is *not* having no thoughts or clearing out one's mind, but rather the ability to take up new ideas and objects of attention. Thus, his "emptiness" is more akin to what nowadays would be called "receptiveness."

[46]Cf. *Laozi*, chapter 47.

compassed therein. So vast and broad is he! Who grasps his true limits? So lofty and broad is he! Who grasps his true Virtue? So active and varied is he! Who grasps his true form? His brilliance matches the sun and moon. His greatness fills all the eight directions. Such a one is called the "Great Man." What fixation could there be in him?

The heart is the ruler of the body and the master of one's spirit and intelligence. It issues orders, but it takes orders from nothing: *it* restrains itself, *it* employs itself; *it* lets itself go, *it* takes itself in hand; *it* makes itself proceed, *it* makes itself stop. Thus, the mouth can be compelled either to be silent or to speak, and the body can be compelled either to contract or to extend itself, but the heart cannot be compelled to change its thoughts. What it considers right, one accepts. What it considers wrong, one rejects. And so I say: If the heart allows its choices to be without restraint, then necessarily it will display its own objects as broadly varying. Its perfected disposition is to be undivided. The *Odes* says,

> I pick and pick the *juan-er* leaves,
> but cannot fill my sloping basket.
> Oh for my cherished one!
> He is stationed on the Zhou campaign.[47]

A sloping basket is easy to fill, and the *juan-er* leaves are easy to get, but one must not be divided with thoughts of the Zhou campaign. And so I say: If the heart is split, it will be without understanding. If it deviates, it will not be expertly refined. If it is divided, then it will be confused. If one guides its examinations, then the ten thousand things can all be known together, and if the person thoroughly develops his original substance, then he will be truly beautiful.

The proper classes of things are not of two kinds. Hence, the person with understanding picks the one right object and pursues it single-mindedly. The farmer is expert in regard to the fields, but cannot be made Overseer of Fields. The merchant is expert in regard to the markets, but cannot be made Overseer of Merchants. The craftsman is expert in regard to vessels, but cannot be made Overseer of Vessels. There is a person who is incapable of any of their three skills, but who can be put in charge of any of these offices, namely the one who is expert in regard to the Way, not the one who is expert in regard to things. One who is expert in regard to things merely measures one thing against another. One who is expert in regard to

---

[47] *Mao #3.*

the Way measures all things together.[48] Thus, the gentleman pursues the Way single-mindedly and uses it to guide and oversee things. If one pursues the Way single-mindedly, then one will be correct. If one uses it to guide one in examining things, then one will have keen discernment. If one uses correct intentions to carry out discerning judgments, then the ten thousand things will all obtain their proper station. . . .

The human heart can be compared to a pan of water. If you set it straight and do not move it, the muddy and turbid parts will settle to the bottom, and the clear and bright parts will be on the top, and then one can see one's whiskers and inspect the lines on one's face. But if a slight breeze passes over it, the muddy and turbid parts will be stirred up from the bottom, and the clear and bright parts will be disturbed on top, and then one cannot get a correct view of even large contours. The heart is just like this.[49] Thus, if one guides it with good order, nourishes it with clarity and nothing can make it deviate, then it will be capable of determining right and wrong and deciding what is doubtful. If it is drawn aside by even a little thing, then on the outside one's correctness will be altered, and on the inside one's heart will deviate, and one will be incapable of discerning the multifarious patterns of things. . . .

In the caves there lived a man named Ji.[50] He was good at guessing riddles because he was fond of pondering things. However, if the desires of his eyes and ears were aroused, it would ruin his thinking, and if he heard the sounds of mosquitoes or gnats, it would frustrate his concentration. So, he shut out the desires of his eyes and ears and put himself far away from the sounds of mosquitoes and gnats, and by dwelling in retreat and stilling his thoughts, he achieved comprehension. But can pondering benevolence in such a manner be called "true sublimeness"? Mengzi hated depravity and so expelled his wife—this can be called "being able to force oneself."[51] Youzi[52] hated dozing off and so burned his palm—this can be called "being able to steel oneself." These are not yet true fondness for it. To shut out the desires of one's eyes and ears can be called "forcing oneself." It is not yet truly pondering it. To be such that hearing the sounds of mosquitoes or gnats frustrates one's concentration is called "being precarious." It cannot yet be called "true sublimeness."

---

[48]Cf. *Analects* 2.12 and the note to that passage.

[49]Cf. *Zhuangzi*, chapter 5, p. 227.

[50]This person is unattested elsewhere, and the pronunciation of the name is uncertain.

[51]For an account of this incident, see D. C. Lau, *Mencius* (New York: Penguin Books, 1970), p. 217.

[52]Youzi, also known as You Ruo, was a disciple of Kongzi.

One who is truly sublime is a perfected person. For the perfected person, what forcing oneself, what steeling oneself, what precariousness is there? Thus, those who are murky understand only the external manifestations, but those who are clear understand the internal manifestations. The sage follows his desires and embraces all his dispositions, and the things dependent on these simply turn out well ordered. What forcing oneself, what steeling oneself, what precariousness is there? Thus, the person of benevolence carries out the Way without striving, and the sage carries out the Way without forcing himself. The benevolent person ponders it with reverence, and the sage ponders it with joy. This is the proper way to order one's heart.

Chapter Twnety-Two:
On Correct Naming[53]

In setting names for things, the later kings followed the Shang in names for punishments, followed the Zhou in names for official titles, and also followed their rituals in names for cultural forms. In applying various names to the ten thousand things, they followed the set customs and generally agreed usage of the Xia. Villages in distant places with different customs followed along with these names and so were able to communicate.

As for the ways the various names apply to people, that which is so by birth is called "human nature." The close connection of response to stimulus, which requires no effort but is so of itself, and which is produced by the harmonious operation of the nature, is also called "human nature." The feelings of liking and disliking, happiness and anger, and sadness and joy in one's nature are called the *qing* 情, "dispositions." When there is a certain disposition and the heart makes a choice on its behalf, this is called "deliberation." When the heart deliberates and one's abilities act on it, this is called "deliberate effort." That which comes into being through accumulated deliberations and training of one's abilities is also called "deliberate effort." Actions performed for the sake of profit are called "work." Actions performed for what is required by the standards of righteousness are called "proper conduct." That by which people understand things is called the "understanding." When the understanding connects to things, this is called "knowledge." That by which people are able to do things is called "ability." When ability con-

---

[53]Cf. *Analects* 13.3 and note 128 to that passage. "Name" in both passages is *ming* 名, which can refer not only to proper names, but to words in general.

nects to things, these are also called "abilities."[54] When the nature is injured, this is called "illness." When one encounters unexpected circumstances, this is called *ming* 命, "fate." These are the ways the various names apply to people. These are the ways the later kings set names for things.

So when the kings established names, the names were fixed, and the corresponding objects were thus distinguished. This way was followed, and the kings' intentions were thus made understood. They then carefully led the people to adhere to these things single-mindedly. Thus, they called it great vileness to mince words and recklessly create names so as to disorder the correct names and thereby confuse the people and cause them to engage in much disputation and litigation. This wrongdoing was considered to be just like the crime of forging tallies and measures. Hence, none of their people dared rely on making up strange names so as to disorder the correct names, and so the people were honest and guileless. Since they were honest and guileless, they were easy to employ, and since they were easy to employ, tasks were accomplished. Because none of the people dared rely on making up strange names so as to disorder the correct names, they were unified in following the proper model of the Way and were conscientious in following commands. Because they were like this, the achievements of the kings were long-lasting. To have long-lasting achievements and to complete great accomplishments is the height of good order. Such is the great accomplishment that comes from conscientiously preserving the agreed names.

Nowadays, the sage-kings have passed away, and the preservation of these names has become lax. Strange words have arisen, the names and their corresponding objects are disordered, and the forms of right and wrong are unclear. As a result, even officers who diligently preserve the proper models and scholars who diligently recite the proper order for things are also all thrown into chaos. If there arose a true king, he would surely follow the old names in some cases and create new names in other cases. Thus, one must examine the reason for having names, the proper means for distinguishing like and unlike, and the essential points in establishing names.

When different forms make contact with the heart, they make each other understood as different things. If the names and their corresponding objects are tied together in a confused fashion, then the distinction between noble and base will not be clear, and the like and the unlike will not

---

[54]That is, when the potential to do something is manifested in a certain activity, it is called a particular ability (e.g. one is said to have the *ability* to drive when one performs the activities specific to that skill).

be differentiated. If this is so, then the problem of intentions not being understood will surely happen, and the disaster of affairs being thereby impeded and abandoned will surely occur. Thus, the wise person draws differences and establishes names in order to point out their corresponding objects. Most importantly, he makes clear the distinction between noble and base, and, at the least, he distinguishes the like and the unlike. When noble and base are clearly distinguished, and like and unlike are differentiated, then there will be no problem of intentions not being understood, and the disaster of affairs being thereby impeded and abandoned will not occur. This is the reason for having names. . . .

Names have no predetermined appropriateness. One forms agreement in order to name things. Once the agreement is set and has become custom, then the names are called "appropriate," and what differs from the agreed usage is called "inappropriate." Names have no predetermined objects. One forms agreement in order to name objects. Once the agreement is set and has become custom, then they are called "names of objects."[55] There *is* a pre-determined goodness for names. If they are straightforward, simple, and do not conflict, then they are called good names.

Some things have a like appearance but reside in unlike classes, and others have unlike appearances but reside in the like class, and these two can be differentiated. For those which have a like appearance but reside in unlike classes, even though they could be combined into one class, they are called two separate objects. If the appearance changes but the object does not become different so as to belong to an unlike class, this is called a transformation. When there is transformation without such difference, it is still called one and the same object. These are what to rely upon in observing the objects and determining their numbers.[56] This is the essential point in establishing names, and the names established by the later kings must not go unexamined.

Claims such as "To be insulted is not disgraceful,"[57] "The sage does not love himself,"[58] and "To kill a robber is not to kill a man,"[59] are cases of confusion about the use of names leading to disordering names. If one tests

---

[55]Xunzi's point seems to be that only after usage is set do the names have any meaning, rather than being mere sound.

[56]Xunzi here seems to be talking about identifying and individuating classes, rather than identifying and individuating particular entities.

[57]This claim was put forth by Songzi.

[58]It is unknown who put forth this claim.

[59]This is a famous Mohist argument.

them against the reason why there are names, and observes what happens when they are carried out thoroughly, then one will be able to reject them. Claims such as "Mountains and gorges are level,"[60] "The natural dispositions and desires are few,"[61] "Fine meats are not any more flavorful," and "Great bells are not any more entertaining"[62] are cases of confusion about the use of objects leading to disordering names. If one tests them against the proper means for distinguishing like and unlike, and observes what happens when they are thoroughly practiced, then one will be able to reject them. Claims such as . . . "Both oxen and horses are not horses"[63] are cases of confusion about the use of names leading to disordering the objects. If one tests them against the agreement on names, using the fact that what such people accept goes against what they refuse, then one will be able to reject them. In every case of deviant sayings and perverse teachings that depart from the correct Way and recklessly innovate, they will belong to one of these three classes of confusion. Thus, the enlightened ruler understands their kind and does not dispute with such people.

The people can easily be unified by means of the Way, but one should not try to share one's reasons with them. Hence, the enlightened ruler controls them with his power, guides them with the Way, moves them with his orders, arrays them with his judgments, and restrains them with his punishments. Thus, his people's transformation by the Way is spiritlike. What need has he for demonstrations[64] and persuasions? Nowadays the sage-kings have all passed away, the whole world is in chaos, and depraved teachings are arising. The gentleman has no power to control people, no punishments to restrain them, and so he engages in demonstrations and persuasions.

When objects are not understood, then one engages in naming. When the naming is not understood, then one tries to procure agreement. When the

---

[60]This claim was put forth and defended by Huizi.

[61]This is another of Songzi's famous claims.

[62]The origin of these last two statements is uncertain.

[63]The text at this point seems corrupt, and the translation is tentative. The claim as presented here appears as an object of analysis in Mohist works.

[64]The word here is *bian* 辨, which literally means "to discriminate among things." This character was interchangeable with another, also read *bian* 辯, which means "to argue, dispute." The text seems to play on a fusion of these senses in the idea that true differences between things will be presented and defended through argument. Therefore, I have rendered it "demonstration" to convey the sense both of pointing out differences and arguing for a position.

agreement is not understood, then one engages in persuasion. When the persuasion is not understood, then one engages in demonstration. Thus, procuring agreement, naming, discrimination, and persuasion are some of the greatest forms of useful activity, and are the beginning of kingly works. When a name is heard and the corresponding object is understood, this is for names to be useful. When they are accumulated and form a pattern, this is for names to be beautiful. When one obtains both their usefulness and beauty, this is called understanding names. Names are that by which one arranges and accumulates objects. Phrases combine the names of different objects in order to discuss a single idea. Persuasion and demonstration use fixed names of objects in order to make clear the proper ways to act. Procuring agreement and naming are the functions of demonstration and persuasion. Demonstration and persuasion are the heart's way of representing the Way. The heart is the craftsman and overseer of the Way. The Way is the warp and pattern of good order. When the heart fits with the Way, when one's persuasions fit with one's heart, when one's words fit one's persuasions, then one will name things correctly and procure agreement. One will base oneself on the true disposition of things and make them understood. One will discriminate among things without going to excess, and one will extend by analogy the categories of things without violating them. When listening to cases, one will accord with good form. When engaging in demonstration, one will cover thoroughly all the reasons. One will use the true Way to discriminate what is vile just like drawing out the carpenter's line in order to grasp what is curved and what is straight. Thus, deviant sayings will not be able to cause disorder, and the hundred schools will have nowhere to hide. . . .

All those who say that good order must await the elimination of desires are people who lack the means to guide desire and cannot cope with the mere having of desires. All those who say good order must await the lessening of desires are people who lack the means to restrain desire and cannot cope with abundance of desires. Having desires and lacking desires fall under different categories, namely being alive and being dead, not order and disorder. Having many desires and having few desires also fall under different categories, namely the numbers of people's dispositions, not order and disorder.

The occurrence of desires does not wait upon the possibility of fulfilling them, but those who seek to fulfill them follow what they approve. That the occurrence of desires does not wait upon the possibility of fulfilling them is something which is received from Heaven. That those who seek to fulfill them follow what they approve is something that is received from the heart. When a single desire received from Heaven is controlled by many things received from the heart, then it will be difficult to classify it as something originally received from Heaven.

Life is what people most desire, and death is what people most despise. However, when people let go of life and bring about their own death, this is not because they do not desire life and instead desire death. Rather, it is because they do not approve of living under these circumstances, but do approve of dying under these circumstances.[65] Thus, when the desire is excessive but one's action does not match it, this is because the heart prevents it. If what the heart approves conforms to the proper patterns, then even if one's desires are many, what harm would they be to good order? When the desire is lacking but one's action surpasses it, this is because the heart compels it. If what the heart approves misses the proper patterns, then even if the desires are few, how would it stop short of chaos? Thus, order and disorder reside in what the heart approves, they are not present in the desires deriving from one's dispositions. If you do not seek for them where they reside, and instead seek for them where they are not present, then even though you say, "I have grasped them," you have simply missed them.

Human nature is an accomplishment of Heaven. The dispositions are the substance of the nature. The desires are the responses of the dispositions to things. To view the object of the desires as obtainable and seek for it is something that the dispositions cannot avoid, but to approve the object of desires and guide them is something that the understanding must provide. Thus, even for a gatekeeper, the desires cannot be eliminated, because they are the necessary equipment of one's nature. Even for the Son of Heaven, the desires cannot be completely satisfied. Yet even though the desires cannot be completely satisfied, one can get close to complete satisfaction, and even though desires cannot be eliminated, one's seeking can be regulated. (Even though what is desired cannot be completely obtained, the seeker can approach complete satisfaction. Even though desires cannot be eliminated, when what is sought is not obtained, one who deliberates about matters desires to regulate his seeking.)[66] When the Way is in ascendance, then one approaches complete fulfillment. When it is in decline, then one regulates one's seeking. In the whole world there is nothing as great as it.

Every person follows that which he approves and abandons that which he does not approve, so there has never been one who knows that nothing

---

[65]Cf. *Mengzi* 6A10.

[66]The repetitive character of these sentences makes them seem very much like glosses that were miscopied into the main text.

is as great as the Way and yet does not follow the Way. Suppose some person had a boundless desire to go south and an unsparing dislike for heading north. How would it be that, because of the impossibility of going all the way south, he would leave off heading south and instead go north? Now people have boundless desire for some things but have an unsparing dislike for others, so how would it be that, because of the impossibility of completely fulfilling their desires, they would leave the Way that will satisfy their desires and instead take up what they dislike? Thus, if one approves of the Way and follows it, then what could detract from this and so bring one to disorder? If one does not approve of the Way and departs from it, then what could add to this and yet bring one to order? Thus, those with understanding judge things by the Way and that is all, and the things those petty schools wish for in their prized doctrines can all fade away.

Chapter Twenty-Three: Human Nature is Bad

People's nature is bad. Their goodness is a matter of deliberate effort. Now people's nature is such that they are born with a fondness for profit. If they follow along with this, then struggle and contention will arise, and yielding and deference will perish therein. They are born with feelings of hate and dislike. If they follow along with these, then cruelty and villainy will arise, and loyalty and trustworthiness will perish therein. They are born with desires of the eyes and ears, a fondness for beautiful sights and sounds. If they follow along with these, then lasciviousness and chaos will arise, and ritual and the standards of righteousness, proper form and good order, will perish therein. Thus, if people follow along with their inborn nature and dispositions, they are sure to come to struggle and contention, turn to disrupting social divisions and disorder, and end up in violence. So, it is necessary to await the transforming influence of teachers and models and the guidance of ritual and the standards of righteousness, and only then will they come to yielding and deference, turn to culture and order, and end up under control. Looking at it in this way, it is clear that people's nature is bad, and their goodness is a matter of deliberate effort.

Thus, crooked wood must await steaming and straightening on the shaping frame, and only then does it become straight. Blunt metal must await honing and grinding, and only then does it become sharp.[67] Now since peo-

---

[67]Cf. Gaozi's metaphor in *Mengzi* 6A1, and opening paragraph of *Xunzi*, chapter 1, p. 248.

ple's nature is bad, they must await teachers and proper models, and only then do they become correct in their behavior. They must obtain ritual and the standards of righteousness, and only then do they become well ordered. Now without teachers or proper models for people, they will be deviant, dangerous, and incorrect in their behavior. Without ritual and the standards of righteousness, they will be unruly, chaotic, and not well ordered. In ancient times, the sage-kings saw that because people's nature is bad, they were deviant, dangerous, and not correct in their behavior, and they were unruly, chaotic, and not well-ordered. Therefore, for their sake they set up ritual and standards of righteousness, and established proper models and measures. They did this in order to straighten out and beautify people's nature and inborn dispositions and thereby correct them, and in order to train and transform people's nature and inborn dispositions and thereby guide them. Then for the first time they were well ordered and conformed to the Way. Among people of today, those who are transformed by teachers and proper models, who accumulate culture and learning, and who make ritual and the standards of righteousness their path become gentlemen. Those who give rein to their nature and inborn dispositions, who take comfort in being utterly unrestrained, and who violate ritual and the standards of righteousness become petty men. Looking at it in this way, it is clear that people's nature is bad, and their goodness is a matter of deliberate effort.

Mengzi says: When people engage in learning, this manifests the goodness of their nature. I say: This is not so. This is a case of not attaining knowledge of people's nature and of not inspecting clearly the division between people's nature and their deliberate efforts. In every case, the nature of a thing is the accomplishment of Heaven. It cannot be learned. It cannot be worked at. Ritual and the standards of righteousness are what the sage produces. They are things that people become capable of through learning, things that are achieved through working at them. Those things in people that cannot be learned and cannot be worked at are called their "nature." Those things in people that they become capable of through learning and that they achieve through working at them are called their "deliberate efforts." This is the division between nature and deliberate effort.[68]

Now people's nature is such that their eyes can see, and their ears can hear. The keenness by which they see does not depart from their eyes, and the acuity by which they hear does not depart from their ears. Their eyes are simply

---

[68]Cf. Xunzi's definitions in the opening section of the "On Correct Naming" chapter. See *Xunzi*, chapter 22, p. 278.

keen, and their ears are simply acute; it is clear that one does not learn these things. Mengzi says: People's nature is good, but they all wind up losing their nature and original state.[69] I say: If it is like this, then he is simply mistaken. People's nature is such that they are born and then depart from their original simplicity and their original material; they are sure to lose these things. Looking at it in this way, it is clear that people's nature is bad. The so-called goodness of people's nature would mean that one would not depart from one's original simplicity but would instead beautify it, would not depart from one's original material but instead make use of it. It would be to cause the relation of one's original simplicity and original material to beauty, and the relation of the heart's thoughts to goodness, to be like the way the keenness by which one sees does not depart from one's eyes, and the acuity by which one hears does not depart from one's ears, so that one can say [being good] is just like the way the eyes are bright and the ears are acute. . . .

Someone asks: If people's nature is bad, then from what are ritual and the standards of righteousness produced? I answer: In every case, ritual and the standards of righteousness are produced from the deliberate effort of the sage; they are not produced from people's nature. Thus, when the potter mixes clay and makes vessels, the vessels are produced from the deliberate efforts of the craftsman; they are not produced from people's nature. Thus, when the craftsman carves wood and makes utensils, the utensils are produced from the deliberate efforts of the craftsman; they are not produced from people's nature. The sage accumulates reflections and deliberations and practices deliberate efforts and reasoned activities in order to produce ritual and standards of righteousness and to establish proper models and measures. So, ritual and the standards of righteousness and proper models and measures are produced from the deliberate efforts of the sage; they are not produced from people's nature.

As for the way that the eyes like pretty colors, the ears like beautiful sounds, the mouth likes good flavors, the heart likes what is beneficial, and the bones and flesh like what is comfortable—these are produced from people's inborn dispositions and nature. These are things that come about of themselves in response to stimulation, things that do not need to await being worked at before being produced. Those things that are not immediate responses to stimulation, that must await being worked at before they are so, are said to be produced from deliberate effort. These are the things that nature and deliberate effort produce, and their different signs.

---

[69]Cf. *Mengzi* 6A6, 6A8, 7A15, and 7B31.

So, the sage transforms his nature and establishes deliberate effort. In establishing deliberate effort, he produces ritual and the standards of righteousness. In producing ritual and the standards of righteousness he institutes proper models and measures. Thus, ritual and the standards of righteousness and proper models and measures are produced by the sage. Thus, that in which the sage is like the masses, that in which he is no different than the masses, is his nature. That in which he differs from and surpasses the masses is his deliberate efforts.

Liking what is beneficial and desiring gain are people's inborn dispositions and nature. Suppose there were brothers who had some property to divide, and that they followed the fondness for benefit and desire for gain in their inborn dispositions and nature. If they were to do so, then the brothers would conflict and contend with each other for it. However, let them be transformed by the proper form and good order of ritual and the standards of righteousness. If so, then they would even give it over to their countrymen. Thus, following along with inborn dispositions and nature, even brothers will struggle with each other. If transformed by ritual and the standards of righteousness, then they will even give it over to their countrymen.[70]

In every case, people desire to become good because their nature is bad. The person who has little longs to have much. The person of narrow experience longs to be broadened. The ugly person longs to be beautiful. The poor person longs to be rich. The lowly person longs to be noble. That which one does not have within oneself, one is sure to seek for outside. Thus, when one is rich, one does not long for wealth. When one is noble, one does not long for power. That which one has within oneself, one is sure not to go outside oneself for it. Looking at it in this way, people desire to become good because their nature is bad.

Now people's nature is originally without ritual and without the standards of righteousness. Thus, they must force themselves to engage in learning and seek to possess them. Their nature does not know of ritual and the standards of righteousness, and so they must reflect and deliberate and seek to know them. So, going only by what they have from birth, people lack ritual and the standards of righteousness and do not know of ritual and the standards of righteousness. If people lack ritual and the standards of righteousness, then they will be chaotic. If they do not know of ritual and the standards of righteousness, then they will be unruly. So, going only by what they have from birth, unruliness and disorder are within them. Look-

---

[70]This seems to be a reference to the story of Bo Yi and Shu Qi. See *Important Figures*.

ing at it in this way, it is clear that people's nature is bad, and their goodness is a matter of deliberate effort.

Mengzi says: People's nature is good. I say: This is not so. In every case, both in ancient times and in the present, what everyone under Heaven calls good is being correct, ordered, peaceful, and controlled. What they call bad is being deviant, dangerous, unruly, and chaotic. This is the division between good and bad. Now does he really think that people's nature is originally correct, ordered, peaceful, and controlled? Then what use would there be for sage-kings? What use for ritual and the standards of righteousness? Even though there might exist sage-kings and ritual and the standards of righteousness, whatever could these add to the nature's correctness, order, peacefulness, and self-control? Now, such is not the case, because people's nature is bad. Thus, in ancient times the sage-kings saw that because their nature is bad, people were deviant, dangerous, and not correct in their behavior, and they were unruly, chaotic, and not well ordered. Therefore, for their sake they set up the power of rulers and superiors in order to control them. They made clear ritual and the standards of righteousness in order to transform them. They set up laws and standards in order to manage them. They multiplied punishments and fines in order to restrain them. As a result, they caused all under Heaven to become well ordered and conform to the Way. This is the order of the sage-kings, and the transformation from ritual and the standards of righteousness.

Now suppose one were to try doing away with the power of rulers and superiors, try doing without the transformation from ritual and the standards of righteousness, try doing away with the order of laws and standards, try doing without the restraint of punishments and fines. Then stand aside and observe how all the people of the world would treat each other. If it were like this, then the strong would harm the weak and take from them. The many would tyrannize the few and shout them down. One would not have to wait even a moment for all under Heaven to arrive at unruliness and chaos and perish. Looking at it in this way, it is clear that people's nature is bad, and that their goodness is a matter of deliberate effort.

So, those who are good at speaking of ancient times are sure to have some measure from the present. Those who are good at speaking of Heaven are sure to have some evidence from among mankind. For any discourse, one values it if things conform to its distinctions, and if it matches the test of experience. Thus, one sits and propounds it, but when one stands up then one can implement it, and when one unfolds it then one can put it into practice. Now Mengzi says: People's nature is good. Nothing conforms to his distinctions, and this does not match the test of experience. He sits and propounds it, but when he stands up then he cannot implement it, and when he unfolds it then he cannot put it into practice. Is his error not great indeed! Thus, if human nature is good then one may do away with the sage-kings and put ritual and the standards of righteousness to rest. If human nature is bad, then one simply must side with the sage-kings and honor ritual and the standards of righteousness. . . .

Someone suggests: Ritual and the standards of righteousness and the accumulation of deliberate effort are people's nature, and that is why the sage is able to produce them. I answer: This is not so. The potter mixes clay and produces tiles. Yet, how could the clay of the tiles be the potter's nature? The craftsman carves wood and makes utensils. Yet, how could the wood of the utensils be the craftsman's nature? The relationship of the sage to ritual and the standards of righteousness can be compared to mixing clay and producing things. So, how could ritual and the standards of righteousness and the accumulation of deliberate effort be people's original nature? In every respect, the nature of Yao and Shun was one and the same as that of Jie and Robber Zhi. The nature of the gentleman is one and the same as that of the petty man. Now will you take ritual and the standards of righteousness and the accumulation of deliberate effort to be a matter of human nature? Then for what do you value Yao and Shun? For what do you value the gentleman? Everything that one values in Yao and Shun and the gentleman exists because they were able to transform their nature and to establish deliberate effort. In establishing deliberate effort, they produced ritual and the standards of righteousness. Thus, the relationship of the sage to ritual and the standards of righteousness and the accumulation of deliberate effort is like mixing clay and producing things. Looking at it in this way, then how could ritual and the standards of righteousness and the accumulation of deliberate effort be people's nature? What one finds base in Jie and Robber Zhi and the petty man is that they follow along with their nature and inborn dispositions and find comfort in utter lack of restraint, so that they turn to greed for profit and struggle and contention. Thus, it is clear that people's nature is bad, and that their goodness is a matter of deliberate effort. Heaven did not favor Zengzi, Minzi Qian, and Xiao Yi[71] and exclude the masses. Then why is it that only Zengzi, Minzi Qian, and Xiao Yi were rich in the true

---

[71] Zengzi and Minzi Qian were both disciples of Kongzi. Xiao Yi (or "Filial Yi") was heir to the throne of Gaozong, ruler of the Shang dynasty. All three were famous for their displays of filial piety.

substance of filial piety and were perfect in their reputation for filial piety? It is because they exerted themselves to the utmost in ritual and the standards of righteousness. Heaven does not favor the people of Qi and Lu and exclude the people of Qin. Then why is it that with regard to the the standards of righteousness for father and son, and the proper distinction between husband and wife, they are not as good at filial reverence and respectful good form as those of Qi and Lu? It is because the people of Qin follow along with their inborn dispositions and nature, take comfort in utter lack of restraint, and are lax in regard to ritual and the standards of righteousness. How could it be because their natures are different?

Anyone on the streets could become a Yu. How do I mean this? I say: That by which Yu was Yu was that he was benevolent, righteous, lawful, and correct. Thus, benevolence, righteousness, lawfulness, and correctness have patterns that can be known and can be practiced. However, people on the streets all have the material for knowing benevolence, righteousness, lawfulness, and correctness, and they all have the equipment for practicing benevolence, righteousness, lawfulness, and correctness. Thus, it is clear that they could become a Yu. Now if benevolence, righteousness, lawfulness, and correctness originally had no patterns that could be known or practiced, then even Yu would not know benevolence, righteousness, lawfulness, and correctness, nor would he be able to practice benevolence, righteousness, lawfulness, and correctness. Shall we suppose that people on the streets originally do not have the material to know benevolence, righteousness, lawfulness, and correctness, and that they originally do not have the equipment for practicing benevolence, righteousness, lawfulness, and correctness? If so, then within the family, the people on the streets could not know the standards of righteousness for father and son, and outside the family, they could not know the proper relations of ruler and minister. This is not so. Now it is the case that the people on the streets can all know the standards of righteousness for father and son within the family, and can know the proper relations of ruler and minister outside the family. Thus, it is clear that the material for understanding these things and the equipment for practicing them is present in the people on the streets. Now if the people on the streets were to use their material for understanding these things and the equipment for practicing them to base themselves upon the knowable patterns and practicable aspects of benevolence and righteousness, then it is clear that the people on the streets could become a Yu. Now if the people on the streets were to submit themselves to the proper arts and practice learning, if they were to concentrate their heart and make single-minded their intentions, if they were to ponder, query, and thoroughly investigate— then if they add to this days upon days and connect to this a long period of time, if they accumulate goodness without stopping, then they will achieve spiritlike powers and understanding, and will form a triad with Heaven and earth.

Thus, becoming a sage is something that people achieve through accumulation. Someone says: Sageliness is achieved through accumulation, but why is it that not everyone can accumulate in this way? I say: They could do it, but they cannot be made to do it. Thus, the petty man could become a gentleman, but is not willing to become a gentleman. The gentleman could become a petty man, but is not willing to become a petty man.[72] It has never been that the petty man and gentleman are incapable of becoming each other. However, the reason they do not become each other is that while they could do so, they cannot be made to do so. Thus, it is the case that the people in the streets could become a Yu, but it is not necessarily the case that the people in the streets will be able to become a Yu. Even if one is not able to become a Yu, this does not harm the fact that one could become a Yu. One's feet could walk over every place under Heaven. Even so, there has not yet been anyone who has been able to walk everywhere under Heaven. It has never been that craftsman, carpenters, farmers, and merchants could not do each other's business. However, none have ever been able to do each other's business. Looking at it in this way, one is not always able to do what one could do. Even if one is not able to do it, this is no harm to the fact that one could do it. Thus, the difference between being able and being unable, on the one hand, and could and could not, on the other, is far indeed. It is clear, then, that [the gentleman and the petty man] could become one another.

Yao asked Shun, "What are people's inborn dispositions like?" Shun answered, "People's inborn dispositions are most unlovely! Why ask about them? When one has a wife and son, then one's filial piety to one's parents declines. When one's appetites and desires are fulfilled, then one's faithfulness to friends declines. When one's rank and salary are full, then one's loyalty to one's ruler declines. People's inborn dispositions? People's inborn dispositions? They are most unlovely! Why ask about them? Only the worthy man is not like that." . . .

---

[72]Cf. *Mengzi* 6A15.

SELECTIVE BIBLIOGRAPHY

Translations

Knoblock, John.

1988–94 *Xunzi: A Translation and Study of the Complete Works*, vols. 1–3. Stanford, CA: Stanford University Press (vol. 1, 1988; vol. 2, 1990; vol. 3, 1994). (The only full translation of Xunzi's works in English. Includes detailed information on historical and philosophical background, as well as an extensive bibliography of works pertaining to Xunzi.)

Watson, Burton.

1963 *Hsün Tzu: Basic Writings*. New York: Columbia University Press. (A highly readable selective translation of the *Xunzi*.)

Secondary Works

Campany, Robert F.

1992 "Xunzi and Durkheim as Theorists of Ritual Practice," in *Discourse and Practice*, Frank Reynolds and David Tracy, eds., pp. 197–231. Albany, NY: State University of New York Press. (Approaches Xunzi as offering a "philosophy of ritual" in the service of larger social, moral, and religious aims.)

Cua, Antonio S.

1985 *Ethical Argumentation: A Study in Hsün Tzu's Moral Epistemology*. Honolulu: University of Hawaii Press. (Examines Xunzi's conceptions of moral reasoning and ethical justification through his views on argumentation and language.)

Goldin, Paul R.

1999 *Rituals of the Way: The Philosophy of Xunzi*. La Salle, IL: Open Court Press. (A wide-ranging study of Xunzi's thought. Examines in detail his views on human nature, Heaven, ritual, and language.)

Ivanhoe, Philip J.

1993 "A Happy Symmetry: Xunzi's Ethical Philosophy." *Journal of the American Academy of Religion*, 61: 639–54. (Examines how, for Xunzi, ritual gains its authority by establishing harmony not just among humans, but also between humans and nature.)

Kline, T. C. III, and Philip J. Ivanhoe, eds.

2000 *Virtue, Nature and Agency in the* Xunzi. Indianapolis, IN: Hackett Publishing Company. (An anthology containing many of the most influential modern philosophical studies of Xunzi's thought in English.)

Machle, Edward J.

1993 *Nature and Heaven in the Xunzi: A Study of the* Tian Lun. Albany, NY: State University of New York Press. (Considers Xunzi as a religious thinker through his views on *tian* ["Heaven"]. Argues against reading *tian* as amoral, scientific "Nature.")

Nivison, David S.

1996 "Xunzi on 'Human Nature'," *The Ways of Confucianism*, Bryan W. Van Norden, ed., pp. 203–13. Chicago, IL: Open Court Press. (Points out how Xunzi's comments on *yi* in chapter nine seem inconsistent with his view of human nature, and proposes a solution.)

Radcliffe-Brown, A. R.

1968 "Religion and Society," in *Structure and Function in Primitive Society: Essays and Addresses*, 153–77. New York: The Free Press. (A revealing exploration of Xunzi's ritual theory.)

Van Norden, Bryan W.

1993 "Hansen on Hsün Tzu." *Journal of Chinese Philosophy* 20: 365–82. (Investigates the extent to which Xunzi may be considered a "conventionalist" in language and in ethics.)

CHAPTER SEVEN

HAN FEIZI

Introduction

The last major thinker of the pre-Qin period is the social and political theorist Han Feizi 韓非子 (c. 280–233 B.C.E.). Han Fei was a member of the
ruling house of the state of Han 韓; a small but influential state, strategically located in the southern portion of China's central plain. The book that
bears his name is a collection of essays on the arts of government and rhetoric, criticisms of historical episodes and existing philosophical doctrines,
commentaries on earlier philosophical works, and collections of historical
and semihistorical anecdotes to be used in the persuasion of rulers. Most of
these works (including all the selections translated here) were written by
Han Fei himself, but some of them appear to be the work of later authors
and were probably added to the text by compilers during the Western Han
dynasty.

According to the historian Sima Qian, Han Fei was "a stutterer who
could not speak his own counsel, but who was skilled at composing written works,"[1] and this may partly explain why, up until the end of his life,
there is no record of Han Fei ever holding an important position in the
government of his home state. Sima Qian also states that at some point
early in his career Han Fei studied under the great Confucian philosopher
Xunzi, and was a schoolmate of the infamous statesman Li Si 李斯—who
went on to become prime minister of the state of Qin—and was largely responsible for Qin's conquest of the Chinese cultural sphere in the year 221
B.C.E. Although Han Fei's ideas seem to have fallen on deaf ears in the state
of Han, his writings eventually brought him to the attention of the reign-

---

[1]See William H. Nienhauser, Jr., ed. *The Grand Scribe's Records* (Bloomington & Indianapolis, IN: Indiana University Press, 1994) v. 7, p. 25.

ing king of Qin (i.e., the future first emperor of China), and as a result, Han Fei was dispatched as an emissary to the state of Qin in either 234 or 233 B.C.E. Unfortunately, Han Fei's former schoolmate Li Si believed that Han Fei posed a threat to his own power, and so he, together with his compatriot Yao Jia 姚賈, slandered Han Fei before the king of Qin, and convinced the king to have him imprisoned. While Han Fei was in prison, Li Si sent someone to offer him poison, and Han Fei, facing the prospect of a cruel execution and unable to defend himself before the king of Qin, accepted the poison and took his own life.

During Han Fei's lifetime, the state of Han was plagued by internal disorder and was in constant danger of being swallowed up by the ever-expanding state of Qin to the west. The fact that Han Fei was operating under these precarious conditions may help to explain why he came to advocate such a pragmatic and largely amoral view of politics. Han Fei does not seem to have been the least bit interested in determining what form of government was most ethically justified. His goal was simply to determine which measures were most effective in ensuring the continued survival of the state and furthering the public interests of the ruler and his people. Han Fei rejected the Confucian and Mohist claim that a ruler should model his government on the values and institutions of the ancient sage-kings. He maintained that each stage in the development of human civilization comes with its own unique set of problems, and so the rulers of each age must be able to come up with new measures for dealing with these obstacles. A truly effective government must be based on an firm grasp of the existing sociopolitical conditions, and not on some ahistorical and overly idealized vision of human social life. Han Fei was also opposed to the traditional model of government because he believed it relied too heavily on the moral character of political agents. He did not deny that it was better to have a good ruler in power than a bad one, but he did not believe that moral goodness by itself was sufficient to guarantee peace and prosperity. Furthermore, Han Fei recognized that while there may be some rulers who are either exceptionally good or exceptionally bad, most fall somewhere in between. If a system of government is to be sustainable over time, it must be stable enough to withstand the occasional bad ruler, and self-supporting enough to be maintained by the numerous mediocre ones. Han Fei was also deeply concerned about the proliferation of what he regarded as politically dangerous or socially useless groups of people. Among the groups singled out for criticism by Han Fei, the most noteworthy are: classical scholars (i.e., Confucians), wandering orators, private swordsmen, draft dodgers, and merchants. In his view, these five groups were nothing more than "vermin" who fed off the resources of the state without contributing anything substantial in return. If these groups were not wiped out or suppressed, Han Fei argued, they would eventually weaken the political structure of society and bring about the downfall of the state.

Han Fei's own political philosophy represents the culmination of a long movement toward institutionalism in early Chinese political theory. Some aspects of this institutionalist view can be seen in Xunzi's emphasis on the political significance of *li* "public ritual" and socially defined standards of *yi* "rightness," but the true proponents of this model of government were the so-called Legalist statesman like Guan Zhong, Gongsun Yang, Shen Buhai, and Shen Dao.[2] Han Fei's role within the Legalist tradition is that of both synthesizer and critic. His major achievement was to show how the individual doctrines developed by the earlier Legalists could be combined into a single theory of government, while at the same time correcting and refining many of the central ideas contained in each of them.

In addition to being a brilliant political theorist, Han Fei was also a great rhetoritician, and the style of his writings has often been praised by later writers. Han Fei not only invented a new genre of writing (*nan* 難, "philosophical critique") he also developed a new style of writing that later became known as the *lian zhu* 連珠, "linked pearl," style. But perhaps Han Fei's greatest contribution in the field of rhetoric lies in his observation that an effective persuasion depends as much on one's knowledge of the person being persuaded as it does on the quality of one's argument, or the style of one's presentation. This observation had important ramifications within the political culture of Warring States China. For the minister, it meant that if you wanted your proposal to be approved, you had to determine what sort of desires and aversions might be "in the mind" of the ruler you were persuading, so that you could adjust the way you presented your ideas to match what the ruler was already thinking. For the ruler, it meant that if you wanted to know the truth behind your ministers' proposals and avoid being misled by their rhetoric, you had to work hard to conceal your own desires and aversions, so that your ministers could not change their words simply to please you.

Han Fei's philosophy had a tremendous influence on later political theory and practice in China. There is no way to determine what role his ideas may have played in shaping the government of the Qin dynasty, but we do

---

[2]See *Fajia* under *Important Terms* and individual entries under *Important Figures*.

know that his theories were often debated and discussed in the succeeding Han dynasty, especially during the height of the so-called Huang-Lao movement. After the Han it is difficult to find any thinker who refers to themselves as a Legalist, but by that point, many of the basic tenets of Legalism had already been incorporated into the ideology of imperial Confucianism, where they continued to be used right down into the modern era.

Chapter Five: The Way of the Ruler³

The Way is the beginning of the ten thousand things and the guiding thread of truth and falsity. For this reason, an enlightened ruler holds to the beginning so that he may know the source of the ten thousand things, and regulates the guiding thread so that he may understand the starting points of excellence and failure. Thus, empty and still he waits, allowing names to define themselves and affairs to determine themselves. Being empty, he grasps the essence of phenomena; being still, he understands the correctness of movements. When a proposal is made, it itself serves to name the objectives. When an affair is carried out, it itself serves to form the results. When form and name are matched and found to be identical, there is nothing for the ruler to do, and everything returns to what is essential. Thus it is said, "A ruler should never reveal what he desires. For if he reveals what he desires, the ministers will cut and polish themselves accordingly. A ruler should never reveal what he intends. For if he reveals what he intends, the ministers will try to make themselves look distinctive." Thus it is also said, "Get rid of likes and dislikes and the true character of your ministers will be plain. Dispense with experience and wisdom and your ministers will be forced to take precautions."

Thus, an enlightened ruler has wisdom, but he does not use it to make plans. He allows the ten thousand things to know their place. He has worthiness, but he does not use it to conduct his own affairs. He observes what his ministers and subordinates base their actions on. He has courage, but he does not use it to express anger. He allows the assembled ministers to fully extend their martial feelings. Thus, by getting rid of wisdom he achieves clarity; by getting rid of worthiness he enjoys achievement; by getting rid of courage he possesses strength. When the assembled ministers keep to their duties, the hundred offices follow a uniform standard, and the

---

³This chapter is noteworthy for its appropriation of Daoist vocabulary. Han Feizi is in fact the author of the first extant commentary on the *Laozi*.

ruler employs them based on their abilities, this is called "exercising the constant." Thus it is said, "Tranquil, he has no position to occupy. Isolated, no one knows his place." When an enlightened ruler practices nonaction above, the assembled ministers will be anxious and fearful below.

This is the way of an enlightened ruler: he makes it so that the wise fully exert themselves in making plans, while he uses their wisdom to manage his affairs. Thus, he is never lacking in wisdom. He makes it so that the worthy refine their natural talents, while he makes use of those talents and employs them. Thus, he is never lacking in ability. He makes it so that when there are achievements he gets the credit for their worthiness, and when there are errors the ministers take the blame. Thus, he is never lacking in reputation. Thus, though he himself is not worthy, he is taught by those who are worthy; though he himself is not wise, he is corrected by those who are wise. The ministers perform the work, and the ruler enjoys the final achievement. This is what is called the guiding principle of a worthy ruler.

The Way lies in not being seen, its use lies in not being known. Remain empty, still, and without concern, so that you may secretly observe the defects of others. See others but do not allow yourself to be seen; hear others but do not allow yourself to be heard; know others but do not allow yourself to be known. Once you understand someone's words, do not alter or change them, but check them using the comparison of form and name. If you put one person in every office, and do not allow them to speak with one another, then the ten thousand things will all be completed. Cover your tracks, conceal your starting points, and your subordinates will not be able to see where you are coming from. Get rid of wisdom, dispense with ability, and your subordinates will not be able to guess your intentions. Hold on to what people have said before, and look to see if they match it with results. Carefully take hold of the handles of punishment and reward and maintain firm control of them. Cut off all hope of using them, smash all intentions to take them, and do not allow people to covet them.

If you do not watch your door and strengthen your gate, tigers will live in your state; if you do not take care with your affairs and conceal your true character, thieves will be born in your country. Some people kill their rulers and take their places, making it so that no one dares not to join them. Hence, they are called tigers. Some people sit by their ruler's side and listen to his secrets for the sake of corrupt ministers. Hence, they are called thieves. If you break up their factions, arrest their benefactors, close their gates, and take away their support, the state will have no tigers. If your greatness cannot be measured and your depth cannot be gauged, if you match up form and name and examine laws and models, making sure that those who usurp powers that do not belong to them are executed, the state will have no thieves.

Thus a ruler of men can be blocked in five ways: when a minister shuts off his ruler from others, this is the first kind of block. When a minister controls the wealth and benefits of the state, this is the second kind of block. When a minister usurps the power to issue commands, this is the third kind of block. When a minister is able to carry out righteousness, this is the fourth kind of block. When a minister can plant his own men in positions of power, this is the fifth kind of block. When a minister shuts off his ruler from others, the ruler loses his position. When a minister controls the wealth and benefits of the state, the ruler loses the power to grant favors. When a minister usurps the power to issue orders, the ruler loses control. When a minister is able to carry out righteousness, the ruler loses his clarity. When a minister can plant his own men in positions of power, the ruler loses his supporters. These are all things that only a ruler of men should control. They are not things that his ministers should be able to manipulate.

The Way of a ruler of men takes stillness and retreat as its treasures. A good ruler does not personally manage his affairs, but he knows the difference between clumsiness and skill. He does not personally calculate or make plans, but he knows the difference between good fortune and bad. Thus, even though he himself does not propose anything, he is good at responding to the proposals of others; even though he himself does not perform any tasks, he is good at increasing his own resources. When a ruler has responded to a minister's proposal by assigning him a task, it is as if he holds the creditor's portion of the *qi* tally.[4] When the task has generated some increase, it is as if he wields the commanders portion of the *fu* tally.[5]

---

[4] The *qi* 契 tally served as a kind of contract or promissory note in Warring States China. When two parties entered into an agreement where one party agreed to provide the resources necessary to fund some item of business in exchange for a portion of the proceeds which that business would generate, the details of the transaction were written or carved on a bamboo or wooden slip, and the slip was then split in half. One half of the slip would go to the person who had provided the funds (i.e., the creditor), and one half would go to the person who would conduct the business (i.e., the debtor). In this passage, Han Fei is using the image of the *qi* tally metaphorically to describe the "debt" that a minister incurs when he proposes to perform some task in the service of his lord.

[5] The *fu* 符 tally was a symbol of legitimacy used to show that an individual had been authorized by his superior to perform some task or speak on the superior's behalf. These tallies were made from a wide variety of materials, including silk, jade, wood, and metal. When a subordinate was sent out on a military or diplomatic mission, he would be given the left-

It is from the matching of the *qi* and *fu* tallies that rewards and penalties are born. Thus, when the assembled ministers lay out their proposals, the ruler assigns them tasks based on their proposals, and then uses the tasks to hold them accountable for their achievements. If the achievements accord with the task and the task accords with the proposal, then the minister is rewarded. If the achievements do not accord with the task or the task does not accord with the proposal, then the minister is punished. The Way of an enlightened ruler is to make it so that no minister may make a proposal and then fail to match it with actions and results.

For this reason, when an enlightened ruler hands out rewards it is generous, like the fall of timely rain, and the hundred surnames all benefit from his bounty. When he hands out penalties, it is terrifying, like thunder and lightning, and even spirits and sages cannot undo his work. Thus, an enlightened ruler does not skimp on rewards or forgive penalties. If he skimped on rewards the successful ministers would become lazy in their work, and if he forgave penalties the corrupt minister would find it easy to do wrong. For this reason, those who make genuine achievements must always be rewarded, even if they are distant and lowly, while those who make genuine errors must always be punished, even if they are close and cherished. If those who are distant and lowly are always rewarded for their achievements, and those who are close and cherished are always punished for their crimes, then those who are distant and lowly will not become resentful, and those who are close and cherished will not become haughty.

---

hand portion of the tally as way of proving that he had the authority to act in his superior's name. The superior would keep the right-hand portion of the tally, and use it as a means of proving to his operatives that the orders he sent via messengers were in fact from him and not from some outside party. In this line, Han Fei seems to be using the image of the *fu* tally to argue that a ruler should check to see that his ministers have only done those things that he has "authorized" them to do, based on their original proposal.

Chapter Six:
On the Importance of Having Standards (A Memorial)

No state is forever strong, no state is forever weak. If those who uphold the law are strong the state will be strong. If they are weak the state will be weak. . . .

Thus, under King Zhuang of Chu and Duke Huan of Qi, the states of Chu and Qi enjoyed hegemony,[6] while under King Zhaoxiang of Yan and King Anxi of Wei, the states of Yan and Wei became strong.[7] Now, however, these states have all deteriorated because their assembled ministers and government officials pursue that which brings about disorder instead of that which brings about order. Since these states are already weak and disorderly, if their ministers and officials abandon the laws of the state and make private arrangements with foreign powers, this will be like carrying wood to put out a fire—the weakness and disorder will only grow worse.

Thus, at the present time, if a ruler can get rid of private crookedness and promote the public law, his people will become secure and his state will become well ordered. If he can expel private conduct and enforce the public law, his troops will grow strong while his enemies grow weak. Therefore, if when examining gains and losses there is a system of laws and standards that can be applied to the claims and actions of the assembled ministers, the ruler will not be decieved by trickery and falsehood. If when examining gains and losses there is a scale of weights and balances that can be used to measure the importance of distant affairs, the ruler will not be deceived by the heaviness or lightness of the parties of the world.

Now if you rely on reputation to advance the capable, the ministers will separate themselves from those above and spend their time colluding with those below. If you rely on political factions to promote men to office, the people will work to develop instrumental relationships and will not seek to be useful with regard to the law. Thus, a ruler who mistakes reputation for ability when assigning offices will see his state fall into disorder.

If a ruler distributes rewards based on reputation, and hands out penalties based on slander, those people who covet rewards and hate penalities

---

[6]Duke Huan of Qi (r. 685–643) and King Zhuang of Chu (r. 613–591) were the first and fourth of China's "five lord protectors." See *ba* "lord protector" under *Important Terms*.

[7]King Zhaoxiang of Yan (r. 311–279 B.C.E.) and King Anxi of Wei (r. 276–243 B.C.E.) were the rulers of the states of Yan and Wei during periods when these states became minor military powers.

will abandon the public law and carry out their private schemes, colluding with one another in order to advance their mutual interests. If ministers forget their ruler and establish relationships with foreign powers in order to advance the interests of their confederates, there will be scant reason for subordinates to obey their superiors. When relationships are profuse and confederates are numerous, so that cliques and factions flourish both inside and outside the state, then even if a minister commits a great transgression, he will have ample means to cover it up. Thus, the loyal ministers will be in danger of being killed even though they have not committed a crime, and the corrupt and wicked ministers will enjoy security and profits even though they have not produced any achievements. When loyal ministers are in danger of being killed even though they have not committed a crime, good ministers will go into hiding. When corrupt and wicked ministers enjoy security and profit even though they have not produced any accomplishments, corrupt ministers will advance in the government. Herein lies the origin of the downfall of the state.

In a situation like this, the assembled ministers will violate the law, strengthen their private influence, and make light of the public legal standards. They will travel repeatedly to the gates of "capable men," but never once go to the court of their ruler. They will deliberate a hundred times about the welfare of their private households, but never once make plans for their ruler's state. So even though the number of ministers may be great, they will be of no use in bringing respect to the ruler; and even though the hundred offices may be filled, they will be of no use in administrating the country. In such a situation, the ruler will have the name of a ruler, but the actual power of the ruler will be shared among the houses of his assembled ministers.

Therefore your servant says, "There are no people in the court of a deteriorated state." The reason why there are no people in the court of a deteriorated state is not because of the degeneration of the court. Rather, it is because the noble houses work to make each other flourish and do not strive to enrich the state; the great ministers work to make each other respected and do not strive to bring respect to their ruler; and the minor ministers look for promotions and stipends by cultivating advantageous relationships and do not attend to the duties of their office. The reason why things are like this is that the ruler has not set the standard from above through laws, and instead relies on his subordinates to take care of things. Thus, an enlightened ruler uses the law to select men and does not try to promote them himself; he uses the law to evaluate accomplishments and does not try to measure them himself. When ability cannot be hidden and errors cannot be covered up, when those who only have a good reputation cannot advance, and denunciations cannot make good men retire, then the relationship between ruler and minister will be clearly defined and the state will be easy to govern. Thus, if Your Majesty would only attend to the law everything would be fine.

When worthy men serve as ministers, they face north,[8] presenting their tokens of allegiance, and are never of two minds about whom they should serve. At court they never presume to excuse themselves from lowly positions, and in the military they never venture to remove themselves from danger. They always follow the directions of their superiors and obey the laws of their ruler. With empty minds they wait for orders and have no predetermined views about what is right and wrong. Thus, although they have mouths they do not use them to speak for their private interests; although they have eyes they do not use them to look for private gain. In all matters they are directed by those above them. Those who serve as ministers can be compared to hands; reaching up they take care of the head, reaching down they take care of the feet. In times of coolness and warmth, hot and cold, they cannot help but aid the body by rubbing or fanning it, and when a sharp sword like *Moye*[9] threatens to strike the body, they dare not fail to bat it away. There are no "private" ministers who are worthy and intelligent, no "private" officers who are useful and capable. Thus, when the people do not establish private relationships outside their own villages, and have no relatives by marriage more than a hundred *li* away, when the noble and the base do not encroach on each other, and the stupid and the wise lift up the balance of the law and stand in their proper places—this is the pinnacle of good order.

Now, if someone thinks little of titles and stipends, and readily leaves a state in order to choose himself a new ruler, your servant would not call him steadfast. If someone uses deceitful rhetoric to go against the law and opposes his ruler with forceful remonstrances, your servant would not call him loyal. If someone doles out favors and distributes benefits, gathering the support of those below him in order to make a name for himself, your servant would not call him benevolent. If someone takes leave of society and goes into seclusion, using his actions to criticize his superiors, your ser-

---

[8]They face north because the ruler traditionally faces south, assuming the position on earth corresponding to the pole star in the heavens. Cf. *Analects* 2.1 and 15.5.

[9]For the legendary sword *Moye* , see *Zhuangzi*, chapter 6, p. 233, n. 57.

vant would not call him righteous. If someone serves as an emissary to the other feudal rulers outside the state and squanders resourses within it, if he takes control of the narrow and dangerous passes and frightens his ruler by saying, "Without me your relationships with friendly states will not be close and the anger of enemy states will not be abated," and the ruler believes him and uses the resources of the state to follow his counsel, if he degrades the name of the ruler while glorifying his own person, and destroys the wealth of the state while benefiting his own household, your servant would not call him wise. These several things are the doctrines of a dangerous age and that which the laws of the former kings sought to minimize. The laws of the former kings say, "A minister should never work to create his own authority or benefit; he should follow the directions of the king. He should never work to create trouble; he should follow the king's road."[10] The people in the well-ordered ages of the past upheld the public law and abandoned private strategies; they focused their intentions and unified their conduct. Everything they did was for the sake of being employed by the ruler.

Now if a ruler of men tries to personally examine each of the hundred offices, he will find that his days are too short and his strength is insufficient. Moreover, if a superior uses his eyes to investigate things, his subordinates will dress up what he sees. If he uses his ears to investigate things, his subordinates will dress up what he hears. If he uses his reasoning to investigate things his subordinates will make their words complex and difficult to understand. The former kings knew that these three things were insufficient to be used in governing, so they put aside their own abilities, based their government on law and method, and carefully exercised the power of reward and punishment. The former kings held on to what was essential, so their laws were simple but inviolable. They alone controlled the land within the four seas, so the intelligent and wise were not able to use their trickery, the flatterers and deceivers were allowed no opening through which they could curry favor, and the corrupt and wicked had nothing to rely upon. Those who lived a thousand *li* away did not dare to change their words, and those who occupied positions of power among the officers of the court did not dare to hide goodness or disguise wrongs. The various subordinates of the court kept to their places and remained unassuming, not daring to overstep the boundaries of their offices or infringe

---

[10]This unattested quotation is similar to a passage found in the *History* that is cited by Xunzi. See *Xunzi*, chapter 2, p. 257 and chapter 17, p. 264.

upon each other's duties. Thus, the affairs of government were not enough to exhaust the strength of the former kings, and they had more than enough time to get things done. It was the way these superiors used the power of their position that made it thus.

When a minister encroaches upon the power of his ruler, it is as if the two of them were in some unfamiliar terrain and the minister, by gradually leading them forward, causes the ruler of men to lose his sense of direction so that he turns from east to west without even knowing it. This is why the former kings set up southward-pointing markers in order to fix the directions of morning and evening.[11] Therefore, an enlightened ruler makes sure that his assembled ministers do not let their intentions wander into areas outside the scope of the law, and does not grant favors in those areas within the scope of the law, so that no action negates the law. Stern laws are what one uses to prohibit transgressions and cast out selfishness; harsh punishments are what one uses to enforce commands and chastise subordinates. The power of the ruler cannot be bestowed on others; control of the state cannot be shared among the gates of several houses. If power and control are shared then a myriad of vices will flourish; if the law cannot be trusted then the status of the ruler will be in danger; but if punishments are not curtailed then wickedness will not prevail. Thus it is said, "The estimate of a skillful carpenter is as accurate as an ink-line, but a good carpenter will always begin by using the compass and square as his standard. The recommendations of the wisest men always strike at the heart of the matter, but a truly wise man will always use the laws of the former kings as a way of checking his conclusions." Thus, when the ink-line is pulled straight, bent wood can be cut true; when the level is even, high sections can be planed down; when the weights and balances have been properly hung, heavy will be shown to be greater than light; and when the size of bushels and piculs has been properly established, more will be shown to be greater than less.

Thus, using law to govern the state involves nothing more than promoting that which accords with the law and abandoning that which does not. The law does not make exceptions for those who are noble, just as the ink-line does not bend around that which is crooked. The wise cannot excuse themselves from what the law commands, and the brave do not dare oppose it. The punishment of transgressions does not bypass the great ministers, and the rewarding of goodness does not neglect the common folk. Thus, when it comes to straightening out the mistakes of superiors and

---

[11]Cf. *Mozi*, chapter 35, p. 106, especially ns. 87–88.

punishing the wickedness of inferiors, ordering the disorderly and untangling the tangled, reducing covetousness, supressing disobedience, and unifying the course of the people, nothing is better than the law. For strictly regulating the offices and overawing the people, thwarting liscentiousness and idleness, and stopping trickery and falsehood, nothing is better than punishments. If punishments are heavy then the noble and the base will not presume to change places. If laws are well defined then those above will be respected and their power will not be encroached upon. When superiors are respected and their power is not encroached upon, then the ruler will be strong and have a hold on what is essential. Therefore, the former kings valued the law and passed it down to their successors. If a ruler abandons the law and relies on private judgments, the positions of superior and inferior will not be properly distinguished.

Chapter Seven: The Two Handles

The way an enlightened ruler controls his ministers is through the use of two handles, and nothing more. These two handles are punishment and favor. What is meant by punishment and favor? To kill or execute—this is what is meant by "punishment." To venerate or reward—this is what is meant by "favor." Those who serve as ministers are fearful of execution and penalties and regard being venerated or rewarded as something beneficial. So if the ruler of men personally exercises his power to punish and grant favors, then the assembled ministers will all fear his might and turn to the benefits he offers them.

With the corrupt ministers of the age, however, this is not the case. When they hate someone, they are able to obtain the power to punish from their ruler and accuse him, and when they love someone, they are able to obtain the power to grant favors from their ruler and reward him. Now if the ruler of men does not make it so that the might and benefits that derive from rewards and penalities come only from him, and instead listens to his ministers when carrying out rewards and penalties, then the people of the state will all fear their ministers while dismissing their ruler, and turn to their ministers while departing from their ruler. This is the misfortune that comes when the ruler of men loses the power to punish and grant favors. The reason why the tiger can subdue the dog is because he has claws and fangs. But if the tiger loses his claws and fangs and allows the dog to use them, then the tiger will instead be subdued by the dog. A ruler of men is someone who uses punishments and favor to control his ministers. Now if the ruler of men loses his power to punish and grant favors and allows his ministers to use them, then the ruler will instead be controlled by his ministers.

Thus, Tian Chang requested the power to grant titles and stipends and exercised it over the assembled ministers above, while at the same time increasing the size of the bushel and picul measures and distributing grain among the hundred surnames below. In this case, Duke Jian lost his power to grant favors and allowed Tian Chang to use it. As a result, Duke Jian was eventually assassinated. Zi Han said to the Lord of Song, "Veneration, rewards, boons, and gifts—these are things that the people all enjoy. Let you, my Lord, take care of these things yourself. Death, mutilation, punishments, and penalties—these are things that the people all hate. Let me, your servant, take care of these." Thereupon, the Lord of Song lost the power to punish and allowed Zi Han to use it. As a result, the Lord of Song was robbed of his authority. Tian Chang gained exclusive use of favor and Duke Jian was assassinated. Zi Han gained exclusive use of punishment and the Lord of Song was robbed of his authority.[12] So if those who serve as ministers in the current age have taken control of both punishments and favor, then the danger facing the rulers of the current age is far greater than that faced by Duke Jian and the Lord of Song. Thus, whenever a ruler is robbed, killed, imprisoned, or overshadowed, it is invariably because he has endangered himself and his state by giving up control of punishments and favors and allowing his ministers to use them.

If a ruler of men wants to put an end to vice, he must examine the correspondence between form and name, and look to see how what is said differs from what is done. When those who serve as ministers lay out proposals, the ruler assigns them tasks based on their proposals, and then uses their tasks to hold them accountable for their achievements. If the achievements accord with the task and the task accords with the proposal, then the minister is rewarded. If the achievements do not accord with the task or the task does not accord with the proposal, then the minister is penalized. Thus, if someone among the assembled ministers proposes something great but the actual achievement is small, he should be penalized. In this case, one is not penalizing them because the achievement is small, but rather because the achievement does not match their named objectives. If someone among the assembled ministers proposes something small but the actual achievement is great, he should also be penalized. In this case, it is

---

[12]For more on Tian Chang and Zi Han see *Han Feizi*, chapter 49, p. 330, n. 41.

not that one is not pleased by the great achievement, but rather that one feels that the harm that comes from achievements not according with named objectives is even greater than the benefit of the great achievement, so he must be penalized.

Marquis Zhao of Han[13] once became drunk and fell asleep. The Steward of Caps, seeing that his ruler was cold, placed the Marquis' cloak over him. When Marquis Zhao awoke he was pleased by this, and asked his attendants, "Who covered me with my cloak?" His attendants replied, "It was the Steward of Caps." Consequently, the ruler punished both the Steward of Caps and the Steward of Cloaks. He punished the Steward of Cloaks because he felt the man had failed to fulfill his appointed task, and he punished the Steward of Caps because he felt the man had overstepped the bounds of his position. It was not that the Marquis did not dislike the cold, but rather that he felt that the harm that comes from ministers encroaching on each other's office is even greater than the harm that comes from being cold. Thus, when an enlightened ruler controls his ministers, he makes it so that ministers cannot get credit for achievements gained by overstepping the bounds of their offices, or make proposals and then fail to match them with actual achievements. If someone oversteps the boundaries of his office, he should die. If someone's proposals are not matched by actual achievements, he should be faulted. If ministers are forced to be virtuous in guarding the duties of their offices and completing the tasks they have proposed for themselves, then the assembled ministers will not be able to form cliques and factions to assist each other.

A ruler of men faces two possible misfortunes: if he employs the worthy, the ministers will use worthiness as a pretext to rob their ruler of his power; but if he promotes men recklessly, his affairs will be neglected and he will not prevail. Thus, if the ruler of men is fond of worthiness, the assembled ministers will dress up their behavior in order to satisfy their ruler's desires and the true character of the assembled ministers will not be apparent. And when the true character of the assembled ministers is not apparent, the ruler of men will have no way of differentiating between good and bad ministers. Thus, the King of Yue was fond of bravery, so his people often

---

[13]Marquis Zhao of Han 韓昭侯 (r. 358–333 B.C.E.) was ruler of the state of Han during the period when Shen Buhai served as prime minister. Although there is no way to be certain, the episode related here is mostly likely a fabrication concocted by Han Fei (or perhaps Shen Buhai) to make a point.

looked lightly upon their own deaths.[14] King Ling of Chu was fond of narrow waists, so there were many starving people in his state. Duke Huan of Qi was jealous and fond of women, so Shu Diao castrated himself in order to take control of the Duke's harem. Duke Huan also liked exotic flavors, so Yi Ya steamed his first-born son and presented it to him.[15] King Kuai of Yan was fond of worthiness, so Zi Zhi made a great show of refusing to accept control of the state.[16] Thus, if the ruler reveals what he dislikes, the assembled ministers will conceal the origins of their actions; if the ruler reveals what he likes, the assembled ministers will feign abilities they do not have. In short, if a ruler reveals his desires, the true character and ambitions of his assembled ministers will be given the resources they need in order to succeed.

Thus, Zi Zhi relied on worthiness to ensnare his ruler, while Shu Diao and Yi Ya used their ruler's desires to encroach upon his power. In the end King Kuai was killed in the chaos following his abdication,[17] and Duke Huan remained unburied until the insects devouring his corpse flowed out from under his door.[18] What is the reason for all this? It is because these rulers of men allowed their natural dispositions to support the misfortunes brought about by their ministers. The character of ministers is not always

---

[14]Both this and the following story regarding the King of Chu are also cited by Mozi. See *Mozi*, chapter 16, p. 71.

[15]After the death of Guan Zhong, Duke Huan of Qi fell under the influence of his harem master Shu Diao 豎刁 and his cook Yi Ya 易牙, each of whom gained the Duke's confidence by pandering to his desires. The activities these two men performed on behalf of the Duke's son Wu Gui 無詭 were responsible for starting the war of succession that erupted following Duke Huan's death in 643 B.C.E.

[16]In the year 316 B.C.E. Zizhi 子之, prime minister of the state of Yan, persuaded his ruler King Kuai of Yan 燕噲王 (r. 320–312 B.C.E.) to yield the throne to him in deference to his superior worthiness. One of the ways he demonstrated this "worthiness" was by repeatedly refusing to accept the throne when King Kuai offered it.

[17]After Zizhi took over the duties of king, the situation in the state of Yan began to deteriorate rapidly. Things eventually became so bad that when the armies of the neighboring state of Qi invaded Yan in 314 B.C.E. (under the pretext of setting up King Kuai's son the Crown Prince Ping 太子平 as ruler), the Yan troops refused to fight, allowing the Qi forces to march right in through the unlocked gates of the capital where they killed both Zizhi and (the former) King Kuai. Qi managed to maintain control of Yan for two years until a popular uprising lead by the Crown Prince expelled the invaders and put Ping on the throne.

[18]During the battle for succession that followed Duke Huan's death, none of his six sons were in a position to bury the former Duke, so his body was simply allowed to rot in his room.

such that they can love their ruler. Some become ministers only to increase their personal benefit. Now if a ruler of men does not cover up his true character and conceal the origins of his actions, and instead allows his ministers to have the means to encroach upon their ruler, then the assembled ministers will not find it difficult to become a Zi Zhi or a Tian Chang. Thus it is said, "Get rid of likes and dislikes and the true character of the assembled ministers will be plain. And when the true character of the assembled ministers is plain, the ruler of men cannot be deceived."

Chapter Eight: A Critique of the Doctrine of the Power of Position

Shenzi says, "The flying dragon rides upon the clouds; the soaring serpent roams upon the mist. But when the clouds disperse and the mist clears, the dragon and the serpent are no different from the earthworm and the ant because they have lost the things on which they travel. If a worthy man bows before an unworthy man, it must be because his authority is light and his position is lowly. If an unworthy man can make a worthy man submit to him, it must be because his authority is heavy and his position is respected. When Yao was a commoner he could not bring order to three people, but Jie, acting as the Son of Heaven, was able to throw the whole world into disorder. By this I know that the power of status and position are sufficient to be relied on, while worthiness and wisdom are not worth admiring.

"If the crossbow is weak but the arrow flies high, it must be because it has been hastened by the wind. If one's character is unworthy but one's commands are carried out, it must be because one has received help from the multitude. When Yao taught among the lower classes the people would not listen to him, but once he faced south and became king of the world his commands were carried out and his prohibitions stopped what they were intended to prohibit. Looking at it from this perspective, one can see that worthiness and wisdom are never enough to subdue the multitude, while the power of status and position are sufficient to make even the worthy bend."

In response to Shenzi some critic says, "As for the flying dragon riding upon the clouds and the soaring serpent roaming upon the mist, I do not deny that the dragon and the serpent depend on the power of the clouds and mist. Nevertheless, if one abandons worthiness and relies solely on power of position, will this be enough to bring about order? I, for one, have never seen this. When there are conditions of clouds and mist, the reason why the dragon and the serpent can ride or roam upon them is that the natural abilities of dragons and serpents are excellent. The clouds may be plentiful, but the earthworm cannot ride on them. The mist may be thick, but the ant cannot roam upon it. When there are conditions of plentiful clouds and thick mist, the reason why the earthworm and the ant cannot ride or roam upon them is that the natural abilites of earthworms and ants are meager. Now, when Jie and Zhou faced south and became kings of the world, using the prestige of the Son of Heaven as their clouds and mist, the reason why the world could not escape falling into great disorder is that the natural abilities of Jie and Zhou were meager.

"Moreover, Shenzi maintains that it was the power of Yao's position that brought order to the world. But how was the power of his position any different from the power of Jie's position that threw the world into disorder? The power of position is not something that can be restricted so that the worthy use it and the unworthy do not. If the worthy use it, the world will be well-ordered; if the unworthy use it, then the world will be disordered. The dispositions and natures of human beings are such that those who are worthy are few, while those who are unworthy are many. So if one uses the benefits of prestige and the power of position to try to save the unworthy men of a disordered age, then those who use the power of position to bring disorder to the world will be many, while those who use the power of position to bring order to the world will be few.

"The power of position is something that can either facilitate order or benefit disorder. Thus, the *Documents of Zhou*[19] say, 'Do not add wings to a tiger, or it will fly into the cities, snatching up people and devouring them.' To allow unworthy men to ride on the power of position is to add wings to a tiger. Jie and Zhou exhausted the strength of the people by building lofty pavilions and deep pools; they injured the lives of the people by creating the punishment of the roasting pillar.[20] That Jie and Zhou were able to complete these unconscionable actions is due to the fact that they

---

[19]The *Zhou Shu* 周書, "*Documents of Zhou*," most likely refers to the set of thirty-two essays that make up the "core" of the work now known as the *Yi zhou shu* 逸周書, "*Lost Documents of Zhou*." The version of *Yi zhou shu* we have today was probably compiled during the Western Han dynasty, but the core chapters may have been in circulation as early as the late fourth century B.C.E. The line quoted here comes from the *Wu jing* chapter in the current text.

[20]The roasting pillar was an extremely cruel form of punishment in which a bronze pillar was laid across a pit containing an open fire, and criminals were forced to walk across the heated pillar until they fell into the flames.

had the prestige of facing south to act as their wings. If Jie and Zhou had been commoners, they would have been punished or executed before they began to carry out even one of them. The power of position is that which nourishes the hearts of tigers and wolves and brings violent and disordering affairs to completion. It is a great danger to the world. The power of position surely has no fixed position in relation to order and chaos. So if the main point of Shenzi's doctrine is that the power of position is sufficient to bring order to the world, then the depth of his wisdom is very shallow indeed!

"If one has fine horses and a sturdy chariot, and one allows a common servant to drive them, people will just laugh at him. If the great charioteer Wang Liang[21] drives them, however, they will speed across a thousand *li* in a single day. The chariot and the horses are no different, but one person travels a thousand *li* and the other is laughed at by people. This is because the distance between skillfulness and clumsiness is vast. Now, suppose one takes the state to be the chariot, the power of position to be the horses, orders and commands to be the reins and bridle, and punishments and fines to be the whip and crop. If a Yao or Shun drives them, the world will be well ordered, but if a Jie or Zhou drives them, the world will be disordered. This is because the distance between worthiness and unworthiness is vast. To understand that one should employ Wang Liang if one wants to travel swiftly over great distances, but not understand that one should employ the worthy and the capable if one wants to promote what is beneficial and get rid of what is harmful—this is the kind of misfortune that comes from not understanding things of the same category. Yao and Shun are the Wang Liangs of governing the people."

In response to the previous critic I say, "Shenzi maintains that the power of position is sufficient to be relied on when governing the offices of the state, but [the previous critic] says one must wait for worthy men before there will be order. This is not the case. The 'power of position' is a single term, but it allows for endless variations in interpretation. If 'power of position' must always refer to naturally occuring differences in power and status, then there really is nothing that can be said about it. What I refer to when I talk about 'the power of position' are the differences in power and status set up by human beings.

---

[21]Wang Liang 王良 is said to have been the charioteer of Viscount Jian of Zhao 趙簡子 (fl. 517–476). He was highly revered in ancient China for his skill at driving horses and teaching the art of charioteering. Cf. *Mengzi* 3B1 (not in this volume).

"Now if one says that when Yao and Shun obtained the power of position there was order, and when Jie and Zhou obtained the power of position there was disorder, I would not deny that this was indeed the case with Yao, Shun, Jie, and Zhou. Nevertheless, differences in power and status are not something that can be set up by a single person. If a Yao or Shun is born into a superior position, then even if there are ten Jies or ten Zhous they cannot cause disorder, because the differences in power and status are well ordered. On the other hand, if a Jie or Zhou is born into a superior position, then even if there are ten Yaos or ten Shuns they cannot bring about good order, because the differences in power and status are disordered. Thus it is said, 'If the differences in power and status are well ordered there cannot be disorder, but if the differences in power and status are disordered there cannot be order.' But this refers only to naturally occuring differences in power and status, and not to the differences in power and status that can be set up by human beings.

"What I am talking about is simply the differences in power and status that can be set up by human beings, and what does worthiness have to do with these? How can I show that this is the case? A guest once told me the following story: There once was a man who dealt in spears and shields. First he would praise his shields saying, 'My shields are so strong that nothing can penetrate them.' Then a moment later, he would praise his spears saying, 'My spears are so sharp that there is nothing they cannot penetrate.' A person in the crowd asked the man, 'If one were to use one of your spears to try to pierce one of your shields, what would happen?' The man could not answer him, because 'impenetrable shields' and 'all-penetrating spears' are two claims that cannot stand together. Worthiness is something that cannot be forbidden by the power of position, but when the power of position is used as a Way of governing, there is nothing that it cannot forbid. So if one says that achieving good order requires both worthiness, which cannot be forbidden, and the power of position, which has nothing it cannot forbid, this is just like saying one has both all-penetrating spears and impenetrable shields. Hence, the fact that worthiness and the power of position are incompatible should be abundantly clear.

"Furthermore, even if a Yao, Shun, Jie, or Zhou only emerged once in every thousand generations, it would still seem like they were born bumping shoulders and treading on each other's heels. But those who actually govern each age are typically somewhere in the middle between these two extremes. The reason why I discuss the power of position is for the sake of these mediocre rulers. These mediocre rulers, at best they do not reach the level of a Yao or Shun, and at worst they do not behave like a Jie or Zhou. If they hold to the law and depend on the power of their position, there will be order; but if they abandon the power of their position and turn their backs on the law, there will be disorder. Now if one abandons the power of position, turns one's back on the law, and waits for a Yao or Shun, then when a Yao or Shun arrives there will indeed be order, but it will only be one generation of order in a thousand generations of disorder. On the other hand, if one holds to the law, relies on the power of position, and waits for a Jie or Zhou, then when a Jie or Zhou comes there will indeed be disorder, but it will only be one generation of disorder in a thousand generations of order. Having a thousand generations of order with one generation of disorder and having one generation of order in a thousand generations of disorder is like getting on two fast horses and riding them in opposite directions—the distance between the two will certainly be great.

"If Xi Zhong[22] had abandoned the models for bending and straightening, or dispensed with the methods of measuring and weighing when he was inventing the chariot, he would not have been able to make even a single wheel. If Yao and Shun had relinquished the power of their positions as rulers and abandoned the law, and instead went from door to door persuading and debating with people, without any power to encourage them with veneration and rewards or coerce them with punishments and penalties, they would not have been able to bring order to even a few households. So the fact that the power of position is sufficient to be used in governing should be clear. Furthermore, if starving people do not eat for a hundred days because they are holding out for fine grain and meat, they will not live. Now if one says that we must wait for the worthiness of a Yao or Shun to bring order to the people of the current age, this is like saying that one should hold out for fine grain and meat in order to save oneself from starvation.

"The critic says that if one has fine horses and a sturdy chariot, and one allows a common servant to drive them, people will just laugh at him, but if Wang Liang drives them they will cover a thousand *li* in a single day. I do not believe this is the case. If one waits for the skilled ocean swimmers of the coastal state of Yue to rescue the drowning people in the states of the central plain, then even though the people of Yue swim very well, those drowning in the central states will still not be saved. To say that we must

---

[22]Xi Zhong 奚仲 is a mythical sage credited with the invention of the horse-drawn chariot during the Xia dynasty.

wait for an ancient hero like Wang Liang to drive the horses of today is just like saying that we should wait for the people of Yue to save the drowning people of the central states. Clearly this will not do.

"If one has fine horses and sturdy chariots, and one places a fresh team every fifty *li* along the road, then even if one allows a mediocre charioteer to drive them, he can still use them to travel swiftly over great distances, and a thousand *li* can easily be traversed a single day. What need is there to wait for an ancient hero like Wang Liang? Moreover, in the case of driving, the critic makes it sound like if one does not employ a Wang Liang, one must employ a common servant who will ruin things; and in the case of governing, he makes it sound like if one does not use a Yao or Shun, one must use a Jie or Zhou who will throw things into disorder. But this is like saying that if something does not taste as sweet as syrup or honey, it must taste as acrid as bitter herbs or mustard greens. The previous criticism is nothing more than a collection of empty rhetoric and meaningless phrases. It presents an argument based on two extreme positions that is entirely opposed to reason and bereft of any method. How can it be used to criticize or find fault with the reasonable teachings of Shenzi! The critic's argument has not reached the same level as his doctrine."

Chapter Twelve: The Difficulties of Persuasion

As for the true difficulty of persuasion, it is not the difficulty of finding something in my knowledge that can be used to persuade the listener, nor is it the difficulty of being able to express myself in a way that elucidates my meaning, nor is it even the difficulty of daring to speak without hesitation so that I can finish everything I have to say. No, the true difficulty of persuasion lies in knowing what is in the heart of the person being persuaded, so that I can use my persuasion to match it.

If the one you are persuading is interested in elevating his reputation, but you try to persuade him using the idea of increasing his profits, you will be regarded as person of inferior character who deals with things lowly and base, so he will surely reject what you have to say and keep you at a distance. If the person you are persuading is interested in increasing his profits, but you try to persuade him using the idea of elevating his reputation, you will be regarded as impractical and removed from the essence of affairs, so the person surely will refuse to accept your advice. If the person you are persuading is secretly interested in increasing his profits, but on the surface he wants to appear to be interested in elevating his reputation, and you try to persuade him using the idea of elevating his reputation, then in the light of day he will welcome you, but in reality he will ignore what you have to say. If you try to persuade such a person using the idea of increasing his profits, then he will secretly use your words while outwardly rejecting you for the sake of appearances. This is something one cannot fail to examine.

Affairs succeed when they are kept secret but fail when they are exposed. The persuader may not be the person who has leaked the information, but if his words touch upon some hidden affair of the ruler, his person will be in danger. If a ruler has some widely known affair he is carrying out, but he is doing it in order to achieve some ulterior objective, and the persuader not only understands what the ruler is doing, but also why he is doing it, his person will be in danger. If a persuader comes up with some special project and the ruler agrees with it, and then some clever person outside the project figures it out and leaks it to the outside world, the ruler is sure to think that it is the persuader who did it, and his person will be in danger. If a persuader does not yet enjoy the full confidence and favor of the ruler, but his words are extremely intelligent, then when his persuasions are carried out and there is some achievement he will be overlooked by the ruler's favor, and when his persuasions are not carried out and there is some failure he will be looked upon with suspicion, and his person will be in danger. If an important person commits some small error, and the persuader ostentatiously discourses on ritual and righteousness in order to challenge his wrongdoing, his person will be in danger. If an important person obtains a plan from someone else and hopes to pass it off as his own achievement, but the persuader also knows where he got it from, his person will be in danger. If a persuader forcefully urges a ruler to do that which he is incapable of doing, or stop that which he is incapable of stopping, his person will be in danger.

Thus, if you talk to a ruler about great men he will think you are implying a difference between him and them, but if you talk to him about little men he will think you are selling your influence. If you talk about what he loves he will think you are trying to borrow resources from him, but if you talk about what he hates he will think you are trying to test the limits of his anger. If you speak too plainly and oversimplify your persuasion he will think that you are unwise and your words are clumsy, but if you speak in too much detail and are too eloquent he will think that you are verbose and your words are confusing. If you make too little of your project and only outline your ideas, he will say you are cowardly and do not dare to say everything that you have to say, but if you make too much of your project and go on and on about it, he will say that you are unmannered and arrogant. These are the dificulties of persuasion. One cannot fail to understand them.

The real work of persuasion is knowing how to highlight those qualities of which the person being persuaded is proud, while eliminating those of which they are ashamed. If a ruler has some private concern, the persuader must use the public standards of righteousness to explain and strengthen it. If a ruler has an intention to do something stupid, and he cannot be prevented from doing it, the persuader should highlight the good points of the plan and scold the ruler for not carrying it out. If a ruler has some lofty ambition in his heart, but in reality he is not up to the task, the persuader should point out the problems with the plan, expose its bad points, and praise the ruler for not doing it. If a ruler wants to be proud of his wisdom and ability, the persuader should bring up several different examples in the same category and give him plenty of room to think, so that he will attribute the final plan of action to himself, and increase his own wisdom without even knowing it.

If you want to make a proposal for peaceful coexistence with other parties within the state, you must use beautiful words to explain the proposal, and subtly make the ruler see how this is in accord with his private interests. If you want to tell a ruler about some dangerous or harmful situation, you must make the potential for destruction or defamation clear, and subtly show the ruler how this may be a personal misfortune for him. Praise other people who have acted in the same way as the ruler you are speaking with, and give examples of other affairs where plans like those of the ruler you are talking to have been used. If there is someone who shares the same vices as he does, you must use their greatness to make it seem as if there is no real harm in it. If there is someone who has suffered the same failures he has, you must use his eminence to make it seem as if there is no real loss. If a ruler believes he has much strength, do not use his past difficulties to correct him. If he believes he is courageous in his military decisions, do not use his past mistakes to anger him. If he believes he is wise in his planning, do not use his past failures to distress him. First make sure that there is nothing in the overall meaning of your proposal that will offend the ruler you are persuading, and nothing in your phrasing or language that will aggravate him, then you can use the full extent of your wisdom and eloquence on him. This is the way to become intimate and close to a ruler without becoming an object of suspicion, so that you will be able to fully express your position.

Yi Yin served as a cook while Boli Xi[23] became a servant. In both cases, this is how they were able to influence their superiors. These two men were both sages, yet even they could not advance without subjugating their persons and demeaning themselves like this. Now if by becoming a cook or a servant you can gain the ear of a ruler and save the world, then this is not something that a capable officer should be ashamed to do. When you have served a ruler for a long time and enjoy his full confidence and favor, so that you are able to plan important matters for him without arousing his suspicion and have disagreements with him without being accused of being disloyal, you should clearly distinguish the beneficial from the harmful in order to promote his accomplishments, and straightforwardly point out the difference between right and wrong in order to glorify his person. When ruler and minister use their relationship to support each other, this is the fulfillment of the ends of persuasion. . . .

The dragon is a creature that can be tamed and trained so that one can ride upon its back. But on the underside of its throat it has inverted scales one foot in diameter, and if any person brushes against them, the dragon will surely kill them. A ruler of men also has his "inverted scales," so if a persuader hopes to succeed, he must be careful to avoid brushing up against them.

Chapter Forty-Three: Deciding Between Two Models of Government

A questioner asks, "Shen Buhai and Gongsun Yang, which of these two men's teachings are most vital to the success of the state?"

In response I say, "This cannot be determined. If people do not eat, then in ten days they will die. But in the depth of the winter, if they do not clothe themselves, they will also die. So if you ask which is more vital to the success of human beings, food or clothing, it is clear that people cannot do without either one of them; both are tools necessary for sustaining life.

---

[23]Boli Xi 白里奚 was prime minister of the state of Qin under Duke Mu of Qin 秦繆公 (r. 659–621 B.C.E.). Tradition holds that he originally came to the state of Qin as a servant, but was set free when Duke Mu recognized his worth as an advisor. Although Han Fei implies that he became a servant willingly, other accounts suggest that he was forced into slavery when Duke Xian of Jin 晉獻公 (r. 676–651 B.C.E.) conquered his home state of Yu 虞, and then given to Duke Mu of Qin when the latter married one of Duke Xian's daughters. Cf. *Mengzi* 5A9.

Now Shen Buhai discussed the use of administrative methods while Gongsun Yang advocated governing through laws. Using administrative methods means to assign offices based on a person's qualifications, to heed the objectives named in a minister's proposal and then hold them accountable for the actual results, to manipulate the handles of life and death, and to test the abilities of the assembled ministers.[24] This is what the ruler controls. Government through law exists when the ruler's edicts and decrees are promulgated among the various departments and bureaus, when the certitude of punishments and penalities is understood in the hearts of the people, when rewards are given to those who respect the law, and when penalties are imposed on those who violate the ruler's decrees. This is what instructs the ministers. If the ruler has no method, he will be obscured above; if the ministers have no laws, there will be disorder below. A state cannot do without either one of these things; both are the tools of emperors and kings."

The questioner asks, "Why is it that one cannot employ administrative methods without government through law, or practice government through law without using administrative methods?"

I respond, "Shen Buhai was counselor to Marquis Zhao of Han,[25] and the state of Han is one of the states formed from the division of the state of Jin.[26] During Shen Buhai's term of office the old laws of Jin had not yet disappeared, but the new laws of Han had already been created; the decrees of the former rulers of Jin had not yet been revoked, but the decrees of the succeeding rulers of Han had already been handed down. Because Shen Buhai did not take control of the state of Han's laws or unify its edicts and

---

[24]Although I translate them somewhat differently, my interpretation of these lines is informed by the arguments put forward by John Makeham in his article "The Legalist Concept of *Hsing-Ming*: An Example of the Contribution of Archaeological Evidence to the Re-Interpretation of Transmitted Texts." *Monumenta Serica*, 39, pp. 87–115. In his own translation of this passage, Makeham omits the line *cao sha sheng zhi bing* 操殺生之柄, "to manipulate the handles of life and death."

[25]See *Hanfeizi*, chapter 7, p. 309, n. 13.

[26]In the year 463 B.C.E., the ducal house of the state of Jin was overthrown by the leaders of four powerful aristocratic clans, the Zhi 智, the Zhao 趙, the Han 韓, and the Wei 魏. The Zhi clan initially tried to take control of the state, but was destroyed by the other three clans in the year 453 B.C.E. Because none of the remaining families were strong enough to defeat their rivals, they decided to divide the territory of the state of Jin into three separate, smaller states (i.e., the states of Zhao, Han, and Wei). These new states were formally recognized by the Zhou king in 403 B.C.E., and continued to exist for almost two hundred years until they were wiped out during the Qin unification. See the *Map of China during the Spring and Autumn Period*.

decrees, there was a good deal of corruption. Thus, if there was something beneficial in the old laws and the former decrees the ministers would follow these, but if there was something beneficial in the new laws and the later decrees they would follow those. Since the old and the new laws were mutually contradicting, and the former and the later decrees were mutually conflicting, even though Shen Buhai ten times instructed Marquis Zhao in the use of method, the corrupt ministers still had the means to deceive him with their words. Thus, in the seventy years since Shen Buhai's death, none of the rulers of the powerful state of Han, which can field ten-thousand war chariots, has ever reached the level of a lord protector or a king; and the reason for this misfortune is that even though Shen Buhai's methods have been employed by the rulers of Han above, the law has not been properly administered within the offices of the state below.

When Gongsun Yang controlled the state of Qin, he set up a system in which people were expected to inform on their associates but were held accountable for the truth of their accusations. He linked the population together into groups of five and ten households and made all the members of each group collectively responsible for crimes committed by any of them. He ensured that rewards were substantial and reliable and that punishments were heavy and certain. Because of this, the people of Qin were industrious and did not rest even when they were tired; they pursued their enemies and did not turn away even when it was dangerous. Thus, their state became rich and their army grew strong. Nevertheless, because the rulers of Qin did not have any method to recognize corruption, the wealth and strength that was generated by this system only increased the holdings of important ministers.

After the death of Duke Xiao and Gongsun Yang, King Hui assumed the position of ruler.[27] At that point the law of Qin had not yet been defeated, but Zhang Yi used the power of Qin to extort profits from the states of Han and Wei.[28] When King Hui died, King Wu assumed the position or

---

[27]Duke Xiao of Qin 秦孝公 (r. 361–338 B.C.E.) was the ruler of Qin during the period when Gongsun Yang enacted his political reforms. When Duke Xiao died in 338 B.C.E., his heir King Huiwen of Qin 秦惠文王 (r. 337–311 B.C.E.) had Gongsun Yang torn apart by chariots because Gongsun Yang had previously mutilated the King's tutor and tattooed his preceptor in retribution for a crime he committed as heir.

[28]Zhang Yi 張儀, a native of the state of Wei, served as advisor to the rulers of a number of prominent states, but in reality he was always an agent of the state of Qin. He used his impressive rhetorical skills to persuade the rulers of Han and Wei into forming a "horizontal" alliance with Qin. As Qin's representative, he was often showered with gifts and titles by the rulers of the states in which he served and amassed a considerable fortune in his lifetime.

ruler, and Gan Mao used the power of Qin to extort profits from the Zhou royal house.[29] When King Wu died, King Zhao assumed the position of ruler, and the Marquis of Rang crossed over the states of Han and Wei to attack the state of Qi in the east. After five years, the state of Qin had not increased its territory by a single foot of land, but Marquis Rang had already enlarged his own fiefdom around the city of Tao.[30] Similarly, the Marquis of Ying attacked the state of Han for eight years, but in the end all he did was enlarge his own fiefdom south of the Ru River.[31] Since that time, all those who have used the state of Qin have been of the same kind as Ying and Rang. Thus, when battles are won it is the great ministers who are respected, and when lands are captured it is their private fiefs that are enlarged. The rulers of Qin have no method by which they can know of their ministers' corruption, so even though Gongsun Yang ten times refined the laws, it is the ministers who have enjoyed the resources his efforts produced. Thus in the several decades since Gongsun Yang's death, none of the rulers of the mighty state of Qin, with all its resources, has ever reached the level of an emperor or king; and the reason for this misfortune is that even though the law has been properly administered within the offices of the state below, the rulers have had no method for dealing with corruption above."

The questioner asks, "What if the ruler uses Shenzi's method and the offices follow the Gongsun Yang's system of law, will this do?"

---

[29]Gan Mao 甘茂 served as Chancellor of the Left under King Wu of Qin 秦武王 (r. 310–307 B.C.E.). He led the attack that captured the city of Yiyang 宜陽 near the East Zhou capital of Loyang 雒陽 in 307 B.C.E., and was a central figure in King Wu's plot to overthrow the last remnants of the Zhou dynasty. It is unclear how he used his position to extort benefits from the Zhou royal house.

[30]Wei Ran 魏冉, the Marquis of Rang 穰, served as prime minister under King Zhao of Qin 秦昭王 (r. 306–251 B.C.E.). In the year 270 B.C.E., he led a force of several thousand men across the territories of Han and Wei to sieze the regions of Gang 剛 and Shou 壽 in the state of Qi. Although the official reason for this attack was to punish Qi for supporting the state of Wei four years earlier, Wei Ran's real purpose was to enlarge the size of his own holdings around the city of Tao 陶.

[31]Fan Sui 范睢, the Marquis of Ying 應候, also served as prime minister under King Zhao of Qin. He opposed Wei Ran's attack on the cities of Qi, and was later responsible for turning the King of Qin against Wei Ran. During his term as prime minister (c. 266–255 B.C.E.), Fan Sui orchestrated a number of campaigns against the state of Han which resulted in the seizure of a substantial amount of territory along the Qin-Han border. However, because these lands abutted Fan Sui's own fief at Ying, their acquisition only served to increase his personal holdings.

I respond, "Shenzi did not fully understand method; Gongsun Yang did not fully understand law. Shenzi said, 'An official should never overstep the duties of his office. Even if he knows something, he should not say it.' Now when Shenzi said, 'An official should never overstep the duties of his office' he meant that if an official attends to his own assignment, that is good enough. As for knowing and not saying anything, this means to not say more than you should. A ruler of men sees with the eyes of the entire state, so no one's vision is more perceptive than his. He hears with the ears of the entire state, so no one's hearing is more acute than his. Now if people know something but do not say it, how can the rulers of men still borrow their eyes and ears?

"The laws of the Gongsun Yang state: 'Anyone who takes the head of an enemy in battle will have their rank raised by one level, and if they want to take an office, they will be given an office with a salary of fifty piculs of grain. Anyone who takes the heads of two enemies in battle will have their rank raised by two levels, and if they want to take an office, they will be given an office with a salary of one hundred piculs of grain.' Thus, in this system, changes in office and rank are linked to success at taking heads in battle. Now if there was a law that said anyone who takes a head in battle is ordered to become a doctor or a carpenter, the result would be that houses would not be built and illnesses would not be cured. Being a carpenter requires skill with one's hands; being a doctor requires a comprehensive knowledge of medicines. So if one uses success at taking heads in battle as the sole criterion for becoming a carpenter or doctor, the position will not match the candidate's abilities. Now managing an office requires wisdom and ability, while taking heads in battle is the result of applying courage and strength. So if one uses those who apply courage and strength to manage offices that require wisdom and ability, this is just like using success at taking heads in battle as the sole criterion for becoming a doctor or a carpenter. Therefore I say, 'Neither of these two gentleman were entirely correct in their understanding of law and method.'"

Chapter Forty-Nine: The Five Vermin

In the age of upper antiquity, human beings were few and animals were numerous, so the people could not prevail against the birds, beasts, insects, and serpents. Then there appeared a sage who taught the people how to build nests out of wood so they could escape all harm. The people were pleased by this and made the man king of the entire world, giving him the name "The

Nester." The people ate fruits, melons, mussels, and clams, but they were putrid and foulsmelling and hurt the people's stomachs so that they often became sick and ill. Then there appeared a sage who taught the people how to start a fire by drilling dry kindling so they could transform their rancid foods. The people were pleased by this and made the man king of the entire world, giving him the name "The Kindler." In the age of middle antiquity, the world was covered by a great flood, but Gun and Yu of the Xia opened up channels to divert the waters. In the age of lower antiquity, the wicked kings Jie and Zhou governed cruelly and created disorder, but Tang of Yin and Wu of Zhou led punitive campaigns to overthrow them.

Now if someone built nests out of wood or started fires by drilling dry kindling during the age of the Lords of Xia, they would surely be laughed at by Gun and Yu. If someone opened up channels to divert the flood waters during the age of the Yin and the Zhou, they would surely be laughed at by Tang and Wu. This being the case, if someone goes around praising the Way of Yao, Shun, Tang, Wu, and Yu in the present age, they will surely be laughed at by the new sages.

For this reason, the sage does not expect to follow the ways of the ancients or model his behavior on an unchanging standard of what is acceptable. He examines the affairs of the age and then makes his preparations accordingly.

Among the people of Song[32] there was a farmer who had a stump in the middle of his field. One day, a rabbit running across the field crashed into the stump, broke its neck, and died. Seeing this, the man put aside his plow and took up watch next to the stump, hoping that he would get another rabbit in the same way. But of course he could not get another rabbit like this, and he soon became the laughing-stock of the entire state of Song. Now if one wants to use the government of the former kings to bring order to the people of the current age, this is all just so much stump-watching. . . .

In upper antiquity, men competed by means of the *dao* 道, "Way" and its *de* 德, "Power;" in the middle age, they tried to oust each other using clever stratagems; these days they battle with strength and spirit. . . .

The past and the present have different customs; the new and the old require different preparations. If one wants to use a lax and lenient govern-

---

[32]The people of Song were the butt of many jokes. Cf. *Mengzi* 2A2, and *Zhuangzi*, chapter 1, p. 207.

ment to bring order to the people of a tense age, this is like trying to drive a spirited horse without reins or a whip. This is the kind of calamity that comes from not understanding.

Now the Confucians and Mohists all claim that the former kings loved everyone in the whole world equally, and looked upon the people like parents look upon their own children. How do they show that this was the case? They say, "When the Minister of Crime was carrying out a punishment, the ruler would not hold any musical entertainment. When he heard report of a death sentence, the ruler would always shed tears." This is how they praise the former kings. But if one holds that when ruler and subject are like father and son there will always be order,[33] this implies that there is never any disorder between fathers and sons. In the nature and disposition of human beings nothing is more primary than the love of parents for their children. All children are loved by their parents, and yet children are not always well behaved. Even if one loves a child deeply, how does that prevent the child from being unruly? Now the love of the former kings for the people was not greater than the love of parents for their children, so if children are not always well behaved even when they are loved, how could the people have been made well ordered simply by loving them!

Furthermore, when punishments are carried out according to the law and the ruler sheds tears because of it, this is in order to demonstrate the ruler's benevolence, and not for the sake of creating order. To shed tears and not want to punish is benevolence, but to not allow offenses not to be punished is the law. The former kings allowed their laws to prevail and did not listen to their tears, so clearly benevolence cannot be relied on to produce order.

People naturally submit to the power of position,[34] but few are able to yield to righteousness. Confucius was a great sage of the world. He travelled throughout the land within the four seas refining people's conduct and elucidating the Way. Everyone in the land within the four seas was pleased by his benevolence and praised him for his righteousness, but those who followed him numbered only seventy men. It seems those who value benevolence are rare while those with the ability to be righteous are difficult to find. Thus, even with the vastness of the whole world, there were

---

[33]Cf. *Analects* 12.11.

[34]For more on the doctrine of shi 勢, "the power of position," see *Han Feizi* chapter 8, pp. 311–16.

only seventy men who followed Kongzi, and only one man who was truly benevolent and righteous.[35]

Duke Ai of Lu was an inferior ruler, but when he faced south and became ruler of the state, none of the people within the borders of Lu dared to not be his subjects. People naturally submit to the power of position, and using the power of position it is truly easy to make people submit. Thus, Kongzi served as Duke Ai's subject despite his moral superiority, and Duke Ai acted as Kongzi's ruler despite his inferiority as a ruler. Kongzi did not yield to the Duke's righteousness, he submitted to the power of the duke's superior position. Thus, if Duke Ai had depended on his righteousness, Kongzi would not have submitted to him, but by taking advantage of the power of his position, he was able to make Kongzi his subject.

These days when scholars counsel the rulers of men, they do not tell them to take advantage of the invincible power of their position as rulers. Instead, they tell them that by striving to practice benevolence and righteousness they can become kings. This is to demand that the rulers of men must be equal to Kongzi and to regard the ordinary people of the world as if they were all comparable to his disciples. This is a scheme that is bound to fail.

Now suppose there is some no-good child. His parents scold him, but he will not reform his behavior because of their anger; his fellow villagers reprimand him, but he is not moved by what they say; his teachers and elders try to educate him, but he does not change his ways despite their instruction. So even with love of his parents, the actions of his fellow villagers, and the wisdom of his teachers and elders—these three "beautiful things"—acting on him, in the end he remains unmoved and will not change so much as a hair on his neck. But when the civil officers of the local magistrate take up the weapons of their office, enforce the public law, and go out looking for evil-doers, he then becomes fearful, changing his demeanor and altering his conduct. Thus, the love of parents is not enough to teach a child to be good. It must be backed up by the harsh punishments of the local magistrate. People naturally grow proud when loved, and become obedient only through coercion.

Even the agile Lou Ji[36] could not climb over a wall ten spans in height because the face is too steep, but a lame sheep can easily graze on a thousand-span mountain if the slope is gradual. Therefore, an enlightened ruler

---

[35]That is, Kongzi himself.

[36]Lou Ji 樓季, the younger brother of Marquis Wen of Wei 魏文侯 (r. 445–396 B.C.E), was a legendary hero renowned for his strength, courage, and skill with horses.

makes sure that his laws are steep and his punishments are severe. An ordinary person will not throw away so much as a yard or two of silk cloth, but even the notorious Robber Zhi would not take a hundred taels of molten bronze. When there is no certainty of harm, even a few yards of cloth will not be thrown away, but when one is sure to injure one's hand, even a hundred taels of bronze will not be taken. Therefore, an enlightened ruler makes sure that his punishments are always carried out.

For this reason, when handing out rewards, it is best to make them substantial and dependable, so that the people will prize them; when assigning penalities, it is best to make them heavy and inescapable, so that the people will fear them; when framing laws, it is best to make them unequivocal and fixed, so that the people will understand them. Thus, if a ruler dispenses rewards and does not revoke them, carries out punishments and does not pardon them, supports his rewards with praise, and acompanies his penalties with condemnation, then both the worthy and the unworthy will do their utmost to serve him.

Now, however, this is not the case. Rulers grant men titles because of their accomplishments in battle, but then look down on them because they are only military officers; they reward people for their agricultural production, but then scorn them because of their family occupation; they banish those who will not accept their rule, but then admire them for their disdain for the world; they blame those who violate their prohibitions, but then praise them for their courage. The things they condemn and praise and the things they reward and penalize are all confused and in conflict with one another. As a result, the laws and prohibitions are undermined and the people become even more disorderly. . . .

The Confucians use "cultural refinement" to confuse the law, the bravos use "martial prowess" to violate the prohibitions, and yet the rulers of men honor them both. This is why there is disorder. Those who depart from the law should be charged with crimes, and yet the learned masters use their knowledge of the arts of culture to get themselves chosen for office. Those who violate the prohibitions should be punished, and yet the bravos use their private swords to get themselves patronized by powerful families. Thus, those whom the law denounces the ruler selects, and those whom the civil officers would punish their superiors patronize. The law and the appointment of officials, the superiors and their subordinates—these four are all turned against each other and there is no way of settling the matter. In such a situation, even if one had ten Huang Di's they still could not bring about order. Therefore, those who practice benevolence and righteousness should not be praised, for if one praises them they will hinder the accomplishments of the state; those who work at the arts of culture should not be employed, for if one employs them they will confuse the law.

Among the people of Chu there was man known for his personal uprightness. When his father stole a sheep he reported the crime to the criminal officers. But the Premier of Chu, thinking that the man had been upright in regard to his lord, but crooked in regard to his father, said, "Kill him!" and had the man arrested and charged. From this it can be seen that someone who is an upright subject to his ruler may be a troublesome son to his father.[37] There was a man of Lu who followed his ruler out to war. Three times they went into battle, and three times the man ran away. Kongzi asked the man why he had run, and the man replied, "I have an elderly father. If I should die there would be no one to take care of him." Kongzi thought the man very filial, so he recommended him and got him promoted to office. From this it can be seen that someone who is a filial son to his father may be a traitorous subject to his ruler.

Thus, the Premier of Chu executed a man and wicked deeds were not reported to the authories in the state of Chu; Kongzi rewarded a man and the people of Lu readily surrendered and ran away. If the interests of superior and inferior are as different as this, and a ruler of men seeks to enjoy the blessings of his altars of soil and millet, while at the same time praising the conduct of private individuals, then surely he will not succeed.

In ancient times when Cang Jie[38] invented writing, he called that which revolved around the self "private" and that which was opposed to the private "public." So the fact that "public" and "private" are mutually opposing ideas was already understood by Cang Jie.[39] Now, believing that public and private interests are the same is the kind of disaster that comes from not being discerning. This being the case, when planning for the good of individuals, nothing is better than to cultivate benevolence and righteousness

---

[37]Cf. *Analects* 13.18.

[38]Cang Jie 蒼頡 is the name of a mythical sage who supposedly created the Chinese written language by looking at the tracks left by birds in the sand.

[39]The argument here is based on the appearance of the Chinese characters for "public" and "private." The graph for the word "private" (*si* 私) was originally written simply as 厶. The graph for the word "public" (*gong* 公) is composed of two elements: the original graph for *si* 厶 and the signific *ba* 八, which can have the meaning "to oppose." Thus, Han Fei's point is that Cang Jie understood the opposition between public and private interests and encoded it into the actual graphs for these words. Cf. *Xunzi*, chapter 2, p. 257, n. 23.

and practice the arts of culture. If you cultivate benevolence and right-eousness you will be trusted, and when you are trusted you will receive employment in the government. If you practice the arts of culture you will become a brilliant teacher, and when you are a brilliant teacher you will become eminent and honored. This is good for the individual. But if this should actually happen, people without merit would receive employment in the government and people without noble titles would become eminent and honored. When government is conducted like this, the state is sure to fall into disorder, and the ruler is sure to be in danger. Thus, two incompatible situations cannot stand together. . . .

What the world calls "worthy" is conduct that is virtuous and honest; what the world calls "wise" is language that is subtle and mysterious. Language that is subtle and mysterious is something that even the wisest people find difficult to understand. So if when making laws for the masses, you use language that even the wisest people find difficult to understand, then no one will comprehend or follow your laws. Hence, if one does not have enough dregs and husks to fill one's belly, one should not strive for fine grain and meat; if one is dressed in a short and tattered robe made out of coarse cloth, one should not hold out for fine stitching and embroidery. The same applies to the business of governing the world: if the critical affairs have not been taken care of, one should not work on the noncritical ones. Now, what government seeks to order is the affairs of the common people. So if you do not use what every man and woman knows clearly, and instead delight in the theories of the wisest men, this is antithetical to good order. Therefore, language that is subtle and mysterious is not the work of the people.

If people regard conduct that is virtuous and honest as worthy, it must be because they value officers who will not deceive them. But those who value officers who will not deceive them also have no methods to keep themselves from being deceived. When the common people associate with one another, they have no wealth or resources that they can use to benefit each other, and no might or position of power that they can use to frighten each other. Therefore, they seek officers who will not deceive them. But the ruler of men occupies a position of power that allows him to control men. He has the resources of an entire state at his disposal, so he can hand out lavish rewards and inflict harsh punishments. If a ruler can manipulate his two handles and use them to refine that which the methods of clarification reveal,[40] then even if he has ministers like Tian Chang and Zi Han,[41] they will not dare to be deceptive. What need is there for him to wait for the kind of officers who would not deceive him?

Now, there are no more than ten officers in the whole world who are virtuous and honest, and yet the offices within the borders of a single state number in the hundreds. So if one insists on employing only officers who are virtuous and honest, there will not be enough men to fill the offices of the state. And if there are not enough men to fill the offices of the state, those promoting order will be few while those promoting disorder will be numerous. Therefore, the Way of an enlightened ruler is to unify the laws and not seek after wisdom, to establish the proper methods and not yearn for honesty. In this way, the law will not be defeated and the offices will all be free of corruption and treachery.

These days when rulers of men listen to people's words, they are pleased by their eloquence and do not require them to match their words with actions. When they evaluate people's conduct, they praise the reputation the person has gained through those actions and do not hold them accountable for the results. For this reason, when the people of the world speak or discuss they strive to be eloquent and ignore the question of usefulnesss. As a result the courts of rulers are filled with people praising the former kings and talking about benevolence and righteousness, and so the government cannot avoid falling into disorder. Similarly, in their personal conduct, the people compete with one another to appear lofty and do not try to produce achievements; the wise officers go into retreat, living in grottos and caves

---

[40]That is, the handles of punishment and reward. For more on Han Fei's notion of "the two handles" (er bing 二柄), see Han Feizi, chapter 7, pp. 307–11. I take the ming shu 明術, "methods of clarification," mentioned here to refer to the various investigative and evaluative techniques that Han Fei believes a ruler must use to see through the rhetoric of his ministers, and learn the truth about their activities and intentions.

[41]Tian Chang 田常 and Zi Han 子罕 are often used by Han Feizi as paradigmatic examples of usurpers who deceived their rulers into granting them the authority to bestow favors and/or administer punishments. (See Han Feizi, chapter 7, pp. 307–11.) Tian Chang was the head of a powerful family in the state of Qi who used his wealth and position to ingratiate himself with the common people and buy the support of important government officials. In the year 481 B.C.E. he assassinated Duke Jian of Qi 齊簡公, exterminated the rival Gao 高 and Guo 國 clans, and set up Duke Jian's younger brother Duke Ping 齊平公 as a puppet monarch. This initial act of treachery paved the way for the Tian clan's eventual usurpation of the rulership of Qi sometime around 356 B.C.E. Zi Han was originally Minister of the City under Marquis Huan of Song 宋桓候. After being appointed to the position of prime minister, he tricked Marquis Huan into giving him the power to administer punishments, and then used this power to steal effective control of the state.

and refusing to accept a government salary or stipend, and so the army cannot avoid growing weak. Why is it that the army cannot avoid growing weak and the government cannot avoid falling into disorder? It is because that which the people praise and their superiors honor are the methods of a disordered country.

These days, everyone in the state talks about the problem of governing, and people keep copies of the laws of Shang Yang and Guan Zhong in their houses. Nevertheless, the state grows poorer and poorer because those who talk about farming outnumber those who actually work a plow. Everyone in the state talks about how to run an army, and people keep copies of the writings of Sun Wu and Wu Qi in their houses.[42] Nevertheless, the army gets weaker and weaker because those who talk about war outnumber those who actually put on armor. Therefore, an enlightened ruler uses the people's strength and does not listen to their words; he rewards their achievements and completely prohibits useless activities. As a result, the people exhaust every ounce of their strength in obedience to their superiors.

The effort required to do farming is exhausting, but people will still do it because they say, "This way I can become rich." Going to war is a dangerous affair, but people will still do it because they say, "This way I can become ennobled." Now if by cultivating the arts of culture and practicing speaking and discussing, one can enjoy the fruits of wealth without the labor of farming, and have the respect of nobility without the danger of battle, what person would not do these things? Because of this, for every one person who uses their strength in farming or warfare there are a hundred who work at being wise. But when many work at being wise, the law is defeated; when few use their strength, the state grows poor. This is why the world is in disorder.

Therefore, in the state of an enlightened ruler there are no texts written on bamboo strips, the law provides the only education; there are no words of learned masters, the civil officers are the only teachers; there are no attacks by private swordsmen, taking heads in battle is the only way to display one's courage. The people of this state, their speeches and discussions are always in accord with the law; their actions and innovations are turned back to accomplishment; and their displays of courage are conducted entirely within the ranks of the army. For this reason, in times of peace the

---

[42]The reference is to *Sunzi bingfa* 孫子兵法 "*Master Sun's Art of War*" attributed to Sun Wu 孫武 (c. 544–496 B.C.E.), and *Wuzi bingfa* 吳子兵法 "*Master Wu's Art of War*" attributed to Wu Qi 吳起 (d. 381 B.C.E.).

state is rich, and in times of trouble the army is strong. These are what are called the "resources of a king." Having amassed the resources of a king, the ruler can then take advantage of the divisions within enemy states and attack them. That which will allow a ruler to surpass the Five Emperors and rival the Three Kings is surely this model.[43]

Now, however, this is not the case. The officers and people do as they please within the state, while the orators enjoy positions of power outside it. To try to deal with a strong enemy when those outside the state and those inside the state are both up to no good, is this not dangerous! Thus, when the ministers discuss foreign affairs, they are either split between vertical and horizantal alliances,[44] or else they are intent on borrowing the strength of the state in order to avenge themselves against some personal enemy. The advocates of the vertical alliance argue that the various weaker states should join together to attack the one strong state (i.e., Qin), while the advocates of the horizontal alliance argue that it is better to serve the one strong state and attack the various weaker ones. But neither of these is the way to preserve one's state.

Now those ministers who advocate a horizontal alliance all say, "If we do not serve the great state then when we are attacked by our enemies we will suffer misfortune." When you serve a great state you cannot be sure of good results, and yet you still must present maps of your territory like a deputy nation, and hand over your official seals when requesting troops. But if you present maps of your territory, your lands will be cut away, and if you hand over your offical seals your name will be degraded. When your lands are cut away, your state will be diminished, and when your name is degraded, your government will fall into disorder. Serving a great state and joining the hor-

---

[43]The Five Emperors are the mythical rulers Tai Hao, Yan Di, Huang Di, Shao Hao, and Zhuan Xu. The Three Kings are Tang, Wen, and Wu (see *Important Figures*).

[44]The "vertical" and "horizontal" alliances are general designations used to describe the various anti-Qin (vertical) and pro-Qin (horizontal) military and political coalitions that were formed in China during the late fourth and third centuries B.C.E. The "vertical" alliances—so named because they united states along a north-south axis—were made up of several smaller states who joined together (under the leadership of whichever of them happened to be the most powerful at the time) to resist the forces of the expanding state of Qin. The "horizontal" alliances—which united states along an east-west axis—were made up of states who, either out of fear or for the sake of political advantage, joined with Qin in their attacks against the other states. These alliances were usually put together by wandering persuaders of uncertain loyalties who travelled from state to state negotiating deals between the various rulers and obtaining official positions within the governments of each of the states they succeeded in rallying to their cause.

izontal alliance will never produce any benefits, but you will lose your lands and your government will fall into disorder.

Those ministers who advocate the vertical alliance all say, "If we do not try to rescue the smaller states and attack the great one then the rest of the world will be lost, and if the rest of the world is lost then our own state will be in danger and our own ruler will be degraded." When you try to rescue the smaller states you cannot be sure of good results, but you still must raise troops and oppose the great one. When you try to rescue the smaller states there is no guarantee that you will be able to preserve them, and you cannot be sure that there will not be division among the states attacking the great one. And if there is division, you will be at the mercy of the strong state. If you send out troops they will be defeated, and if you withdraw to protect your own lands your cities will be taken. Trying to rescue the smaller states and joining the vertical alliance will never produce any benefits, but your lands will be lost and your armies will be defeated.

Thus, if you choose to serve a strong state, the agents of a foreign power will take over the offices inside your realm; and if you try to rescue the smaller states, the influential ministers within your own land will use their position to gain benefits from abroad. Long before any benefits to the state have been realized, fiefdoms and lavish stipends will have already come to the ministers. So even if their ruler and superior is degraded, the ministers will still be respected, and even if the territory of the state is diminished, their private households will still be enriched. If their plan succeeds, they can use the authority this gives them to extend their influence. If their plan fails, they can still take the riches they have gained and retire in comfort. But if the rulers of men, when listening to counsel, honor their ministers with titles and stipends before their plans have even succeeded, and do not punish their ministers even when their plans have failed, then who among the wandering persuaders would not hazard putting forward some profit-seeking proposal in the hopes of benefiting from it afterward? So why is it that rulers continue to destroy their states and ruin themselves by listening to the groundless advice of these orators? It is because the rulers of men do not understand the difference between public and private benefit, do not distinguish between appropriate and inappropriate words, and do not ensure that punishments and penalties are imposed after a plan does not succeed.

Rulers all say, "If I attend to foreign affairs, then at best I may become a king, and at worst I can keep myself secure." To be king is to be able to attack others; to be secure is to be invulnerable to attack. When one's state is strong, one can attack others; when one's state is well ordered, one cannot be attacked. But strength and good order cannot be brought about by anything outside the state, they belong to the realm of internal government. Now if a ruler does not implement the proper laws and methods within the state, and instead depends on employing wisdom outside the state, his state will never become strong or well ordered. . . .

The natural aspirations of the people are such that they all move toward security and benefit and avoid danger and poverty. Now when the ruler launches an attack against another state, the people know that if they advance they will be killed by the enemy, and if they retreat they will die by execution, so either way it is dangerous. When they are forced to put aside the work of their own households and labor like sweating horses in the armies of their ruler, they know that their families will face hardship and their superiors will not compensate them, so they are sure to become poor. These situations of poverty and danger, how can one expect the people not to avoid them? Therefore, the people hasten to serve within the private gates of powerful ministers and get themselves exempted from all military service,[45] because by getting themselves exempted from all military service they can distance themselves from battle, and if they distance themselves from battle they will be safe. They offer gifts and bribes and use those "on the road" to power to get what they need, because if they get what they need they will be personally secure, and when they are personally secure they will enjoy benefits. These situations of security and benefit, how can one expect the people not to move toward them? For this reason, public-spirited people are few while private-minded individuals are numerous.

The method of governing used by an enlightened ruler to bring order to his state is to keep the number of merchants, craftsman, and wandering tradesmen low and their status humble. In this way he promotes the primary occupations, and discourages the auxillary ones. In the current age, however, the requests of those dear to the ruler are granted, so offices and titles can be bought, and when offices and titles can be bought, the status of merchants and artisans will not remain humble. When ill-gotten wealth and peddlers gain circulation in the marketplace, the number of merchants will not remain low. When those who collect taxes and exploit the farmers are more respected than officers who till their own land and go off to battle, then righteous and upright officers will be few while merchants and peddlers will be numerous.

Thus, these are the customs of a disordered state: its scholars use the pretexts of benevolence and righteousness to praise the Way of the former kings. They put on a grand appearance and speak in elegant phrases in

---

[45]The meaning of this line is somewhat unclear and the translation here is tentative.

order to cast doubt upon the laws of the current age and create division in the hearts of the rulers of men. Its orators concoct fabrications and make false claims, borrowing the strength of foreign powers in order to achieve their private aims, while neglecting what would benefit the altars of soil and millet. Its swordsmen gather bands of followers, establishing their own standards of deportment and conduct in order to make a name for themselves and violate the prohibitions of the five offices. Those who worry about being driven into battle gather within the private gates of powerful ministers, offering gifts and bribes and using the recommendations of influential people to get themselves exempted from the labor of military service. Its merchants and craftsmen deal in crude and inferior products, accumulating undeserved wealth by hoarding goods until the best time to sell and looking to make a profit from the farmers. These five groups of people are the vermin of the state. If the rulers of men do not get rid of these five vermin and nurture just and upright officers, then even if the states of the land within the four seas are broken and perish and their ruling houses are eaten away and destroyed, it should come as no surprise.

Chapter Fifty:
On the Prominent Schools of Thought

The prominent schools of the age are Confucianism and Mohism. The greatest of the Confucians was Kong Qiu [i.e., Kongzi], and the greatest of the Mohists was Mo Di [i.e., Mozi]. Since the death of Kongzi, there has been the Zi Zhang school of Confucianism, the Zi Si school of Confucianism, the Yan family school of Confucianism, the Meng family school of Confucianism, the Qidiao family school of Confucianism, the Zhongliang family school of Confucianism, the Sun family school of Confucianism, and the Yuezheng family school of Confucianism. Since the death of Mozi, there has been the Xiangli family school of Mohism, the Xiangfu family school of Mohism, and the Dengling family school of Mohism. Thus, after Kongzi and Mozi, the Confucians split into eight factions and the Mohists split into three.[46] The doctrines and practices that each of these factions accept and reject are divergent and conflicting, and yet each faction claims that they are the true representatives of the Way of Kongzi

---

[46]Although some scholars have gone to great lengths to try to correlate the names given here with specific figures in the Confucian and Mohist movements, the historical truth behind these eight schools of Confucianism and three schools of Mohism is still the subject of much scholarly speculation and debate.

or Mozi. Kongzi and Mozi cannot come back to life, so who will determine which of the current schools are the right ones?

Kongzi and Mozi both followed the Way of Yao and Shun and both claimed that they were the true transmitters of the Way of these sages, and yet the doctrines and practices that each of them accepted and rejected are not the same. Yao and Shun cannot come back to life, so who will determine whether the Confucians or the Mohists are correct? The traditions of the Yin and Zhou dynasties go back more than seven hundred years, and the traditions of the Yu[47] and Xia dynasties go back more than two thousand years before that. Yet none of these can determine if the Confucians or the Mohists are right. Now then, if someone wants to examine the Way of Yao and Shun that existed more than three thousand years in the past, how can they possibly be certain about their ideas! Someone who is sure about something without supporting evidence is a fool. Someone who bases their views on something they cannot be sure about is a charlatan. Thus, those who depend on the teachings of the former kings and are absolutely sure about the Way of Yao and Shun are either fools or charlatans. The teachings of fools and charlatans and codes of conduct that are inconsistent and contradictory— these are things an enlightened ruler will not accept.

When participating in funeral rites, the Mohists wear winter clothes if it is winter and summer clothes if it is summer. Their inner and outer coffins each measure only three inches thick, and they only wear their mourning garments for three months. The rulers of the age consider this to be frugal and honor them. The Confucians, on the other hand, will bankrupt their entire household in order to provide a lavish funeral. They wear their mourning garments for three years, and so destroy themselves with mourning practices that they are forced to walk with a cane. The rulers of the age consider this to be filial and honor them. But if one applauds Mozi for his frugality, one should condemn Kongzi for his wastefulness, and if one applauds Kongzi for his filial piety, one should condemn Mozi for his irreverence. Filial piety and irreverence, frugality and wastefulness—these are all features of the teachings of the Confucians and the Mohists, and yet their superiors honor them both equally.

According to the code of conduct taught by Qidiao,[48] a person should never cringe before an angry expression or run away from a challenging

---

[47]The name Yu 虞 is sometimes used to refer to the "dynasty" of the ancient sage-emperor Shun.

[48]No information about this figure is available. Most commentators agree that he was not part of the Qidiao family school of Confucianism mentioned in the opening paragraph.

stare. If someone's conduct is crooked, they should be disobeyed even by a common slave; if someone's conduct is upright, they should be willing to show their anger even to one of the feudal rulers. The rulers of the age consider this to be steadfast and honor him. According to the code of conduct taught by Songzi, a person should always speak out in opposition to fighting and conflict, and never take part in revenge against an enemy. They should never resent being captured or imprisoned, and never consider it disgraceful to have been insulted. The rulers of the age consider this to be tolerant and honor him. But if one applauds Qidiao for being steadfast, one should condemn Songzi for being too forgiving, and if one applauds Songzi for being tolerant, on should condemn Qidiao for being too violent. Now being tolerant and being steadfast, being too forgiving and being too violent—these are all features of the codes of conduct taught by these two gentleman, and yet rulers listen equally to both of them.

These are the teachings of fools and charlatans and debates between confused and contradictory doctrines, and yet the rulers of men listen to them all. As a result, the officers of the land within the four seas use no fixed method in their speech, and follow no uniform standard of behavior in their conduct. Hot coals and ice cannot coexist for long in the same vessel; cold and hot weather cannot arrive at the same time. Similarly, one cannot allow two inconsistent and contradictory teachings to both stand and expect there to be order. Now if you pay equal attention to inconsistent teachings, and try to harmoniously carry out principles that are in disagreement with each other, how can there be anything but disorder? If a ruler's way of listening and acting are as disorderly as this, his government of his people will surely be the same.

When the educated officers of the day talk about governing, they often say, "One should give land to the poor and destitute in order to provide for their lack of resources." Now if there are some people who, having the same opportunities as everyone else, are able to keep themselves fully supplied even without the benefits of a good harvest or some additional source of income, it is either because they are industrious or because they are frugal. If there are some other people who, having the same opportunities as everyone else, still fall into poverty and destitution even without the misfortunes of famine, sickness, and natural disasters, it is either because they are wasteful or because they are lazy. Those who are wasteful and lazy become poor, while those who are industrious and frugal become wealthy. Now if a superior imposes taxes on the rich in order to redistribute their wealth among the families of the poor, this is stealing from the industrious and frugal and giving to the wasteful and lazy. If a ruler does this and then expects his people to be industrious in their work and frugal in their expenditures, he is going to be disappointed. . . .

Tantai Ziyu[49] had the appearance of a gentleman, so Kongzi became acquainted with him and took him on as his disciple. But after he had lived with him for some time, he found that his conduct did not measure up to his looks. Zai Yu's[50] speech was elegant and cultured, so Kongzi became acquainted with him and took him on as his disciple. But after he had lived with him for some time, he found that his wisdom did not measure up to his eloquence. Therefore, Kongzi said, "Should one select men on the basis of their appearance? I made that mistake with Tantai Ziyu. Should one select men on the basis of their words? I made that mistake with Zai Yu." Thus, even with the wisdom of Kongzi it is still possible to mistake the facts about people. Now the eloquence of these new orators today is far more excessive than that of Zai Yu, and the rulers of the age are far more muddled in their hearing than was Kongzi. So if the rulers of today choose to employ people based solely on the fact that they are pleased by how they speak, how could they possibly not make any mistakes? Thus, the state of Wei employed Mang Mao because of his eloquence and met with misfortune south of Mount Hua,[51] and the state of Zhao employed the Lord of Mafu because of his eloquence and met with

---

[49]Ziyu 子羽 is the secondary name of Tantai Mieming 澹臺滅明 (b. 512 B.C.E.). He is mentioned briefly in the *Analects* (cf. *Analects* 6.14, not in this volume), but nothing is said about his physical appearance. Sima Qian includes Tantai Mieming among the ranks of Kongzi's disciples, but whereas Han Fei describes him as a beautiful man who disappointed Kongzi with the baseness of his conduct, Sima Qian states that he was an ugly man whose exemplary conduct lead Confucius to reverse his original judgment that he was a man of limited abilities. See *The Grand Scribe's Records* v. 7, p. 76.

[50]Zai Yu 宰予 (a.k.a. Zai Ziwo 宰子我, 520–481 B.C.E.) was one of Kongzi's less enthusiastic disciples. Kongzi once praised him for his eloquence (cf. *Analects* 11.3), but he was also scolded by the master for falling asleep during the day (cf. *Analects* 5.10, not in this volume), and criticized for the "lack of feeling" he displayed in his attitude toward the traditional three-year mourning ritual (cf. *Analects* 17.21).

[51]In the year 273 B.C.E., the Qin general Wei Ran 魏冉, Marquis of Rang 穰, attacked the states of Zhao, Han, and Wei and won a great battle against the Wei general Mang Mao 芒卯 (a.k.a. Meng Mao 孟卯) near the foot of Mount Hua 華 in modern-day Shanxi 山西 province. The reason for Mang Mao's defeat is sometimes said to be that he gained his position through *zha* 詐, "verbal trickery," rather than ability.

disaster at Chang Ping.[52] These two are both examples of what a mistake it can be to employ people based solely on their eloquence.

Even the great blacksmith Ou[53] could not determine the quality of a sword simply by looking at the quantity of tin used in forging it or examining the amount of green and yellow coloring. But if one uses the sword to strike down swans and geese in the water and cut the heads off young colts and horses on the land, even a common slave would have not doubts about its sharpness. Even the great horse trainer Bo Le[54] could not determine the quality of a horse simply by inspecting its teeth and breath or scrutinizing its shape and appearance, but if one hitches it to a chariot and drives it forward to see how fast it covers a length of road, even a common slave would have no doubts about whether the horse is good or bad. Even Kongzi could not determine the quality of an officer simply by looking at his features and dress or listening to his manner of speaking. But if one tries out the person in some office or assignment and then examines the nature of his achievements, even an ordinary person would have no doubts about whether he was a fool or a wise man.

Therefore, in the administration of an enlightened ruler, the prime minister always rises up from the position of district magistrate, and the powerful generals always emerge from the ranks of soldiers. Because individuals with merit are always rewarded, their titles and stipends soon become substantial and they are inspired to work even harder. As these individuals move from office to office and are promoted to higher and higher levels in

---

[52]In the year 262 B.C.E. the state of Qin launched a campaign to retake lands it had won from the state of Han, but which the local governor of the region had surreptitiously handed over to the state of Zhao. The Zhao general Lian Po 廉頗 was able to hold back the invading Qin troops at Changping 長平 for more than three years, but then the King of Zhao, listening to rumors being spread by Qin spies within his own state, removed Lian Po and appointed Zhao Kuo 趙括, the Lord of Mafu 馬服君, as supreme commander of the Zhao forces. Zhao Kuo persuaded the king that he could win a swift victory through a massive frontal assault, but his inexperience led the Zhao troops into an ambush which divided the army in two and severed their supply lines. In the end, 450,000 men of Zhao lost their lives. Many of these either starved to death or were massacred after the war was already over in order to punish the region and keep it from rising up in rebellion.

[53]Master Ou the Blacksmith 區冶子 was a famous swordmaker of the *Spring and Autumns Period*.

[54]Bo Le 伯樂 was a talented horse trainer known for his ability to recognize and develop the hidden abilities of the animals under his care.

the government, their offices and assignments become more significant and the government becomes even more well ordered. To ensure that titles and stipends are substantial and offices and assignments are well ordered is the Way of a king.

Someone who owns a thousand square *li* of rocks and boulders cannot be called rich; someone with an army of one million funerary dolls[55] cannot be called strong. It is not that the rocks are not big or that the funerary dolls are not numerous, but such a person cannot be called rich or strong because boulders cannot grow grain, and funerary dolls cannot be used to oppose an enemy. Now, those officers who are clever artisans or merchants who have purchased their offices, eat without ever having cultivated any new land; and land that is not cultivated is just as useless as land covered with rocks and boulders. Similarly, because the Confucians and the bravos have found a way to become eminent and honored without ever having to serve in the army, the people refuse to be employed in battle, making them as useless as funerary dolls. To understand that it is disasterous to have nothing but boulders and funerary dolls, but not understand that it is equally disasterous to have these office-buyers, Confucians, and bravos making it so that new land is not cultivated and the people refuse to be employed in battle is to not understand things of the same category.

Thus, even though the rulers or kings of enemy states may be pleased by my righteousness, I cannot make them offer up tribute and become my subjects; even though rulers within my own passes may denounce my conduct, I can always make them present the ceremonial tribute of birds and pay court to me.[56] Thus, when your strength is greater, others will pay court to you, but when your strength is weaker, you must pay court to others. Therefore, an enlightened ruler works to accumulate power. In a stern household there are no impertinent servants, but a compassionate mother will often have spoiled children. By this I know that might and the power

---

[55]In ancient China, small human figures made out of straw, wood, or clay were often buried in the tombs of high-ranking members of society. It was believed that these "funerary dolls" would serve the occupant of the tomb after death. The enormous terracotta army arrayed before the tomb of the First Emperor of China can be seen as the furthest extension of this ancient mortuary ritual. Mengzi quotes Kongzi as cursing the man who first gave these dolls a life-like appearance, because this might lead to a revival of the ancient practice of sacrificing real people and burying them along with the dead. See *Mengzi* 1A4 (not in this volume). For an image of such a terracotta army, see the web site for this volume.

[56]In ancient China, vassals would present offerings of birds to their rulers as ritual symbols of their loyalty. The type of bird presented differed according to the rank of the person presenting it.

of position can be used to put an end to violence, while even the most profound Virtue is not enough to stop disorder.

When a sage governs a state, he does not wait for people to be good in deference to him. Instead, he creates a situation in which people find it impossible to do wrong. If you wait for people to be good in deference to you, you will find that there are no more than ten good people within the borders of your state. But if you create a situation in which people find it impossible to do wrong, the entire state can be brought into compliance. In governing, one must use what is numerous and abandon what is scarce. Therefore, the sage does not work on his Virtue, he works on his laws.

If people had to wait for arrow shafts that are naturally straight, then for a hundred generations there would be no arrows. If they had to wait for wood that is naturally round, then for a thousand generations there would be no chariot wheels. If in a hundred generations there is not a single arrow shaft that is naturally straight, or a single piece of wood that is naturally round, how is it that every generation is able to ride around in chariots and shoot down birds with arrows? It is because they use the Way of straightening and bending. Indeed, even if one found an arrow shaft that was straight without having been straightened, or a piece of wood that was round without having been bent, a good craftsman would still not value it. Why? Because those who need to ride in chariots are more than just one person, and archers require more than just one shot. Similarly, even if there are a few people who are naturally good without having been trained through rewards and penalties, an enlightened ruler will not value them. Why? Because the laws of the state cannot be abandoned, and those who need to be governed are more than just one person. Therefore, a ruler who has the proper method does not rely on accidental goodness. He follows the Way that is certain to succeed. . . .

Now those who do not understand the art of governing always say, "One must win the hearts of the people."[57] If one could bring about order simply by seeking to win the hearts of the people, there would be no need for great counselors like Yi Yin and Guan Zhong. All one would have to do is listen to the people. But the wisdom of the people cannot be used because their minds are like the minds of infants. If an infant's head is not shaved, its stomach will hurt; if its boils are not lanced, the swelling will become worse. Nevertheless, whenever an infant's head is shaved or its boils are lanced, someone has to hold the infant while its loving mother takes care

---

[57] Cf. *Mengzi* 4A9 (not in this volume).

of these things, and the infant will still scream and cry endlessly because it does not understand that enduring this little bit of discomfort will bring about a great benefit.

Now, those above encourage the people to plow their fields and cultivate new land because they want to increase the people's means of livelihood, but the people think their superiors are just being cruel. They draw up penal codes and establish heavy penalties in order to put an end to wickedness, but the people think their superiors are just being harsh. They levy taxes in money and grain in order to fill the coffers and granaries of the state so that they can fund military expeditions and rescue the people in times of famine, but the people think their superiors are just being greedy. They ensure that everyone in the state knows how to put on armor and see to it that there are no private exemptions from military service because they know that in order to capture enemies in battle the people must be able to combine their strength and fight fiercely, but the people think their superiors are just being violent. These four things are the means to good order and security, but the people do not know enough to be pleased by any of them.

The reason why rulers seek out officers with sagelike understanding is because they know that the wisdom of the people is not sufficient to guide them. In the past, Yu opened up a new channel for the Chang Jiang and dredged out the bottom of the Huang He, and yet the people collected tiles and stones to throw at him. Zichan opened up acres of land for cultivation and planted mulberry trees for the raising silk worms, and yet the people of Zheng slandered and cursed him.[58] Yu's efforts benefited the entire world and Zichan's efforts preserved the state of Zheng, but both men became the objects of slander. So clearly the wisdom of the people is not good enough to be of any use. Thus, to look for worthiness and wisdom when promoting officers, to expect to please the people when governing them—these policies are the sprouts of disorder. One can never govern properly using them.

---

[58]Zichan 子產 was the prime minister of the state of Zheng 鄭 under Dukes Jian 鄭簡公 (r. sixth century B.C.E.) and Ding 鄭定公 (r. 529–514 B.C.E.). He introduced a number of agricultural and economic reforms that greatly strengthened the state of Zheng, but that were initially opposed by the populace.

SELECTIVE BIBLIOGRAPHY

Translations

Liao, W. K., tr.

1939/   *The Complete Works of Han Fei Tzû: A Classic of Chinese Political Science.*
1959   Probsthain's Oriental Series, v. XXVI. London: Arthur Probsthain. 2 vols.
        (The only complete English translation currently available. Although
        Liao's rendering of the text is sometimes difficult to follow, it remains an
        invaluable resource for examining how Han Fei's views on politics and
        rhetoric are informed by his historical investigations and criticisms of
        other theorists.)

Watson, Burton, tr.

1964   *Han Fei Tzu: Basic Writings.* Columbia College Program of Translations
        from the Oriental Classics. New York: Columbia University Press. (An
        extremely readable, though at times rather loose, translation of Han Fei's
        best-known philosophical treatises, prefaced by a brief introduction ex-
        plaining the overall content and intellectual background of Han Fei's
        thought.)

Waley, Arthur.

1994   "Lao Tzu and Han Fei, Memoir 3," in William H. Nienhauser, Jr., ed.,
        1994, *The Grand Scribes Records. Volume VII: The Memoirs of Pre-Han
        China*, 21–32. Bloomington: Indiana University Press. (Currently the
        best translation of Sima Qian's biography of Han Fei. Includes numerous
        textual and explanatory notes.)

Secondary Works

Chen, Ellen Marie.

1975   "The Dialectic of Chih (Reason) and Tao (Nature) in the 'Han Fei-Tzu'."
        Journal of Chinese Philosophy. 3:1 (Dec), 1–22. (Argues that the Han Fei
        conceives of the ideal ruler as someone who tries to imitate the passivity
        and objectivity of *Dao* 道 "Nature" by using laws and punishments—in-
        stead of subjective human *zhi* 知 "reason"—to eliminate selfishness and
        promote the common good.)

Lundahl, Bertil.

1992 *Han Fei Zi: The Man and the Work*. Stockholm East Asian Monographs, No. 4. Stockholm: Institute of Oriental Languages, Stockholm University. (A scholarly monograph focusing on the problem of the authenticity of various chapters in the *Han Feizi*. Useful primarily for its summaries of modern Chinese and Japanese scholarship.)

Moody, Peter R., Jr.

1979 "The Legalism of Han Fei-tzu and Its Affinities with Modern Political Thought." *International Philosophical Quarterly*, 19:3, 317–30. (A thoughtful examination of Han Fei's political philosophy that argues that Han Fei's amoralized, autocratic, and institutional conception of politics presages the "modern" political theories found in the works of thinkers like Machiavelli and Hobbes.)

Wang, Hsiao-po, and Leo S. Chang.

1986 *The Philosophical Foundations of Han Fei's Political Theory*. Monograph no. 7 of the Society for Asian and Comparative Philosophy. Honolulu: University of Hawaii Press. (Examines five so-called Daoist chapters in the Han Feizi and argues that Han Fei's political philosophy represents an attempt to legitimize Legalist theory by grounding it in a Daoist conception of the underlying patterns and processes of the natural world.)

▪ APPENDIX ▪

Note: All dates earlier than the beginning of the Eastern Zhou are traditional dates (i.e. dates that have not been verified by modern archaeology), and all individuals and events earlier than the Shang dynasty are mythical or semi-mythical.

Bo Yi 伯夷. Elder brother of Shu Qi. The brothers were royal princes in a small state loyal to the Shang dynasty (see *Important Periods*). The younger brother was designated as heir by his father but, upon the latter's death, he deferred to his elder brother. However, Bo Yi refused to contravene his father's wishes, and with both brothers mutually deferring to one another they decided to withdraw from the state and live in isolation at the foot of Mount Shou Yang. When King Wu (see below) subsequently defeated the Shang and established the Zhou dynasty (see *Important Periods*), the brothers refused to serve the Zhou, regarding it as an illegitimate regime established by brute force. As a consequence, they starved to death. They are regarded as paragons of propriety and right.

Fu Xi 伏羲 ("Tamer of Oxen"). The first of three mythical cultural heros known as the "Three Sovereigns" (see Huang Di and Shen Nong below) who were credited with discovering or implementing the inventions and institutions that made Chinese civilization possible. Fu Xi is credited with the domestication of animals, inventing methods for fishing and trapping, and with establishing the basic structure of the family.

Gongshuzi 公輸子. Famed craftsman and contemporary of Kongzi whose skill was so great that he was said to have made mechanical birds of bamboo that could continue flying for three days and wooden horses propelled by springs that could draw carriages. He became the patron deity of carpenters.

Gongsun Long 公孫龍 (b. 380 B.C.E.?). Along with Huizi (see below) an important figure within the *Mingjia* "School of Names" (see *Important Terms*). Gongsun Long was renowned for his paradoxes; the most famous is his "White Horse Paradox," which claims that "A white horse is not a horse."

Gongsun Yang 公孫鞅 (d. 338 B.C.E.). Also known as Shang Yang 商鞅 or "Lord Shang." He was chief minister for Duke Xiao of Qin 秦孝公 (r. 361–338 B.C.E.) and the purported author of the *Book of the Lord of Shang* 商君書, an important work of the *Fajia* "Legalist School" (see *Important Terms*). Gongsun Yang is credited with developing the notion of government through "laws" or "legal standards" (*fa* 法), in which a ruler establishes clearly defined and easily understood standards of duty and behavior for his subjects, and then motivates his people to accord with them through the use of rewards and punishments. This idea directly influenced the thought of Han Feizi.

Guan Zhong 管仲 (d. 645 B.C.E.). Guan Zhong was chief minister for Duke Huan of Qi 齊桓公 (r. 685–643 B.C.E) and the purported author of the Legalist (see *Fajia* under *Important Terms*) work the *Guanzi* 管子. Under his guidance, Duke Huan became first of the *ba*, "Lord Protectors" (see *Important Terms*). Primarily as a consequence of this event, Guan Zhong was either praised or criticized by later thinkers.

Houji 后稷 ("Duke of Millet"). Originally an official title but now regarded as a proper name for Qi 棄, who served as the minister of agriculture under Emperor Shun (see below).

Huang Di 黄帝 ("Yellow Emperor"). Third of the "Three Sovereigns" (see Fu Xi above and Shen Nong below). He is credited with the invention of wooden houses, boats and carts, and with the implementation of the earliest forms of writing. His wife is credited with inventing the methods of sericulture (raising silkworms to produce silk).

Huizi 惠子 (c. 380–305 B.C.E.). Also known as Hui Shi 惠施, and along with Gongsun Long (see above) a prominent figure within the *Mingjia* "School of Names" (see *Important Terms*). Though a prodigious author, few of Huizi's works are extant today. He is most well known for his ten paradoxes, which purportedly show that there is an underlying unity to the universe. He concludes from this that we should show compassion to all things. Huizi was a friend and perhaps a teacher of Zhuangzi.

Jie 桀 ("Tyrant Jie"). Purportedly, the evil last ruler of the Xia dynasty (see *Important Periods*). His traditional reign dates are 1818–1766 B.C.E.

Li 厲 ("King Li"). An incompetent, cruel Zhou dynasty ruler. He ascended to the throne in 878 B.C.E.

Li Lou 離婁. Also known as Li Zhu 朱. A contemporary of Huang Di (see above), Li Lou was renowned for his acute vision. It was said that at a hundred paces he could see the tip of an autumn hair. (In autumn an animal's hair is thinnest and most fine.)

Pengzu 彭祖 ("Ancestor Peng"). The Chinese Methuselah, purported to have lived seven hundred years.

Robber Zhi (*Daozhi* 盜跖). On some accounts, a contemporary of Huang Di, but more commonly regarded as an infamous and shameless brigand of the *Spring and Autumn Period* (see *Important Periods*). Some sources say that he came from Lu, Kongzi's home state.

Shen Nong 神農 ("Divine Farmer"). Second of the "Three Sovereigns" (see Fu Xi and Huang Di above), he is credited with the discovery of the hoe and the plough, the invention of agriculture, and with establishing the basic institutions of trade and commerce.

Shen Buhai 申不害 (d. 377 B.C.E.). Prime minister of the state of Han under Marquis Zhao of Han 韓昭侯 (r. 358–333 B.C.E.) and an important figure within the *Fajia* "Legalist School" (see *Important Terms*). Shen Buhai is credited with developing the idea of "administrative methods" (*shu* 術), an elegant, though somewhat inflexible, system for evaluating the performance of government officials by comparing the objectives or duties that ministers "name" (*ming* 名) for themselves when they propose an action or accept a government position, with the actual "form" or "situation" (*xing* 刑 or 形) that results when they carry out said duties. If "form" and "name" match, the minister has properly performed his duties and should be rewarded; if they do not match, the minister has failed in his duties and should be punished. This idea directly influenced the thought of Han Feizi.

Shenzi 慎子 (c. 350–275 B.C.E.). Also known as Shen Dao 慎到, an important figure within the *Fajia* "Legalist School" (see *Important Terms*). Shenzi developed the doctrine of "the power of position" (*shi* 勢), an idea that directly influenced Han Feizi's thought. According to the doctrine of *shi*, the key to a ruler's success lies in his ability to maintain his sociopolitical superiority over his subjects so that he can use the power and prestige of his position to intimidate people into obeying his commands. This idea can be understood as an amoralized, institutional version of the earlier notion of government through "moral charisma" (*de* 德) advocated by the Confucians. But whereas the Confucians maintained that the power of moral charisma is generated through the cultivation of the ruler's character, Shen Dao and Han Fei believed that the power of status is simply a concomitant feature of the ruler's sociopolitical position.

Shi Kuang 師曠 ("Music Master Kuang"). A blind musician of the sixth century B.C.E. who, reportedly, could foretell the outcome of a battle by listening to the hoofbeats of the enemy cavalry or the fortunes of a king by listening to the grumblings of his people. He is often cited as the standard for musical taste and a paradigm for connoiseurs in general.

Shun 舜 ("Emperor Shun"). Second of the mythical "Three Sage-Kings" (see Yao and Yu below). His traditional reign dates are 2255–2205 B.C.E. Renowned for his filial piety, Shun's own father—known as the "Blind Man"—and stepmother treated him remarkably badly and even attempted to kill him on several occasions in order to benefit his spoiled and generally worthless half-brother. Shun's continued love and respectfulness in the face of this abuse eventually won over his parents and brother, moving them to reform.

Shu Qi 叔齊. Younger brother of Bo Yi (see above).

Sima Qian 司馬遷 (c. 145–90 B.C.E.). A Han dynasty (see *Important Periods*) figure who completed the *Shiji* 史記 (*Records of the Historian*), a work begun by his father, Sima Tan. The *Shiji* is the first comprehensive account of Chinese history from its beginnings to the time of composition. It had a tremendous influence on later Chinese views of history and historiography and was treasured as a fount of moral and political exemplars and insights.

Songzi 宋子 (c. 360–290 B.C.E.). Also known as Song Rongzi 宋榮子, Song Xing 宋銒, or Song Keng 宋牼, a pacifist who encouraged people to simplify their lives and avoid conflict by minimizing their desires, particularly what he considered to be artificial desires for things such as prestige, wealth, and power.

Tang 湯 ("King Tang," also known as 成湯 "Tang the Successful"). His traditional reign dates are 1766–1753 B.C.E. Defeated the tyrant Jie (see above) and founded the Shang dynasty (see *Important Periods*).

Wen 文 ("King Wen"). A virtuous vassal of the tyrant Zhou (see below), his name means "cultured." King Wen ruled over a state called Zhou 周. (Note that the name of this state, though romanized the same way as the name of the tyrant Zhou—see above—is written with a different graph.) While having good warrant for rebellion, King Wen remained loyal to his ruler, sustained by the hope of reforming him.

Wu 武 ("King Wu"). His traditional reign dates are 1122–1115 B.C.E. Son of King Wen (see above). His name means "martial." After succeeding his father, he overthrew the tyrant Zhou (see below) and founded the Zhou dynasty (see *Important Periods*), which was named after the state over which he ruled.

Yao 堯 ("Emperor Yao"). First of the mythical "Three Sage-Kings" (see Shun above and Yu below). His traditional reign dates are 2356–2255 B.C.E. He is credited with the invention of the calendar, developing rituals and music, and establishing the basic structure of government. Yao skipped over his own unworthy son and designated a peasant named Shun as his successor, based upon the latter's remarkable filial piety. Yao is said to have trained Shun to rule and shared power with him during the last twenty-eight years of his reign.

Yi Yin 伊尹. An able minister of King Tang's (see above). According to some accounts, Yi Yin was working as a farmer when his talents were recognized and he was promoted by the king. Others say that he attracted the king's attention through his cooking.

Yi Ya 易牙. Famed as a remarkably talented chef who worked in the kitchen of Duke Huan of Qi (see Guan Zhong above). Yi Ya's ability to harmonize various flavors in ways that people in general found delicious and appealing was seen as emblematic of the way sages are able to hit upon those ethical principles and practices that all people approve of and take delight in.

You 幽 ("King You"). An incompetent, cruel Zhou dynasty ruler. He ascended to the throne in 781 B.C.E.

Yu 禹 ("Emperor Yu"). Third of the mythical "Three Sage-Kings" (see Yao and Shun above) and founder of the Xia dynasty. His traditional reign dates are 2205–2197 B.C.E. Yu is credited with overseeing the first successful state efforts at flood control, a remarkably important project given the topography of central China. Yu is said to have so selflessly dedicated himself to this work that he wore off all the hair of his thighs and shins. In carrying out his duties, Yu is said to have passed by his own house three times without pausing, even though he could hear his wife and children weeping over his absence. While cited by many early thinkers, Yu was a particular favorite of Mozi, perhaps because his dedication to public duty seemed to trump his devotion to his own family.

Zhou Gong 周公 ("The Duke of Zhou"). Brother of King Wu (see above). According to traditional accounts, when King Wu died, his infant son became ruler of the newly founded Zhou dynasty (see *Important Periods*). The Duke purportedly served the young king as a wise and virtuous regent and did not attempt to wrest power from him for his own gain. The Duke of Zhou served as a paragon for selfless devotion to the greater good.

Zhou 紂 ("Tyrant Zhou"). The evil last ruler of the Shang dynasty (see *Important Periods*). His traditional reign dates are 1154–1122 B.C.E. See also the entry for Wen, above.

■ IMPORTANT PERIODS ■

Xia 夏 ("Xia dynasty"). Traditional dates: 2205–1766 B.C.E. See Yu and Jie under *Important Figures*.

Shang 商 ("Shang dynasty," also known as the 殷 "Yin dynasty"). Traditional dates: 1766–1122 B.C.E. See Tang and Zhou under *Important Figures*.

Zhou 周 ("Zhou dynasty"). Traditional dates: 1122–256 B.C.E. Often divided into "Eastern" and "Western" Zhou (see below).

> Western Zhou (*Xizhou* 西周). The earlier part (1122–771 B.C.E.) of the Zhou dynasty. Widely regarded as a golden age of peace, stability, and prosperity. See Wen, Wu, and Zhou Gong under *Important Figures*.

> Eastern Zhou (*Dongzhou* 東周). The latter part (770–256 B.C.E.) of the Zhou dynasty. It began when disgruntled vassals, together with "barbarian" (i.e., non-Chinese) forces, sacked the Zhou capital and killed the ruling king. Remnants of the Zhou royal family escaped and founded a new capital far to the east at Loyang and installed the king's son as ruler. However, the dynasty never again controlled China.

>> Spring and Autumn Period (*Chunqiu* 春秋). The period 722–481 B.C.E. covered by the court chronicle of Lu, Kongzi's native state (see *Spring and Autumn Annals* in *Important Texts*). This period saw the rise of the institution of *ba* 霸 ("lord protector," see *Important Terms*).

>> Warring States Period (*Zhanguo shidai* 戰國時代). The period 403–221 B.C.E. It began when the Zhou king officially recognized the partitioning of the state of Jin 晉, which had been carved up by and divided among the members of an alliance of other states in 453. Soon after, in 335, the rulers of these and other allegedly "vassal" states began to usurp the title *wang* 王 "king" (see *Important Terms*) which rightfully only the Zhou king could claim.

Qin dynasty 秦. A short-lived dynasty (221–207 B.C.E.) that marked the end of the "Warring States Period" by unifying the various states into a single empire. It is from the name "Qin" that we get our word "China."

Han dynasty 漢. A long lasting and largely stable dynasty consisting of an "Earlier" or "Western" and a "Later" or "Eastern" period, on either side of a brief interregnum (see below).

"Earlier" or "Western Han" (206 B.C.E.–8 C.E.)

"Later" or "Eastern Han" (25–220 C.E.).

The *Changes* 易 (*Yi*). A multilayered composition whose earliest strata originate in divinatory texts of extremely old provenance, perhaps as early as the beginning of the first millennium B.C.E. There is little evidence of it playing a major role in the thought of any of the philosophers covered in this volume, though it was known to them in some form. It becomes profoundly important to the history of Chinese thought after the addition of various *Appendices*. This occurred sometime around the third to second century B.C.E.

The *History* 書 (*Shu* or *Shangshu* 尚書). The original text purportedly contained the pronouncements and judgments of important figures at critical junctures in history. Along with the *Odes* (see below) the *Shujing* was regarded as a classic from the very earliest period. Both were seen as repositories of traditional wisdom and cited as support by a wide range of Chinese thinkers. The present version of the text contains some genuine Zhou dynasty (see *Important Periods)* era writings, though its purportedly pre-Zhou material remains suspect.

The *Spring and Autumn Annals* 春秋 (*Chunqiu*). The court chronicle of Lu, Kongzi's native state. It takes its name from the generic name for such chronicles, which literally meant "Springs and Autumns" (i.e., the regular passage of time). Tradition says that Kongzi edited this remarkably terse work. Two influential commentaries on it, the *Gongyang zhuan* and *Guliang zhuan*, present interpretations of the text that see it as offering "praise and blame" judgments of various historical individuals and events. A third text, the *Zuozhuan* (see below) is not so much an interpretation as a complement to the text. It fills in historical details of the events recorded in the *Spring and Autumn Annals* rather than offering interpretations of its cryptic pronouncements.

The *Odes* 詩 (*Shi*). A collection of rhymed poems derived from early folk songs and ceremonial incantations. Tradition claims that Kongzi edited an earlier group of three thousand poems down to three hundred, but modern scholars regard this as myth. The text existed in a number of versions during the early period and like the *History* was regarded as a classic. The message of the *Odes* was thought to be more allusive and allegorical in nature and interpreting the poems has been a preoccupation of thinkers from Kongzi on down to contemporary times. The text we have today, called the *Mao* version, is named after and can directly be traced to a student of Xunzi's. It contains three hundred and five poems divided into three types: *Feng* 風 ("The Airs"), *Ya* 雅 ("The Elegies"), and *Song* 頌 ("The Hymns").

The *Music* 樂 (*Yue*). A no longer extant text that probably was more concerned with the proper effects and meaning of music and its contribution to social and ethical well-being rather than an analysis of the nature of music itself. The *Liji* (see the *Rites* below) contains a chapter called the *Record of Music* 樂記 (*Yueji*) but the relationship between this text and the ancient classic is uncertain at best.

The *Rites* 禮 (*Li*). By the end of the Han dynasty (see *Important Periods*) there were several texts that purported to describe the proper form of ancient ceremonies and their significance. Among the most important of these are the *Rites of the Zhou Dynasty* 周禮 (*Zhouli*), *On Etiquette and Rites* 儀禮 (*Yili*), the *Rites* 禮記 (*Liji*), and the *Rites of the Elder Dai* 大戴禮記 (*Da Dai Liiji*). While none of these descend from any known pre-Han text it is clear that at least large sections of the first two texts existed and were known as early as the fourth century B.C.E.

Zuozhuan 左傳 ("Zuo's Commentary"). A substantial historical text that augments the *Spring and Autumn Annals* by providing a wealth of detail concerning the events recorded in the original court chronicle.

ba 霸 ("lord protector" or "hegemon"). Lord protectors were rulers of states who, although nominally vassals to the Zhou king, actually ruled in the king's place, supported by the mutual political and military support of their fellow "vassals." See *Spring and Autumn Period* under *Important Periods*.

baijia 百家 ("Hundred Schools"). A collective name for the various schools of thought that proliferated during the late *Spring and Autumn* and *Warring States* Periods (see *Important Periods*). The notion of a "school" of thought in early Chinese philosophy is quite loose. Only rarely does it describe a set of thinkers who shared fundamental beliefs or doctrines. More often it is a concept applied retrospectively to identify groups of thinkers who shared common themes or approaches or who studied with or were inspired by a common thinker.

dao 道 ("Way"). One of the basic meanings of early forms of this character was a physical "path," but it came to refer more generally to a way of doing something, an oral or written account of such a way, and, when used as a verb, to give such an account. Depending on the context, the *dao* in question can be *a* way of doing something, or it can refer to *the* right way. Daoists appropriate the term to refer to what is responsible for the overall, underlying pattern of the universe.

Daojia 道家 ("Daoist School" or "Daoism"). A term applied retrospectively, in the Han dynasty (see *Important Periods*), to a varied collection of thinkers, especially Laozi and Zhuangzi, who rejected both the particular conceptions of ethical cultivation of the Erudites and the rationalistic consequentialism of the Mohists.

de 德 ("Virtue"). One of the most important senses of early forms of this character was "Royal Virtue"—the spiritual force a king cultivates through proper sacrifice and deportment that allows him to gain and maintain his rule. This sense of *de* being a kind of power remains central for many of its later meanings. Most generally, it could designate the natural effect or power—good, bad or indifferent—that a person or thing had upon those nearby. For Kongzi, *de* came to mean something like "moral charisma"—a property that any good person could cultivate and have. It retained the connotation of having a "magnetic" capacity to draw, influence and inspire others that was part of the earlier notion of "Royal Virtue." Daoists too embraced a related but distinctive sense of *de*, describing it in terms of the natural therapeutic effect Daoist sages have upon the people, creatures and things within their presence.

Fajia 法家 ("Legalist School" or "Legalism"). A term applied retrospectively in the Han dynasty (see *Important Periods*) to an intellectual movement centered on the writings of Gongsun Yang (Lord Shang), Shen Dao, Shen Buhai (see *Important Figures*), and others that took an amoral approach to the problems of social and political organization and management.

junzi 君子 ("gentleman"). Literally, this term means "son of a lord," and hence originally referred to someone possessing a particular social status. However, Kongzi emphasized living up to the ethical implications of this social role, so that being a genuine gentleman is a goal to strive for, rather than something simply bestowed by noble birth.

li 禮 ("rites," "rituals," or "propriety"). This term originally referred to religious rituals, such as sacrifices of food and wine to the spirits of one's ancestors, but it came to have a much broader application, including matters of etiquette and aspects of one's entire way of life, including dress, behavior, and demeanor. *Li* sometimes seems coextensive with all of ethics and can even extend to what seems like the patterns of nature. Mengzi also uses the term to refer to a virtue associated with following the rites.

li 里. A unit of length equal to about one-third of a mile.

ming 命 ("fate" or "mandate"). Most broadly, *ming* refers to what is determined independently of human agency or choice. It is a concept closely related to *tian* ("Heaven"), and like *tian* has both descriptive and normative senses. Thus, unavoidable future events (such as one's death), and inescapable natural facts (such as the need to eat) are said to be *ming*. However, *ming* can also refer to what is normatively mandated, such as the right to rule of a sage-king (which is referred to as *Tian Ming*, the "Mandate of Heaven").

Mingjia 名家 ("School of Names" or "Sophists"). A term applied retrospectively in the Han dynasty (see *Important Periods*) to a varied collection of thinkers who shared a common interest in the nature of language, debate, and paradox, including Gongsun Long and Huizi (see *Important Figures*).

Mojia 墨家 ("Mohist School" or "Mohism"). The school of thought that grew around and out of the teachings of Mozi.

mu 畝. A unit of land measure equal to about 733 square yards, a little less than one-seventh the area of a football field.

qi 氣. Perhaps originally referring to the mist that arose from heated sacrificial offerings, this term later came to refer to vapor in general and human breath in particular. In a more technical sense, *qi* was thought of as a kind of vital energy found in both the atmosphere and the human body and existing in various densities and levels of clarity or turbidity that is responsible for, among other things, the intensity of one's emotions. Zhuangzi recommends being guided by the *qi*, presumably because he regarded it as more objective and impersonal than the promptings of one's own heart. In later Chinese philosophy, *qi* was thought of as the fundamental "stuff" out of which everything in the universe condenses and into which it eventually dissipates.

qing 情 ("the genuine," "essence," or "disposition"). The *qing* of something is what it genuinely is, as opposed to what it might appear to be. This is often conceived of in terms of how it would spontaneously behave and develop if given a proper environment and support. More specifically, some interpreters have argued that the *qing* of a thing can be the essential characteristics of that thing. Toward the end of the Warring States Period, *qing* came to refer to human emotions or dispositions (perhaps because some thinkers regarded these as essential to humans beings).

ren 仁 ("humaneness" or "benevolence"). For Kongzi, this term refers to the sum total of virtuous qualities, or the perfection of human character. (It is etymologically related to the character for "human," and thus has previously been rendered "manhood-at-its-best."). For Mohists it is the universal and impartial concern one should manifest toward all people. For certain later thinkers, like Mengzi, *ren* came to be understood as a specific virtue akin to benevolence or compassion. However, for Mengzi and other Erudites, benevolence is "graded," stronger for family members than for strangers.

Ru 儒 ("Erudites"). Traditionally translated as "Confucian," this term has no etymological relationship with the name "Kongzi" (Confucius). The term appears to have been in use prior to the time of Kongzi, but there is considerable scholarly debate over exactly what its original meaning was. After Kongzi, however, it clearly is used to refer to those who think of themselves as carrying on the tradition of culture and learning that Kongzi defended and came to represent. However, the Erudites often disagreed vehemently among themselves about how to interpret this tradition.

shen 神 ("spirit," "spiritual," or "spiritlike"). *Shen*, like *gui* 鬼 ("ghost"), can refer to a spiritual being, such as the spirit of a dead ancestor. However, some philosophers speak of living people as *shen*, "spiritual" or "spiritlike," when they accomplish things beyond the range of normal human capacities, such as morally transforming people through the power of Virtue.

sheng 聖 ("sage"). A *sheng* is a person who has achieved the greatest possible human excellence. Sages may possess special abilities (see *de* above), but they are still human beings. See also *shi* and *xian*.

shi 士 ("scholar" or "knight"). Speaking most generally, a *shi* is a member of the social elite. However, the precise nature of that elite varies with historical period and society. Early on, the *shi* were members of the warrior nobility (hence "knight"), but already by the time of Kongzi "*shi*" often referred to someone who was literate, hence it is sometimes translated "literatus." (Much later, in Japan, *shi* refers to the *samurai*, who were often both warriors and scholars.) As with *junzi* (see above), later philosophers emphasize living up to the duties implied by the social role rather than enjoying the prerogatives of one's often hereditary position. See also *sheng* and *xian*.

si 思 ("to concentrate or reflect on"). *Si* refers to a directing of the attention on something either external or mental. Although the term is often translated as "thinking," it does not generally refer to ratiocination or theoretical reasoning. However, *si* does not exclude what we would commonly call "reflection."

tian 天 ("Heaven"). This term can refer to the sky, hence the standard translation "Heaven." However, Heaven can also be a sort of higher power. Various thinkers conceive of this higher power in different ways, though. Thus, Heaven seems to be very much like a personal god in the Mohist writings, but is more like the impersonal processes of nature in the writings of Zhuangzi and Xunzi, and is somewhere in the middle in the sayings of Kongzi and Mengzi. In the period covered in this anthology, Heaven is *not* primarily thought of as a place, and is not connected with any explicit views about an afterlife.

tianzi 天子 ("Son of Heaven"). A title for the legitimate ruler of the world (i.e., a true king, see *wang* below).

wang 王 ("king"). A genuine king should rule by Virtue (see *de* above) not by brute force. In addition, there should be only one genuine king at a time. As in the case of *junzi* and *shi* (see above), there is a distinction between the de facto social and political role and its idealized, normative conception. See also the entry on *ba* ("Lord Protector") above, and the entries for *Spring and Autumn Period* and *Warring States Period* in the list of *Important Periods*.

wuwei 無為 ("nonaction"). Although it literally means "the absence of doing," *wuwei* does not refer to acting like an inanimate object. Rather, non-action is acting in a way that is natural, unforced, and unselfconscious. The *Laozi* and

Zhuangzi both advocate nonaction, but the latter text strongly suggests that it can be achieved only through years of self-conscious practice. The term also appears in "Confucian" works and the Erudites also take nonaction as a goal, but they disagree with Daoists about the means to achieve this goal, and the kinds of activities in which one manifests it. See also *ziran*.

xian 賢 ("worthy"). A term designating a level of cultivation in general somewhere between a *shi* and a *sheng*.

xin 心 ("heart," "disposition," or "feeling"). This term can refer to the physical organ in the chest, but it also can refer to the psychological faculty of thinking, perceiving, feeling, desiring and intending. (These were not regarded as separate functions by Chinese philosophers, as they sometimes are in Western philosophy.) By synecdoche, *xin* can also refer to "feelings" or dispositions to feel or perceive things in a certain way.

xing 性 ("nature" or "human nature"). For most thinkers in the classical period, this term refers to the characteristics of a paradigmatic instance of the sort of creature that one is. (This is much like one of the senses that "nature" has in Western philosophical writings, hence the translation.) These tendencies are more likely to be realized if one is given a healthy environment. Thus, the sprout of a willow tree has a tendency to grow into an adult willow tree, but it may die from a lack of water, or be warped through techniques such as those used to grow *bonsai*. Xunzi insists that *xing* be used only to refer to the characteristics something has innately. Often in philosophical texts the nature under discussion is specifically "human nature" (*renxing* 人性), so the character *xing* by itself will sometimes be translated that way.

yi 義 ("right" or "righteousness"). One early definition states that "The right is the appropriate," where "appropriate" (*yi* 宜) refers to what is appropriate for one to do and to be, given the situation and one's social role (e.g., ruler, minister, father, son, etc.). However, *yi* can also refer to what is right or appropriate for a person in general. By extension, the term refers to the character of one who does what is *yi* (hence "righteousness"). Note that "human rights" is a very different notion that belongs to a distinct and unrelated conceptual framework.

yin 陰 and *yang* 陽. In their earliest use, *yin* and *yang* may have referred to the shady and sunny sides of a hill respectively. Eventually, the terms were associated with *qi* (see *qi* above) and understood either as two distinct modes of *qi* or as two fundamental forces that shape and guide *qi*. In general, *yin* and *yang* designate two broad sets of phenomena characterized by associated states, tendencies, or qualities. For example, day, hot, above, active, masculine, speech, Heaven, etc. are *yang*; night, cold, below, still, feminine, silence, Earth, etc. are *yin*. The various phenomena and the states, tendencies, and qualities within each set are thought to be related to one another and all are regarded as natural aspects of different situations, things, or events. *Yin* and *yang* are thought to be complementary forces or qualities and a given situation, thing, or event can often be described in terms of one or the other. Used early as technical terms in Chinese medicine, the pair eventually became part of the standard vocabulary of Chinese cosmology.

zhi 智 ("wisdom," "cleverness"). *Zhi* typically has a positive connotation and refers to a virtue that manifests itself in such things as good judgments about the consequences of various actions. However, sometimes *zhi* refers to amoral intelligence or cleverness, and in some contexts clearly is regarded as a human vice or defect.

zi 子 ("Master"). An honorific term, often used after someone's family name, typically referring to a teacher who has disciples (e.g., "Kongzi" = "Master Kong"). It may be used by someone in reference to teachers who are not one's own "master."

ziran 自然 ("natural"). Literally meaning "self-so," this term describes anything that occurs of its own accord, without external coercion. A number of thinkers of this period regard such unselfconscious spontaneity as a mark and necessary constituent of a well-lived life. See also *wuwei*.